Diva

Diva

Defiance and

University of Texas Press Austin

Passion in Early Italian Cinema

by Angela Dalle Vacche

Foreword by Guy Maddin

Material included in Chapter 4, "Wings of Desire: Aviation, Fashion, Circus Stunts," is reprinted from Angela Dalle Vacche, "Femininity in Flight: Androgyny and Gynandry in Early Cinema," in *A Feminist Reader in Early Cinema*, 444–475, edited by Jennifer Bean and Diane Negra. Reprinted by permission. Copyright © 2002 by Duke University Press.

Material included in Chapter 5, "Acting: Prostitution, Vertigo, Close-up," is reprinted from Angela Dalle Vacche, "Asta Nielsen: Motion, Emotion, and the Close-up," *Framework* 43:1 (Spring 2002), 76–94, by permission of Wayne State University Press. Copyright © 2002 by Wayne State University Press, Detroit, MI 48201-1309.

Material included in Chapter 8, "Nino Oxilia: Blue Blood and Satanic Rhapsody," is reprinted from Angela Dalle Vacche, "Lyda Borelli's *Satanic Rhapsody*: The Cinema and the Occult," *Cinémas* 16:1 (Autumn 2005), 91–115; special issue on "Femmes et cinéma muet: Nouvelles problématiques, nouvelles méthodologies," edited by Rosanna Maule. Copyright © 2006 by Cinémas. Reprinted by permission of the publisher.

Printed in the United States of America
First edition, 2008

♾ The paper used in this book meets the minimum requirements of ANSI/NISO Z39.48-1992 (R1997) (Permanence of Paper).

Library of Congress Cataloging-in-Publication Data
Dalle Vacche, Angela, 1954–
Diva : defiance and passion in early Italian cinema / by Angela Dalle Vacche ; foreword by Guy Maddin. — 1st ed.
p. cm.
Includes bibliographical references and index.
ISBN 978-0-292-71661-2 (cl. : alk. paper) — ISBN 978-0-292-71711-4 (pbk. : alk. paper)
1. Women in motion pictures. 2. Motion pictures—Italy. I. Title.
PN1995.9.W6D35 2008
791.430945—dc22 2007036402

This book is dedicated to

Professor J. Dudley Andrew

Professor Robert P. Kolker

Ms. Adrienne Mancia

Ms. Giuliana Mazzotti

Publication of this book was aided by generous support from The School of Literature, Communication and Culture at The Georgia Institute of Technology.

Contents

Attached inside the back cover is *Diva Dolorosa* by Peter Delpeut, a companion DVD of film clips from 1914–1920.

Foreword

SILENT DIVAS OF ITALIAN CINEMA

When on a shopping spree for anguish, rapture, martyrdom, comas, counts, rapes, bastards, orphans, dogaressas, philtres, sirens, suicides, mistaken identities, flower festivals, and sudden fatal loves—even a tattooed baby—one need look no further than the Italian Diva Film, a vast clearinghouse of art nouveau decors and nineteenth-century melodramatic devices still in wondrous working order.

Within these pages are the gaudy inventories of these diva films, which flourished on the continent between 1910 and 1920, and which starred cinema's first divinities: Lyda Borelli, Pina Menichelli, Francesca Bertini, and other Olympian ancestors of the merely mortal stars of Hollywood history.

Gathering into one deeply conscious glance all the beauty scattered so sublimely through that last hour of the fin de siècle, the Italian film diva is both the movie's center and the movie itself; she is the eye and the hurricane. Indolently we bathe in her fragrant mysticisms and sensualities, while all about her, rent hearts and havoc are strewn with the violence of Armageddon. Even she is consumed by the force of her own storm—babies are ripped from her arms, leering roadmen are thrust into their place. She is buffeted by betrayals. Her purses are torn away. Her hands are pelted by ducal kisses innumerable.

Savagely lashed by her own tresses while Destiny blasts her soul, the diva cries out for vengeance, cries out with her entire body, and this is what is most spectacular about the diva film—the vocabulary of the body! Aided only in part by as many as thirty drool-inducing costume changes per film, the diva's body twists and ripples in endless metamorphoses expressing wave upon wave of inner tumult. Ever so slowly—for the film's time is the diva's time!—and in a fashion completely alien to our New World eyes, do the torso and its limbs strain toward an unprecedented posture of prurience enmarbled, and upon achieving this shocking pose, move on to the next astonishing attitude, unfurling the fingers first, languidly allowing these digits to splay about the face and the bosom of the diva and in so doing inscribe upon those marvelous surfaces the plots of all stories from all times.

During the screenings you can't help but imagine you sit next to Wayne Koestenbaum, that great curator of history's taxidermied opera divas, chronicler of their conduct, and exegete of their every signifier. You pretend you've introduced him to these florid films and by doing so you've struck him dumb. The cine-diva's vocabulary smites him with its vastness, strangeness, and uncanny accessibility—like hieroglyphics made suddenly readable.

Penny-dreadfully named—*Satanic Rhapsody, Royal Tiger, The Painting of Osvaldo Mars*—and aggressively assembled by genuine but forgotten Italian *auteurs,* the diva films are hugely watchable. Packed with melodramatic non sequiturs, dazzling and long-abandoned editing tropes, and sometimes outright peculiar toning and tinting strategies, these compact little dramas—most of them run under an hour—induce the most arcane intoxication.

The films' morbid and degenerate yoking of sex and death, and their closety devotion to costumery and decors, spritz the bruised-fruit aromas of Decadence from one end of the program to the other. One can feel in all the scenarios the pervasive influence of Gabriele D'Annunzio—a kind of Italian Walt Disney of his day, his long-gloved fingers in a bit of everything. It seems plausible that D'Annunzio, the great sensualist author and poet, ghost-wrote the screenplays, and with his one tin eye shining, oversaw the production of these movies like the construction of so many death-rides at a great Liebestod theme park.

While the cult of the diva grew within the Italian populace, Mussolini could perceive the fevers of degeneracy in this great film genre. Preferring more subservient women for his country's ideal, he especially disapproved of an art form that celebrated the fearsome power and savage suffering of the feminine. After his rise to power, the diva film went into eclipse.

Now, exalted by the imminent return of the diva, if only between the covers of this book, I'm determined to throng her portico with the other ardent suitors. Then, at first sight of her and her heartsick entourage, I shall toss my unworthy self headlong at the hem of her dress, hoping to plant there just one kiss before being swept into oblivion by the delicious fury of the Divine.

—*Guy Maddin*

Acknowledgments

THE GEOGRAPHY OF A BOOK

On a cold winter day of 1990, the late Anne Coffin Hanson, my senior colleague in the Department of the History of Art at Yale University, and I went to lunch to discuss my first professional evaluation. In chapter six of my then-forthcoming book, *The Body in the Mirror* (Princeton University Press, 1992), I had a sentence on the Italian diva of silent film. As we were talking about the progress of my scholarship, Anne said: "Write about her."

Between 1990 and 1995, while I was writing and completing my second book, *Cinema and Painting: How Art Is Used in Film* (University of Texas Press, 1996), I traveled to Venice, Rome, and Milan with grants from Yale to research my diva project. After spending incredibly long hours in the libraries of each city, and despite endless lines at the photocopy machine, I managed to gather a respectable quantity of data on my topic and its historical context. This first international trip climaxed at the lake resort of Gardone Riviera, where I was able to visit Gabriele D'Annunzio's mansion, called Il Vittoriale. I had also arranged for screenings in Turin, but the only visual detail that struck me was that the logo of the Turin Film Museum did not appear at the bottom of the film print I was looking at. On the contrary, the logo said NFM, Nederlands Filmmuseum. So I began to think about Amsterdam.

Back in New Haven, during a phone call with Paolo Cherchi Usai, I learned that the Cineteca di Bologna had diva films—but how to get to the list of its archival holdings? Then, Robert Haller, the director of Anthology Film Archives, in New York, invited me to a screening of *Lyrical Nitrate* (*Lyrisch Nitraat*, 1991), by Peter Delpeut, an archival compilation film that contained footage from *Malombra*, with Lyda Borelli, and from *Il Fior di Male*, again with the famous Lyda. Of course, I had seen the diva's films before, during my trip to Rome, but encountering Borelli again through Delpeut was even more hypnotic. In addition, Antonia Lant's introduction to the film was most inspiring. In 1995, I set my mind on Bologna first, since I had no contact whatsoever in Amsterdam. I managed to get the list of films from the Bologna archive: it held a lot of diva films. Shortly after, I decided to go to the African Film Festival in Ouagadougou, Burkina Faso.

Unable to go to the movies by myself at night because it was too dangerous, I teamed up with my Nigerian colleague, Frank Ukadike, who needed help with his French. One day, before enlisting my language skills to talk to Air France, he proposed a lunch at a local restaurant, where he would introduce me to a few people from Holland. It was there that I fortuitously met Peter Delpeut, who at the time was the deputy director of the Nederlands Filmmuseum. He gave me his business card and confirmed that the NFM had many diva films.

As soon as I got back to America, I applied for another Yale travel grant and arranged to go to Bologna and Holland the following summer. My head was swimming: I saw so many films that the level of fatigue was truly unbearable, and I started thinking that the only way to handle this topic would be to bring the films to America so that I could watch them over and over again. By the time I met Peter Delpeut at the NFM, inspired as I still was by his *Lyrical Nitrate,* all I had to do was to say to him: "I am writing a book on the Italian diva. Why don't you make a new film about her?" And he did. In the wake of a two-week journey all over Italy, which included more screenings for Peter and myself and interviews with documentary filmmaker Gianfranco Mingozzi and historian Vittorio Martinelli, NFM producer Frank Rhoumen swiftly organized the finances and the shooting schedule.

Now that I had enlisted the collaboration of the Dutch museum and the Bolognese film archive, I felt more confident, so I approached Adrienne Mancia, who, at the time, was a senior film curator at the Museum of Modern Art in New York. She spoke to Bologna again, and Italian film historian Gian Piero Brunetta also joined the project. Richard Peña, at the Film Society of Lincoln Center, expressed interest and agreed to host a series of screenings during the New York Film Festival at Lincoln Center as soon as appropriate funding could be secured. The result was that Peter Delpeut premiered *Diva Dolorosa* in Amsterdam in 1999, and in 2000 I cocurated, with Gian Luca Farinelli, a film retrospective at Lincoln Center of some diva films restored by the Cineteca di Bologna.

But it was really Federica Olivares who brought all the pieces together, at a point when we had the research, the films, and the location, but no money. A very intelligent and dynamic lady from Milan, Federica Olivares persuaded the Italian company La Perla to fund the retrospective. Last but not least, in 2004 my Dutch colleague Ivo Blom organized a wonderful symposium to celebrate the jubilee of the Dutch Institute in Rome. *Diva Dolorosa* was screened, and Ivo Blom, Peter Delpeut, and I met Queen Beatrix of the Netherlands, who had come with all her entourage. Seen as a female type, the Dutch queen, elegant but simple in manner, could not have been less like a diva.

Whereas conducting the research and organizing the retrospective took a certain number of years, writing the book took even longer. I decided to use as many books from the period as possible in my analyses, and I became fascinated with words that were popular then but no longer exist today: for example, *cerebrismo* (cerebralism) and *lussuria* (lust). And, finally, I became involved with topics I had never explored before, such as occultism and the history of the airplane. I must say that during all these years I had a terrific time; in fact, I met so many different people and explored so many different archives that I wonder whether I will ever be able to let the period of early and silent films go out of my life, despite my interest in other areas as well.

Of course, I am deeply grateful to all the institutions that helped me: the Archivio del Gazzettino, Venice; the Archivio Storico of the Biennale in Venice; the Biblioteca Luigi Chiarini of the Scuola Nazionale di Cinema, Rome; the Biblioteca Nazionale of Rome and the Biblioteca Nazionale of Florence; the Braidense Library, Milan; the Brera Art School Library, Milan; the Burcardo Theatre

Library, Rome; the Cineteca di Bologna; the Cineteca Italiana, Milan; the Cineteca Nazionale, Rome; the Danish Film Institute, Copenhagen; the Film Society of Lincoln Center, New York; the Fondazione Giorgio Cini, Venice; the Fondazione Il Vittoriale degli Italiani, Gardone Riviera (Brescia); the George Eastman House, Rochester, New York; the Hertziana Library, Rome; the School of Literature, Communication and Culture at the Georgia Institute of Technology, Atlanta; the Institute of Forensic Medicine and the Lombroso Museum, Turin; the Library of Congress, Washington, D.C.; the Mario Praz Museum, Rome; MART (Museo di Arte Moderna e Contemporanea di Trento e Rovereto), Rovereto; the Film Study Center of the Museum of Modern Art, New York; the National Museum of Cinema, Turin; the Netherlands Filmmuseum, Amsterdam; the New York Public Library; the Pigorini Museum, Rome; the Querini-Stampalia Library, Venice; the Rockefeller Foundation's Bellagio Program, Bellagio; the Whitney Humanities Center at Yale University, New Haven; the Wolfsonian Museum, Miami Beach; and Zeitgeist Films, New York.

In all these places, it was the people I met who really made a difference. It was clear that we shared a passion for the study of film. This list of additional persons is so long that I can only express my sincerest gratitude to all who helped me intellectually, financially, and organizationally: Richard Abel, Stefano Albertini, Paula Amad, Dudley Andrew, Adriano Aprà, Pierre Apraxine, Laura Argento, Shannon Attaway, Mariella Bacigalupo, Aldo Bernardini, Emily Braun, Joseph Brodsky, Leslie Camhi, Paola Castagna, Thomas Christensen, Antonio Costa, Donald Crafton, Paola Cristalli, Monica Dall'Asta, Guido Dalle Vacche, Eric de Kuyper, Mary Ann Doane, Susan Emerson, Marguerite Engberg, Franca Farina, Lucy Fischer, Mary Gibson, Giovanna Ginex, Tom Gunning, Rodney Hill, Marjorie Kaufman, Kenneth Knoespel, Robert Kolker, Michele Lagny, Adrienne Mancia, Guy Maddin, Rosanna Maule, Luca Mazzei, Mario Musumeci, Linda Nochlin, Jean-Loup Passek, Mario Portigliatti Barbos, Leonardo Quaresima, Riccardo Redi, Elisabeth Riani, Paolo Riani, Mark Seymour, Pierre Sorlin, Luciana Spina, Elliott Stein, Ian Stimmler, Edward Stratman, Jean Sudrann, Casper Tyberg, Karole Vail, William Valerio, Patrizia Veroli, William Weaver, Judith Wechsler, Jamie Wolf, and Daniela Zamburlin.

I also wish to acknowledge two colleagues in early cinema, Charles Musser and Jennifer Bean, who read the manuscript and helped me revise it. This book came into being thanks to the endless copyediting and image research of Nadine Covert and Wendy Wipprecht, who worked with an amazing mix of calm and precision. I also want to recognize the excellent help I received from the University of Texas Press, in particular from Laura Bost, Nancy Bryan, Jim Burr, Joanna Hitchcock, Kip Keller, Stephanie Nelson, and Leslie Tingle.

All the translations are mine, as are the mistakes. I have tried to write *Diva* in such a way that anyone can follow the story I tell, and not just specialized readers. On the other hand, I hope this book will stimulate more comparative work on early Italian cinema and, for example, prerevolutionary Russian films. For all these reasons, I have kept footnotes to the necessary minimum, provided a contextualizing bibliography, and tried to convey the flavor of the period as much as possible.

Angela Dalle Vacche
New York City

Time Line

CULTURAL EVENTS AND THE DIVA FILM

My time line begins with Edgar Allan Poe, because the filmic image was associated with occult powers, and it ends with the legalization of divorce, because this issue was a central topic in the diva-film genre. The turning point of the time line is 1913, the official birth date of the diva as a cultural phenomenon. Although this study argues for a close relationship between filmic form and Bergson's philosophy, the time line includes references to Freud, because some of his most famous case studies belong to this period and function as a signifying absence in the context of early Italian cinema.

1839	Edgar Allan Poe, "The Fall of the House of Usher"
1840	Edgar Allan Poe, *Tales of the Grotesque and Arabesque*
1859	Charles Darwin, *On the Origin of Species*
1860–1870	Italian unification; Rome chosen as capital
1863–1901	Nationwide effort to reduce illiteracy; population increases 30 percent and number of teachers grows from 34,000 to 65,000
1870–1890	Expansion of railway network from 1,250 to 8,060 miles
1871	Charles Darwin, *The Descent of Man*
1873	Giovanni Verga, *Tigre Reale; Eva*
1876	Gustave Moreau paints *Salome Dancing Before Herod*
1877	Mandatory elementary instruction in Italy (implemented by Minister Michele Coppino)
1881	Antonio Fogazzaro, *Malombra;* premiere of Jacques Offenbach's *Tales of Hoffmann,* featuring an automaton called Olympia in Act I
1882	Age requirement for male suffrage lowered from twenty-five to twenty-one; two years of elementary education and military service also required
1886	Villiers de L'Isle-Adam, *Tomorrow's Eve*
1888	Anna Vertua Gentile's best seller for young women, *Come Devo Comportarmi* (How Should I Behave)—eleven editions through 1921
1892	Edmondo De Amicis, *Amore e Ginnastica*
1893	Cesare Lombroso, *The Female Offender;* Luigi Pirandello, *L'Esclusa*
1895	Wilhelm Roentgen discovers X-rays

1896 Battle of Adwa (Adowa); Henri Bergson, *Matter and Memory*

1898 Repression of riots against the increased cost of bread; art nouveau arrives in Italy at an exposition in Turin; Pierre and Marie Curie publish their discovery of radium

1900 Italian-born anarchist Gaetano Bresci comes from America and kills King Umberto I in Monza; Vittorio Emanuele III becomes the new king; Henri Bergson, *Le Rire (Laughter)*; Sigmund Freud, *The Interpretation of Dreams*

1901 Piombino steel mills established

1902 Benedetto Croce, *Estetica*

1903 Pius X becomes pope; Otto Weininger's best seller *Sex and Character;* Wilhelm Jensen, *Gradiva: A Pompeian Fantasy;* Benedetto Croce begins publishing *La Critica* (1903–1944); *Leonardo* (magazine) published (1903–1907); Luca Comerio films *Ballo Excelsior:* film of twelve tableaux vivants about the scientific advances of mankind; Giulio Marconi's wireless telegraph establishes contact between Europe and America; first successful powered, piloted flights by Wilbur and Orville Wright in Kitty Hawk, North Carolina

1904 Grazia Deledda, *Cenere;* encounter between Bergson and Papini

1905 Filoteo Alberini films *The Capture of Rome:* first Italian fiction film based on historical subject; Einstein introduces special theory of relativity; Sigmund Freud, *The Joke and Its Relation to the Unconscious*

1906 Prime Minister Giovanni Giolitti begins an era of social reforms; Sibilla Aleramo becomes famous for her autobiographical novel *Una Donna;* eruption of Vesuvius near Naples

1907 Giovanni Papini, *Philosophy of the Cinematograph;* Henri Bergson, *Creative Evolution;* Freud, *Dreams and Delusions in Jensen's "Gradiva"*; Edmondo De Amicis, *Cinematografo Cerebrale*

1908 Georges Sorel, *Reflections on Violence;* Luigi Pirandello, *L'Umorismo; La Voce* (magazine) published (1908–1916); Ernest Rutherford awarded Nobel Prize for his work on atomic decay and the chemistry of radioactivity; Adolf Loos, *Ornament and Crime*

1909 Mario Calderara designs and flies lightweight biplane; Nobel Prize to Marconi for wireless telegraph; F. T. Marinetti publishes first futurist manifesto, in *Le Figaro* (February); death of Cesare Lombroso; Serge Diaghilev establishes Ballets Russes and goes to Paris; F. T. Marinetti, *Mafarka, the Futurist: An African Novel*

1910 Gianni Caproni establishes Caproni Company and Flight School; Maria Tarnowska tried in Venice as an accomplice to murder; eruption of Etna near Catania, in Sicily; Lyda Borelli triumphs in *Salomè; il cinematografo* (masc.) shifts to *la film* (fem.)

1911 Italy declares war on Turkey for the conquest of Libya; Luigi Pirandello, *Suo Marito;* Anton Giulio Bragaglia begins work on photography; Ricciotto Canudo, *La Naissance d'un Sixième Art;* first time an Italian woman wears pants in public (Turin); Ballets Russes arrives in Italy; Ida Rubinstein performs in *Saint Sebastian*

1912 Universal male suffrage in Italy; Valentine de Saint-Point issues *The Manifesto of Futurist Woman;* Anton Giulio Bragaglia, *The Typist;* Nijinsky, *L'Après-Midi d'un Faune;* Vatican bans all film screenings inside religious buildings

1913 Valentine de Saint-Point, *Futurist Manifesto of Lust;* Anton Giulio Bragaglia, *Manifesto of Photodynamism* and *L'Attrice Fotodinamizzata* (The Photodynamic Actress); establishment of formal network of film censorship; first male suffrage vote on October 26; maximum flow of Italian immigration to United States; Rosina Ferrario is first Italian woman to earn civil pilot's license; Papini launches a new periodical, *Lacerba;* **Lyda Borelli stars in Mario Caserini's *Ma l'Amor Mio non Muore* (Everlasting Love)—the first diva film, from Gloria Film, Turin**

1914 Italy is torn about going to war; Gabriele D'Annunzio, "Del Cinematografo come Strumento di Liberazione e Trasfigurazione"; Sigmund Freud writes the case study of his analysis of Sergei "The Wolfman" Pankejeff; Ricciotto Canudo, *Il Manifesto dell'Arte Cerebrista;* June 28—Austrian Archduke Francis Ferdinand assassinated in Sarajevo; Caproni builds the first of many bombers to be deployed in World War I

1914–1918 World War I

1915 Italian alliance with France and England and declaration of war on Austria; Giovanni Pastrone, *Cabiria,* with Italian diva Almirante Manzini as Sofonisba and nonprofessional actor Bartolomeo Pagano as Maciste; Freud, "A Case of Paranoia Running Counter to the Psycho-Analytic Theory of the Disease"

1916 Guido Gozzano, *Il Nastro di Laocoonte e I Serpi di Celluloide; The Futurist Manifesto of Cinematography*

1917 Caporetto defeat; Henrik Ibsen, *A Doll's House;* F. T. Marinetti envisions the *Dance of the Aviatrix;* Valentine de Saint-Point organizes a "Festival of Metachory" at the Metropolitan Opera House, New York

1918 Italian victory on the Piave River and armistice with Austria; Gabriele D'Annunzio flies over Vienna and drops patriotic leaflets; Freud publishes "The Wolfman" case history

1919 Blocking of proposed Sacchi Law; Sebastiano Arturo Luciani, *L'Idealità del Cinematografo;* Gabriele D'Annunzio drafts the Carta del Carnaro in Fiume

1920 Occupation of factories; the beginning of Fascism; Ricciotto Canudo, *Hélene, Faust et Nous: Précis d'Esthétique Cérébriste*

1921	Founding of the Italian Communist Party
1922	Fascist March on Rome; Mussolini becomes the dominant figure in Italian politics
1939–1945	World War II
1945	Italian women granted the vote
1958	The Merlin Law bans prostitution in brothels and decriminalizes prostitution if practiced privately
1974	National referendum confirms legality of divorce

Diva

Introduction

MATER DOLOROSA

The diva is the most important female singer, the prima donna, on an opera stage, but the word can also describe an arrogant or temperamental woman. Closely related to the English word *divine*, *diva* means "goddess," and thus one labeled a diva competes for the spotlight with God, the ultimate divine maker of stars. Whereas God coincides with eternity, stars live and die. The point here is that the word *diva* connotes timelessness and infinity. By contrast, the word *star* is about someone special, exceptional, or superhuman, but not comparable to a divinity.[1] In her best moments, the diva involves a certain kind of ineffable spirituality, a ritualistic otherness, and an intuitive aura about invisible things. In short, the diva is an anomalous star compared to the Hollywood model that has defined film stardom for the rest of the world. The diva's unusual contribution to the history of stardom stems from the cultural specificities of Italian modernity.

In early Italian cinema, *diva* meant a female star in a feature film that ran at least sixty minutes and included some close-ups for the heroine and a fairly static use of the camera. The point-of-view shot and the shot–reverse shot, two basic features of classical American cinema, did not exist in the Italian films made between 1913 and 1918. However, the point-of-view shot began to appear around 1919 or 1920 in diva films.

The three most famous divas of this period were Francesca Bertini (1892–1985), Lyda Borelli (1884–1959), and Pina Menichelli (1890–1984). One could say that Italian stardom was more hierarchical or stratified than the Hollywood model. This is why I will also discuss minor stars who specialized in playing heroines in short adventure films: to show how divas in the so-called "long" feature film were preceded by lesser-known female colleagues. In the end, my discussion of divas is based more on the films I have been able to see than on the stars' degree of celebrity. Hence, my study includes sections about divas less famous than Bertini, Borelli, and Menichelli: Diana Karenne, Maria Jacobini, Soava Gallone, Mercedes Brignone, Stacia Napierkowska, Elena Makowska, Italia Almirante Manzini, and Leda Gys. Notwithstanding my list, there are other divas who are linked to possibly surviving films and warrant further examination: Elena Sangro, Gianna Terribili-Gonzales, Hesperia, Rina De Liguoro, Carmen Boni, Maria Carmi, and Vera Vergani.

Since my method is not biographical, I have included available information about the lives and careers of the divas in the Biographical Profiles at the end of this study.[2] Besides underlining iconography to show that the diva was a mélange of old clichés and new fads, my approach is based on bringing out the richness of the diva's visual form as a cultural type.[3] Notwithstanding the obvious context of art nouveau, what was the cultural paradigm containing the diva as a signifying figure? The answer: time-conscious narratives concerned with social issues. The first short fiction film produced in Italy was Filoteo Alberini's *La Presa di Roma* (1905; *The Capture of Rome*). Hence, one can easily understand that Italian cinema was born out of an obsession with history and time, perhaps because national unification occurred as late as 1860—that is, well after France, England, and Germany had become nation-states.

After starting out with a historical film, the Italian film industry, trying to establish itself in the emerging international market for the cinema, quickly turned to history, religion, literature, and opera as storehouses of historical narratives. This historical obsession resulted in Enrico Guazzoni's *Quo Vadis?* (1913); Mario Caserini and Eleuterio Rodolfi's *Ultimi Giorni di Pompeii* (1914; *The Last Days of Pompeii*); *Cabiria* (1914), by Giovanni Pastrone (1883–1959); and *Christus* (1916), by Giulio Antamoro (1877–1945), to name only a few of the most important box-office hits at home and abroad. For his production of *Intolerance* (1916), D. W. Griffith (1875–1948) himself was inspired by the Italian industry's penchant for monumentality, spectacle, and accuracy of detail in the sets and costumes.

The two most important genres of the early and silent period became the historical film and the diva film. Besides these two dominant generic specialties, the industry produced plenty of adventure films and comedies. But while the adventure film embraced the long format in 1913, comedies remained mostly short and socially self-conscious. The most successful star of the adventure film was Emilio Ghione (1879–1930), a close friend of Francesca Bertini, who gave life to the serial, *I Topi Grigi* (The Grey Rats). The most acclaimed comedians of the silent period include André Deed (1884–1938), as Cretinetti, and Ferdinand Guillaume (1887–1997), as Polidor. No complete, in-depth study of the Italian silent-film industry has ever been written in English, a problem linked to the lack of translations of Italian and French film scholarship for monolingual English audiences and specialists.

Whereas Gian Piero Brunetta has argued that the historical genre was more important both aesthetically and commercially than melodrama,[4] my findings indicate that, first, the diva film was at least competitive with, and perhaps equal to, the historical film in popularity. Second, the diva film was a specific genre in and of itself, not an occasional specialization of melodrama in general. Diva films became a genre because of the intense social consciousness they exhibited in denouncing the corruption of adult young males. Given that, according to the diva film, many adult males cheat, steal, lie, pimp, kill, disappear, or loaf, the most important topics of this genre were courtship, first love, seduction, pregnancy, virginity, marriage, adultery, abandonment, divorce, child custody, prostitution, public reputation, employment, relatives, and financial power.

Third, and what is most important, the diva film was concerned with history—namely, time—since its primary topic was the change from old to new models of behavior in the domestic sphere and between the sexes. Besides the historical film and melodrama, Brunetta also addresses short comedy films, which he places at the bottom of the generic hierarchy. It is worth noting, however, that the topic of gender roles in transition was central to the comedies produced before World War I. At the same time, issues of sexual confusion or role reversal also appear in the context of adventure and science-fiction films, such as Mario Roncoroni's *Filibus* (1915) and André Deed's *L'Uomo Meccanico* (1921; The Mechanical Man). My guess is that many other examples relevant to genre, gender, and stardom in the history of early Italian cinema are waiting to be discovered and analyzed.

In short, were we to compare the diva film to the historical film genre one more time, it would become apparent that the diva film's preoccupation with men and women redefining themselves is absolutely dominant in the social and cinematic imagination of the period. This interest in the boundaries of identity is not surprising, since Wilhelm Roentgen discovered X-rays in 1895, Pierre and Marie Curie discovered radium and polonium in 1898, Albert Einstein developed his special theory of relativity in 1905, and Ernest Rutherford was awarded the Nobel Prize in chemistry in 1908 for his studies of radioactive decay. Clearly, the turn of the century was marked by several scientific discoveries challenging notions of energy, being, substance, and visibility. Needless to say, all these categories not only upset the equivalence between surface and depth, but they also reshaped definitions of masculinity and femininity, gender roles and sexual orientation, biological features and physical appearances.

In contrast to the more private focus of the diva film, depictions of antiquity and battles in historical films offered opportunities for spectacle, but not much regarding the new couple or the new family. Everybody had something to say or to learn about love, passion, and betrayal, and that was why everybody went to the cinema. Since historical characters were most predictable in their dominant male and subordinate female roles, the epic genre attracted its mass audience through its use of settings, its deployment of crowds of extras, its staging of rapid or highly choreographed actions, and its reliance on special effects such as crumbling temples, erupting volcanoes, and sea storms. All this enormous effort was meant to pay tribute, so to speak, to lofty and legendary topics.

In contrast to the historical film's spectacular and external emphasis on public, heroic action, the diva film struck a more domestic, hidden, personal, yet highly sensitive chord. So complicated and controversial were the issues at stake that the diva grew out of the struggle for change in Italian culture. This icon became a model of transition for Italian women and a figure of temporality for the society at large. So intensely preoccupied was she with the theme of transformation that her sinuous, ever-shifting outline stood for the ways in which Italian men and women experienced change and looked at modernization with both eagerness and fear. The diva's corporeal plasticity was nothing else than a symptom of ambiguity and uncertainty about breaking away from the past and moving into the future.

As Aldo Bernardini has argued, female stardom in the sense of *divismo* was no domestic discovery, but a systematic form of mass cult that Italian cinema imported from abroad.[5] Although she was trained in the theater, the Danish actress Asta Nielsen (1881–1972) was the first European star to invent film stardom. Nielsen's name and way of being became a trademark of emancipated femininity in innumerable countries. She launched herself into this more subliminal and

Danish actress Asta Nielsen in a scene from *Afgrunden* (1910; *The Abyss*). Courtesy Danish Film Institute, Copenhagen.

far-reaching form of iconicity with *Afgrunden* (1910; *The Abyss*). And Nielsen became the first star because she introduced an unprecedented vertical tension into her acting style for the screen. The vertigo in Nielsen's acting brought out film's power to make visible otherwise invisible psychological states.

Before Nielsen, the divine Sarah Bernhardt (1844–1923) rose to stardom through her sensationalistic way of living and her flamboyant yet tragic acting style.[6] Eleonora Duse (1858–1924), instead, distinguished herself by the spiritual slant of her quiet but intense introspective approach.[7] Whereas Sarah Bernhardt always played herself, regardless of her ostensible role, Duse's fusion with her characters is worth commenting upon. In fact, she anticipated Stanislavsky's method and the Actors Studio technique, which were based on the performer's psychological merging with the character.

Just like Nielsen, Duse strove to make visible the depths of interiority, but she never used her acting to openly display the erotic dimension of the female body on stage. Extremely private in daily life, Duse was capable of great passions, but she was also modest and idealistic. In contrast to Nielsen's assertive language of desire on-screen, Duse brought to the stage the corporeal geography of medieval mysticism by using her hands, props, silence, stillness, and emptiness as departure points toward something either invisible or overwhelming. Duse's inconspicuous but open-ended acting style recalled Italian women's habit of assuming expressions of re-

Lyda Borelli in *Malombra* (1917).

ligious absorption. The so-called "mystical look," with eyes raised to the sky and hands brought together in prayer, was how most women posed for a photographic portrait. This Catholic cliché was adopted by innumerable aunts and mothers in the family album of every home, and even by Sarah Bernhardt, who was Jewish.

Although she was influenced by Bernhardt's exuberance, Duse's spirituality, and Nielsen's independence, the film diva also differed from all her predecessors because her frantic acting underlined a negative view of the female body. And this is perhaps why the Italian film diva has been confused with the femme fatale of northern European painting and literature. The twisting human figure of the diva became a site of hysteria, out of which some new positive shape might emerge. With a mute eloquence comparable to a suffragette's speech, the Italian diva expressed the struggle of women caught between old-fashioned standards and new options for the future. Yet despite the musical and dance-like qualities of her acting, the diva's characters in film were unable to develop further and embrace a truly feminist, avant-garde practice. Indeed, the film diva came up against too many obstacles and could not prevail, and so her melodramas could not evolve into more interesting narratives and visual forms. In the aftermath of World War I, the Italian film industry, after several golden years of great success, collapsed. Between 1919 and 1922 the rise of Fascism reversed all the advances of the women's emancipation movement and repressed the debate about divorce that had been triggered by the proposed Sacchi Law.[8]

Even though *diva* means "star," the Italian diva was much more erratic and complicated than the Hollywood star, possibly because American mainstream cinema was tied to values of narrative coherence and depth of character, which the diva film overlooks for the sake of dazzling visual display and an operatic heightening of emotions. Thus, the diva was an anomalous star in the Hollywood sense of this term. At the same time, it would be wrong to assume that the diva did not incorporate or borrow traits from the femme fatale and from all sorts of other legal, scientific, and artistic definitions of femininity typical of her cosmopolitan period.[9] She was so mixed that to study this topic is daunting due to the cross-national, intertextual, cross-cultural, and intrageneric connotations.

Symptomatic of twentieth-century traumas and neuroses, the diva's acting was double-edged, for her characters are torn between the artificial, statuesque posing of a respectable woman, and the animal swiftness and sly ferocity that Cesare Lombroso (1835–1909) attributes to thieves, prostitutes, and anarchists.[10] The combination in one type of these two extreme postures—rigidly elegant and callously flexible—demonstrated that the diva's cultural function was to embody a conflicted answer to major changes within sexual and social relations. On-screen, the diva is afraid of, but also eager for, new behaviors and fresh situations. By contrast, Hollywood stardom as a whole was built on the belief that, on the one hand, greedy vamps were always evil, and, on the other, that any new way of being, either personal or economic, was, by definition, always good. This kind of trajectory is comparable to that of an arrow, hurtling forward without doubts or hesitations, trusting in a sort of blind faith in improvement or, in any case, massive change.

Regardless of any painful adjustments it might require, change, in American cinema, was considered the equivalent of progress within a linear and goal-oriented trajectory valuing effort, success, and the future. The Hollywood female star's inclination toward change, therefore, did not correspond to the mixture of subordination and anticonformism, suffering and rebellion that was typical of Italian female divismo. As Mira Liehm remarks in *Passion and Defiance* (1984), the Italian diva generally looked sad or melancholic, whether she portrayed a single mother, a prostitute, an abandoned wife, or an artist's model.[11]

The diva's acting was often overreactive, spectacular, and operatic instead of psychologically motivated and introspective.[12] This is because her character's sense of self does not stem from a level of personal entitlement, but rather from the approval of her family and society at large. Typically, she looks alone even when she is with a lover or a husband. She feels obliged to stand beside the man who betrays her, either because children are involved or because she doubts whether she can take on a more independent role for herself than the traditional personae of mother and wife.

Betrayed by men and in competition with female rivals, the diva is often a woman with no real or productive function in society; she can make herself useful only as the unhappy nurturer or passive relative of those around her. At the same time, there are enough moments of repressed desire and stifled anger in these films to indicate that the diva longs for social justice. The diva dreams about some kind of miraculous transformation or redemption that would ensue if she finds the

Pina Menichelli (film source unknown). Author's collection.

(top) Soava Gallone in *La Cavalcata Ardente* (1925; The Fiery Squadron). Author's collection.

Diana Karenne in *Christus* (1916; directed by Giulio Antamoro). Courtesy Cineteca Nazionale, Rome.

courage and the energy to break away from her submissive and duty-bound existence.

In short, within an oscillation between mystical-visionary and hysteric-melancholic postures, the diva's acting style mostly fits the stereotype of the *mater dolorosa,* or sorrowful mother, depicted by Michelangelo Buonarroti in his sculpture *Pietà* (1500; Compassion), to cite one of the most famous examples. But there is also a twist to this comparison. While the Virgin Mary is a willing and loving mater dolorosa toward the sacrificial son of God, the diva is mostly a woman who suffers because she was born a woman, whether she has children or not. In fact, the society in which the diva lives accepts a woman only if she fits within a self-effacing role of some kind. Furthermore, Michelangelo's mater dolorosa underlines the strength of the bond between a "virginal" mother and a "divine" son.

Although the diva's pain can derive from the loss of a child, her general way of suffering stems from either the painful choice to remain in the past or the lonely decision to break the rules. From this fundamental lack of acceptable options, it is not surprising that, at the end of most melodramas, she returns to the status quo or she is punished or killed. On the other hand, in many diva films the diva kills in self-defense. In *La Piovra* (1919), for instance, Bertini kills her stalker, and in *La Storia di Una Donna* (1920; The Story of One Woman), Menichelli nearly succeeds in shooting her rapist.

Installed in the basilica of Saint Peter's inside the Vatican, Michelangelo's *Pietà*—this

Michelangelo, *Pietà* (1497–1500). St. Peter's Basilica, Vatican State. Photo: Alinari/Art Resource, N.Y.

Titian (Tiziano Vecelli), *Assumption of the Virgin* (1516–1518). Santa Maria Gloriosa dei Frari, Venice. Photo: Scala/Art Resource, N.Y.

poignant episode of maternal mourning and total devotion to the crucified son—depicts an event preceding Christ's resurrection. According to Catholicism, this rebirth was a divine event defeating human time and evolutionary history alike; similarly, the diva dreams of liberating herself into a new persona above and beyond the constraints of the present and the disappointments of history. Yet it was the crucified Christ who experienced a glorious and public resurrection, well before the quieter and more private ascension to heaven of his suffering mother. Most importantly, according to Catholic dogma, her virginity was what allowed Christ's mother to reach heaven corporeally, with her mortal body intact.

For the film diva, the Catholic legacy of the mater dolorosa underlines a model of only patient nurturing, with no rebirth, no defeat of human time, no new beginning. In the drudgery of daily life, the diva's forced devotion or excessive attachment to her male companion degenerates into a self-destructive act through which she stubbornly holds on to an ideal love that cannot last. The desires of the Italian diva oscillate between sacred and profane poles: between impossible dreams of heavenly transcendence and the temptations of primitive bestiality, shown whenever she looks like a feline, an owl, or a snake.

Both personae, the mystic and the animal, are, in the end, male projections meant to erase or frame female sexuality. But the extremes of mystic or animal also mean that the very unfolding of modern life is an ambiguous realm of painful uncertainties about where things might be heading. Indeed, around the turn of the century, conceptions of space and time changed so radically that their previously accepted linear contours twisted themselves on the screen, diva film after diva film, and especially in the minds of men and women who did not know how to restructure their ways of thinking and behavior in a modern way.

Whereas order, control, metonymy, efficiency, and monotony prevailed in American modern culture at the beginning of the century, in early Italian cinema, anxiety, utopia, excess, metaphor, and imagination won out. The premise of this book is that Italian modernity was delayed and dysfunctional, but also ambitious and spontaneous. Thus, the organization of my chapters is divided between two sets of basic forces: the pull toward the past against the leap into the future, the falling down into regressive practices in antithesis to the search for spiritual elevation. One could say that the debates over the modern self and the nature of the new woman used the diva's body, on the one hand, to produce arabesques or loops that piled up with unprecedented energy, and, on the other, to spawn a deformed body with grotesque outlines hinting at monstrous births.[13] In other words, the new woman either looked unrecognizable because she was too abstract, or became nonrepresentational because she was too strange. Finally, one may wonder why I am using these terms—*arabesque* and *grotesque*—and one may also be curious about their origin or relevance to the diva as a moving image about change, or, in Gilles Deleuze's words, a time-image.[14]

Let us argue for a moment that a Victorian optical toy called a phenakistoscope, developed around 1833, left its special trace inside the moving images of early cinema. While standing in front of a mirror, let us rotate the phenakistoscope's disc, a single human form repeated all around its border. At first, if the speed is not too great, the figure will begin to deform itself into a doodle, and later, at maximum speed, it will unravel into a quasi-abstract graphic pattern. Not only did the disfiguring and deforming principles of the phenakistoscope stay on inside the apparatus of early cinema, but its fast or slow spinning was also relevant to the way in which a whole society perceived people and things. The arabesque and the grotesque conveyed the mixed and chaotic rhythms of modern life.

Thus, the diva's arabesques and grotesqueries signaled how difficult it could be to move toward change steadily but effectively. Indeed, such a warping of space and time was constantly staged by the diva film, whose roller-coaster narratives were about the absence of a systematic temporal trajectory. Such a lacuna may be put into relation with a society lamenting the loss of responsible adult males. Often reduced to disobedient children or vulnerable sons whom the diva tolerates, supports, or accepts, these carefree or exploitative partners stood for a void in modern, constructive, and responsible historical agency. This is why, in the diva film, to compensate for the proliferation of dandies and Don Giovannis, of male artists and loafing aristocrats, old and tough patriarchal figures stay on. It is as if the narrative needs the previous male generation in order to reach some kind of closure. Yet these grandfathers or old uncles, representing an antimodern and anachronistic regime, behave either overprotectively or despotically toward their young female relatives.

Through the arabesque and the grotesque, the acceleration or the slowing down of my

Phenakistoscope disc (c. 1833). Courtesy of Stills Collection, Motion Picture Department, George Eastman House, Rochester, N.Y.

imaginary phenakistoscope relies on two opposite but complementary rates of motion. These two speeds—slow and fast—greatly differ from the always-identical rhythms of the assembly line in the American factory. There, production proceeds step by step, each step calculated in advance to maximize profit. Although the images of a Hollywood film may seem faster or slower according to the external reactions they trigger, generic Hollywood narratives are fairly predictable in their internal pace: by a certain point, the story achieves a climax, a resolution, and a closure, as if the whole process had been timed on an invisible clock. Hollywood is like a factory in the sense that the creativity of storytelling is there—live and strong—but it is also either channeled or regulated.

By contrast, diva films, both singly and as a genre, are much more accidental, erratic, uneven, badly plotted, and unpredictable in their developments. This much more nonsystematic, emotional, and subjective handling of temporality greatly differs from the Tayloristic, measurable protocols of time used in both the American factory and the Hollywood studios. But the key questions, at this point, are what was the cultural source of this more improvisational model of time and why did the diva film embrace it? My study will argue that the handling of temporality in the diva film was influenced by the irrational, impulsive climate produced by the great popularity in Italy of the philosophy of Henri Bergson (1859–1941).[15] For the French thinker, energy battles against death, and spontaneity and subjectivity are in conflict with logic and measurement. In the history of early Italian film theory, the genealogy of this philosophical legacy goes from Bergson to Giovanni Papini (1881–1956), from the former futurist critic Sebastiano Arturo Luciani (1884–1950) to painter-turned-film-producer Pier Antonio Gariazzo (1879–1964), and from filmmaker Nino Oxilia (1889–1917) to Ricciotto Canudo (1879–1923), an Italian expatriate in Paris who was at the center of the cine-club movement in the twenties. All these writers and artists celebrated an obscure stream-of-consciousness tempo in film at the expense of the models of thought deployed by Hollywood narratives.

In line with Bergson's sense that flights of the imagination are more important than reality or science, and despite the absence of the point-of-view shot and of the shot–reverse shot, a profoundly subjective gaze was in charge of the diva film. It was as if the whole genre were a sort of delirious phenakistoscope through which Italian audiences watched themselves struggling and suffering with outdated gender roles. The diva film's internal, diffused subjective gaze accounts for its amazing mixture of lyricism, paralysis, and desperation, while it also subtends its spellbinding décor, the escapist mise-en-scènes, the Gothic schemes, the futurist allusions, and the utopian or mystical yearnings.

Divas, Industry, and the Arts

The film historian Aldo Bernardini has demonstrated that the Italian film industry was organized (or scattered) according to either city or region.[16] Production houses in different areas of the country tended to specialize in competing genres. The diva film, with its aristocratic, art nouveau, and often protofeminist slant, was produced more in northern Italy (Milan, Turin) than in the south. Naples, instead, was the most important city for the realist handling of crime-ridden melodramas, often inspired by popular songs in the local dialect. The Italian film industry's organization was structurally weak. Its major failure was the absence of Hollywood's vertical integration—that is, stable links across production, distribution, and exhibition to ensure a steady and fast diffusion of films throughout the territory without too many interlopers to drain the original company's profit. Creativity was also a problem in the young Italian film industry, for if Hollywood quickly came to behave like a factory, it also knew how to be creative enough to update and differentiate its products. By contrast, genre films in Italy were often redundant.

Already during the silent period, the American vertical system of integration, by which a film moved smoothly from production to the box office, enabled Hollywood to quickly conquer the rest of the world with action, romance, and suspense. In short, cinema was a more organized business in America than in Italy. The wealthy aristocracy and the entrepreneurial upper bourgeoisie were heavily involved in early Italian filmmaking because these two groups included the investors in films and the producers. Their personal agendas, however, did not interlock into an overall industrial system, and their financial adventures with the cinema could lead to quick success or sudden bankruptcy. In *Life to Those Shadows* (1990), Noel Burch correctly links early Italian cinema to the middle class, which did not enjoy the financial means of the aristocracy, although it embraced the latter's nationalistic and decadent ethos.[17] In France, the film industry became experimental and anticonventional while also managing to remain in touch with the democratic values of the working class. In the United States, cinema was made of narratives appealing to the masses, and showed no interest in strange experiments or elitist creative solutions. Early American cinema addressed the recent immigrants who could not afford other forms of entertainment and who were drawn to the humblest form of representation, in contrast to more prestigious media, such as theatre.

Without a doubt, cinema too, had a populist appeal in Italy, but it was also mainly an urban phenomenon. The tension of old and new, which placed the diva between the nineteenth-century operatic stage and the twentieth-century filmic screen, ended up performing a strange detour through the ancient form of the commedia dell'arte: this old but fluid tradition turned out to enable women to refashion their own image in the new industry according to new fictional roles and professional models.

As Bernardini and Martinelli explain, leading players or "first actors" could easily become "artistic directors" at the production house that had originally hired them. During the era of the short film, whenever a performer arrived on the shooting set, he or she became one of the many elements of the company; specializations were still rather vague, and everybody would help, according to what needed to be done. Within this framework, the performer would learn about directing, writing, costumes, and sets.[18]

To be sure, this interchangeability of professional roles came from the commedia dell'arte: a lowbrow kind of stage, open to improvisation without a rigid division of labor. In this context, the *capocomico* was simultaneously the leading actor and the director of the performance. It was exactly in this kind of flexible climate that Duse started her career. From the stage to the shooting set, professional roles remained blurred and potentially less prejudiced against women's leadership during filmmaking. In other words, the commedia dell'arte's loose working method made room for an enabling alliance between women and the cinema.

Besides opera and theater, other art forms were called upon to feed the creative vein of the emerging Italian film industry. The famous titles of Italian and international literature were widely used for all sorts of adaptations, but in the most superficial fashion. The weakness of the Italian novel—mostly limited to the historical genre—in comparison with its French and English psychological counterparts was notorious, and widespread illiteracy explained opera's monopoly on the imagination of the Italian masses.[19] The humble status of early cinema and the lack of enough indigenous novels with a flair for personal drama meant that the literary sources for the diva film were often imported from France and belonged to the lowbrow category of the feuilleton. Four diva films, however, stand out for their domestic literary origins. Carmine Gallone's *Malombra*

Francesca Bertini in *Assunta Spina* (1915). Courtesy Cineteca Nazionale, Rome.

(1917), with Borelli, is based on the eponymous novel (1881) by Antonio Fogazzaro. Giovanni Pastrone's *Tigre Reale* (1916), with Menichelli, is based on a novelette (1873) by Giovanni Verga (1840–1922), a Sicilian writer known for his realist (*verismo*) fiction rather than for his symbolist-decadent works. In fact, it is worth noting that, besides *Tigre Reale*, Verga wrote *Eva* (1873), the story of a Sicilian painter who ruins all his romantic and artistic ideals for the sake of a female dancer, and, under the influence of the French naturalist Émile Zola, *Eros* (1875), an analysis of psychological and social conflicts between men and women. The third diva film in this list, Gustavo Serena's *Assunta Spina* (1915), with Bertini, was based on a loose, elliptical adaptation of Salvatore Di Giacomo's play in Neapolitan dialect (1909), combined with his short story of the same title (1914) written in mainstream Italian. Finally, Febo Mari's *Cenere* (1917), with Eleonora Duse—the only film role the famous actress ever performed—comes from a story (1904) by Grazia Deledda (1871–1936).[20]

As film historian Giovanni Marchesi explains in his essay on the relation between cinema and literature:

> *French literature's great influence on silent Italian cinema fits within a more general climate of French intellectual dominance during the whole nineteenth century and for a good part of the twentieth century: one must keep in mind that since the Enlightenment,* Italian culture had found itself in a situation of backwardness and isolation *that was compensated for through the appropriation of French authors—Balzac,*

twenty-one films; Sardou, sixteen; Xavier de Montepin, ten films; Henri Bataille, Dumas fils, and Ponson du Terrail, eight films; Georges Ohnet and Eugene Sue, seven films; Feuillet and Bernstein, five films; Dumas père and Gyp, four films; Feydeau, three films; Zola, seven films; Gautier, four films; Maupassant, two films; Flaubert, one film; Stendhal, one film—and foreign literature in general. The great Russian novelists, for instance, reached Italy through French translations; likewise, a few years later, Soviet cinema, once again, arrived in Italy by way of Paris; finally, one must remember that Svevo, who, with Pirandello, is the only Italian literary figure of European stature at the beginning of the twentieth century, achieved recognition thanks to the intervention of French literary criticism.[21] (*emphasis added*)

Marchesi's examples apply to film production beyond the diva film. Yet there is no doubt that Victorien Sardou, Henri Bataille, and Georges Ohnet ranked among the most famous and prolific producers of melodramatic novelettes and theatrical sources that were later adapted into diva films not just once, but sometimes through several remakes, interpreted by the same or by different divas.

Besides opera, theater, and literature, dance is another appropriate term of reference for the diva as a cultural phenomenon. In his book *Paris/Manhattan: Writings on Art*, the cultural critic Peter Wollen writes:

The decadents articulated a view of sexuality which rigorously refused any conventional ascription of sexual nature. They portrayed a world of androgyny in which desire could run against the grain, in the wrong direction and toward the wrong object. They contested the conventional division of sexuality into active and passive. This scandalous disruption of conventional sexual stereotypes allowed modern women to identify with Salome and, along with parallel identifications with the maenad (Isadora Duncan) and the witch (Mary Wigman), to lay the foundations of modern dance, the single art form dominated by women, from Loie Fuller and Ruth Saint Denis, through Mary Wigman and Martha Graham, up to Pina Bausch and Yvonne Rainer, and beyond.[22]

The diva film was comparable to a new kind of dance, one meant to illustrate an intense and fascinating page in the history of the battle between the sexes. Many diva films feature the image of a couple involved in the most spectacular step in the tango: the drop, or throw, in which one partner picks up the other, who pretends to be falling to the floor. One could say that the history of the diva film is all about this alternation of drops: the female partner is often doing the falling, but the male lead sometimes surrenders to the choreographic direction of the new woman of modernity.

The tango, however, is a dance with rigid gender roles, which the futurists made sure to condemn, along with the museum-city of Venice and the moonlight; on the other hand, the iris shot with Amleto Novelli on top and Lyda Borelli at the bottom of the frame for the closure of the very first diva film, *Ma l'Amor Mio non Muore* (1913; *Everlasting Love*), not only became a common way of ending diva films or setting up photographs, it also resonated with a stubborn longing for a romantic ideal of stylized gracefulness.

Needless to say, painting and sculpture are also relevant to an understanding of the diva film as a visual form and as a genre concerned with temporality and women's issues; references to futurist and metaphysical art, and to decadent and neoclassical styles, will be scattered throughout this study.

Lyda Borelli in *Ma l'Amor Mio non Muore* (1913; *Everlasting Love*). Courtesy Cineteca Nazionale, Rome.

Diva, Vamp, and Femme Fatale

In Leopoldo Carlucci's *Caino* (1918), Elda, a betrayed country wife, dies of sheer pain, while her sister Cecile, the femme fatale played by the diva Elena Makowska, remains unpunished and eventually marries a wealthy evil Frenchman. This example notwithstanding, the equivalence between the diva and the femme fatale, in the genre of the diva film, was more an exception than a rule. To be sure, in Giovanni Pastrone's *Il Fuoco* (1915; The Fire), Pina Menichelli is the ultimate femme fatale. In Febo Mari's *Il Fauno* (1917; The Faun), Elena Makowska, playing an evil seducer and crafty mistress, has nothing of the mater dolorosa about her. On the other hand, the films I examine closely in the present study make it clear that the Italian diva was no simple national variation on the international figure of the femme fatale.

In other words, she was not always and only a projection of male paranoia about the other sex, as has been argued until now, a stance that grossly confuses the Italian diva with the American femme fatale or vamp. There are many Hollywood performers who deserve the designation of star, vamp, or femme fatale, but only Theda Bara (1890–1955) can be said to be the American answer to the phenomenon of the Italian diva.

As Janet Staiger explains in *Bad Women: Regulating Sexuality in Early American Cinema* (1995), Theda Bara's overnight success in 1915 was symptomatic of male anxieties stirred by the unprecedented degree of freedom enjoyed by immigrant girls in large American cities.[23] Bara's sudden rise to fame was sustained by the film industry's aggressive marketing, which constructed a whole legend around her modest origin. Bara was born Theodosia Goodman, the daughter of a Jewish tailor, in Cincinnati. Yet Bara was billed as a woman of mystic powers, born in the Sahara, the love child of a French artist and his Egyptian mistress. The studio publicists came up with an anagram of "Theda Bara": "Arab Death." Onscreen, Theda wore indigo eye makeup to emphasize her pallor, and she surrounded herself with symbols of death, such as skulls, ravens, and serpents—clearly imitating Bernhardt's morbid necrophilia.

In Frank Powell's *A Fool There Was* (1915), based on "The Vampire," a poem by Rudyard Kipling, Bara is a generic social evil, comparable to alcohol or bankruptcy. The concern with alcoholism here strikes a meaningful note of similarity between early American and early Danish cinema. By contrast, alcohol was not a major theme in early Italian cinema. Furthermore, it is worth noting that supporters of women's emancipation in the United States were often involved in temperance campaigns. Feminism, antialcohol leagues, and the negative reputation of cinema as a source of female employment leading young, naïve women into white slavery was another triptych of social concerns common in America right before Bara's success.

Because Bara's character is only an enigmatic symptom of social disturbance, she has no family and no circle of friends. Thus, she is a sort of abstract negative force that operates independently. She is evil for evil's sake, since it never becomes clear whether she is acting out of personal revenge. In Powell's film, as a character with no name, literally called the Vampire, Bara strikes, succeeds, transforms each man into a social outcast, and then exits the narrative completely unscathed and unpunished. Bara always wins, but feels nothing. There is no anger, there is no past; likewise, there is no compassion, there is no delusion, there is no confusion. The diva film, by contrast, continues to be moving and thought-provoking, precisely for all the opposite reasons: naïve girls fall in love and are abandoned; lonely mothers are punished despite their good qualities; and women are worthless unless they are young and beautiful. The genre is a feast of paradox and oxymoron. Most importantly, in *A Fool There Was,* the betrayed American wife, played by Mabel Frenyear, does suffer during the adultery, but she also has a community of friends that supports her. Everybody is quick to condemn her husband's betrayal.

In contrast to Theda Bara's vamp, who has a superficial taste for blood, Italian divas kill not so much for sheer cruelty but because their characters rebel against sexual harassment, rape, or adultery. In this respect, the Italian diva does not embrace the traditional femme fatale's gratuitously or egotistically murderous vocation. In other words, the diva does not kill for social advancement. The diva, ethically conscious, divides the world into those who have power and money and those who do not, into those who are fair and empathetic and those who take advantage of vulnerable people. As a woman, the diva always knows that, regardless of her own economic situation, she has hardly any recourse when misfortune strikes. The society in which she lives is so misogynistic that even wealthy women are often the victims of a patriarchal system.

The Feminization of Film

During the first decade of the twentieth century, neither women nor the cinematograph were taken seriously by the establishment, although everybody was aware of the suffra-

Theda Bara in *Sin* (1915). Photographer unidentified. Author's collection.

(right) Margaret Livingston as the vamp in F. W. Murnau's *Sunrise* (1927). Author's collection.

Italian women leaving the theater after watching Giovanni Pastrone's *Cabiria* (1914), with diva Italia Almirante Manzini in the role of Sofonisba. This metacinematic image comes from *Maciste* (1915), with Clementina Gay. Author's collection.

gettes' movement and of the threat that the cinema posed to good literature and the traditional theater. One way to demonstrate how powerful women were in early Italian cinema is to look at the trade journals. Based on the frequency of photographs, there were far more female stars than musclemen climbing the ladder of fame before World War I. And there were so many of these photographs—all of different divas—that some of the women appeared and disappeared overnight. As a result, the popular impact of husbands, dandies, pimps, brothers, and fathers in the diva film was tangible but limited. Amleto Novelli as the perverse Russian expatriate in *La Piovra* (1919), Febo Mari as the vulnerable artist in *Il Fuoco* (1915), and Emilio Ghione as the rough guy in *Ivonne, La Bella Danzatrice* (1915) represented the three most important categories of masculinity in the diva film as a genre. Notwithstanding the talents or looks of these male stars, they all remained subordinate to the diva on-screen. In real life, however, some of them—Paolo Azzurri, for example—were able to develop their own production companies, just as Francesca Bertini did. Through Bertini Films or Azzurri Films, for example, they tried to exercise more control over their earnings. Still, Francesca Bertini and Emilio Ghione died in abject poverty.

It might be fair to say that early cinema in Italy was born a woman. In other words, the diva's dominance of the visual register stays on, regardless of her punitive elimination at the end of most narratives. She dominates not because she is in control but because, rich or poor, she is beautiful; and beauty was a positive value in a culture sensitive to an ancient aesthetic practice at odds with the glitches and rough spots of mechanical reproduction.

Even the history of the appropriation of the English word *film* into the Italian language spells out a strong alliance between the medium and femininity. Around 1913, the diva film in Italian was commonly called *la film*, a feminine noun. Before this grammatical reincarnation, however, film was still referred to as *il cinematografo*, a masculine noun. At the very beginning, *il cinematografo* was nothing more than a fun topic included in booklets and magazines along with crossword puzzles, cartoons, songs, anagrams, nursery rhymes, and all sorts of other linguistic, technological, and quotidian curiosities for children and adults.[24]

Most importantly, in the days of short films, the masculine noun in daily speech, *il cinematografo*, had a negative connotation—it meant mental confusion. This pathological definition of the cinema was adopted by the socialist Edmondo De Amicis for his novelette *Cinematografo Cerebrale* (1907), a sort of light-hearted divertissement about patriarchy in a state of crisis.[25] De Amicis's text is worth summarizing because it describes the shift from a weak sense of male self-confidence to a feminization of patriarchal authority.

In De Amicis's novelette, the wife is out in the world and the husband is home alone. Loneliness and idleness lead to introspection about a father's worst fears and fantasies. However, this turn to repressed materials within the psyche does not involve a complete loss of control. In *Cinematografo Cerebrale*, De Amicis relies on a traditional use of grammar. His sentences do not give up logical organization; they do not yield to the power of free association, dangerous analogies, or ambiguous puns. His mind wanders through a gallery of old-fashioned fantasies about women without opening up to modernism's stream of consciousness.

De Amicis's placement of masculinity in the domestic sphere suggests that the bourgeois man was lagging behind the times despite major innovations in society: the department store, the airplane, pants for women. De Amicis's feminization of the male protagonist enables the writer to position the cinema as *cinematografo* inside daydreaming and memory, but also outside technology and productivity. By the end of the novelette, when his wife returns home, the pater familias is relieved: he

Emilio Ghione. Author's collection.

Lyda Borelli, in mourning and surrounded by fading flowers, in a scene from Carmine Gallone's *Malombra* (1917). Courtesy Cineteca di Bologna.

no longer has to face his inner cinema, and he is much happier having some female company over which to reestablish his power as the head of the family. Despite the protagonist's attempt to maintain the status quo in language and at home, it was around 1910 that *il cinematografo* began to shift to *la film*.

Divas and dandies—it is expected that they all live, love, succeed, suffer, cheat, kill, and die. But early Italian cinema yields a more subtle and surprising discovery: the pulsing beat of time in the inanimate things that surround these fictional human beings. The world of objects looms large in the diva film: clocks, hourglasses, cigarettes, roses, veils, curtains, photographs, rings, hats, gloves, shoes, clouds, trains, rocks, gates, and fireplaces are as important as acting styles or narrative structures in this genre. Indeed, the problem of historical change and its impact on gender roles is the topic of the diva film. Once again, time feels and looks subjective in this genre, for it is depicted between the extremes of cigarette smoke trailing away and perfect neoclassical statues. And there is more: the withering roses and the cigarettes wasting away in the air are also about melancholia and loss. In a sense, they remind viewers that everything passes: painting is replaced by cinema, but no matter how young the new medium is, it already knows that its own life span is limited. Roses, cigarettes, and clocks are all memento mori or *vanitas* images about human frailty and the passage of time, which, in turn, is an indifferent and cold reminder of mortality. Veils, curtains, and draperies suggest mobility and revisions, but even these objects are volatile and unreliable. Yet to better understand why the diva was a figure of temporality split between a life-giving impulse that overrides all forms of history, on the one hand, and the memories of a soon-to-be-bygone era, on the other, my reader will have to learn about the ideas of Henri Bergson and their impact on the construction of the diva at the turn of the century.

Theory and Technology

CHAPTER I

The Shape of Time

ÉLAN VITAL AND MEMENTO MORI

The cinema owes its emotional power, unique status in mass culture, and medium specificity to one particular feature: it was the first technology to split time into two clashing but complementary directions. The first is a scientific measure of change, a quantitative, objectively verifiable succession or metonymy: a chain or sequence following many clear steps. Here the cinema mimics the assembly line of the rational modern factory. By contrast, the cinema's alternative approach to time involves a metaphorical sensibility and a qualitative, subjective definition of change as a visionary leap from one state to another, from one freewheeling association to an odd analogy—the way it happens in the literary stream of consciousness and in futurist visual collages or poetic montages of words. For women and the diva film, time is, of course, linked to physical beauty, aging, and biological reproduction in ways that men do not need to worry about as intensely. Through film stardom, exceptional beauty is preserved and made endlessly available to the masses. In this way, aesthetics marries serialization. By defying time and uniqueness, the cinema, in a sense, offers an aura of beauty and timelessness, one untouchable by physical aging.

Women suffer from the problem of either not having enough time or having too much of it. Temporality for them is suffused with feelings of anxiety about aging too rapidly or with waiting alone for a real love that may never come. Women's condition is modern in the sense that "being modern" means to worry about time. Yet their situation is eccentric because whether they experience time as accelerated or slow, they are emotionally out of synch with the comparatively more controllable time of clocks and calendars that pace men's careers and industrial production. In early cinema, a human figure moving too fast or moving slow may have looked funny or surreal because these two rhythms were at odds with a more consistent linear motion in space over time. Likewise, hysteric convulsions and shifting fabrics are two hypnotic features deeply associated with the image of the film diva. As a result of the diva's emphasis on motion as curvature, it is impossible not to think of a special kind of feminine temporality—one that proceeds by leaps and bounds, in contrast to the relatively straight, causal trajectory of a more predictable and productive patriarchal teleology.

Notwithstanding the different and subjective meanings of temporality for women and men, everybody was intrigued by the cinema's power to play with time. Viewers were amazed by the uncanny doubling of the human figure on screen; by the possible reversal

Francesca Bertini (film source unknown). Courtesy Cineteca Nazionale, Rome.

(left) Francesca Bertini (film source unknown). Courtesy Cineteca Nazionale, Rome.

of its motion in space; and by the appearance on-screen, alive and walking, of someone dead or absent. By resurrecting ghosts and setting them in motion, early cinema added living life to the theme of eternity. All of a sudden, the aura of still painting could handle process, change, and development. In this climate of new visual and philosophical possibilities, the cinema began to reset the balance between Italian women's burdensome past and a potentially more feminist future. At the movies, just because images changed over time, the odds for improvement looked more favorable for the feminine sex. If any human image, male or female, could move in space, change, and simultaneously last forever, there might also be enough time to live better and even achieve, after so many struggles, "everlasting love," the utopian title of the first diva film, in 1913.

During the first steps of the cinema as a mass medium, the strongest advocate of an endless sense of energy in the natural world and in human life was the French philosopher Henri Bergson. In *Creative Evolution* (1907), he theorized about the existence of the élan vital, a sensualist impulse mobilizing all matter all the time, in defiance of either the cold chronology of history or of time's linearity. Bergson's élan vital was no predictable biological urge; it was a fluid, erratic, and continuous force activating change.[1] While it should not be confused with Charles Darwin's instinct for survival, the élan vital involves leaping forward by accumulating energy from memory and the past, together with the impulse to create anew out of a sense of intuition that overcomes the present. In the philosopher's own words, intuition, memory, and imagination feed personal creativity and historical transformations. For Bergson, life never stands still, because it is movement itself. This is why perceptual reality, for Bergson, is a human illusion produced by analyses and schemes.[2] In other words, Bergson's sense that everything changes all the time is a reminder that human control and rational thought have limits. For the French philosopher, what is truly "real" is movement, which, in turn, inhabits the deepest regions of subjectivity, where time deposits its mysterious traces and secret wishes: "But we must accustom ourselves to think being directly, without making a detour . . . We must strive to see in order to see, and no longer to see in order to act. Then the Absolute is revealed very near us and, in a certain measure, in us. It is of psychological and not of mathematical nor logical essence. It lives with us. Like us, but in certain aspects infinitely more concentrated

Pina Menichelli. Author's collection.

Henri de Toulouse-Lautrec, *Jane Avril* (1899). Lithograph, printed color, 22 1/16 × 14 1/16 in. Gift of Abby Aldrich Rockefeller (167.1946). Museum of Modern Art, New York. Photo: Digital Image © Museum of Modern Art. Licensed by Scala/Art Resource, N.Y.

and gathered up in itself, it *endures*" (emphasis in the original).[3]

With the word *evolution* next to *creative* in his title, Bergson criticized Charles Darwin's theory of gradual, small, and verifiable changes over time. Bergson also disagreed with the idea of a single line in the world of instincts, a view upheld by the criminal anthropologist Cesare Lombroso. Finally Bergson's ambition was to overcome a Hegelian model of history, in which the dialectic of old and new settles into a form of compromise. In contrast to Hegel, Bergson thought that history is made of an inefficient mixture of change and chance.

Although Bergson and Lombroso were both popular in Italy, their theories were far apart. Thus, a bit more needs to be said about Lombroso's negative impact on women's struggle for emancipation. In the wake of his 1893 publication of *The Female Offender* (*La Donna Delinquente*), Lombroso's theory about the biological inferiority of women had spread everywhere.[4] For Lombroso, biology was destiny with no recourse—he admired Darwin's theory of evolution—so time could only be cruel to women as they aged. Lombroso's women fell into three categories: mothers, prostitutes, and criminals. Lombroso was persecuted by the Catholic Church because his work rallied against the concept of soul, or anima, in favor of environmental, nutritional, behavioral, anthropometric, and physiological factors, but also because of his Jewish background. Lombroso was a socialist and a reformist who believed science could improve the world.

In contrast to Bergson's unintentional openness to women's energy for the future, Lombroso's influence led the construction of the film diva to include the worst possible stereotypes. It is much easier to recognize Lombroso's ideas in the diva as a cultural type and as a performer than to realize to what extent other schools of thought and art movements also contributed to the formation of this powerful icon. Without a doubt, it is correct, and yet a bit too obvious, to state that the diva was a hysteric. By contrast, it is a lot more interesting to discover the diva's links with antipositivist tendencies that, despite their overreaction against science, were equally capable of theorizing about modernity, time, and women's expectations.

Weary of industrialization and homogeneity, Bergson distinguished between *indivisible movement in time* and *homogeneously divisible space*. Needless to say, with this distinction he celebrated real or meaningful *duration* (*durée*) in contrast to the artificial grids and schedules produced by the rules and conventions of labor patterns and gender roles at home and in the public sphere. Because space, for Bergson, could be fragmented and calculated, it was both analytical and illusory. Its intensely visual status and its compliance with geometry accounted for its external nature and an inability to be in touch with the most formless, most internal, yet richest levels of imagination hidden in the human self. In fact, Bergson's theory of creativity is predicated on a subjective definition of time: namely, on "real" time belonging only to mental life and not to the calendar.[5]

For Bergson, time, just like sound or smell, is invisible, and its rhythms seem fast or slow according to one's state of mind or physical condition. Antiscientific, antimathematical, anti-Cartesian, Bergson's model of the self privileges not only time over space, but also sound over sight, abstraction over figuration, and emotion over logic. The diva and all her spectators, male and female alike, were in an ideal position to identify not so much with Bergson's theories or books, but with a general atmosphere valuing irrationalism and fantasy, spirituality and spiritism, visionary experiences triggered by haunting memories and utopian yearnings. In short, Bergsonism became the new flag of a rebellious modern sensibility open to occult phenomena, operatic extremes, and esoteric practices.

For Italian women with feminist inclinations, the élan vital came to signify a will to reinvent oneself no matter the obstacles.[6] Yet just as the diva does not entirely belong to Lombroso, she cannot be reduced to a visualization of Bergson's concepts. Rather, she can also function as a reminder of regressive and disabling forces mostly associated with a Catholic emphasis on human frailty, subordination to authority, and finite temporality.[7] As a negative figure of time passing, the diva embraces Bergson's belief in the powers of internal and creative transformation without giving up a sense of resignation and passivity imposed by Catholic memento mori. Instead of underlining renewal through the élan vital, as Bergson's duration does, the theme of memento mori argues that we are all human—not because we are all creative, but rather because we are all subject to death. Consequently, the diva film's mise-en-scène is riddled with ambiguities. The theatrical opening and closing of curtains, the trails of cigarette smoke, the withering of roses, and the emphasis on ephemeral pleasures linked to wine and gambling seem to suggest a shallow and superficial world that, just like love and life, happens and disappears in the grip of death's corrosive power over time.

On the other hand, the flickering of fireplaces, the shimmering of pearls and exotic decorations, along with the diva's frequent use of veils, screens, feathers, and curtains, can also be read in the light of a theme of fluidity, which, instead of functioning as a memento mori, paves the way for rebirths and hallucinations. In short, influenced by Bergson's philosophy of timeless creativity and by the pressure of Catholic mores, Italian women—and the Italian diva as well—operated between the "new" woman of modernity and the mater dolorosa.

While the word *mater* clearly refers to gender, *dolorosa* implies that women suffer because they take on Christ's pain, and, therefore, they suffer for and about someone else. Needless to say, in clear contrast to the indestructible energy of the élan vital, the idea of martyrdom built into the image of the crucified Christ transfers itself over to the female condition. The film diva's contemporaries demonstrated quite an understanding

Lyda Borelli in Amleto Palermi's *Carnevalesca* (1918). Courtesy Cineteca di Bologna.

of the contradictory facets involved in the construction of the diva. This awareness of interrelated yet separate pieces making up the diva's puzzle emerges from Lyda Borelli's use of a prism at the beginning of Amleto Palermi's *Carnevalesca* (1918). Each section of the film is introduced by a close-up of the diva's hand pointing the viewer toward a piece of cut glass. This optical object has several sides that refract light and dissolve its hard angles into a source of splendor with no volume and no origin. It is not clear if this luminous effect was meant to dazzle the viewers into reverie or shock them into alertness. In a word, the diva as a cinematic type and as a cultural phenomenon is comparable to the prism in *Carnevalesca*.

Did any diva ever manage to defy the Catholic components of her filmic type? The answer is definitely yes: for example, Pina Menichelli's bad girl, who enjoys being as bad as she can, but still has moments of light playfulness that differentiate her from all the other, much more serious divas. In *La Storia di Una Donna* (1920) by Amleto Palermi, Menichelli wears a long, long necklace of glistening white pearls with a crucifix dangling from it. There it is: a figure of temporality who twirls painfully in her memories of sexual abuse, and whose secularly opulent jewelry is grotesquely combined with the Christian cross, no longer a relic, or even a memento mori, but a fashion statement tinged with camp.

Bergson's Reception in Italy

Despite this serendipitous alliance between women's fight against marginalization and Bergson's attack on the positivist scientific establishment, the story of Bergson's reception in Italy is complex enough to warrant further examination, especially because Bergson himself wrote against motion studies in *Creative Evolution,* in a section titled "The Cinematographical Mechanism of Thought and the Mechanistic Illusion." It is most likely that by "cinematographical mechanism" Bergson really meant Étienne-Jules Marey's analytical research with strips of still photographs.[8] As a result, Bergson aligned the cinematograph with a machine-like intelligence and positivism rather than with his own brand of *lebensphilosophie* (life philosophy). Until now, Bergson's subjectivism has been associated with the avant-garde 1920s films of Germaine Dulac and with the music of Claude Debussy.[9] Most importantly, the present study argues that the origins of the cinema should not be associated only with Sigmund Freud and the development of psychoanalysis, but also with the precursor of French phenomenological thought. Notwithstanding Bergson's negative opinion of mechanically produced still images, the film culture surrounding the diva demonstrated that many Italian intellectuals and artists relied on *Creative Evolution* as a source of inspiration when theorizing about the cinema.

In the world of Italian philosophy, Bergson's stress on intuition and imagination greatly appealed to Benedetto Croce (1866–1952), Italy's most prominent philosopher from the turn of the century until after World War II. Agreeing with Bergson, Croce contended in his *Estetica* (1902) that the work of art should not be reduced to a physical object or external manifestation, because it derives from an inner state of knowledge (intuition) that, aided by the imagination, transforms and unifies impressions.[10] For Croce, at the aesthetic level, the emotional and the intellectual aspects are fused. Thus, the Italian philosopher could approve of Bergson's downplaying of abstract reason because, in Croce's eyes, Cartesianism was a tradition unable to deal with history and subjectivity. On the other hand, in *Matter and Memory* (1896), Bergson makes clear that he is really much more interested in the exchangeability of subject and object than in historical method.[11] For Bergson, an image involves a mind, and a mind does not come into being unless it finds some matter onto which to project itself.

Bergson's sense that the self is an image and that images are cosubstantial with the perception of matter implies the possibility of reversing time to the extent that the memories of the past and the imagination of the future partake of an equivalent level of creativity. The result of this isomorphism between the past and the future leans toward a cyclical view of the historical process (*corsi-ricorsi*) dear to the Italian philosophical tradition stemming from the anti-Cartesian stance of Giambattista Vico (1668–1744) and culminating in the impact on Italian thought of Friedrich Nietzsche (1844–1900) and his theory of eternal return.[12] While Bergson's élan vital became more and more contaminated with Nietzsche's model of the superman, the Vichian roots of Croce's training were strong enough to allow him to appreciate Bergson's emphasis on the primacy of poetical and metaphorical vision over analytical and mathematical thinking.

According to Martin Jay, Bergson was very interested in emotions and sensations because of their ability to destabilize the links between body and mind, thus potentially reconfiguring the hierarchy of the senses.[13] By contrast, Croce continued to rely on a notion of classical equilibrium. He was also weary of powerful sensations in art, so that, as we shall see in greater detail later on, he despised the diva and her baroque, excessive image. However, Bergson's and Croce's comparable attention to free will was significant in Italian intellectual culture, since Catholic thinkers were eager to defend the concepts of soul and guilt dismantled by Lombroso's atavism.[14]

Croce and Bergson had a common enemy in scientific positivism. Moreover, both had an interest in paranormal phenomena: psychic energy, hypnotic powers, and recent discoveries about invisible life inside brute matter. They had the opportunity to meet each other in 1911 while attending a conference in Bologna devoted to topics halfway between science and occultism. After this brief encounter, however, Croce moved away from Bergson's phenomenological stance and turned more toward Hegelian historicism. Bergson asserted that he had never read Hegel, and, as a matter of fact, the French philosopher's open-ended and more spontaneous sense of temporality stood as an alternative to Hegel's organic, dialectical, and totalizing model of historiography.[15]

According to the Italian film historian Luca Mazzei, Giovanni Papini (1881–1956), a Florence-based thinker with antiestablishment leanings, had read Bergson by 1900, being dissatisfied with positivist philosophy. At the age of twenty-two, Papini's intellectual aspirations brought him into contact with other artists and writers. He founded and managed, with Giuseppe Prezzolini, the influential but short-lived magazines *Leonardo* (1903–1907) and *La Voce* (1908–1916), the latter of which Papini directed during 1912 and 1913. Papini tried to modernize Italian culture by introducing significant French, British, and American ideas (such as William James's pragmatism). Papini attacked Gabriele D'Annunzio, whose work he considered too traditionalist. Around 1913, the year of the diva's birth, Papini joined the futurists and launched a new periodical, *Lacerba*. By 1920, however, Papini had detached himself from Marinetti's futurist movement and converted to Catholicism. A complex and contradictory figure, Papini intertwined himself with as many aspects of Italian culture as did the Italian diva.

In his groundbreaking essay on philosophy and the cinema, Luca Mazzei reports that Papini was already corresponding with Bergson by 1903, that the two thinkers met in person in Geneva in 1904 during a conference, and that they met again, in 1905, when Papini paid Bergson a courtesy visit. As soon as Bergson made the connection between cinema and intelligence at the end of *Creative Evolution*, in the spring or summer of 1907, Papini responded in two ways: in August he published a book review of *Creative Evolution* in *Leonardo*, and as early as May 18, 1907, he published his independent take on film and philosophy, titled *Philosophy of the Cinematograph* (*La Filosofia del Cinematografo*), which he sent to *La Stampa*, Turin's daily newspaper.[16] Turin has been considered the entry point of French culture into Italy.

In Papini's journalistic piece, Bergson is never mentioned, and anonymous philosophers are described as a bunch of pedantic professors who never go to the cinema, even if, according to Papini, they really should. Papini's omission of any reference to Bergson's "Cinematographic Mechanism of Thought and the Mechanistic Illusion" is problematic: Bergson was the first philosopher to address the question of the cinema as a philosophical problem, even though he did so by thinking about motion studies. Furthermore, Mazzei proposes, the 1905 encounter between the two philosophers might have included an exchange of views about the scientific vocation of the cinema, upheld by Bergson as the only direction then available to the new medium.[17]

Papini, Mazzei suggests, had probably learned about Bergson's negative views on the cinema, illusion, and intelligence two years before the publication of *Creative Evolution*. Hence, the Italian thinker was able to exploit the release of Bergson's book for a sort of personal journalistic scoop. Thus, my impression is that the short time between the publication of the French scholarly book and the Italian journalistic article would explain why Papini wrote against Bergson's equivalence between cinema and intelligence without identifying it as Bergson's view. The more obscure Italian disciple was probably eager to outdo the internationally famous mentor by riding the wave of his immense popularity not only among practitioners but also with the general public.

Only one year before Bergson's *Creative Evolution*, Papini, with his best-selling *Il Crepuscolo dei Filosofi* (1906; The Twilight of the Philosophers)—a title taken from a book planned but never written by Friedrich Nietzsche—had already proclaimed the death of philosophy.[18] But the Florentine did all this with a tone by far more incendiary than the one used by Bergson to argue against the limitations of science. The reference to Nietzsche within Papini's Bergsonism is significant. Bergson's élan vital was already beginning to lose its existential and regenerative force because it had begun to consolidate into a more nationalistic stance. The whole concept of élan vital, so important to an understanding of the diva's resilience and the futurists' passion, quickly became politicized, along with the Nietzschean "will to power." All this marked an escalation of radical ideas pushing for that alliance between art and politics, war and aesthetics, that Walter Benjamin was to describe so eloquently in 1936.[19]

There is not enough in Papini's journalistic piece to prove that he plagiarized Bergson word for word, since he embraces the opposite stance and celebrates the cinema. In the section devoted to the cinema in *Creative Evolution*, Bergson relies on a binary structure of argumentation that opposes the cinematograph and intelligence on one side with duration and intuition on the other. By contrast, in his piece for *La Stampa*, Papini justifies the connection between philosophy and the cinema by saying that the new medium is the world "spiritualized."[20] And here is how, thanks to Luca Mazzei's brilliant article, we come to understand where the most interesting and original part of Papini's essay really begins. The Florentine thinker gets to this conclusion by setting up an alternation of subjective and objective processes, human and cosmic perception. By amplifying Bergson's compenetration of memory and matter into a similar osmosis between the spiritual and the mundane realms, Papini adds a cosmological, animistic twist that cannot be found in Bergson.

The cinema, Mazzei reports, combines two eyes, one for fantasy and the other for realism:

> *Images that are projections of the cosmos (namely, imitations of something infinite not only spatially but also qualitatively) transform themselves, during the process of looking, from subjective views coming from a known and verifiable spectator into objective views; thus, the same images become portions of a much bigger subjective view stemming from the gaze of another kind of spectator, one*

who is much bigger, omnipresent, and omniscient, although completely unknown.[21]

All of a sudden, the cinema for Papini involves a machine made of a mise-en-abyme of mirrors orchestrating a series of exchanges and reversals between a human eye and a cosmic eye, thus anticipating a protosurrealist understanding of how unbridled fantasy and daily life are intertwined. Mazzei goes on to cite Papini's own words from *Philosophy of the Cinematograph:*

We have the feeling that the events depicted in film are the true events, viewed as if they were seen inside a mirror that could keep up with them very rapidly in space. . . . The only method we have to understand the world is to reduce it to something similar to our spirit, to imagine it animated by something that looks like a bigger Self, animated by some universal form of psychic activity. This method is called animism.[22]

Needless to say, the connections between Bergson and Papini are strong but garbled. Papini's early film theory stands out because he realized that film is not just about narrative, but involves a mysterious, hieroglyph-like inscription, namely, a figural level that cannot be decoded. This view had already been explored by the German Jesuit Athanasius Kircher (1602–1680), who believed in a mysterious stone alphabet, a pictorial language of nature inscribed by God inside the world. In addition, Kircher, a sort of engineer-philosopher, wrote a treatise called *Ars Magna Lucis et Umbrae* (1646; The Great Art of Light and Shadows), about the construction of a machine for projecting images on a screen; to this day, the work remains a controversial piece of scholarship because of its blatant technological mistakes or omissions.[23] But the point here is not about the viability of the machine or the obvious religious implications of Kircher's theological thesis. From the point of view of rethinking film theory, what is interesting is the connection between animism and cinematic movement, across the figural level that eludes reading, and the photographic register that expands visibility.

Papini's animistic understanding of film is also valuable because it anticipates Deleuze's redefinition of the cinema in *L'Image-Temps* as a spiritual automaton.[24] Compared to Papini, Deleuze has a more phenomenological and secular theory of the cinema, whereas Papini's animism (or vitalism) is, comparatively speaking, more cosmic and religious. The contemporary reader can now begin to see where, between Papini and Deleuze, lies the contribution of another major figure in the history of classical film theory. Drawing inspiration from the surrealist principle of photography, the French critic André Bazin (1918–1958) argued that the filmic image is both a fact and a hallucination. For Bazin, the cinema is about bearing witness to the presence of the Others, a falling in love with the world while sensing new undercurrents of emotional affinities in the most unpredictable, alien, or impenetrable elements, such as animals, landscapes, nonprofessional actors, and children.[25] Once again film is about a visual reading that is both outside and beyond words, even though cinema works like a language.[26]

Finally, when thinking about the diva film's alleged escapism, one could profitably turn again to the echo of Kircher's pictorial language of nature as inscribed by God. Kircher's alphabet as a form of divine writing is not far from the surrealist taste for the most bizarre phenomena in the heart of nature. Carnivorous plants and seahorses defy the boundaries between the animal and the vegetable kingdom, sea and earth, while at the same time they are comparable to an image that is both natural and monstrous. And the etymology of the word *monster* (from the Latin *monstrum*) refers to an evil omen, a warning susceptible to various interpretations. In a sense, the diva film, too, combines the two kinds of eyes described by Bazin, required by surrealist photography, and appropriated by Federico Fellini in one of his most famous statements. In fact, to defend himself from the polemics surrounding his turn to fantasy, and away from neorealism, with *La Strada* (1954), the Italian director stressed that the cinema has two eyes—namely, fact and hallucination, exotic fantasy but also, and most importantly, social docudrama.[27]

Papini's eventual disappointment with all philosophy based on metaphysics and his rejection of the extremely fashionable Bergson did not occur overnight. For a while the Florentine was the Italian spokesperson of the French philosopher. In 1909 he published an anthology titled *La Filosofia dell'Intuizione* (*The Philosophy of Intuition*) in the series *La Cultura dell'Anima* (*The Culture of the Soul*), sponsored by the publisher Carabba.[28] Papini also devoted chapters to Bergson in his 1913 collection of essays *Ventiquattro Cervelli* (*Four and Twenty Minds*), which was reprinted in 1922.[29] Unlike Croce, who was in charge of the journal *La Critica* (1903–1944) and who vehemently attacked the avant-garde, Papini's *Leonardo* and *Lacerba* gave voice to futurism and held on to much more extreme views against logic and abstract rationalism than Bergson himself ever did. In the end, Mazzei contends, the French philosopher apparently did not even bother to keep up with Papini's translations of his own work in Italy.[30] Nevertheless, through Papini, accurate as well as distorted knowledge of Bergson's ideas spread in Italian culture and made its meaningful impact on the highly musical (operatic), subjective, and ritualistic style of the diva film.

Sebastiano Arturo Luciani

Eager to reconfigure the mapping of the senses in order to defy Descartes's emphasis on disembodied, mental vision, Bergson argued that sound and smell were more important than the eye or even the visualization of touch. It is significant that Bergson's interest in sound and interiority reappears in the writings of Sebastiano Arturo Luciani (1884–1950) on the cinema and actresses. In 1919, for example, the theorist Luciani argued that the best cinema is the one that makes visible the invisible without showing too much. Were the cinema to abandon a musical inspiration for the sake of too strong a visual or plastic one, it would degenerate into theater or dance. To maintain its cosmic soul, or metaphysical vocation as a spiritual automaton for the invisible, the cinema had to hold on to some mystery. Luciani entitled his essay "L'Idealità del Cinematografo" (1919), thus openly linking his work to Platonic theory.[31] Yet his overall stance was influenced by Bergson: at one point Luciani declares that life—and, I would add, reality as well—is pure movement, namely, in Bergson's words, indivisible duration or subjective temporality. As far as the title of Luciani's essay is concerned, words such as *idealismo* and *idealità* are a way to signal a Bergsonian affiliation, for even if the French philosopher had tried to develop a position located between idealism and materialism, his disciples, commentators, and imitators in Italy would have quickly pushed Bergson's work under *idealismo*, possibly as a nod to Croce's undeniable authority in this field.

This facile use of philosophical labels immediately fostered confusion, even misreadings. After all, Bergson, in *Creative Evolution*, had argued against the artificiality of Platonism, which he considered equivalent to the cinematographic mechanism of intelligence, an area of the mind linked to space and quantity rather than to imagination and memory.[32] At any rate, for Luciani just as for Papini, Bergsonism and film aesthetics are compatible. In fact, cinema is an art form that is closer to music and poetry than to theater, literature, or painting; it thrives on an elusive, half-glimpsed form of visuality, one that has to do more with the inner rhythms of the spirit or abstraction than with physical beauty or spatial display. By rejecting spectacle and celebrating a plastic, but also ineffable, kind of image, Luciani seems to prefer the highly expressive yet self-chastising style of the diva film over the openly intelligible images and mass-exhilarating feats found in the historical epics of the period.

Luciani's "L'Idealità del Cinematografo" was published in *Penombra*, a journal traditionally devoted to divas, their professional accomplishments, and romantic biographies. On the pages of this rather frivolous magazine, Luciani wrote about time, space, and even actresses:

The inevitable and instinctive pairing of music with cinematographic projection stems from a series of analogical relationships. The cinema can and should be like a music for eyes: a music sustained by rhythm, but a particular kind of rhythm that unfolds in time and space and that is not perceptible unless one is gifted with a very special combination of musical and pictorial sensitivity. Only by obeying this rhythm is it possible to figure out the unfolding and the ordering of the various scenes, which go by according to the actual duration of their happening, either in the foreground or in the background, until they integrate themselves in space. As soon as poets are able to visualize what they think, when their aesthetic visions are high enough to prevail over any interest in a more or less pretty actress, then the cinema will be an art form. And the only one that our so deeply misunderstood epoch has been able to discover.[33]

In this passage Luciani seems to advocate an agenda that is not far from the triple analogy between musicality, cinematic flow, and a poetical sensibility upheld by Germaine Dulac (1882–1942), the French avant-garde feminist filmmaker. This is not surprising, because Luciani was a good friend of theorist and filmmaker Marcel L'Herbier (1888–1979), who belonged to the cine-club movement in the twenties, as did Dulac. Luciani also seems to anticipate Bazin's tenet of *montage interdit*, in the sense that too much editing risks interfering with cinema's animistic vocation, that is, the mysterious yet living force of an image in motion.[34]

To return to Luciani, as long as silent cinema strives for poetry, the word can become image, and music can turn into visual movement. Most importantly, motion, for Luciani, is about the life of an inner self whose transformations may elude even individual consciousness. Just like time and music, motion, too, is difficult to grasp. Cinema, in a sense, provides a tracing of motions not simply in the sense of literal, visible movement in space, but also in regard to the microscopic changes that occur inside the natural world and through human behavior. In Kircher's words, we have, with cinema, a pictorial language of nature that, on the one hand, is inscribed by forces we can decipher. Pictorialism is readable in the sense that, like Egyptian hieroglyphs, pictorial alphabets can be decoded.

On the other hand, when we are in front of a film, we also sense that there are other forces whose languages we are unable to fully master because they are not human. For instance, objects in film acquire an unusual degree of energy. And this is because nature or matter as such is alien to humankind. We decipher it, predict it, and control it, but only to a limited extent. Its excesses and surprises, however, cinema's indifferent, cold, mechanical eye can record most revealingly yet unobtrusively. From his pronounced interest in movement rather than in singing or voice, Luciani manages to bring cinema closer to dance than to opera. In fact, throughout "L'Idealità del Cinematografo," he juxtaposes the static and verbose features of theater to the lyrical feeling and fluid movements of film. Although Luciani was also involved with the futurist avant-garde before World War I, by 1919 he was clearly in touch with the so-called impressionist film movement of Germaine Dulac and Marcel L'Herbier.

Like Papini, Luciani, too, associates cinema with the two extremes of pure dream or fantasy, and of unfettered reality or candid documentation. In the theater, Luciani explains, fake sets stand next to real people, but the actors are not themselves, and the sets are truly cardboard clouds and nothing else. Luciani does not envision the filmic image as a mixture of truth and fiction in space, but more as a double-edged surface caught in a process of exchange between inside and outside, surface and depth. This is why movement discloses the vicissitudes of visible and invisible levels of experience. And in true Bergsonian or animistic fashion, à la Papini, the elements that make the difference during this osmosis of inside and outside are imagination and memory, for every moment is different from the previous one as well as from the next one, within an ever-shifting flow of energy between spectator and screen.

But for Luciani, time and timing much more than spatial architecture bring out the qualities of poetry, atmosphere, and nostalgia. Again, Luciani's Bergsonism asserts that temporality, or the dance-like rhythm of acting, is what makes visible the invisible, while the value of this externalization of inner life (soul) on film is one of preservation or memory, not far from Bazin's "mummy complex."[35] After all, Bergson's choice of time over space was informed by the awareness that precisely because time is outside human control, duration—the subjective experience of time passing—is the deepest and truest level of subjectivity, one that should be shown as such in its own "real" time without charting it into an artificial system of numbers and hours.

Unfortunately, Bergson's legacy in Italy was catastrophic. On the eve of World War I, a whole generation rallied behind either Marinetti's futurist avant-garde or D'Annunzio's militaristic ambitions, or else defected from the less extremist wing of the socialist party in favor of the revolutionary syndicalism of Georges Sorel (1847–1922). Influenced by Bergson's rejection of materialism in Marxist ideology, Sorel published *Reflections on Violence* in 1908, just one year after Bergson's *Creative Evolution*.[36] Clearly, Italian Bergsonism, and the notion of the élan vital in particular, had degenerated into a celebration of the creative power of violence, thus turning many artists and intellectuals in favor of World War I. By incorporating decadent echoes of "art for art's sake," Bergson's philosophy in Italy lost touch with genuine efforts toward social renewal and personal reinvention rooted in peace and cooperation. In the wake of these regressive developments, the diva began to shrink into the rigid cliché of the hysteric femme fatale.

Despite the negative outcome of the diva's story, the debate on the cinema and gender roles could not have been richer or more widespread than it was. Within the classical-humanist-liberal tradition and in Marxist circles, however, the two most important voices, i.e., Benedetto Croce and Antonio Gramsci, respectively, did not support the diva film and the cinema. Only Luigi Pirandello, who was familiar with Henri Bergson's ideas about laughter, showed a genuine appreciation of women's struggles. Yet he also understood the threat that mechanical reproduction posed to traditional ideas about masculinity.[37]

Laocoön's Filmstrip

CLASSICISM, MARXISM, VITALISM

In early Italian film culture, the process of dropping old stereotypes about femininity and coming up with new configurations was an experience riddled with ambiguity. This process found its best summary in a 1912 cover for the film trade magazine *Cines:* a young woman stretches her arms out to hold up a snake-like strip of film celluloid. *Cines* reappropriates the famous icon of Laocoön, the Trojan priest who fought the giant sea serpents that attacked him and his two sons. In comparison with this classical tale, the *Cines* logo is less tragic and much more ambivalent.

Cover of *Cines* review (1912). Author's collection.

The Laocoön group. Marble; height: 95½ in. (2.42 m.). Roman copy, perhaps after Agesander, Athenodorus, and Polydorus of Rhodes (present state, former restorations removed), 1st century AD. Museo Pio Clementino, Vatican Museums, Vatican State. Photo: Scala/Art Resource, N.Y.

Because she has no clothing on, the *Cines* woman amounts to a pleasant outline rather than a character with a psychological identity. Her neoclassical hairstyle refers to the high culture of antiquity to which Laocoön belongs. In addition, her idealized beauty sets her apart from living women; she might be an ancient goddess fallen into the crass world of modernity, but she also represents a figure larger than herself. Either she is a beneficent patroness of the cinema, or else she is the origin of a black shadow, the *mal ombra* that defines her silhouette and supplies the title to Carmine Gallone's wonderful film *Malombra* (1917), with Lyda Borelli.

The headband worn by this young muse of the cinema is the only accessory featured in the film magazine's logo. Perhaps the containment of her hair reassures the readers that she is no Medusa with wild curls and a dangerous stare. Indeed, her face in profile is hardly recognizable because the woman sits on her bent legs like someone asking for help or forgiveness. Despite her kneeling posture, the muscles of her lower torso indicate strength and a certain degree of androgyny. She is the muse of motion after all, hence her slightly athletic look.

In contrast to the young woman's nudity, the convoluted filmstrip can be seen as a sort of substitute for a cloth, textile, or fabric. In fact, the extension of her arms evokes the threading of wool into a shapely ball of yarn. In addition, her slightly drooping position brings to mind someone bending toward the neckline of a dress about to be worn. This visual ambiguity between the threading of film into a reel and the threading of fabric into a dress is a powerful analogy between cinema and fashion. Both linked to industry and the market, cinema and fashion tend to empower and enslave women at the same time. In *Il Fior di Male* (1915), Lyda (Lyda Borelli) becomes the director of a fashion empire. In *Il Processo Clémenceau* (1917), Pierre's old mother raises her son alone by running a tailoring business. The livelihood of the Marchesa Luisa Casati (1881–1957), a socialite, trendsetter, and sort of diva-like creature outside of film, was based on profits from the Milanese textile industry.

Laocoön's struggle with the snakes is a famous image because of the way it combines beauty with horror, a painful twisting of the body with the spectacle of its perfect limbs. Likewise, the *Cines* muse is an image fraught with ambiguities. It is hard to tell whether the logo's woman is imprisoned by the constraints of fashion and social habit, or whether she is engaged in reinventing her own appearance by means of a dress that has not yet been sewn together. However, the comparison between the subject of the *Cines* illustration and Laocoön's tale does involve one fundamental difference. Laocoön and his children died fighting the snakes. In contrast to this negative legacy, the *Cines* logo marks a creative and exciting period in the history of the relation between Italian women and the cinema.

Poets, political theorists, philosophers, and writers all contributed to a climate of opinion that warrants close discussion in order to understand the cultural connotations attached to the diva and the diva film. While the famous image of Laocoön and the snakes appears in the writings of Guido Gozzano and Gabriele D'Annunzio, in other instances such iconography is completely absent. The idea of the arabesque, however, comes up with Pirandello, who, along with Anton Giulio Bragaglia, was influenced by Henri Bergson, and represents the vitalist camp. The playwright described male anxiety about changes in gender roles while equating the diva with the "new" woman of modernity. By contrast, Benedetto Croce and Antonio Gramsci—defenders of classicism and Marxism, respectively—voiced negative opinions about the diva, the cinema, and the lowest levels of popular culture, which were often cherished by women readers. Indifferent to Marxism and to Bergson's *lebensphilosophie*, D'Annunzio and Gozzano produced ambivalent texts about film, the diva, and women in general. Despite her disappearance or taming with the advent of Fascism, it is amazing to consider how successful and powerful the diva managed to become, given the mostly negative terms of the intellectual and artistic debate surrounding her and the new medium. As a type and against all odds, she dominated her epoch and its imagination.

Guido Gozzano and Gabriele D'Annunzio

In 1914, Gabriele D'Annunzio wrote an essay, "Del Cinematografo considerato come Strumento di Liberazione e come Arte di Trasfigurazione"; two years later, Guido Gozzano published "Il Nastro di Celluloide e i Serpi di Laocoonte" in *La Donna* (5 May 1916).[1] Just as the diva was caught between an oppressive past and an unknown future, the cinema also received mixed evaluations from D'Annunzio, the ultimate decadent poet, and from Gozzano, a poet with a much stronger feeling for the provincial everyday than his heroic and cosmopolitan colleague.

Gozzano's "Laocoön" piece offers a negative overview of the new medium. After describing a production-house logo that depicts snakelike chunks of film ensnaring a male figure instead of a female one, Gozzano depicts the cinema as an ugly trap of money, creativity, and technology. Most interestingly, in this article written for a woman's magazine, Gozzano distinguishes between film and traditional art by invoking the opposition between a rich American painter and a refined European lady. Gozzano also condemns the appeal the new medium has for young American women like Ketty. It seems that she was a traveler from Baltimore with whom Gozzano had a brief flirtation during a trip to India. In contrast to the elegant European lady called "art," the American girl spits, smokes, and plays with men. The Italian poet clearly disliked the type of the new woman from the New World.

Despite Gozzano's rejection of Ketty's nonconformist ways, he was involved in a long platonic relationship with Amalia Guglielminetti, a poet from Turin who was widely known as a rebellious woman. Whereas Gozzano became famous as a result of his literary achievements, Guglielminetti achieved celebrity through her transgressive manners. In her novels, she failed, unable to move beyond conventional melodramas. But as one of the first Italian divorcées, she was, without a doubt, the new woman of the highest Turinese intellectual circles: free, unconventional, gossiped about. She addressed all sorts of contradictions between private choices and public opinions in her novels and short stories about women.[2]

For Gozzano, the Turinese film industry—where he tried, without much success, to find work—was the land of the grotesque, home of an endeavor rooted in confusion, artistic mediocrity, and the enslavement of art to money. This overall negative view pervades the three short stories Gozzano devoted either to actresses or to the shallow business of the moving pictures.[3] "Pamela-Film" is the tale of a spinster who inherits a sinful film-production company and turns it over to the Catholic Church. "The Scissors' Reverberation" ("Il Riflesso delle Cesoie") is about a couple who work in the cinema as performers. During a shoot set in a convent, as they watch the virginal female students playing among the quiet nuns, they realize how they have gone wrong. They mourn their lost youth and artistic purity, and they regret the artificial lives they portrayed in films—probably in diva films—about adultery, scandals, and vice. Gozzano does not specify what kind of cinema his two protagonists were decrying; as a result, the sociological commentary of the diva film against male abuses is turned into a general indictment of the cinema as a medium. This kind of rhetorical move was extremely common in the film criticism of the diva's days.

"The Diva's Sandals" ("I Sandali della Diva") is the most interesting of Gozzano's three short stories because the story's descriptive parts act as a sort of cabinet of curiosities displaying the archeology of the cinema. During a childhood sojourn in the villa of the former film diva Palmira Zacchi, now a widowed baroness, Gozzano recalls his infantile fascination with all kinds of protocinematic technologies and toys:

And photographs, endless photographs of men and things, mechanical toys that were so marvelous I could hardly breathe: the Trocadero with multiple waterfalls, made of crystal in a spiraling shape; the Tour Eiffel made of gold, with visitors going up and down; a tree filled with shiny hummingbirds, singing and flapping their wings; a small Greek temple where a male and a female dancer would perform pirouettes together as soon as a mechanically produced melodic sound would come on. . . . And landscapes visible through the mutoscope, a gadget I had never seen before: London, Paris, Niagara Falls, a surface of frozen snow with skaters, the Pyramids with the camels and the Bedouins.[4]

All these gadgets connected with motion and travel fill the child's mind with wonder, but they also hide horrible secrets about the diva's past. In the same way, the mixing of the mechanical with the organic produces strange results halfway between the marvelous and the repellent.

To be sure, Palmira Zacchi's association with the grotesque begins with her appearance: long, muscular, masculine-looking legs stem out of a frilly, pink, cloudlike skirt. But Zacchi is most helpless when she throws her purple sandals at two mysterious male visitors from Vienna. These men, who may be the representatives of her nasty relatives abroad, turn her from a wealthy baroness into a shriveled dance teacher. Furious, Zacchi throws her shoes, one by one, against the door, which bangs shut behind the two lawyers. For Gozzano, this gesture of rage completes the violent trajectory of Zacchi's somewhat disjointed body. Just as her thin, childlike waist and her huge wet-nurse breasts do not seem to belong to the same person, her colorful sandals clash against an abstract legal indictment she cannot overcome. On the screen and in real life, the diva is a montage of old and new, and therefore she is an unstable construct of discordant parts.

We do not know if Gozzano was familiar with Wilhelm Jensen's *Gradiva: A Pompeian Fantasy* (1903), but it is possible that he read this German tale about an archeologist, Norbert Hanold, in love with antiquities and chasing his dream woman, Gradiva, among the ruins of Pompeii. The subtitle alone, *A Pompeian Fantasy*, might have caught Gozzano's attention and motivated him to read this example of Nordic fascination with Italy as a land of hidden mysteries and archeological treasures. It is also unclear whether Gozzano knew Freud's case study, "Dreams and Delusions in Jensen's *Gradiva*" (1907).[5] Despite this lack of reliable information in regard to Gozzano's sources for "The Diva's Sandals," the iconographic similarities between the Italian and the German writer are so numerous that they make the story worth recounting.

Norbert Hanold, a young German archeologist, falls in love with the plaster-cast relief of a young woman walking with graceful and self-confident steps; her sandals, an androgynous accessory, facilitate motion. Hanold names his fantasy figure "Gradiva," which in Latin means "the girl who steps along." The tale proposes, through Hanold and Gradiva, a new version of Pygmalion's wish that Galatea, his beautiful statue, would come to life, Jensen's story becomes much more complicated once the archeologist dreams of witnessing the destruction of Pompeii by Vesuvius in AD 79. During the dream, Hanold catches sight of Gradiva, but she is no longer walking. Rather, her body has become a motionless mold of condensed lava among the ruins.

In short, regardless of Freud's psychoanalytic reappropriation, Jensen's story stands out as a beautiful fable about the feminine origin of the cinema and the function of drap-

"Gradiva" relief, perhaps representing Aglauros, daughter of Cecrops, the mythical first king of Attica. Museo Chiaramonti, Vatican Museums, Vatican State. Photo: Scala/Art Resource, N.Y.

ery in suggesting movement. In fact, Hanold's fascination is based not only on the empty space between Gradiva's lifted heel and her sandal's sole, but also on the fluid and quasi-three-dimensional motion of her tunic's folds. Whereas Gozzano's childhood memories about the archeology of the cinema evoke Edison's amazing laboratory in Villiers de L'Isle-Adam's *Tomorrow's Eve* (1886), Jensen's *Gradiva* looks like a fantastic literary translation of Muybridge's motion studies, in which an endless series of women and men perform the act of walking, with or without props in their hands. But unlike Gradiva, Muybridge's models posed naked to allow the scientific audience a better view of the muscles involved in the achievement of motion. The issue of clothing is no small detail, since in "The Diva's Sandals," Zacchi is the first woman who arouses the writer's sexual curiosity.

As a child, Gozzano shares a bedroom with the diva while a guest in her villa. Ortensia, Palmira's old servant, asks him not to look when the baroness is undressing for bed. A curious and disobedient child, the future writer secretly peeks until he learns from glancing at the diva's naked body that men and women are anatomically different. Again the parallel with Muybridge, motion studies, and the archeology of the cinema is relevant here, for the marvelous toys of landscapes, birds, and clothed dancers do not align movement with sexual difference, but the nude models inevitably characterize their walking patterns with anatomical information. Just as Muybridge's motion studies intertwine the birth of cinema with the awareness of masculinity and femininity, Gozzano performs a mental leap from anatomy to autobiography, from biology to memory. In fact, he remarks that Zacchi's wrinkled skin looked like a textile of human temporality in ways reminiscent of the filmic image's mummy-like ability to embalm time past.

Sandals loom large in Gozzano's story. Sandals, however, do not help Zacchi win the race against patriarchal legal power. Furthermore, even though Gozzano uses the word *sandals* in the title, Zacchi does not wear the same kind of flat sandals usually shown in any visual reference to Jensen's Gradiva. To be sure, the diva's last name is Zacchi, which is extremely close to *tacchi,* "heels." While women's sandals may have a small heel, it is intriguing that Zacchi's last name evokes the idea not just of shoes that are elegant—because their open design lengthens the leg—but also of heels that turn the footwear into a sort of female phallus with a castrating knife. On the other hand, her first name, Palmira, is not far from the semantic fields of Pompeii and palm trees, suggestive of southern Italy.

Given these similarities and discrepancies between Jensen and Gozzano, what is the Italian writer trying to say about women and early cinema? Since his short story ends with an unmistakable emphasis on the sandals, Gozzano seems to seal his piece with a reminder to the reader that women involved in a career are threatening. The Viennese lawyers interrupt her income from a powerful former lover. Zacchi loses her title and her villa and ends up as a poorly paid employee at La Scala, in Milan. Gozzano repeatedly underlines how Zacchi's heeled sandals carried her from the domestic sphere to the cinema, into the aristocracy, by virtue of her diva-like status, and now back to dance where she originally started. Sadly, the final stage of her life is disappointing. As a teacher at La Scala, she is still lifting her silk gown and showing the lower half of her leg. Unlike Gradiva, who, unknowingly, shows the bottom of her foot because she is walking fast, Zacchi is at odds with her former cunning power. Now this gesture is no longer designed to seduce, but to demonstrate ballet techniques to her female pupils. Someone could say that Jensen's archeologist indulged in a motion-filled fantasy, but his dream has been replaced by Gozzano's hidden and subtle association between the diva and a prostitute, who uses her body to attract her customers' attention. The lifting of the skirt not only does not precede a formal bow in an elegant salon but, outside the safe classroom, may even signal a shameful availability. Such a reading of Zacchi's exhibition of her legs suggests that the teaching role is only one step away from the streetwalker's. And this is why the sandals are not in the Roman style—flat, colorless, and sober—but were upgraded to a more modern and sadistic version of stiletto pumps in purple, the color of shame.

Two years before the publication of Gozzano's "Laocoön" article, Gabriele D'Annunzio wrote an essay titled "Of the Cinema Considered as a Medium of Liberation and as an Art of Transfiguration" ("Del Cinematografo Considerato come Strumento di Liberazione e come Arte di Trasfigurazione"), which covers his views about the cinema and deploys the very same term of reference. Because of his attachment to high culture—that is, classical mythology and Renaissance art—D'Annunzio at one point characterizes the cinema of his own days as *sconce buffonerie,* which means something like "dirty jokes."[6] Yet compared to Gozzano's angry provincialism and dismissal of American ingenuity, D'Annunzio's stance is much more ambiguous and potentially open to the new medium. In ways that unexpectedly echo the futurist predilection for the *monello,* or street urchin, D'Annunzio is willing to accept the cinema as long as it paves the way for a new type of masculinity: "a boy who is both refined and strong" ("*un fanciullo delicato e forte*"). Of course, this *homo novus* (new man), or delicate athlete, is the adolescent version of the Nietzschean superman, who will, as he grows up, acquire all the additional refinements of the adult D'Annunzian dandy. "*Un fanciullo delicato e forte*" embodies what D'Annunzio himself would like to become through a rebirth of literary creativity.

The phrasing, "medium of transfiguration and art of liberation," in the title of D'Annunzio's essay benefits only men; it definitely does not apply to women. Women are not even mentioned until the last paragraph, and then are referred to only once, when D'Annunzio brings in the nymph Daphne. An athletic lover of sports and chases, Daphne's youthfulness and love of independence bring to mind the new woman of modernity, who, in aristocratic circles, embraced horseback riding and, in the cinema, played dangerous roles on the screen. Driving, bicycling, playing tennis, and horseback riding were all fashionable sports among upper-class women.

D'Annunzio did not allude to Daphne in order to encourage women to modernize and liberate themselves. Instead of achieving a higher degree of mobility and freedom in the wilderness, D'Annunzio reminds us, Daphne was turned into a tree. And to further legitimize his futuristic faith in young men rather than dynamic women, the poet diligently refers to Ovid's recounting of the Daphne myth in *Metamorphoses.* When considering D'Annunzio's view of the cinema, where the transformation of women into marvelous, decorative, quasi-supernatural fetishes involves no liberation, it is worth noting that as early as 1909, Ovid's poem had been the source of D'Annunzio's first, unrealized project for the silent-film industry. Furthermore, that same year, already longing for the aura of youth—a fashionable icon to be achieved through the outfit of a dashing aviator—D'Annunzio dedicated his first *velivolo* (aircraft) to Ovid , since he was the poet of all transformations.[7] Of course, D'Annunzio counted on the wings of his imagination rather than on the rules of technology to achieve miracles, including the rejuvenation and metamorphosis of his own body.

Gozzano's reference to Laocoön in his 1916 article echoes, but also darkens, the historical

Gabriele D'Annunzio's ex libris. Courtesy Il Vittoriale, Gardone Riviera.

(right) School of Arcimboldo, *Alla donna di buon gusto.* Schloss Ambras, Innsbruck, Austria. Photo: Erich Lessing/Art Resource, N.Y.

antecedents of the feminine logo on the 1912 *Cines* cover. The Turinese poet's mythological allusion is mostly about film as a source of trouble and confusion for men and women alike. D'Annunzio's use of Laocoön is hidden, but possibly more positive than Gozzano's. In his essay about film, D'Annunzio does not refer to the famous Trojan priest. Yet his use of the word *liberation* in the title invokes the idea of getting out of a trap. For D'Annunzio, the new medium can be about liberation as long as the ending of Laocoön's struggle is reversed: were he to succeed in defeating the snakes, the film industry, too, would avoid the filmstrip's coils, especially the ones marring the diva film's convoluted and redundant narratives.

To be sure, D'Annunzio not only hides but also rewrites the reference to Laocoön in the second half of his title, where the cinema is defined as an art of transfiguration. In contrast to liberation, this second idea of metamorphosis is linked not only to Ovid's famous poem, but also to the twists and turns of Laocoön's body. His motions are as curvilinear and as unpredictable as the wavy corset the snakes build around him and his sons. The motions of Laocoön, his children, and the snakes are none of them believable, as if human beings and animals were trying to refashion their bodies into impossible shapes. Ironically, the attackers as well as the victims rely heavily on motion, and their agitation confuses animal and human parts, as if it might produce a new, mixed creature made of displaced limbs and dangling coils. Halfway between the marvelous and the grotesque, D'Annunzio hides his Laocoön behind the term *transformation*, for his own Ovidian and buried metamorphoses are far too chiseled, and they may upset the traditional reading of this kind of iconography.

More is at stake in D'Annunzio's hidden Laocoön than the clustered meanings of liberation and entrapment, or the confusion between the animal and human forms leading to some kind of wondrous transformation. That Laocoön's story is the subtext behind D'Annunzio's choice of words emerges from his analogy between the filmstrip (*la pellicola*) and a mass of entangled bowels (*budelli*). At first, such a word releases a visceral image of all the lowbrow, Grand Guignol sources out of which film was born. The circus, fairgrounds, vaudeville, cabaret, magicians, and mountebanks—all these venues and performers, however, operate well below D'Annunzio's elitist credo of art for art's sake.

Secondly, the image of bowels is not just about the messy business of digestion taking place in the depths of the male or female body, but is also comparable to a laboratory of artistic creativity. As soon as the possible meaning of *bowels* shifts from the digestive to the creative, the negative connotations of Laocoön as a deadly web of pain and violence recede in favor of a new, intricate apparatus regulating birth instead of digestion, invention instead of destruction.

D'Annunzio, however, is quick to claim the power of creativity for the male artist alone, so that the term *bowels* belongs to a section of his essay in which Laocoön's subjugation is effaced by Leonardo's use of animal bowels for the construction of a beautiful musical instrument:

> *Modeled on Leonardo's fantastically arranged bowels and imbued with powerful breaths to the point of becoming huge, the filmstrip will be eventually able to take over all the sets and chase away the misery and embarrassment of contemporary film productions. Only then shall we hope to see coming toward us the true messiah of this new art: a refined and strong boy conceived in the shade of harmonious hills whose curving shapes resemble the winds of Spring as they carry in their mouths the taste of strange herbs, and as they arrange a flock of wild birds in the shape of Dionysus's thyrsus or in the guise of Apollo's lyre.*[8]

Were we to combine Laocoön's snakes with D'Annunzio's bowels, it is easy to see how the hidden thesis of this misogynist iconography is that women are confused by and with the cinema; that the cinema is below the other arts; and that the female body itself shares a sort of embarrassing kinship with the abject, visceral materials of which the cinema is made. As a result, just like film, the woman is the snake of temptation, for the medium whose convoluted strip resembles her curvy but also deceptive body satisfies its audiences with very little, just a few "dirty jokes" (*sconce buffonerie*). D'Annunzio's insistence on the obscene potential of film indicates that, for him, the diva film, with its scandals, fell somewhere between the novelette and pornography.

For both Gozzano and D'Annunzio, the only way out of this situation lay in a mystical, poetical, transfigurative, quasi-abstract, or metaphysical use of the cinema, one involving as little corporeality as possible and a maximum of melody. This is why Gozzano devoted time and effort to a nearly experimental, antinaturalistic film project about Saint Francis.[9] Just like Gozzano and the film critics of the period, D'Annunzio blamed the diva and the cinema for the adultery, rape, and financial exploitation that men perpetrated against women.

Chasing after a seductive yet disruptive kind of fantasy, D'Annunzio concludes his essay by celebrating the mode of the marvelous, but with no clear explanation of what this approach would entail. In the end, D'Annunzio comes across as an ambivalent thinker about the cinema. He is someone willing to side with a new technology, but he is also unable to shake off his classical education. His concluding imagery, the flying birds and blowing winds, leans toward an understanding of the medium as a liberating force, one capable of defying the physical laws of time and space. Yet the poet's futuristic stance coexists next to a heavy horizon of erudite citations, Ovid and Leonardo.

Echoing the futurists' dislike for mother earth and their passion for flying, the poet's essay on film states that the earth itself, just like the female body, is both desirable as well as threatening for the free-spirited male artist. *Il fanciullo delicato* can tolerate a landscape of hills as long as they form a nurturing womb in whose shadow the new man can grow. The hills' harmonious profile means that their feminine curves offer no obstacle on the ground. By contrast, they stand in the background, looking as light as a spring breeze. Meanwhile Leonardo, a figure between art and science, just like the medium of cinema, makes art out of the least appealing section of the body, the intestines—a section of the digestive tract near the reproductive apparatuses of women and animals alike.

A Nietzschean touch: the two possible forms that a D'Annunzian cinema of poetry can take are the peaceful Apollonian tempo of historical pageants and the frenzied, Dionysiac rhythms of diva films and their hysterical scenes.

Benedetto Croce, Walter Benjamin, and Mario Praz

The diva's worst sin is that her excessive and convoluted image is "baroque." Shortly before World War I, *baroque* meant something negative, as *kitsch* does today: it stood for bad taste. It described something exaggerated, outdated, and, worst of all, insubstantial. Most importantly, for the Neapolitan philosopher Benedetto Croce, the word *baroque* meant something completely different from what it did for Walter Benjamin (1892–1940), in his *The Origin of German Tragic Drama* (1916).[10] In his *Estetica* (1902; Aesthetics), Croce condemns allegory for subordinating the spiritual dimension of life to the materiality of writing: he feels that allegory is not a direct mode of spiritual manifestation, but a kind of shortcoming.[11] As a secret way of speaking through a stereotypical surface level, allegory is a good antidote to censorship, since it mostly thrives on indirect communication. While the first level tells a story that is safe, something else much more controversial writes itself below.

For Benjamin, it is the written message below the surface that matters. The allegorical level is made of ruins, or secrets eager to be unlocked. For the allegorist, the writing below is visible, but difficult to decipher. Benjamin's ruin is a time capsule written in code. It contains many histories, including the lost experiences of those who could not speak or write at the time of their defeat or elimination. It is these marginal histories that Benjamin, as an allegorist, wishes to release from a landscape made of death.

As a philosopher, Croce was concerned about the future of Italian society, which was attempting to shift from feudal mores to bourgeois liberalism. For Croce, allegory belongs either to the dark and mystical Middle Ages or to the frivolous manners of the baroque. As a shortcoming, allegory is a roundabout, oblique way of writing, symptomatic of the absence of something fundamental. According to Croce, liberalism and freedom were not quite present in Italy. By contrast, for Benjamin, even though God has forsaken mankind, ruins and their allegories are pivotal in developing an alternative history that counters the official version.

For both Croce and Benjamin, there are links between allegory and inscription, or between allegory and cryptic systems of communication. Croce concludes that in baroque allegory all interiority is evacuated into the exteriority of the page: for him, in allegorical personification there is no spiritualization of the physical.[12] For Croce, history is no landscape of power and death; instead, history is supposed to be a narrative describing the achievement of liberty. Croce envisions history as the positive story of humankind's effort to transcend its material and physical limitations and grow toward a set of humanistic, liberal values. The ideological limitations of such a position are self-evident.

As a classicist, Croce did not understand that the crisis in consciousness brought about by the turn of the century was irreversible, profound, and unprecedented in its radical reconfiguration of perceptual and social categories. Neither the self nor liberty, neither art nor history, could be discussed in the terms used in the previous centuries, especially once the Enlightenment had marked the leap from absolute monarchies to a bourgeois world of nation-states.

Croce believed that the referent of allegory is a world of individuals reduced to mechanical puppets and shallow figurines, since the allegorist must use a predetermined, and somewhat rigid, key to unlock the secrets stored in the text. As a liberal, Croce relied on historical change when moving from the level of superficial appearances and events into the regions of spiritual depth and well-cherished civic values. Croce condemned the baroque period and, therefore, the diva, for they both embodied superficiality, seduction, ornament, and artifice. By reading against the grain of the surface text, Benjamin showed he had no trust in traditional, linear history, whereas Croce felt that historical knowledge went hand in hand with social progress. Croce was a lay philosopher and a passionate advocate for the separation of state and church, but he was also an idealist, a reformist thinker rather than a materialist, radical one. This is also why he, at first, supported Mussolini's Fascism. Later, Croce chose to occupy a sort of intellectual ivory tower, where he remained until the end of World War II, but his influence in Italy persisted well beyond the forties.

So eager was Croce to tame the antihumanist effects of modernity for the sake of preserving classicism in daily life that he railed against the work of Mario Praz (1896–1982), the author of *The Romantic Agony* (1930). A scholar of the Romantic period, Praz specialized in European and American literature, writing about Poe and Rimbaud, Keats and Flaubert. More literary critic and historian than philosopher, Praz was perfectly at ease accepting D'Annunzio's work and French decadent-symbolist culture. For Praz, these two areas amounted to the last crucial burst of Romantic energy in the nineteenth century, just before the rise of the twentieth-century, modernist avant-gardes—the futurists, for instance. Unlike Praz, who understood the links between Romanticism and modernism, Croce despised Marinetti's bombastic rhetoric and intense militarism. These two problematic features of the Italian avant-garde were also condemned by Gramsci, a Marxist—after his initial and enthusiastic interest in the futurists' rejection of the past. As a result, Gramsci's antifuturist stance unwillingly echoed Croce's, since they were both opposing the only area of fertile experimentation Italy had produced as a modern country.

During and after the period of the diva film, however, Croce was seen as having more intellectual authority than Praz. The latter's legacy was appreciated only in the 1960s, when Italy became more open to psychoanalysis, and when the links between Poe and Freud became the fashionable new topics in the wake of the 1968 student upheavals. Until then, history textbooks had ended with a cursory discussion of World War I, and issues of ideology and style had hardly ever been raised, the favored approach being instead a heavily mnemonic one based on high and low periods in a formal sense. In addition, because of Croce's lasting influence on the Italian national school system, it was not until the 1970s and 1980s that the whole modernist component of French decadent and symbolist D'Annunzian culture was reevaluated.[13]

Croce espoused the classical values of equilibrium and rationality. In "The Advance of Culture and Spiritual Unrest, 1901–1914" (1928), Croce criticized several major figures in Italian culture because they were all prey to some kind of baroque-like excess. Lombroso's positivism, for instance, with its blind faith in science, was too arrogant; D'Annunzio was "steeped in sensuality and sadism,"[14] and also wallowed in an "imperialistic style, with vast solemn movements of phrase, seeming to say great things but losing themselves in vagueness";[15] and futurism was "romanticism of the most distorted type."[16] For Croce, *baroque* was a derogatory adjective, applicable to popular literature of the lowest kind, namely, the serialized novelettes written for the masses:

> *To read the reviews and books of the day was to come under an incessant fusillade of ideas, sometimes happy, at other times ill-conceived; some intelligent, others confused, but not one of which in its rapid flight was stayed for closer consideration and analysis in order that it might be developed and made productive. They revealed more excitement than ardor, more initiative than persistence, more restlessness than movement, more curiosity and dilettantism than serious interest.*[17]

Carolina Invernizio (1851–1916), the wildly popular Italian author of Harlequin-style romances, was clearly a nuisance for the influential philosopher.

For Croce, the diva's baroque style catered to the masses' sense of disorientation, offering only an artificial and temporary intensity of sensations and emotions: "The innermost feeling of the age, the feeling that expresses itself freely and irresistibly, was chiefly made up of a sense of satiety and weariness, of passive skepticism and bitter mirth, of an inclination to tears."[18]

It was not until 1948, at the height of the neorealist period, that Croce made his first positive reference to the cinema's potential as an art form, in a letter to Luigi Chiarini, the director of the prestigious film journal *Bianco e Nero*.[19]

Antonio Gramsci

Croce was not the only major Italian thinker to look down on the cinema and the diva. His strongest ideological opponent, the Marxist Antonio Gramsci, also reached a negative conclusion about female stardom. For Gramsci, too, the diva was overly baroque; she embodied a sort of poisonous role model for working-class women. It is intriguing that Gramsci limited his understanding of the diva to aristocratic roles. He never addressed the fact that divas impersonated economically oppressed or sexually abused heroines. For example, Borelli played a prostitute in *Il Fior di Male*, and Francesca Bertini sold herself to a petty lawyer in *Assunta Spina*. It is also worth noting that despite his arguments in favor of a national popular literature for the masses and about the masses, Gramsci despised serials and feuilletons precisely because those genres were associated with a female consumer having lots of time to waste. Someone who could indulge in reading for many hours, Gramsci assumed, was likely to be outside the working class. In regard to the so-called women's novelettes, Gramsci wrote: "It is a lachrymose literature suitable only for stupefying the women, girls, and youngsters who feed on it. It is also often a source of corruption. . . . Millions of women and young people read these fables."[20]

What is even more disturbing is that on the topic of the detective novel, a genre that might have raised some questions about the boundaries of the law, Gramsci flatly repeats the conclusions reached by Lombroso's student, the positivist Enrico Ferri: "The detective novel . . . may perhaps have influenced the increase in crime among adolescent loafers."[21] Just as the detective novel was teaching criminal behavior to young readers, the diva film was a school for immorality. Here Gramsci echoes the indictment of cinema put forth by innumerable Catholic censors. Clearly, Marxism, melodrama, and crime did not belong together on the screen.

Gramsci's comments reveal his dislike of scandalous and sensationalistic films and show that his Marxism ran into difficulties when confronted by lowbrow forms of entertainment, especially those catering to women and young people. Those two audiences were outside Gramsci's ideal readership: the wholesome adult working-class man and his female companion.

Gramsci subordinated an analysis of changing gender roles to class identity. More specifically, Gramsci's writings on the theater and the cinema offer a conflicting array of statements about Lyda Borelli and the new woman. In his 1917 review of Henrik Ibsen's *A Doll's House*, written for the socialist paper *L'Avanti*, Gramsci celebrates Nora Helmar's sense of self and her desire to seek an independent life.[22] Unfortunately, Gramsci argues, this model of emancipation has not fully implanted itself in Italian life, because the bourgeois Italian woman tends to prefer the freedom of coquetry or the hypocrisy of charitable sacrifice to Nora's dignity and sincerity. Instead of analyzing the differences between Danish and Italian definitions of modernity, Gramsci concludes that Italian middle-class women live between the stereotypes of the frivolous socialite and the mater dolorosa.

In my view, such an assessment is insightful, for it denounces the power of Catholic morality and points to the power of the upper classes. Yet it does not take into account the meaningful but modest impact of the suffragette, or the criminal but political role of the prostitute—two marginal social types that the diva addresses over and over again. The prostitute meddled not only in the world of crime, but also in the sphere of the bohemians, the so-called *Scapigliati.* In Italy, the literary movement of Scapigliatura was critical of the capitalist order and sensitive to the arrival of Émile Zola's novels about psychological flaws and social issues.

By contrast, Gramsci cites the case of two proletarian women who, with the consent of their husbands, left their families to achieve a fuller inner life.[23] With his contextualization of Ibsen's heroine in post–World War I Italy, Gramsci indicates that the sources of a new moral code leading to legal reform can be found only in the ethos of the working class. The bourgeois woman, for him, either embraces independence because she confuses psychological emancipation with the excitement of a new fashion, or she avoids independence entirely because she is afraid of change and of being on her own financially.

It is certainly true that only wealthy or celebrated women, such as the socialite Marchesa Luisa Casati or the extravagant writer Amalia Guglielminetti, made the news, whereas the conquests and choices of less notorious, average Italian women were represented only through the diva's attitudes of rebellion.[24] But the diva film was not enough to capture Gramsci's sympathy. Nevertheless, it was really the cinema—especially the diva film—that spoke to all the women who fell between the cracks of competing stereotypes or ideological affiliations.

Gramsci's faith in the potential of the working class to change the perception of gender relations stemmed from his positive view of modernity and industrialization. Even though proletarian ethics were more in touch with historical change, Gramsci himself exhibited fairly traditional tastes when it came to matters of art. In a 1916 essay on the rivalry between the theater and the cinema, after arguing that the stage needs to revitalize itself from within, Gramsci makes it clear that he tolerates the moving image as a fad linked to just an expansion of "visual curiosity."[25]

To him, moving pictures were a sort of escape, merely an entertainment that would lead to a degeneration of taste among the general public. In the light of this definition of the cinema, Gramsci seemed to believe that the theater, although more expensive than the cinema, was a much better kind of nourishment for the minds of the working class. If the cinema either stimulated a superficial form of mental engagement or else appealed to the spectators' lowest instincts, we should not expect a high opinion of film actresses from Gramsci.

With a Lombrosian ring, Gramsci wrote that the diva Lyda Borelli was pure "sex" without one drop of talent or any claim to art.[26] Because she was the ultimate expression of cinematic allure but had no acting skills, Gramsci saw her as a prehistoric entity with no level of psychological complexity—in short, Borelli was a sex animal. We sense the discomfort of a man still tied to nineteenth-century aesthetic categories, such as decorum; in this respect, the socialist leader mirrored the liberal Croce.

Both of them were attached to a cohesive, organic view of the self: for Gramsci, the best social model was the working class; for Croce, it was Prime Minister Giolitti's thrifty management style. In either case, these two social orientations were the guarantors of rationality and progress. The diva's discontinuous motions and unpredictable choices did not fit within the two thinkers' different yet comparable models of subjectivity. Nevertheless, it is important to recognize that, Gramsci's personal opinions aside, socialist circles were most open to and supportive of women's issues. Steeped in a positivistic faith in science, hygiene, and self-improvement, socialist women like Paola and Gina Lombroso and Anna Kuliscioff ceaselessly worked on health issues, embraced anticlerical positions, and participated in the debate on divorce.[27]

Instead of placing the cinematic screen at the very center of the culture of modernity, Gramsci felt that this new medium was just another drug for the working class. Thus he could not see that there might be some connection between the phenomena of the diva and the new woman. In fact, these two types are clearly separate and exist in antithesis to each other in Gramsci's writings. For the socialist, the new woman came from the factory and Ibsen's theater. This is why, for Gramsci, Borelli represented both an old type of femininity and a beautiful brainless animal. Furthermore, Gramsci's celebration of working-class ethics in response to Ibsen's Nora discloses that, in his theory, class origins have a key impact on the relations between men and women, so much so that shifting the class setting from the bourgeoisie to the proletariat would suffice to solve the biggest problems in the battle of the sexes.

Gramsci's tendency to assimilate women's needs to a class imperative was further confirmed by his comments on the sexual question in the *Prison Notebooks* (*Lettere dal Carcere*), which were written from 1926 to 1934, but not published until 1947.[28] According to Renate Holub, thanks to his concept of hegemony, Gramsci "was capable of probing relations of power on a micro-structural level" and of understanding "sexuality as a site of domination and oppression."[29] For Gramsci, the personal was political. His conclusions, however, could not but have disappointed the pre–World War I feminist agenda. Holub goes on to explain that for the Italian thinker, "the modernist intensification of the rationalization of production does not elicit new possibilities for sexual expression and freedom for women, but requires modern women to adjust to the requirements of disciplined structures of time."[30] Without a doubt, for Gramsci, the adjustment of the Italian working class to a Tayloristic routine (1911) was a necessary evil of industrialization in a heavily rural country.

Here Gramsci shows he understood the double-edged meaning of the assembly line in the factory: on the one hand, it was dehumanizing for the worker to repeat the same gesture again and again robotically. On the other, Gramsci figured out that the metonymic chain involved in the assembly line was just one example of a broader style of time management, a rule-bound relation to temporality that enabled the individual to maintain a certain degree of control in the workplace and in the modern city. Rule-bound temporality is an unavoidable feature of mass society. More and more people's lives are made to run according to the same schedule. Before industrialization, the meaning of time was based on an individual, a seasonal, or a ritualistic framework. After transforming time into a controllable routine to help increase productivity, modern industry compensated its workers with the development of leisure activities.

Unlike the futurists, who glorified spontaneity, violence, improvisation, and performance, Gramsci felt that modern rules, with their step-by-step approach, offered the Italian working class an opportunity to make itself indispensable, and therefore more powerful in the nation as a whole. Despite their celebration of technology, the futurists had no real knowledge of industrial manufacturing. Likewise, they did not show great or systematic concern for the workers' movement and the peasant class. Gramsci's point here reflected his overall belief that in a nation with a delayed process of industrialization, class must take precedence over gender, even if he passionately rejected a mechanistic view of Marxism in favor of the interweaving of the personal and the political spheres. In other words, if the political interests of male workers required an increase in production, women had to put aside their own grievances and support their mates as best they could.

Luigi Pirandello

A man of the theater who was also a novelist and an essayist, Luigi Pirandello (1867–1936) thought that the cinema leaned toward dance, and the futurist Anton Giulio Bragaglia reported that he proposed the name *cinemelograph*, which meant a kind of kinetic writing in which words melted into music.[31] The Italian playwright knew well Henri Bergson's *Le Rire* (1900; *Laughter*) when he produced an essay titled *L'Umorismo* in 1908. Bergson defined the comic as a sort of relief we experience when we find ourselves free from the mechanistic, repetitive, and materialistic sides of daily life. For Pirandello and Bergson alike, a situation is always comic if it participates simultaneously in two series of events that are independent of each other, and if the situation can be interpreted in two quite different ways. However, for the French thinker, laughter was based on an unrecognized intention to humiliate and consequently to correct our neighbor. With Pirandello, the juxtaposition of the comic and the tragic led to a quasi-surreal sense of the grotesque. Pirandello's work is characterized by a radical pessimism that never becomes nihilistic, but it does envision the modern self as perpetually alienated and alien to the worlds of nature and society.

The Sicilian playwright was enough of a modernist to understand that because of the overstimulation of modern life, consciousness was becoming more and more like an "elastic net."[32] Despite this modernist stance, Pirandello was enough of a pessimist that even Croce thought of him as a "humanist" and dared not discard the Sicilian writer along with D'Annunzio and the futurists. In his famous novel *Shoot! The Notebooks of Serafino Gubbio, Cinematograph Operator* (1915), Pirandello's protagonist, Serafino, is, in P. Adams Sitney's words, a metonymy of the cinematic apparatus.[33] And the word *apparatus* is appropriate here for specific historical reasons. In the very early days of the cinema, the operator—meaning whoever turned the handle of the box-like recording camera—was, unlike today's cinematographer, the person in charge of how things would look in the end. In addition, filmed scenes in early cinema often consisted of one take and were unedited. The mere motion of characters and objects was the marvel of the period. In short, Serafino was a combination of director, editor, writer, and cinematographer.[34]

Serafino keeps telling the reader how many meters of footage in how many minutes he has been able to shoot, without ever acknowledging that his own choice of rhythm has a creative component. The reason Serafino does not consider his own speed to be a form of creativity is that he is gradually transformed into a mechanical man. By contrast, Pirandello's diva, the beautiful Russian Varia Nestoroff, faces a much richer situation: the impassive lens of the camera makes Varia, and everybody else, aware that the individual is never only one person, but always a series of multiple, coexisting possibilities in flux. And it is in this plural and unstable definition of identity that the legacy of Bergson becomes apparent in Pirandello.

As *Shoot!* unfolds, it slowly becomes clear that Pirandello's views on the cinema are not negative, as many critics have argued. The alchemical kinship between Serafino's impassive lens and Varia's supple body suggests that it is not the apparatus that is mechanical, noncreative, and dehumanizing; rather, it is the man behind the machine, Serafino himself, who feels insecure and frustrated about relations between men and women in daily life and, consequently, between men and machines during his working time on the set.

This is not to say, however, that the cinema is always easy to handle, even for the open-minded diva Varia Nestoroff. Pirandello writes:

She herself remains speechless and almost terror-stricken at her own image on the screen, so altered and disordered. She sees there one who is herself but whom she does not know. She would like not to recognize herself in this person, but at least to know her. Possibly for years and years, through all the mysterious adventures of her life, she has gone in quest of this demon which exists in her and always escapes her, to arrest it, to ask it what it wants, why it is suffering, what she ought to do to soothe it, to placate it, to give it peace. . . . She is really tragic: terrified and enthralled, with that somber stupor in her eyes which we observe in the eyes of the dying . . . she is quivering with rage. . . . Enemies, to her, all the men become to whom she attaches herself, in order that they may help her to arrest the secret thing in her that escapes her: she herself, yes, but a thing that lives and suffers, so to speak, outside herself.[35]

Cinema brings out the diva's existential complexity to the fullest. As she looks at herself, Varia is not worried about makeup or beauty in general; she is thinking about existential issues, and this ability to think in philosophical terms about the human condition is precisely what Serafino assumes Varia cannot do. In the passage above, Pirandello describes the inner self of the Italian diva with an acumen and a sensitivity unparalleled by anyone else from that period.

In antithesis to Varia's curiosity about the new technology, Serafino's last name is "Gubbio," a word that refers to the hill town where Saint Francis was born, and also to the Italian word *dubbio* ("doubt"). Clearly Pirandello's protagonist is doubtful about the cinema, seeing it as a medium of vulgar melodramas featuring crass characters steeped in the cult of sensuality and material possessions. Like a modern Saint Francis, he yearns for a more ascetic, metaphysical, and mystical use of the new technology. One wonders whether Pirandello was aware of

Gozzano's unfulfilled plans for making a film about Saint Francis.

Already linked with variability by the operatic cliché from Giuseppe Verdi's *Rigoletto* (1851), "*la donna è mobile,*" Varia's reputation as a cosmopolitan femme fatale is encrusted with layers and layers of negative connotations, and was therefore dehumanized well before the invention of the cinema. This is why she can interrogate her disorderly, protean appearance on the screen. She has nothing to lose to begin with. She does know, although she does not know why, that she is by definition and at all times a negative image. Through any kind of doubling of the negative image she already is, Varia has the potential of bringing about another being—even a positive one! Perhaps some kind of new female being will be born, one capable of standing up against the operatic and literary clichés presiding over her negative origin as a woman of spectacle and death.

For Serafino, the problem posed by mechanical reproduction is not one of plurality, choice, and direction, but one of complete effacement. One old self is being defeated by a modern one that has nothing to do with its previous, self-assured, stable origin. This radical sense of detachment between the original and the copy could be read as Serafino's inability to adjust, or as a commentary on his arrogant rejection of any form of self-evaluation through an alter ego. As Pirandello remarks, he is even afraid of his shadow.[36]

The stakes in relation to the impact of cinema on identity are thus very different for Serafino, whose definition of individuality and masculinity depend on the brain controlling the coordination of eye and hand. When he uses the newly invented cinema apparatus, Serafino's head is no longer unique or even attached to his body. Its two most important functions—seeing and believing—have been replaced by a box. In fact, the early cinema's combination of recording and projecting, receiving and transmitting, in a single heavy box, seems to repeat the conjunction in the brain between vision and presence. In other words, the mind trusts that matter exists if it looks as though it can be touched. But what about the cinema, in which absolutely nothing is there except the shadow-like photographic and moving impression of everything being exactly where it should be?

On the strength of its flair for optical illusion, the cinema has reorganized the map of Serafino's senses to such an extreme that the predictable turning of the handle is what now enables human vision; the eye no longer regulates the hand. But fate has worse things in store for Serafino than the transformation of his brain into a rotating mechanical handle. Serafino's old humanist self feels so unnecessary to the camera that all his humanity, soul included, is about to evaporate into a puff of cigarette smoke inside a crowded movie theater.[37]

Like Gramsci, Pirandello favored the theater over the cinema. This is why Pirandello decried the situation of the actor in film in comparison with that of the performer in theater. But Pirandello differs from Gramsci in that the novelist, intentionally or not, allowed for a connection to a new understanding of fleeting temporality. And it is this sense of life, or élan vital, being timeless, unlike finite human experience, that links Pirandello to Bergson's philosophy of vitalistic becoming in defiance of historical conclusions.

It is difficult to find an object better than a cigarette to mark the sense of time passing inevitably but uselessly. With both Bergson and Pirandello, the blind technological frenzy of modernity boils down to a strange combination of accidental waste and unavoidable fatality, of mass tragedy and passive superficiality. It is also worth noting that both Pirandello and Croce decried the loss of soul in the wake of increasing industrialization. Neither Croce nor Pirandello meant "soul" in a religious sense, but they were both referring to the cultural clash between materialism and spiritualism.

That Pirandello's stance about the cinema contained a feminist streak and that it was not entirely negative are confirmed by a letter the writer sent to Anton Giulio Bragaglia in 1918 about the possibility of adapting *Shoot!* for the screen and casting Pina Menichelli in the role of Varia Nestoroff.[38] Pirandello's choice was intriguing, for Francesca Bertini, tall and commanding even in the slums of Naples for *Assunta Spina,* had too much personality of her own to fit Serafino's shallow view of the diva. And Lyda Borelli was too refined to satisfy the axiom that the cinema was crass entertainment. Menichelli, on the contrary, was the diva who had been turned into a femme fatale by one director, Giovanni Pastrone. Furthermore, only Menichelli could be the female threat Serafino was eager to complain about. Likewise, only Menichelli could be the new woman nobody had quite figured out. Notwithstanding her stereotypical role in Pastrone's *Il Fuoco,* there was also a lot more about Menichelli the camera could sense and bring out, far beyond the limits of the femme fatale. As a result, there was nothing personal or professional to come between her and the screen. She was the most malleable performer and the best image to shuttle between Serafino's fears and the writer's sympathy.

It is hard to tell whether Pirandello's willingness to work with Bragaglia on a screen adaptation was motivated by a desire for profit or by the sense that something new might be learned from a closer engagement with the cinema. It is possible, however, to see Pirandello begin to support the cinema in the scene in which Serafino's eyes discover that the diva is neither animal-like nor a mechanical creature.

This unexpected discovery happens all of a sudden, and it is comparable to an epiphany. At last Serafino realizes that Varia is made of light, an icon of temporality comparable to the camera obscura. His new perception is linked to the moment the sun dances on her face: "The sun . . . through the vine leaves of the pergola, was beating upon her face. It was true; and a wonderful sight was the play, on that face, of the purple shadows, straying and shot with threads of golden sunlight, which lighted up now one of her nostrils, and part of her upper lip, now the lobe of her ear and a patch of her throat."[39] At least for a while, in Serafino's eyes, Varia's face becomes as abstract as an arabesque of light in motion. She becomes a movie—an image of life unfolding irregularly, through unforeseeable, minute transformations he can relate to and feel touched by emotionally and, therefore, very humanly. And this is the value and power of the cinema: that moment when motion becomes emotion for everybody in the theater, but also secretly and differently for each viewer. Of course, the reason for this magic remains either unknown or difficult to explain in words.

Most importantly, Pirandello transforms nature—namely, the sun—into the artist or the filmmaker, thus disposing, once and for all, of Serafino as the alienated cinema operator. By allowing the sun, the ultimate source of life, to make the film, without human artists or human performers in control, Pirandello seems to anticipate André Bazin's insight that nature can produce images that look like surrealist photographs: a flower or a snowflake.[40] The sun's arabesque-like tracery of light on Varia's face is an important moment in the relation between Serafino and the diva on the set. Until then, Serafino had known of her only through negative hearsay, and as his last name suggests, it was this prior gossiping that had deepened his doubts about her and the cinema.

Serafino knows Varia as a femme fatale, a malefactor rather than a victim: besides flirting with his friend Baron Aldo Nuti, she apparently led a previous lover, Giorgio Mirelli, another friend of Serafino's, to commit suicide. Notwithstanding Varia's negative reputation, the temporary transformation of her appearance from negative to positive, thanks to the sunshine, is as stunning as the mechanical reproduction of the human figure in its moving double on the screen. By realizing that, thanks to the cinema, he is capable of seeing the same object anew and differently, Serafino begins to accept that the diva's sunlit face can be by far more interesting and, paradoxically, more natural than the cliché he has always perceived her through. In other words, it is the copy that has the power to extrapolate the truth hidden in the original, and the mechanical handle is not heartless, but functions as a device for cleaning up Serafino's clogged mind and eyes.

So entranced is he by this epiphany that all of a sudden Nestoroff's name, Varia, sheds its traditional association with female duplicity and deception. Instead, the word *varia* is an allusion to Heraclitus's idea that nothing lasts forever, that everything changes all the time. Thus the diva's name, "Varia," comments on cinema's ability to preserve a moment in motion as no previous art form had been able to do. Stunned by the discovery that Varia's image delivers a unique visual experience, he declares: "How in the world did she not understand that I was not her enemy?"[41] The image of the diva under the sunlight exemplifies a life-giving use of the cinema. This means that the medium of shooting—cinema—besides being used to kill the soul in favor of superficial appearances, can be also deployed for an opposite and most worthwhile purpose. By the end of the narrative, Pirandello's novel is not about shooting a film and killing a humanistic premodern notion of male individuality. It is, instead, about shooting old ideas, getting rid of the past, so that a positive view of the cinema, love for life, and femininity might prevail.

Most importantly, one final episode proves that the alignment of cinema with hunting and death is a masculine choice. During the production, Baron Aldo Nuti comes to the set to play the role of courageous explorer and kill a beautiful tigress that the production house Kosmograph has bought from the zoo nearby. Nobody knows, however, that Varia's rejected lover, livid with humiliation, has a secret and revengeful plan against her. Instead of aiming at the tigress, he turns the gun on the diva. But the loyal animal seizes the opportunity to star as the protector of a helpless woman: the beast devours the evil baron, in complete defiance of the script for *The Lady and the Tiger,* a colonial adventure set in India for the British film market. In the end, the diva turns out to be a peace-loving professional, and the tigress, previously accused of all sorts of misbehavior, becomes the new heroine of the day.

In his essay on Pirandello's *Shoot!* Tom Gunning remarks: "One senses on Pirandello's part a premonition of the often deadly role the male gaze played in the history of cinema, as described by feminist film theorist Laura Mulvey. Nestoroff inspires a desire that leads men to despise rather than admire her."[42] Hoping to add to Gunning's agenda of reading Pirandello's novel in light of feminist film theory, I would underline that Baron Nuti and Serafino, instead of Varia, are the objects of the writer's criticism. Such an interpretation may seem more persuasive in light of some of Pirandello's lesser-known works that favored women's issues and preceded the composition of *Shoot!* Pirandello asserted his concern for the female condition by writing two novels with surrealist underpinnings, based not so much on the exploration of the Freudian unconscious but on paradoxical situations in daily life. The first was *L'Esclusa* (also titled *Marta Ayala*, written in 1893 but published in 1901), which means "the female outsider," the story of a young woman unjustly accused of adultery.[43]

Pirandello's aim was to expose the delirium of traditional masculinity and bourgeois conventions: when the husband throws his wife out of the house, she is innocent; when he takes her back, she has in fact committed adultery. Pirandello's sensitivity to women's issues might have been due to his having taught for many years in an *istituto magistrale*, a vocational state school for future female teachers. When Pirandello met Marta Abba (1900–1988), a talented actress and the true love of his life, he could not live with her openly because he was still married and taking care of his sick wife, Antonietta, the daughter of a wealthy partner of Pirandello's father in a Sicilian mining business. Bound together through a coldly arranged marriage, Pirandello and Antonietta produced three children and had to face many financial hard times. Unable to handle any anxiety about money, Antonietta became seriously violent and dangerous to the rest of her family. Yet Pirandello took care of her for seventeen years because he did not have the heart to see his wife end up in an asylum.[44]

In 1911, Pirandello worked on *Suo Marito* (Her Husband), originally titled *Giustino Roncella Nato Boggiolo*, a novel inspired by his friend the writer Grazia Deledda's complicated personal and professional life in a world dominated by men.[45] Well aware of his novel's sympathetic portrayal of Silvia Roncella, a writer, Pirandello decided to avoid a second edition. The novel was so controversial that he feared a second printing might harm Deledda's career.

Anton Giulio Bragaglia

Primarily trained as a man of the theater, Anton Giulio Bragaglia (1890–1960) became famous in 1913 as the founder of photodynamism, the controversial branch of the futurist movement devoted to photography.[46] The relations between photodynamism and futurism are difficult to chart because they were marred by personal tensions between Umberto Boccioni (1882–1916), the painter, and Anton Giulio Bragaglia, the self-appointed promoter of nonrealistic photography. In 1912, Bragaglia met Marinetti, who decided to finance photodynamic research. This official support led to photodynamic portraits of futurist members, including the 1913 "poly-physiognomical" portrait of Boccioni. This image shows a general awareness about a major shift in culture: the singular, organic, coherent self of classical-humanist culture has been replaced by the multiple and shifting identities of modern life.

To be sure, Boccioni engaged in photo-performances with well-positioned objects. These props stressed the iconic, even symbolic, power of the images. Based on a strong sense of staging, such an approach was not far from the controlled compositions of academic painting. As a result, the photographs were weakened at an indexical level. In other words, the iconic power of objects was so strong, but also open-ended, that the human element was inevitably either subordinated to the props or defined by them. This reinsertion of human intentionality through the staged placement of objects in the picture ran up against the idea of photography as the only mechanical medium that could operate by exploiting the absence of the human element. Supposedly, chance and randomness would guarantee photography's indexical stance well outside any notion of craftsmanship or artistry.

It is hard to know exactly why Bragaglia and Boccioni became rivals: after all, they were both downplaying photography's indexicality for the sake of imaginative setups, ghostly results, and a shared desire to debunk the link between science and photography. In addition, Boccioni and Bragaglia were both using photography to make visible the invisible, to reveal the perceptual inner lining of motion itself, the overall trajectory or movement through change, without compartmentalizing each separate stage or final result in the scientific wake of Marey and Muybridge. Needless to say, Bragaglia's theoretical statements in his *Manifesto of Photo-Dynamism* (1913), and in other writings as well, are replete with Bergsonian echoes about the indivisible flow of movement and its lyrical power:

Movement is the expression of an object's trajectory as it comes to occupy different spaces filled with the memories of other objects that have been there and in motion; movement is the revelation of life and of the mystery of its evolution. Movement is the most lyrical essence of life, while its expression is the trajectory. The latter is the expression of a gesture that has taken place, a dynamic result made of visible air, of speed that can be seen.[47]

The real question, however, has to do with how Bragaglia managed to reconcile his kind of Bergsonism with his attachment to photography. Photography's stillness was an impediment to the unpredictable or spontaneous flow of images Bergson situated inside duration. According to film theorist Mary Ann Doane, the only possible answer to this problem is that Bragaglia's photographic work waged a battle against the valuing of the single moment in a vacuum or the capturing of the instant by itself and outside a broader stream of experience. Doane's argument is persuasive in the sense that for the futurist photographer, the visibility of sensation and the trajectory of motion were more important than the single moment in isolation or the analytical breakdown of different kinetic phases.[48] What is peculiar, though, is that Bragaglia's interest in the subjective experience of movement never produced an interesting enough range of photographic topics.

Anyone would agree that Bragaglia achieved pretty much the same kind of photograph over and over again and was unable to develop a precise typology of sensations based on different movements, performers, actions, props, and other kinds of variables. Bragaglia's overall result was based more on how the image looked, on its internal quasi-ghostly vibration, than on its usefulness in differentiating the movements of sewing from the movements of climbing. Considering that Bragaglia's priorities were more aesthetic than scientific, it is all the more ironic that he was rejected by Boccioni, the self-appointed advocate of painting. In fact, Bragaglia's choice of photography did not completely rule out painting, which he continued to depend on for his sets in the theater. He considered photography and painting to be exchangeable forms, but not opposite and competitive ones, as Boccioni did. There is a way in which Bragaglia's photodynamic, trembling, and multiple contours remind us of the texture of paint, of the artist's brushstroke turning into a sort of cinematic swish-pan, whenever a casual splatter or dripping erases a previous image. It was likely that Bragaglia conceived of photodynamism as something that could range from a pictorial, quasi-abstract use of photography to something similar to musical rhythm, and partaking of both kinetic energy and perceptual stimulation.

In the end, Boccioni chose a very traditional and, in principle, antifuturist position by claiming that no matter what Bragaglia did, photography was irreconcilable with the realm of art as a form of individual manual creativity. By so doing, he managed to arrogate to himself alone the humanist, outdated, but still prestigious ego ideal linked to the artist's hand, the aura of the signature, and the uniqueness of the work of art. Without the official support of the futurist movement, Bragaglia kept working on photodynamism with his brother, Arturo, but clearly the two of them continued their research in the margins of the futurist avant-garde.

It is sad to think that personal rivalries prevailed over intellectual dialogue, especially when we consider that both Boccioni and Bragaglia were influenced by Bergson. Painting prevailing over photography amounted to the rehashing of an old chapter in the history of the system of the arts, which futurism had not seriously bothered to rewrite but had simply proclaimed dead. Boccioni's marginalization of experimental photography confirmed that there were areas of contradiction and insecurity on the topic of technology inside the most powerful ranks of the movement.

Within a comparably narrow horizon, Bragaglia did not expand his photodynamic experiments as much as he could have. In contrast to Muybridge and Marey, who had studied motion by using men, women, animals, and all kinds of objects and environments, both indoors and outdoors, Bragaglia mostly used male models or male friends for his photodynamic experiments. Only two portraits of women stand out: "The Typist" (1911) and "The Photodynamic Actress" (1913). In "The Typist," the movement trails stem from the kinetic intensity hovering over the hands of this modern young workingwoman. That typewriting was one of the few professions open to women before World War I is also demonstrated by a short film entitled *The Typist* (*La Dattilografia*, 1911). In this short modern drama, a secretary is disturbed by the advances of her lecherous boss. It is hard to know whether Bragaglia had seen this little film, yet the intertextual connection between the film and the photograph, as well as the interface of woman and machine, suggests that female labor makes women more vulnerable instead of emancipating them. In fact, in Bragaglia's photograph, typing is charged with both a kinetic and a dangerously erotic energy that, in turn, can be said to trigger the male's advances in the film.

Bragaglia's second female portrait is a bit closer to the diva as a cultural type, for he relied on photodynamism to explore the sensation of smell. In "The Photodynamic Actress" ("L'Attrice Fotodinamizzata," 1913), his model was an obscure theatrical performer from the Talli Company, Zarina de Sylvain. She stood in front of Bragaglia's camera, enjoying the perfume of a rose. "The Photodynamic Ac-

Anton Giulio Bragaglia, *Dactylographie* (1911). Gelatin silver print (gold-toned) 4 5/8 × 6 5/8 inches. Metropolitan Museum of Art, Gilman Collection, Gift of the Howard Gilman Foundation, 2005 (2005.100.244). Photograph, all rights reserved, Metropolitan Museum of Art. © 2006 Artists Rights Society (ARS), New York/SIAE, Italy.

tress" is an important image simply because the combination of actress and rose was to become one of the strongest clichés inhabiting the diva film.

In the wake of photodynamism, one scene from Edoardo Bencivenga's *La Piovra* (1919) exemplifies the sensation-based visual style of the diva film. There is no blurring of the image, but the acting style acknowledges subatomic movements that signify something powerful being felt below the visual surface. In *La Piovra,* the evil Baron Petrovic persecutes Francesca Bertini, who plays the role of a loyal wife tormented by an insanely jealous husband. During a theatrical performance, the baron's face appears in close-up against a black background: his eyes stare obsessively at Bertini with a fixed glare. Bertini is sitting in a theater box, turning her beautiful naked white back to the man who, shrouded in complete darkness, continues either to look at her or to think of her so intensely that the cut between the two shots underlines a telepathic connection between the diva and the baron. Bertini turns her head and looks behind her. For a moment she sees nothing, and yet she has the feeling that a dangerous pressure is hovering around her. Instead of freezing its object into a statue, the baron's desire makes the diva move. While Bertini is the moving image and her back is a screen, Petrovic's gaze has become comparable to a projector, beaming energy that brings to life motionless shadows, empty surfaces.

By visualizing the movements of actors as they express sensations, whether large or small, Bragaglia may have been trying to warm up the cold and precise eye of photography through a passionate celebration of the fact that nothing stands still, that everything feels and flows, even if it does so inside a single photograph, and not from shot to shot, as in the best moments of *La Piovra.* In a word, photodynamism was the vitalistic answer to photography's associations with scientific positivism. Furthermore, one wonders whether photodynamism was also a sort of humanist rejection of the mechanical. It might be more accurate to say that Bragaglia replaced the organic with a sensualistic model as a way to amplify minutiae and exacerbate detail, following an aesthetic not far from D'Annunzio's penchant for baroque excess or symbolist overrefinement. Bragaglia made each of his photographic images look as if the picture were either remembering or imagining the experience of movement with a sort of metaphysical accuracy for detail.

The diva film and photodynamism became two comparable reactions against technological advances. Bragaglia, for example, deeply admired the spiritualist reputation hovering around the 1911 arrival of the Ballets Russes in Italy. In his book *L'Evoluzione del Mimo* (1930), Bragaglia writes about the transformation of choreographed movement into a medium for spiritual inquiry. Considering that he was writing in 1930 and looking back at the first decade of the century, it is possible to detect Bragaglia's disapproval of shallow Fascist spectacles of physical prowess:

Today I would be inclined to rely on the fusion of dance with pantomime and to abolish regimented dancing, to reject the great movements of crowds in order to privilege the small mimicry of subordinate roles, and I would also rely on the contrast between personalities instead of showcasing superficial technical dexterity—all this would help overcome the materialist or sport-oriented approach, based only on the muscles, and reinvigorate dance through the inner life of the performer, in the light of spiritual epiphanies.[49]

After learning the ropes from his father, Francesco, at *Cines,* Bragaglia decided to bring together dance, theater, and photography in a film project. In *Thaïs* (1917), Bragaglia's film style is limited to cuts from one self-contained tableau to another. This framework is typical of an early cinema still ruled by theatrical staging. Yet as the exotic name in the title suggests, this film is orientalist, as a costly diva film should be; most importantly, it is a film about personal change, and thus about transformation over time: just like a drug, orientalism opens the doors of perception to unknown dimensions that supposedly lead to the reinvention of oneself.

In *Thaïs,* the most interesting handling of motion concerns the characters' sartorial transformations and the quasi dissolution of the diva's death chamber into an array of vapors. In Bragaglia's terminology, this technique of dissolving sets from a solid material to a fluid one was called *scenoplastica.*[50] To be sure, Bragaglia's theory of scenoplastica was about the temporary and mixed nature of any set, because solid materials have the potential to change into liquid or gaseous ones. Likewise, in *Thaïs,* floral motifs can switch to geometric ones. The plasticity of the onstage world was Bragaglia's valuable insight into the cinema as a medium made of presence and absence, the medium that can exchange what is full with what is empty, and vice versa.

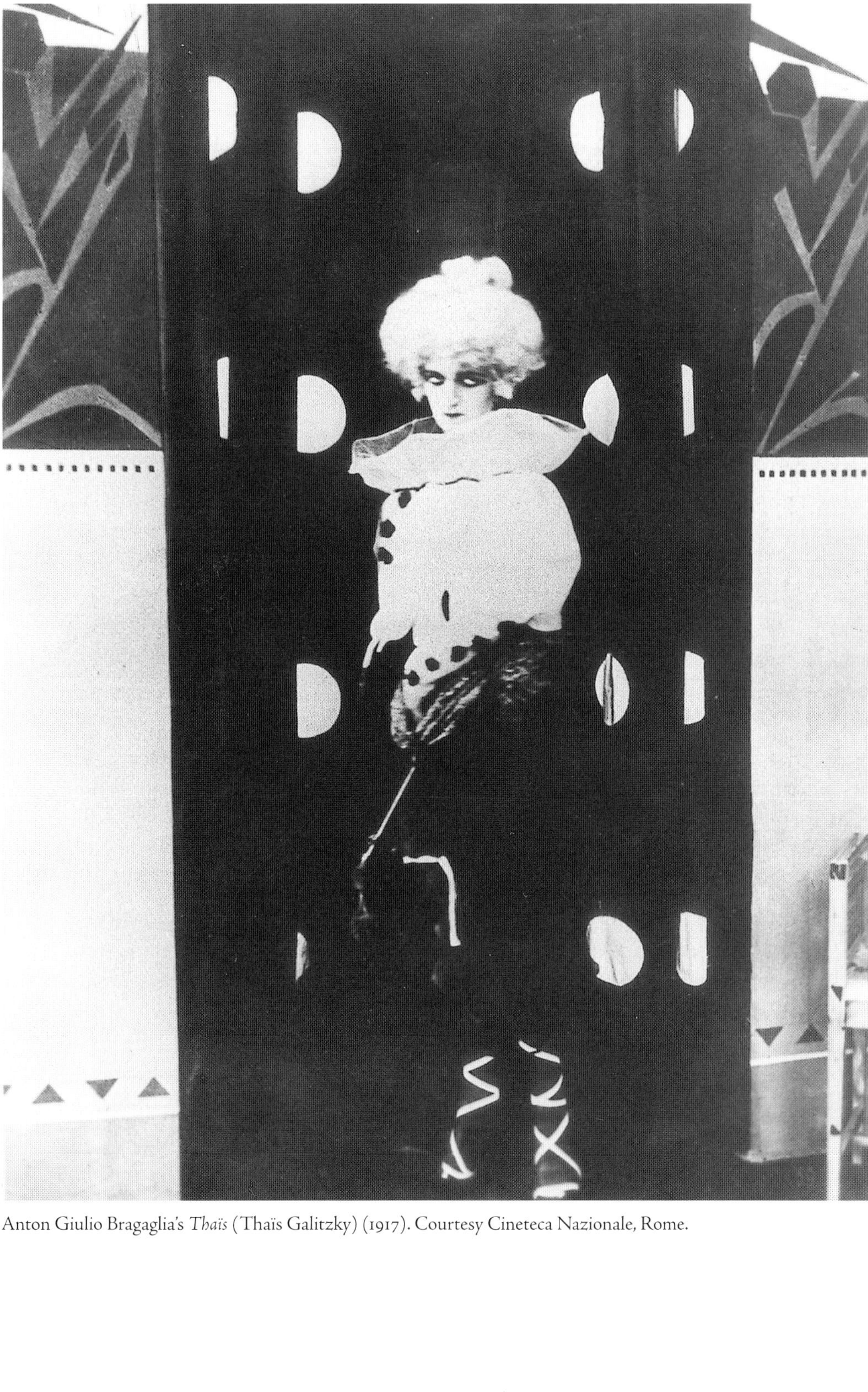

Anton Giulio Bragaglia's *Thaïs* (Thaïs Galitzky) (1917). Courtesy Cineteca Nazionale, Rome.

In *Thaïs*, a sort of self-conscious conceptual essay on the diva as a cultural and philosophical type, Bragaglia's main star, Thaïs Galitzky, plays the triple role of Thaïs, Countess Vera Preobrajenska, and Nitchevo (Nothing)—a veritable photodynamic triptych, evolving from the credits in full title to the empty screen, with the character in the middle functioning like an optical illusion. Less famous than her colleague Galitzky, Ileana Leonidoff plays the Countess Bianca Stagno-Bellincioni. In contrast to traditional diva films, in which a man chooses between two women, in *Thaïs*, Galitzky shares herself between Bianca and Count San Remo, who, in turn, is also involved with Bianca. Instead of a love triangle with one man and two women, the narrative is organized around a lesbian couple and three potentially rotating and competing centers of power. This is the case because, for a while, it is unclear which of the three characters is in charge of which temporary triangular configuration. Circles and triangles, conceived by set designer Enrico Prampolini (1894–1956), proliferate throughout the film, along with painted eyes and peacock feathers, voyeurism and vanity, narcissism and paranoia, delusion and obsession.

Inasmuch as Prampolini's sets amplify the problems of love, they also repeat to the point of redundancy the patterns printed on the clothes worn by Galitzky. This match between clothes and sets resolves itself in favor of Thaïs, who becomes the protagonist at the center of all triangles. On the one hand, Prampolini's visual spectacle hides Bragaglia's sense of intellectual crisis in tackling the gender question. On the other, the orientalist motifs of arabesque-like plants and grotesque mythological creatures reappear on the decorated walls and on the costumes so congruently and regularly that the diva appears to be imprisoned not only in her airless, overly decorated rooms but also, worse, in her own fashionable clothes. Despite their eccentric and unconventional look, these dresses do not help Thaïs refashion herself; their visual rhyming with the painted walls makes her look less and less like a person and more and more like a piece of furniture. Unfortunately, this sense of architectural entrapment goes against her unconventional, liberated life with lovers of both sexes.

Notwithstanding the drawbacks of Prampolini's sets and costumes, Bragaglia thought very carefully about the diva as a mixed type. In a few scenes, for example, Bianca wears acceptable modern clothes, such as a *tailleur*—a comfortable, sporty skirt with a longish jacket on top. Yet Bianca's costuming continues to celebrate the nurturing side of femininity, since the tailleur does not prevent her from holding a huge bunch of freshly cut flowers in her arms. Thaïs, the character, incorporates all three types: the film diva inhabiting a world of optical tricks, the trouser-wearing whip-wielding lesbian, and the cruel femme fatale. Bianca, on the other hand, is a mixture of the new and the traditional woman: she may wear a tailleur, but in one famous publicity still, she wears her hair pulled back into a bun and parted in the middle, while Thaïs is sitting down, leaning back in her chair, and offering her smiling face to the camera.

Bianca's vertical and Thaïs' diagonal postures grow out of each other, but they also begin to resemble the hand of a clock ticking away toward either death or liberation. In contrast to Bianca, who dresses all in virginal white or in serious black, Thaïs puts on outrageous black-and-white garments: her shoes have long white laces that are crossed over her black knee-high hose and make her look like a mountebank; her puffy white rococo wig

Anton Giulio Bragaglia's *Thaïs* (1917). Courtesy Cineteca Nazionale, Rome.

Anton Giulio Bragaglia's *Thaïs* (1917). Courtesy Cineteca Nazionale, Rome.

and large white collar with black spots over a shortened pilot's ensemble or black balloon trousers insist that she can be an aviatrix, a clown, or even some kind of dashing, sexually ambiguous eighteenth-century rake.

While most of *Thaïs* takes place indoors or in elegant gardens, the central long sequence of the film unfolds outdoors on a river—possibly the Tiber, for the film was shot in Rome. After being driven onto the deck of a

Anton Giulio Bragaglia's *Thaïs* (1917). Courtesy Cineteca Nazionale, Rome.

huge barge, the car belonging to Thaïs's carefree male friends is slowly pulled across the water by a system of ropes and pulleys stretching from each bank. A large portion of the sequence is shot from a high angle, all of it in long shot and also in long take, with no cuts. The episode stands out from the rest of the film because it is an isolated scene of uninterrupted labor happening in real time, and carries a strong and unexpected documentary flavor. Furthermore, the camera keeps its distance from any recognizable character, so that the viewer feels as if a nonfiction film about the river had taken over the previous drama based on dangerous liaisons. The only way to explain this break in a farce of jealousies and betrayals that unfold in medium shot is to read the sequence as a commentary on temporality, history, and change. All of a sudden the film drops its nervous rhythm and acquires the solemn, nearly somber tone of a slow-moving funeral on the water as observed by a respectful and godlike eye. It is easy to see how Thaïs's tightrope act between sexual orientations and this painstaking crossing of the river spell out the imminent death of old clichés and the exhausting search for new formulas. The importance of this search is shown by the placement of the word *novissima* (newest) in Prampolini's film logo.[51]

This change of tempo from previous slapstick moments, which imitated action-filled American silent comedies, to the slow dragging of the heavy barge through the water occupies too central a position in the narrative to be dismissed as some stray footage accidentally left in the final version. Since the modern car sits still on an old system of transportation, there is a sense in which an allegorical journey over the troubled waters of modernity might be taking place. Indeed, Thaïs and her friends are not simply modern; they even pose as futurists. The men engage in mechanical motions like a bunch of marionettes, while Thaïs pretends to be a stuntwoman from the circus, bouncing up and down on a large trampoline.

The possibility of an overall allegorical reading of the film is further confirmed by its last four minutes, during which, after Bianca's death, Thaïs enters her own secret chamber, a place of magic powers, the other side of the looking glass, or the hidden world of the fourth dimension. In line with Bergson, time *is* the nonfigurative but most fundamental element of human experience. In this special place made of time beyond human space, Bragaglia seems to contrast two kinds of temporalities. The first mode is linked to the female body twisting and turning in a mixture of freedom and pain. Here Thaïs reminds the viewer that the film diva is like Laocoön—for her the challenge is not to combine pain with beauty, but to reinvent herself; she must move from a trite, heavy form into one that is both new and unknown. The consequences of modernity are still completely under discussion, which explains the use of irony during the barge sequence. As heavy and large as a house, the modern car stands for a whole architecture of old habits and behaviors. By contrast, the barge, motorless and unstylish, is the only reliable way to cross the barrier of the river. No wonder Thaïs's struggle to regenerate herself takes place among weightless and ever-shifting substances such as perfume, gas, odors, smoke, and clouds. The aerial metaphors of tightrope walking and circus acrobatics represent an attempt to completely overturn the pull of gravity, and strange odors win out over sight.

Yet the second mode of temporality for the secret chamber has nothing to do with Bergson's élan vital leading to rebirth. By

Anton Giulio Bragaglia's *Thaïs* (1917). Courtesy Cineteca Nazionale, Rome.

contrast, it uses a big clock to allegorize a gloomy view of a rule-bound modernity, the countdown toward the death of imagination and spontaneity. Besides the big clock, the chamber's scenoplastica relies on a forest of knives that gradually traps the diva's body. These blades make time look even more inevitable, surgical, linear, accumulative, and systematic—with no intervals, no room for marvelous metamorphoses. And yet in the midst of this punitive mise-en-scène directed against the diva, Prampolini's sets—or, perhaps, the dream-like, eroticized memories of her ever-changing clothes—manage to avoid aggression by evaporating into colorful whiffs of smoke. In fact, the print of *Thaïs* from the Cinémathèque Française includes some tinted sections.

The ultimate icon of chronometric temporality decried by Bergson, Bragaglia's oversized clock, shown in close-up, is not far from Giorgio De Chirico's obsessive iconography in his metaphysical painting of that very same period. For the famous painter, public reminders of time passing mark time but are also frozen in time, for they always remain identical to themselves; these clocks are static and detached from lived experience. De Chirico's clocks are the empty shells of a scientific notion of temporality in crisis. It is this kind of homogeneous, predictable, rule-bound time that humanist culture, in small Italian towns sheltered by Renaissance arcades, can afford to ignore. The changing interface of body and building produces shadows, and in De Chirico's world, they are enough to mark the unraveling of the day. Thus, the sun is the one and only clock.

Augusto Genina's *La Signorina Ciclone* (1916; Miss Hurricane). Courtesy Cineteca di Bologna.

(bottom) Suzanne Armelle in *La Signorina Ciclone*. Courtesy Cineteca di Bologna.

The world has become an eerie camera obscura.

Besides the detour into De Chirico's metaphysical painting, which, I repeat, occurred in the same period that Bragaglia worked on *Thaïs,* it is also worth analyzing the representation of time in a little-known film by Augusto Genina, *La Signorina Ciclone* (1916; Miss Hurricane), based on an idea from Lucio D'Ambra. Only a fragment of Genina's film has survived, but those 421 meters, preserved at the Cineteca di Bologna, are enough to recount the plot and explain its purpose. *La Signorina Ciclone* tells the story of a dynamic Gibson girl—an enterprising American, Fluffy Ruffles—who, like a master puppeteer, controls the strings attached to her seven boyfriends and their seven dogs. The point is that her suitors behave like a bunch of automatons working on an assembly line, and their level of coordination triggers plenty of comic effects. Genina's film is a parody of industrial time—the homogenization of time into something artificial, which Bergson clearly considered a negative aspect of the industrial society in which he lived.

To return to Bragaglia's death chamber, it is significant that Thaïs herself, the diva, turns on the switch that releases the poisonous floating substances. Yet is this just a masochistic suicide, or a temporary effacement preceding the birth of something new? It is well known that Bragaglia was interested not only in Bergsonism, but also in color theory and the physics of light. All these scientific efforts, however, were meant to find an answer that could not quite be reached. This is perhaps why one of Thaïs's names is Nitchevo, "nothing," which could refer to a complete mental blankness or to a privileged level of insight, both possibilities staying on at the very same time.

For example, in her essay on *Thaïs*, Millicent Marcus notes that Bragaglia started his own periodical of esoteric pantheism, entitled *La Ruota* (1915–1916), "whose letterhead, designed by Prampolini, featured a peacock as 'the epitome of colors unified in light.'"[52] Without a doubt, color is the foremost site of subjectivity and motion, or of subjective time rendered visible, so that this utopian possibility of discovering a secret alchemy that fuses all colors into sheer light was not unrelated to the period's search for an ideal modern creature that perfectly integrated body and brain, male and female. But this bisexual creature, who was to replace the male humanist subject after the explosion of the so-called modern sexual question, was difficult to bring to life.

As a film, *Thaïs* must content itself with being only a limited yet brave answer to the call for the types of *capricci meravigliosi* (marvelous fancies) theorized by the futurists in their manifesto *Futurist Cinematography* (1916).[53] In many ways, *Thaïs* is difficult for the contemporary film viewer because it is so

An esoteric image from Gabriele D'Annunzio's Il Vittoriale. Courtesy Fondazione Il Vittoriale, Gardone Riviera.

steeped in the iconography and issues of the period. In addition, the original tinting is not always available, and the black-and-white chromatic effects of Prampolini's sets suffer whenever the print shown is not a properly restored one. *Thaïs* is also a film with a very self-conscious aesthetic thesis, and this fact alone makes its overloaded conceptual allegory somewhat difficult to digest. On the other hand, it displays an amazing amount of lucidity about the philosophical challenges of the period.

It may be that the film's failure lies in its author's indecision about whether to be an artist or a critic, his attempt to be spontaneously creative and rigorously analytical, all at the same time. One thing is certain: of all the diva films of the period, Bragaglia's *Thaïs* is the one that, through the negative use of the clock of science, most explicitly associates the sinuous acting style of the diva with the Bergsonian concept of "subjective duration."

Francesca Bertini and Amleto Novelli in *La Piovra* (1919, directed by Edoardo Bencivenga). Author's collection.

(bottom) Francesca Bertini in *La Piovra*. Courtesy Cineteca di Bologna.

In addition, *Thaïs* also makes clear that the curvilinear style of art nouveau was first and foremost the representation of a historical challenge, specifically, of the élan vital required to change from old to new. In the aftermath of Gotthold Lessing's *Laokoon* (1766), the canonical treaty on the relations among the arts, Bragaglia proposed a new system of relations among twentieth-century media; in it, thanks to the quasi-cinematic dissolve of scenoplastica, the inorganic elements of the sets were transmuted into the marvelous beginnings of unforeseeable but perhaps desirable hieroglyphs.

From Laocoön's Snakes to the Octopus's Web

Like photodynamism, the question of the new woman was another major blind spot or controversial area for futurism, one that highlighted the contradictions of futurist rhetoric. As Marinetti declared in the founding *Manifesto of Futurism* (20 February 1909), printed in the pages of *Le Figaro:* "We will glorify war—

the world's only hygiene—militarism, patriotism, the destructive gesture of the anarchist, beautiful ideas worth dying for, and scorn for women."[54]

Despite this misogynistic beginning, Marinetti did not hesitate to modify his stance; by 1913, in the "Imagination without Strings" manifesto, he advocated the "semi-equality of man and woman and the lessening of the disproportion in their social rights."[55] It is possible that futurism's initial "scorn for women" was based on the movement's absorption of Lombroso's widely believed theory of female inferiority. The point here is that this whole historical period was marked by a sense of confusion about what constituted a man and what constituted a woman. It is this very loss of reliable reference that propels the narrative of *La Piovra* (1919), with Francesca Bertini and Amleto Novelli.

In Edoardo Bencivenga's *La Piovra*, the extensive use of the split screen calls attention to how the clash of good and evil, and of deceiving femininity and moralizing masculinity, is a completely inadequate explanation for the kind of visual solution that emphasizes separation as sexual difference. During the theater sequence, it is Simone's husband who invites the dishonest Baron Petrovic to visit his wife in the intimacy of their theater box. By contrast, Simone, a married woman, firmly rejects another suitor, Georges Morel, when he proposes an affair.

The repeated blocking of two characters on one side of the screen, next to an empty section of the same frame, calls attention to an area of dark desire that circulates back and forth between the faithful wife and the jealous husband. The editing also underlines the reversible nature of male and female desire by positioning Simone and her husband in a way that achieves an unsettling mirror-like effect from shot to shot. Throughout the film, it never becomes clear to whose desire the empty screen belongs, but it is precisely through all these visual ambiguities that *La Piovra* stands out as a protopsychoanalytic film. To begin with, the female character is entitled to as much complexity as the male, to the point of being awarded a double or evil self through the metaphor of the octopus in the title: "*la piovra*." That octopus, Simone's evil self, is Baron Petrovic, a strange figure who oscillates between feminine and masculine features. For instance, he steals from Morel's bank to provide Simone with plenty of luxuries, but by leading Morel to the edge of financial ruin, the Russian baron also becomes a sort of femme fatale in a tuxedo. Petrovic's looming shadow functions as the hidden masochistic self of Simone and also as the extension of her husband's sadistic efforts to separate mother and child and to push his own wife into prostitution.

La Piovra's narrative organization is remarkable, for it plays on the idea of an unconscious, the repression of which turns the husband into a dictator and the wife into a demimondaine. Considering that the film was made in 1919, when Freud's ideas were known but hardly popular in Italy, *La Piovra* stands out as an experiment in orientalist, erotic iconography.[56] During the second half of the film, after the child's death and the husband's disappearance from the narrative, Simone and her new suitor, Georges Morel, go together to a charity event held in Japanese style.

Shortly after their departure, the whole pavilion catches fire. Once the couple arrives home, Simone realizes that the stalker is there, and she decides to confront him on her own, once and for all. Thus, she locks herself up in a dark room and ignores Morel's efforts to break down the door and come to her res-

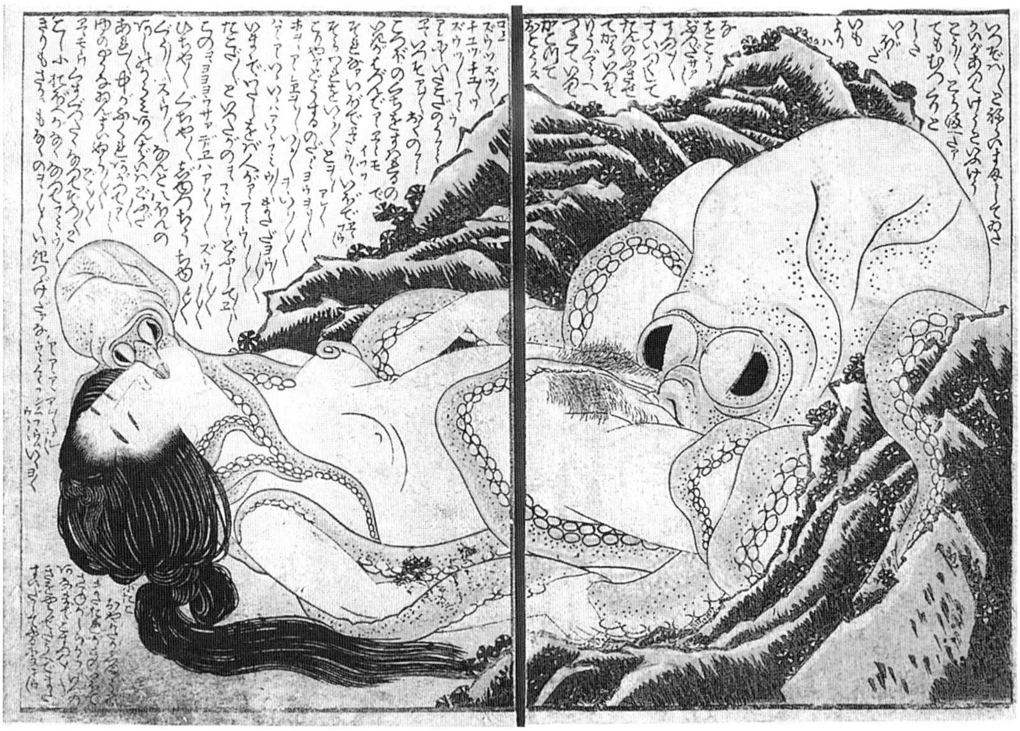

Katsushika Hokusai, *Woman and an Octopus* (1814). Print from *Kinoe no Komatsu* (1820; Young Pines) album (OA+.0.109). British Museum, London. © Copyright the Trustees of the British Museum.

cue. Simone's choice is dangerous, and the darkness of the room is somewhat unnecessary. On the one hand, it looks as if she is hiding from Morel to be alone with Petrovic. On the other, she may be trying to protect her good suitor from the baron's evil scheme. Most importantly, Simone's strange choice follows her visit to a gazebo with Japanese art, a tradition famous for its explicitly erotic iconography involving female pleasure. Furthermore, the dark room in her house is a space comparable either to the Catholic confessional or to a mind obscured by unspeakable thoughts. Likewise, it is hard to tell whether the fire in the Japanese gazebo is about passion consuming the body or punishment meant to burn all sinners.

One way to explain this level of secrecy and ambiguity in Simone's behavior is that the Japanese setting may have kindled a dangerous orientalist fantasy inside her mind. In her book on art nouveau, Ghislaine Wood writes:

The octopus, for instance, which had particular erotic significance in shunga, *surfaced in many Art Nouveau objects. The sculptor Rupert Carabin, who produced some of the most explicitly erotic objects of the period, used the octopus on the exterior of a chest to suggest the erotic nature of the sculpture contained within. Rather more typically of Art Nouveau objects, Auguste Ledru's vase of 1895 brings the octopus and woman together in a suggestive rather than explicit erotic relationship.*[57]

Overall, *La Piovra* is a basic yet difficult

Amleto Palermi's *Carnevalesca* (1918) with Lyda Borelli. Courtesy Cineteca di Bologna.

film to read. Although it has elements of a happy ending—Simone and Morel are united at last and the evil baron dies—there is so much iconographic excess that a babel or a Babylon of images prevents the viewer from settling on a single final interpretation. It is as if each sequence undoes the previous one, so that it becomes impossible to decide whether the ending is stable. Likewise, negative and positive connotations overlap inside the very same image. The more Simone falls into a depression, the more she is associated with a train speeding across the horizon. On the other hand, as soon as she liberates herself from a sense of helplessness, she climbs downward along a steep rock until she ends up running alone by the sea. No clear destination is in sight; the camera looks down on her small figure from inside a high angle that never moves sideways to show either the vast expanse of the sea or a more spacious environment within which to live or dream.

The only possible conclusion regarding the film is that, with its erotically ambiguous images and unresolved narratives, the diva film as a genre managed to occupy a much more subliminal and private place in the feminine imagination than Lombroso's popular and rigid theories would have granted it. Nevertheless, *La Piovra* marks a sort of dead end in the genre because the iconography begins to cave in on itself as it loses the ability to tell a story with a resolution. This crisis of imagery was probably a signal that times were ripe for social change.

There is one more example from a diva film that I would like to mention in conjunction with *La Piovra* and Francesca Bertini. The image of a horrible octopus—its tentacles evoking Laocoön's snakes—reappears in Amleto Palermi's *Carnevalesca* (1918), with Lyda Borelli. The periodic insertion of this monster from the sea is intercut with shots of entangled carnival streamers. Such an iconographic analogy expands further: all together, the streaming ribbons, the mobile tentacles, and Laocoön's snakes underline a widespread crisis of linearity. It is precisely this climate of confusion, deception, and innuendo that is devastating the fairy-tale kingdom of Malazia depicted in *Carnevalesca*. Of course, the word *Malazia* is well chosen because it reminds the viewer of intentional bad faith or malice (*malizia*). A film about the entanglements among the members of a royal family vying for the throne, *Carnevalesca* takes the disruptive impacts of the cinema, modernity, and mechanical reproduction to their most negative limit.

Orientalism

BALLETS RUSSES, OCCULTISM, CANUDO

Cultural historian Linda Anna Saladin has demonstrated that the ultimate femme fatale is Salome.[1] Such a claim is not difficult to contextualize through the diva film. Salome is the most important referent because she is the youngest and most recognizably orientalist icon available. She was also a beautiful dancer, and as such, she blurred the boundary between cinema and dance, situating these two arts of movement within the opposition of time and physical beauty. In contrast to some well-known transgressive Roman female figures, such as Messalina or Agrippina, Salome had the additional advantage of possessing an innocent kind of cruelty. Salome was more acceptable to Italian audiences than Messalina and Agrippina, who consciously schemed for power, because she turned the beheading of John the Baptist into a game. In a word, Salome was both thrilling and mindless.

Salome became very popular through the paintings of Gustave Moreau (1826–1898), which appeared when French artistic culture was already the most influential European model in Italy. In comparison with Italy's restrictive morality and small economy, Paris stood for a combination of cosmopolitan pleasures and dangerous situations. This is why the most reckless characters in Leopoldo Carlucci's *Caino* (1918) are all French or Francophile. Salome's cruelty clashes with the Italian diva's suffering as a mater dolorosa. Hence Salome could turn out to be a problematic source to be associated with the diva. To further complicate the situation, this type also represents the culture of the nineteenth century, which the diva would like to reject because of her leanings toward the personality of the modern woman. In addition, because of her associations with veils that both cover her and expose her nudity, Salome might be too sensual for the psychology of the Italian diva as a mixed icon of emancipation and mysticism.

In a climate of opinion dominated by Cesare Lombroso's criminal anthropology, Salome's combination of eroticism and cruelty implied prostitution so readily that her icon needed some adjustment before it could adhere to the pictorial and aristocratic standard required by the aesthetic and ideological issues of the diva film. In *Il Quadro di Osvaldo Mars* (directed by Guido Brignone, 1921), Salome's image by itself is enough to spell out nudity, even if the naked body is not actually shown in the fatal portrait. Nevertheless, Brignone's film demonstrates how dangerous it could be for a respectable woman to be associated with an image whose international and artistic repute was not enough to neutralize accusations of promiscuity and mur-

Gustave Moreau, *Salome Dancing Before Herod* (1876). Armand Hammer Collection. Gift of the Armand Hammer Foundation. Hammer Museum, Los Angeles. Photo: Robert Wedermeyer.

der. While Brignone's film relies on a long, convoluted narrative to salvage a good wife's reputation in *Rapsodia Satanica* (1915), with Lyda Borelli, Nino Oxilia does not seem overly preoccupied with taming Salome's lethal effects. On the contrary, during the first half of the film, the diva, as Salome, leads one of her male suitors to commit suicide. Guilt, however, is not an issue, because Borelli, as Alba D'Oltrevita (Dawn-Beyond-Life), was operating under the devil's influence. Mindlessly seductive, the diva enjoys dancing as much as Salome does, without thinking about the effect of her actions. In the second half of the narrative, however, as soon as Borelli rebels against the devil's influence, she embraces a completely new role model, the famous American dancer Loie Fuller. Yet this switch of inspiration is more forced than gradual. Although the character of Salome belonged to Fuller's repertory, Oxilia's film can find only one justification, based on a strange union of chance and time, to account for the diva's schizophrenic identity. While making her pact with the devil, Borelli does not realize that her statuette of Cupid, representing romantic love, interferes with the reversal of her aging process. In *Rapsodia*, by downplaying all the evil associations with crime, the devil, and criminal anthropology, Oxilia's diva becomes the new woman of modernity. Pure freedom, she exudes an energy full of positive promises for the future

Beloved by the futurists and by the scientists Pierre and Marie Curie, Loie Fuller was about modernity, mystery, imagination, and technology. While dancing with colored electric lights, Fuller produced luminous swishes, waves, and streaks in the darkness, and would dematerialize into a phantasmagoria of flying veils. In short, the two terms of reference in *Rapsodia Satanica* are Salome and Loie Fuller, the magic orient and the industrialized New World. These two models articulate a dialectic of old and new that also defines the Italian diva as a composite and contradictory being.

While art nouveau is always orientalist because of its arabesque-like or abstract designs based on patterns from nature, orientalism does not limit itself to art nouveau, referring generally to the ancient fascination Europeans felt for distant lands.[2] Within this alliance of art nouveau and orientalism, Salome means exoticism. Thus, the diva film frequently exhibits a fanciful, colonial, and cosmopolitan component in the extraordinary luxury of its sets and costumes. Orientalism in the diva film can be seen as any kind of stylistic citation that evokes a more sensual, unrulier, and more extravagant life than the daily routine experienced by film viewers. In many diva films, the actress playing the diva role may go from rags to riches and back again. This roller-coaster pattern across social classes is typical of the melodramatic mode to which the diva film belongs. The high production values of the orientalist diva film distinguish this genre from the short contemporary dramas and adventure films featuring the modern woman. Despite the diva's economic ups and downs, orientalism was the marker of wealth, luxury, consumption, and

Lyda Borelli in Nino Oxilia's *Rapsodia Satanica* (1917). Courtesy Cineteca di Bologna.

(right) Henri de Toulouse-Lautrec, *Loïe Fuller at the Folies Bergères* (1893). Oil on cardboard, 24.9 × 17.8 in. (63.2 × 45.3 cm.). Musée Toulouse-Lautrec, Albi, France. Photo: Scala/Art Resource, N.Y.

waste. As such, it was also an entry point for fantasies of social advancement.

The escapist, aristocratic, transgressive component of orientalism found its most typical expression in the serpentine line of art nouveau. Later, the 1920s saw the logical, mechanical, and unnatural contouring of art deco, its straight line linked to rationality, patriarchy, metonymy, Taylorism, and technology. By contrast, the wavy line of art nouveau resembles vines and tendrils, trees and flowers, hair, flowing garments—in a word, the energy of nature and its ever-changing flow of phenomena: clouds and rivers taking on different outlines in the wind and rain.

With its arabesque-like profile, the style of art nouveau embodies an ever-resurging creativity that twists and twirls on and on in ways reminiscent of Bergson's description of the élan vital—reshaping, unstructuring, and reenergizing all matter fortuitously.[3] Yet, despite its endless energy, the loops of art nouveau do not seem to allow for radical breaks or definitive disruptions. Through an intricate work of curves and reroutes, the so-called flowery style of art nouveau manages to preserve continuity by contouring the past into the present within a web whose beginning and end intersect and diverge at the same time. To be sure, the arabesque can degenerate into a labyrinth instead of feeding a vitalistic impulse.

From the turn of the century until World War I, orientalist furniture with Japanese and Chinese motifs appeared in the houses of both the aristocracy and the middle class. This exotic, art nouveau look kindled the freewheeling imagination of the petit-bourgeois viewer who could afford to go to the *cinematografo* but not to the theater. In his discussion of the diva and her spectatorship, film historian Gian Piero Brunetta argues that this kind of star appealed to certain groups in society that felt excluded from social advancement and were seeking some kind of compensation or revenge.[4] At first the gains promised by colonialism were touted as a quick way to mobilize economically stagnant sectors of the population. Italy had won Libya from the Turks in 1911, but the conquest of Tripoli was not as easy or as profitable as the Italian establishment had hoped. The difficulties of the Libyan campaign opened old wounds from the failed colonial expeditions in Somalia and Abyssinia at the end of the nineteenth century. In 1896, for instance, during the Battle of Adwa, 18,000 Italian soldiers were defeated by a much larger force (80,000–100,000) of Emperor Menelik's Abyssinian fighters armed with spears, arrows, and sticks. This defeat was especially demoralizing because it marked the first and only time an African army managed to prevail over a European enemy equipped with guns and cannons.[5]

Moving from East Africa to Libya, for Brunetta, the diva stemmed from a mixture of envy, compensation, and anger among those who continued to be impoverished and without hope for a better future after the Tripoli campaign. Because the diva could play an aristocratic woman who was either a dangerous temptation or a kept woman who lived and sinned in a world of luxury, she was an ideal fantasy for lower-middle-class male viewers seeking the thrills of the good life and the challenge of a forbidden object of conquest. Typically, the diva leads wealthy men to ruin and causes them to lose control over their family fortunes. The diva's power to annihilate both herself and a wealthy man satisfied the audiences' appetite for the punishment of the upper classes. Without a doubt, Brunetta's thesis captures the femme fatale side of the diva, but it does not deal with her mater dolorosa component or her "new woman" aspect.

La Donna Nuda

Before 1913, it was possible though rare to encounter orientalist elements in the short adventure film or the contemporary drama. The short adventure film *Come una Sorella* (1912; Like a Sister) features the character of Nelly, who sings and dances in a tabarin (cabaret) called Alhambra. The name alone of this locale triggers images of faraway lands and exotic civilizations. Hence, this film stands out as an exception to the important rule that the contemporary drama before 1913 did not include orientalist elements; as a result of its ordinary settings, it was less expensive than the diva film, born the following year. On the other hand, it would also be erroneous to claim that all diva films were lavish orientalist spectacles. Carmine Gallone's *La Donna Nuda* (1914; The Nude Woman) avoids exotic references in favor of the bohemian world of artists and models, a milieu inspired by Paris and Montmartre. Hence, this diva film is an exception to the equally important rule of an alliance among orientalism, aristocracy, and stardom that echoes the diva's power through the cost of the sets and the variety of her wardrobe.

La Donna Nuda is imbued with resistance to historical change. A whole new class of doctors, lawyers, bankers, architects, engineers, accountants, and teachers fantasized about the sexual scandals and the family inheritances of the rich, preindustrial aristocracy. As we learn from the diva film, the wealthy spent their lives shuttling between the grand hotel and the health spa, between the racetrack and the airfield. In addition, the development of the internal combustion engine, hydroelectric power, the automobile, and the airplane enabled the new rising middle class to feel superficially confident about the future even as it began to erode the privileges of the feudal aristocracy.

Historian Adrian Lyttelton points out that the use of Egyptian and oriental motifs to celebrate the development of a family dynasty in the textile industry can express a family's arrogance.[6] A pompous monument, the Crespi mausoleum near Milan, dominates, without shame or guilt, the nearby humble workers' cemetery. In other words, as Lyttelton points out, the Crespi family used new money to espouse authoritarian and paternalistic ideals rather than liberal, progressive, and democratic ones. They were enthusiastic about the present, but they did not sufficiently plan for the future. These new leaders had studied and traveled abroad, so they were knowledgeable about more advanced industrial methods. Still, their managerial models were more exploitative and short-term than growth oriented and liberal. They continued to privilege a tight family nucleus over the civic rights of the individual, and, especially in their private lives, they remained attached to premodern, archaic concepts: machismo, honor, bloodline, and suffocating double standards for men and women.

Set against this ambivalent panorama of new technologies and old values, *La Donna Nuda* is the best film to discuss the tension between old and new during the art nouveau period, even if it does not rely on a full-blown orientalist style. Directed by the otherwise talented Carmine Gallone (1886–1973), *La Donna Nuda* is technically conservative, and its narrative is tedious and repetitive. In his close analysis of Gallone's handling of time and space through the tableau vivant and a flat development without much stress on

Mario Roncoroni's *Filibus* (1915). Courtesy Nederlands Filmmuseum, Amsterdam.

causality, the Italian critic Alberto Boschi concludes that *La Donna Nuda* looks more like filmed theater than a set of moving pictures.[7] The rare changes in angle, the lack of variation in the distance between the camera and the actors' bodies, and the weakness of the contrasts between similar situations occurring in different locations leads Boschi to pronounce the film "archaic." As far as Gallone's direction of actors, Boschi concludes: "The centrality of the diva's body sets up, far in advance, the whole filmic mise-en-scène, even if this may mean downplaying the expressive power of objects and sets."[8]

Based on a text by Henri Bataille (*La Femme Nue*, 1908), *La Donna Nuda* was shot in Turin, and many outdoor scenes were done in the city's famous Parco del Valentino. Because of its proximity to Paris, Turin was the Italian city most influenced by French culture. Hence, Gallone may have chosen to focus on a bohemian rather than an orientalist atmosphere in an attempt to replace Montmartre's experimentation in the arts with a much more provincial avant-garde phenomenon, *la Scapigliatura*. Referring to Milan, Turin's competitor in matters of modernity, Lyttelton remarks:

> *Milan was the only city where there existed something more or less comparable to the Parisian bohème, a sort of counterculture or alternative society, contesting the values of the bourgeoisie while living on its margins. This was the* scapigliatura, *which literally means long or disheveled hair, always a mark of the bohemian. It was linked, as in Paris, to radical politics. However, the* scapigliatura *movement was a temporary phenomenon which did not reproduce itself.*[9]

A story of love, art, and betrayal, *La Donna Nuda* features two competing love triangles: two men plus a negative mother figure in the first, and two women plus a positive father figure in the second. The oedipal situations embedded in the potential development of these three competing couples revolve around the following: an ambitious young painter, Pierre; Lolette (Lyda Borelli), an innocent and self-sacrificing model; an old painter, the paternal and protective Rouchard, whom Lolette leaves in order to join Pierre and become both his model and a sort of unrecognized wife; and an older female aristocrat who is a painter also. The first part of the narrative involves the romantic moments and financial struggles of Pierre and Lolette; during the second half, the aristocratic lady—a femme fatale as well as a painter—seduces Pierre, who abandons the desperate Lolette. After becoming famous for his paintings featuring Lolette as a model, Pierre is ready to fall in love with a wealthy older woman, especially one who can be both colleague and patron. Pierre's change from carefree bohemian to manipulative host, from ambitious artist to lazy womanizer, captures the overall social conformism of the emerging upper middle class during the art nouveau period in Italy.

The narrative trajectory of *La Donna Nuda* demonstrates that the polished surfaces of quick wealth proved more attractive than stylistic experiments and substantial breakthroughs in the arts and in the national economy alike. Evidence of this failure to embrace genuine renewal, even on the part of the young, emerges in the way Lolette models for Pierre. He portrays her according to the tritest conventions of the classical nude: her eyes stare blankly into the void, and her passive body is offered to the male gaze. This handling of Lolette's image is not only traditional, but also racier than Rouchard's picturesque portraits of his former model in a decorous costume. An older man and a paternal presence in Lolette's life, Rouchard is in touch with Lolette's humble roots and with Italy's rural past, which the morals of the large city tend to discard in favor of more daring images of nudity.

Ironically, however, the bohemian Pierre is far more conservative than his older colleague, for his ideal is the Renaissance courtesan instead of the new woman of modernity. Finally, Lolette is hardly the film's prima donna; her clothes are modest and she is seen in either poor or middle-class settings, without any orientalist elements added to the basic art nouveau style of the period. Lolette's humbleness comes through when she tries to endear herself to Pierre with a little domestic flirting: she teases him by hiding behind her back a spoon she has used to whip cream. Fearing that Pierre is about to abandon her for a stronger female rival, Lolette, with her humorous and childlike game with the spoon, exposes the gap between two irreconcilable roles: that of wife and that of model—or better, that of maid and that of lover.

Russian Fever

The period of art nouveau in Italy coincided not only with the advent of the cinema but also with the women's movement, so the rise of the diva is grafted onto the changing perception of gender roles. At a basic level, the visual culture of art nouveau is always embedded in the diva film's iconography, and it owes its most extravagant orientalist features to the 1911 arrival of Serge Diaghilev's Ballets Russes in Italy.[10] The Ballets Russes mixed folkloric, premodern, and antimodern sources with avant-garde modernist materials. Its definition of modernity included both the remembered past and a dynamic present. This is why Russian fever in Italy stood for the merging of scientifically based technologies with "higher," occult, and unknown phenomena. This new sensibility was variously referred to as magic, spiritualist, or the "fourth dimension."[11] The mystical, scientific, orientalist, Slavic model of modernity spread within early Italian film culture. Early cinema slanted the imaginary geography of art nouveau's orientalism toward eastern Europe, to the point of exhibiting the symptoms of a veritable Russian fever, or Slavophilia. Without a doubt, Diaghilev's dance company had an enormous impact on fashion, taste, and the debate on gender roles.

Whereas the tradition of classic Italian dancing was centered on the ballerina and her subordination to the male lead, the Ballets Russes turned gender roles upside down, situating the effeminate Nijinsky and the androgynous Ida Rubinstein at center stage. The Ballets Russes' integration of various art forms greatly inspired the newborn film industry, which was eager to acquire respectability by incorporating the legacies of older art forms and the distinctive visual styles of bygone eras and remote regions of the world.

Paris, Rome, and Venice became the home away from home for the Ballets Russes; their British and American receptions were much less enthusiastic. In fact, the London and New York audiences, with their Victorian and Puritan values, did not approve of the strange cocktail of folk-primitivist, cubo-futurist, and cosmopolitan-orientalist ingredients emphasized by the overall style of Leon Bakst's set designs. In Paris and Italy, what was going on onstage was as important as the dinners, salons, receptions, scandals, and improvised artistic collaborations happening on and off the stage. For example, Jean Cocteau (1889–

Vaslav Nijinsky dancing in Debussy's *L'après-midi d'un faune.* Victoria and Albert Museum, London. Photo: Victoria and Albert Museum, London/Art Resource, N.Y.

1963) belonged to a group that included Erik Satie, Pablo Picasso, and Igor Stravinsky. Thanks to Diaghilev's genius for public relations, every Parisian hostess, every dandy, every person of talent or in search of notoriety wanted to belong to the group of "*fervents des russes.*"

The arrival of the Ballets Russes in Rome was especially welcome because it tapped into a late-nineteenth-century decadent sensibility rather than an early-twentieth-century modernist regimentation. In other words, the high aesthetic standards of Diaghilev's company spoke to the symbolist-decadent ethos of art for art's sake. In Italy, this extreme sensibility loomed large as the last and most intense antimodern battle in defense of an ideal notion of beauty. The exasperated aestheticism of the decadent period was a reaction to modernity's rapid changes. Likewise, hesitations about technology stemmed from an uneasiness with the simplifying, functionalist, streamlining imperative of industrialization.

On the other hand, the Ballets Russes' experimentations with sets, music, dance, and color were so daring and genuinely innovative that they also appealed to the Italian futurist avant-garde. Although the futurists' technocratic statements were meant to battle the nostalgic aestheticism of symbolist-decadent circles, and of the diva film in particular, the Italians, too, were swept away by the exotic and rejuvenating spirit of Bakst's colorful sets, in which folkloric and primitivist elements stood next to Byzantine and mystical icons.

From the stage, the Ballets Russes overflowed into daily life and became a formula for grandiose parties organized by the Mi-

Marchesa Luisa Casati (1881–1957). Courtesy Fondazione Il Vittoriale, Gardone Riviera.

lanese Marchesa Luisa Casati.[12] Installed in Ca' Venier dei Leoni, an unfinished eighteenth-century Venetian palace on the Grand Canal, the marchesa would feast with her friends in Saint Mark's Square, the open-air ballroom of Venice. Painted or photographed by a string of major artists, such as Kees Van Dongen, Gabriele Boldini, Augustus John, Giacomo Balla, Man Ray, Joseph Paget-Fredericks, Romaine Brooks, Casati hired Paul Poiret, Leon Bakst, Vionnet, and Erté (Romain de Tirtoff) to design some of her outfits. As a result, her wardrobe included an array of strange items, including an all-white Pierrot costume of translucent silver silk, and a Vionnet dress of black velvet accessorized with a tiger-skin top hat and a pirate eye patch. Rumor has it that during a performance of the Ballets Russes, the extravagant aristocrat showed up wearing a gown composed entirely of egret plumes. Her movements caused the garment to shed clouds of feathers, thus leaving its wearer almost nude by the evening's end.

Casati, who squandered one of the largest fortunes in Italy, was far more eccentric and unpredictable than the hardworking film divas. Nevertheless, the eye-catching style set by the Ballets Russes became a must for all socialites and performers. Italian divas soon started wearing bizarre headbands and hair jewelry inspired by Bakst's designs. In *L'Arzigogolo* (1924; The Doodle), Italia Almirante Manzini, for example, sports a conelike headdress made of strings of white pearls; in *Carnevalesca* (1918; Carnival Fantasies), Lyda Borelli replaces a royal tiara with a snug-fitting crown contoured of long peacock feathers; in *Il Fuoco* (1915), Pina Menichelli is memorable for her famous owl-shaped hat.

So rampant was this Italian fever for anything with an eastern European flavor that the writer and filmmaker Lucio D'Ambra invented a new orientalist proverb about the femme fatale's irresistible power of seduction: *occhi slavi non te la cavi* (Slavic eyes ensnare you in their guise). Originally D'Ambra had dedicated this saying to the diva Soava Gallone, formerly Stanislava Winawer (1880–1957), with the intention of celebrating her delicate yet extreme form of beauty: the rosy color of her skin was enhanced by her blue-green eyes, and just a touch of Asian charm was conveyed by her high cheekbones. Gallone's delicate screen persona as a major diva was suggested by her adopted Italian name: Soava, or suave.

Over the years, the Russian fad embraced even the vaguest Slavic connection. Its allure was so powerful that it erased the Polish origins of a few women who were recruited by the Italian film industry and raised to the rank of divas. In the magazine articles of the time, film critics generally discussed these foreign-born ladies without too much concern for the accuracy of biographical details. In fact, the Slavic contingent was mostly Polish rather than Russian; it included Diana Karenne (1888–1941), originally Leocadia Konstantin, and Elena Makowska (1893–1964), born in the Ukraine to Polish parents. Finally, in the footsteps of Ida Rubinstein, one

Lyda Borelli in Amleto Palermi's *Carnevalesca* (1918). Courtesy Cineteca di Bologna.

(right) Italia Almirante Manzini in Mario Almirante's *L'Arzigogolo* (1924). Author's collection.

Publicity from Jacques Feyder's *L'Atlantide* (1920) with Stacia Napierkowska. Author's collection.

more Russian dancer enjoyed some brief fame in Italian cinema: Stacia Napierkowska (1886–1945) worked at Film d'Art Italy and became famous for her femme fatale role in Jacques Feyder's *L'Atlantide* (1920).

The expensive balls and eccentric fashions inspired by Russian fever were reserved for the elite, but crime stories and sexual scandals involving Russian characters became legendary in all social groups. The wild designs and primitivist leanings of the Ballets Russes can be said to have been anticipated by an even more savage and alluring creature: Maria Tarnowska, a Russian socialite condemned for her lover's murder in 1906. In *Le Nostre Attrici Cinematografiche* (1919; Our Cinematic Actresses), Tito Alacci mixes a dose of criminal lore with names from film history: "The most recent fatal women, whose names spread all over the world, were Draga Maskin and Sofia Chotek, not too mention Natalia Obrenovich, Eugenia Bonaparte, Alexandra Romanov, and Countess [Maria] Tarnowska. All six received from Mother Nature wild hair, stormy eyes, and charming smiles."[13] No wonder that while the notorious Russian countess was in a Venetian jail on the Giudecca, a film about Tarnowska's cause célèbre was produced in

1910.[14] Annie Vivanti (1866–1942), an Italian writer of novelettes, wrote about visiting Tarnowska in jail. Vivanti used such a mystical style that her subject's identity as a femme fatale slipped into that of a Christian martyr.[15]

Long before Diaghilev's arrival in Paris, Cesare Lombroso authoritatively anticipated the Russian fad. Upon the publication of *The Female Offender* (1893), the best-selling Turinese criminal anthropologist declared that a female Russian colleague with the surname Tarnowsky had provided the photographs of Russian female criminals and prostitutes upon which he based his theories about femininity and crime.[16] In the wake of Lombroso's popularity, this completely imaginary criminal and sexual connection via Russia deformed the diva's corporeal iconography into hysterical convulsions that twitched across early Italian film culture.

In fact, the "Tarnowska Effect," constructed out of the last name shared by Lombroso's colleague and Maria, was nothing but another orientalist fiction. After Lombroso, the popularity of the Ballets Russes reinforced the stereotype that Russian women were irresistible, strange, and dangerous. Appropriating the name "Tarnowsky/Tarnowska" allowed Lombroso to enhance his topic, but there is a kernel of truth stored in the scientist's controversial data: Pauline Tarnowsky was a female physician in the late nineteenth century. She wrote in the tradition of her father, V. M. Tarnowsky, who was the author of the standard study on Russian prostitution, which appeared in both Russian and German editions. In a later paper, Pauline Tarnowsky provided a scale of the appearance of prostitutes in an analysis of the "physiognomy of the Russian prostitute." At the upper end of the scale is the "Russian Helen," and this is where Annie Vivanti's Maria becomes the "Elena" of Lombrosian discourse. The cultural historian Sander Gilman concludes that Lombroso, with his son-in-law, Guglielmo Ferrero, reworked and mismatched all these Russian sources for their joint project on women in 1893.[17]

The combination of sexuality, scandal, sensation, and sensationalism, both in the newspapers and in the movie theaters, threw a negative light on the cinema, which began to be blamed as a source of corruption. The diva's sinuous outline quickly turned into a snake's coils, and orientalism began to slide toward pornography. Although it was used as a form of self-censorship, or as a veil behind which to hide erotic material, orientalism accelerated the development of film censorship.

In his book *I Pericoli Sociali del Cinematografo* (1922; The Social Dangers of the Cinematograph), Piero Pesce-Maineri describes the evils of the cinema in a language so imbued with mystery and emotion that he sounds more like an aroused spectator than a detached censor: "In the silent darkness of the movie theater . . . the young boy's heart beats more rapidly: the ghosts of irreality take shape in his feverish mind, his sexual emotions become awake, and evil ideas take on an alluring quality."[18] The mixture of fascination and prohibition that characterizes Pesce-Maineri's view of the cinema echoes the threatening yet irresistible aura men attribute to the diva as the ultimate exotic icon.

The use of orientalism to increase the pictorial artistic value of an otherwise ghostly filmic image is further confirmed by a double equivalence between cinema and lust, and between lust and femininity. In a little article titled "Il Fascino della Bellezza Muliebre nella Cinematografia" (The Appeal of Feminine Beauty in the Cinema) and published in the popular trade journal *La Vita Cinematografica* of 15 May 1914, the obscure but enthusiastic professor Arnaldo Monti declares that cinema is the art of "*lussuria estetica*" (aesthetic lust).[19] Imagine Professor Monti as a fairly boring academic who becomes a film journalist without paying the price exacted from the old male teacher in *The Blue Angel* (1930) by the most dangerous and humiliating of all vamps: the blond, cold, androgynous Marlene Dietrich.

The view that the cinema was a seductive Eastern temptress leading the whole nation astray began to be debated in a vehement editorial in the pages of *La Gazzetta del Popolo* and continued in 1910 in *Il Corriere della Sera*, an even more prestigious newspaper. Films were compared to novelettes for illiterate people, corrupting the morally healthy Italian audiences. The director Mario Caserini organized an academic conference in 1910 to defend his newborn art. In 1912 the Vatican banned all screenings inside religious buildings. On the other hand, as long as they did not wear religious vestments, priests were allowed to go to the cinema. In 1913 the efforts of G. B. Avellone, a judge from Rome, led to the establishment of the first formal network of censorship committees across the country. The final effort to contain the cinema came in 1913 when Prime Minister Giovanni Giolitti (1842–1928) issued a memorandum to all regional governors, encouraging them to monitor screenings. They were to make sure that audiences did not sit in total darkness and that the seats were reasonably distant from one another, thus preventing any illicit contacts.[20]

Despite the cinema's bad reputation, the Vatican did not hesitate to rely on the new medium for propaganda purposes. Pope Pius X appeared in person in the documentary *The Great Religious Holidays of 1913*.[21] To top it all off, the very organized German theater owners were cited as exemplars: even when screenings were approved for minors, the room was divided into two sections, one for boys and one for girls. By September 18, 1924, each Italian censorship board included a mother as a regular member. A final look at writings that denounced the cinema as a source of corruption or a social evil will reveal to what extent the diva's visual form was hidden between the lines.

In 1901, Enrico Ferri published *Studi sulla Criminalità ed Altri Saggi* (Studies on Criminality and Other Essays), a treatise in which Darwinism was woven into Marxist theory and Herbert Spencer's sociology. A student of Lombroso, Ferri writes: "Murders and murderers, so proteiform and numerous, [have become] daily events in social life. Art had to sense the passionate shivering of this criminal wave spreading itself . . . in snake-like patterns . . . and in more or less bloody bursts of violence."[22] Ferri's adjective *proteiform* is a synonym for *protean* and shares connotations with *arabesque*, a word that stands for both orientalism and the diva's shifty silhouette. The term *arabesque* is the trademark of the semiabstract flowery shape of art nouveau. It also encapsulates the diva's filmic image, the female body, and the exotic look of the sets. For Ferri, this overlayering of elements instigated a crime wave.

The arabesque expands to orientalism, and this style of the diva film meant that the genre included both a fascination with the East and cosmopolitan references in general. Despite its luxurious look, orientalism in the diva film discloses the practice of colonization and prejudice, since two kinds of narrative solutions emerge and often involve male figures. Evil seducers end up working in the colonies as a form of punishment after various transgressions instigated by a femme fatale. Orientalism also functions as a sort of screen for

Marlene Dietrich in Josef von Sternberg's *Der Blaue Engel* (1930; *The Blue Angel*). Author's collection.

anti-Semitic allusions. In Mario Caserini's *Ma l'Amor Mio non Muore* (1913; Everlasting Love), for example, the name of the spy, Moise Sthar (played by Gian Paolo Rosmino), is clearly an anti-Semitic jab. Not only does he steal military plans from Elsa's father, thus causing the innocent daughter's ruin (Elsa is portrayed by Lyda Borelli), but when he sees her again on a boat trip with Prince Maximilian (Mario Bonnard), he immediately turns this accidental encounter into a profitable journalistic scoop. In Caserini's film there are also many characters with German names: the impresario Schaudard, the father Julius Holbein, the colonel Theubner. All these figures are reminders that, in 1913, areas of northern Italy were still territories occupied by the Austro-Hungarian Empire of the Hapsburgs. The assassination of Archduke Francis Ferdinand was approaching in Sarajevo (28 June 1914), although the Balkans had been unstable since 1908.

Orientalism marks a fascination with, as well as fear of, the blurring of boundaries. In *Malombra* (1917), with Lyda Borelli as Marina di Malombra, the threat of Germany is figured again through the accountant Steinegge, possibly an Italian version of the German Jewish name "Stein," and his daughter Edith. *Malombra*'s narrative is difficult to evaluate because sections of the film are missing. Steinegge, since he keeps all the Ormengo family's financial records, seems to be constructed as a vaguely anti-Semitic stereotype. Thus he makes sure that the money and power remain in the hands of a patrilinear genealogy under the control of his employer, Cesare D'Ormengo, who is also Marina's uncle and legal guardian. It slowly becomes clear that Marina, an orphan, might have more economic rights than her cruel relative is willing to acknowledge. In the end, Steinegge's loyalty to the family is admirable. Yet the narrative not only imposes on this professional character an odd, foreign-sounding surname, but it also places him on the side of the male oppressor, as if his accounting skills were comparable to the anti-Semitic cliché of the Jewish pawnbroker.

The practice of putting characters with foreign last names in diva films also allowed filmmakers to explore stories of divorce, separation, and adultery. Except for the most powerful members of the aristocracy, who were able to negotiate separation agreements regardless of the well-known veto imposed by the Catholic Church, this solution was plainly illegal in Italy, in the eyes not only of the Vatican but also of the state. In a published lecture I found in D'Annunzio's archive at Il Vittoriale, entitled "La Femme dans la Littérature Italienne," futurist suffragette Valentine de Saint-Point writes: "In contrast to what one might think, modern Italian women's literature does not look like modern French women's literature. This difference comes from the fact that, unlike French legislation, Italian laws and manners have not allowed certain freedoms and rights to women. For instance, there is no divorce, so women who are unhappily married cannot be free and start their lives again in a new way."[23] The use of English, French, and German names for film characters was, therefore, a convenient way to move the narrative abroad or make it refer to some imaginary parallel universe and thereby overcome the generally negative reputation of the medium and the restrictions of the Italian legal system from 1913 onward.

An over-the-top example of orientalism intertwined with cosmopolitanism comes from *Tigre Reale* (1916; Royal Tigress), with Pina Menichelli. The diva plays the unpredictable Countess Natka, a Russian married woman who has an affair with Giorgio La Ferlita, a young Italian diplomat. The diplomatic profession appears frequently in the diva film because it is tightly interwoven with aristocratic and transient lives. In *La Storia di Una Donna* (1920), Menichelli's first love ends up working for a mining company in a colonial outpost. In *Maman Poupée* (1919), with Soava Gallone, the protagonist's childhood friend and true love is dispatched to Cuba for several years. The upper-class nomadic flavor of international diplomacy also contributes to the plot of *Il Processo Clémenceau* (1917), with Francesca Bertini. There, the best male friend of Pierre Clemenceau, Constantino Ruiz, is a representative of the Italian government abroad. Finally, foreign names are also used to protect national reputation when a man abuses a woman. In *Il Fior di Male* (1915), Lyda Borelli plays a reformed prostitute who heads an extremely profitable fashion house. However, she loses her career and her reputation because the lecherous Mr. Rogers, a banker married to a philanthropist, harasses her in secret.

Last, it is important to mention that the narrative geography of orientalism and cosmopolitanism found a correspondence in accounts of film exports in the trade journals of this period. Between 1910 and 1915, in addition to Latin America, where Italian cinema was very popular because of a shared cultural taste for melodrama, excess, and spectacle, the three foreign areas where Italian diva films succeeded the most were Egypt, Russia, and the Balkans. In turn, all sorts of information about daily life, fashion, sports, technological advances, and scientific discoveries came from America, France, Germany, and Denmark; these were the countries whose films were imported most frequently in Italy.[24] Until 1917, however, American releases were routed through England before reaching southern Europe.[25]

Ricciotto Canudo

It may seem that orientalism is only about space and avoids the theme of time. Yet among philosophers and scientists of this period, there was a strong interest in the problem of time as such, and especially in forms of communication between the dead and the living, the past and the present. Film itself was already considered a time capsule, since dreams or hallucinations dealing with the dead appear in diva films. In *Malombra,* Marina's flashbacks involving her female ancestor, Cecilia, are a case in point. In contrast to the measurable and controllable space of geography and colonial expansion, the invisible, uncontrollable "fourth dimension" of time was symptomatic of a widespread sense of crisis: not a single system of beliefs appeared to hold up. The transformation of something unknown, absent, or past into representable, present, yet intangible apparitions was a practice the cinema was fueling through a combination of movement and the uncanny doublings of mechanical reproduction. In this respect, *Malombra* stands out as an example of modernist realism: while it calls attention to male abuses against women, it is also a wonderful meditation on the nature of cinema itself. Without relying on any special effects, the story summarizes all the key issues of its period, ranging from technology to philosophy, from the battle of the sexes to female fantasies.

The intertwining of cinema, the arts, the occult, and orientalism revolved around the Italian film critic Ricciotto Canudo (1877–1923), who moved to Paris around 1902; his initiatives and ideas contributed to the whirlpool of ideas shaping early Italian film theory and hovering over the diva film.[26] This genre's specific concerns, however, such as the crisis of the family, the development of the new woman of modernity, and the problem of children born outside of marriage, were far from Canudo's mind. An aesthetician by training, the Italian expatriate paid no attention to social evils, being instead eager to celebrate Italian national culture abroad. Canudo was weary of bourgeois theater, or "the theater of adultery," because it rehashed the modern couple's problems. Likewise, for him, the diva film was too bogged down by the battle of the sexes and out of touch with more experimental aesthetic goals.[27] Without a doubt the diva film was the continuation of a melodramatic bourgeois theater centered on the jealousy and the deception Canudo disapproved of, since he was a free spirit living on the edge. This is perhaps why there are no writings by Canudo on this genre. In Paris, he enjoyed the bohemian lifestyle. Though lacking original ideas, he focused on making a name for himself.

Canudo's bibliography is riddled with republications, revisions, and retitlings in French and Italian; he also announced definitions and agendas chaotically, copying the format of the futurist manifesto. An admirer of Claude Debussy's antiromantic music, Canudo advocated a daring kind of cinema, one featuring grotesque and marvelous images from the Italian artistic tradition. He was also fond of action and comedy films from America. The highlights of his contribution to the historical record amount to the article "La Naissance d'un Sixième Art—Essai sur

Enrico Imoda (Italian, active 1900s), "Materialization of a Young Woman Produced by the Medium Linda Gazzera," June 28, 1909. Gelatin silver print, 9.4 × 6.8 in. (24 × 17.3 cm.). Metropolitan Museum of Art, Gilman Collection, Gift of the Howard Gilman Foundation, 2005 (2005.100.385.1).

le Cinématographe" (1911); the foundation of CASA (Club des Amis du Septième Art) in 1921; the launching of the *Gazette de Sept Arts* (1922); the revision of cinema's definition from the sixth to the seventh art in his "Manifeste du Septième Art" (1924); and his posthumous book, *L' Usine aux Images* (1927).

Canudo was involved in a cultural scene that included Abel Gance, Marcel L'Herbier, Louis Delluc, Léon Moussinac, and Jean Epstein—namely, the most important names of the French cine-club and impressionist avant-garde movements of the 1920s. Whereas this decade was fertile for French film, it was sterile for the Italian film industry. Thus, Canudo's establishment of a Parisian profile followed the best years of the diva film. Notwithstanding this chronological discrepancy, his theories about the cinema are nevertheless worth discussing in relation to the diva film because of his inclination toward orientalist and gothic details, namely, two stylistic registers relevant to the genre of the mater dolorosa.

Canudo knew Bergson's *Le Rire*. He admired Richard Wagner's concept of *gesamtkunstwerk* (complete work of art, i.e., opera as the combination of all media) and André Antoine's naturalist theater and cinema *en plein air*.[28] He also had a fascination for Cézanne's ability to make movement out of light and color.[29] All these elements indicate that the Italian critic was eager to tone down film's scientific origin in favor of a much more visionary yet primitivist sensibility, one with a penchant for abstraction, purity, and music. The connection with Bergson's vitalist philosophy is the most important body of knowledge shared by the Italian critic and the progressive impetus of the diva film. Yet Bergson's influence on Canudo was also mediated by the philosopher's imitators. According to Germana Orlandi Cerenza, the variations on Bergson were numerous: A. Lacuzon was associated with integralism; E. Florian-Parmentier with impulsionism; A. M. Gossez with dynamism; N. Beauduin with parossism; and H. M. Barzun with dramatism.[30] In a word, all these obscure artistic tendencies had to do with a vulgarized Bergsonism based on the triumph of emotions. Canudo, in the meantime, never missed an opportunity to make himself noticed by one intellectual community or another. This is why Bergson's critique of positivist science was not enough to deter Canudo's organizational abilities in regard to the world of science. In 1922 and in 1923, for example, he fought for a scientific use of cinema, even though his best contacts were mostly in the arts.

Bergson's élan vital was not only compatible with Canudo's sense of life as a mystery set in motion by invisible energies, but it was also in line with his approval of cinema's internationalist and humanitarian mandate.[31] Just as Bergson's vitalistic impulse redeemed humanity and nature from death, likewise the cinema was meant to be the universal language of the future. Yet the alignment of Canudo with Bergson's vitalist, antiscientific philosophy can become clearer only if the Italian critic's contempt for the cold eye of photography is clarified. According to Canudo, cinema is divorced from photography, since the moving image is the equivalent of a dream that can only be seen and felt, but never dissected. Canudo's stance was, therefore, antithetical to the analytical motion studies conducted by Marey. In the footsteps of Cézanne, who used photography as a tool to develop his portraits but never approved of it as an art form, the Italian critic wanted the movement of film to separate cinema from photography, so that the emotions triggered by moving images could transfigure the world into a quasi-surreal musical manifestation of everlasting life.[32]

Canudo's cinema was the modern equivalent of both a mystical experience and of a mythical force comparable to Wagner's overwhelming spectacles in Bayreuth. All forms of art fed into Canudo's cinema, just as painting and opera, theater and music were all relevant to the rich visual style of the diva film in all its orientalist display. Only cinema, the total form of art of Wagner's gesamtkunstwerk, Canudo argued, could release the worn-out masses of humble people from some deeper and more painful sense of inadequacy exasperated by modernity.[33] Likewise, the great historical spectacles of the Italian silent-film industry and the diva's operatic melodramas were supposed to strive for magnificence, musicality, and catharsis in order to achieve a sort of purifying return to the origins of myth and the roots of all passions. Canudo's cinema was the ultimate modern mass ritual. For the Italian aesthetician, it is this primitivist intensity that distinguishes film's emotionalism and ambition from the stillness and limitations of photography, in which each image is separate and cut off from the energy of modern life. The critic writes: "Now the cinema brings to fruition the representation of life of motion, but only by doubling its external visibility. This is the climax of an artificial kind of reproduction that *Cézanne called with disdain:* 'the photographic eye.'"[34]

Canudo's suggestive definition of cinematic representation was modeled on the antimimetic vocation of music, a medium close to all the levels of subjectivity that were of interest to Bergson: intuition, memory, and imagination. An admirer of Nietzsche, Canudo saw cinema as the will to collective fantasy and as an outlet for individual creativity. Despite the fact that Canudo agreed with Arthur Schopenauer about modern alienation, the naturalist flavor of André Antoine's film *La Terre* (1922) did not persuade the Italian to take the cinema completely out of the Wagnerian theater and the noisy city and put it into the fresh air of the countryside. Canudo's writings show that, for him, volition and vitalism—even more than scientific discoveries or Cézanne's personal immersions in the natural landscape—spell out that people's dreams control the world. In a sense, for Canudo, the step from Wagner to Nietzsche was inevitable. This is also perhaps why Canudo wanted at all costs to demonstrate that cinema was an art form, even if he kept stating that the cinema he knew had not quite become an art, thus relying on a commonplace of his period. In a sense, Canudo never resolved the problem of film's undeniable photographic origin, which André Bazin was to celebrate in 1945. The French film theorist, in fact, argued that the cinema is a medium, and not an art, and its specificity thrives on a photographic ontology that implies the rejection of the link between the human hand and creativity.[35]

Besides the shared legacy of Bergson's philosophy, the connections between Canudo and the diva film are shaped by the explosion of popularity surrounding the arrival of the Ballets Russes in Paris by 1909. At first, dance did not belong to Canudo's system of the arts, hence the confusing use of titles in which cinema is called first "the sixth art" and later on "the seventh art." It took Canudo's professional involvement with the Ballets Russes, plus his romance with the well-connected Valentine de Saint-Point, before he made room for dance in his work. In the wake of Diaghilev's success, Canudo became, in 1911, one of the first critics to praise the art of the

Russian painter Marc Chagall. The painter reciprocated by producing a work titled *Hommage à Apollinaire, Walden, Cendrars et Canudo* (1911–1912). At the end of his booklet *Hélène, Faust et Nous: Précis d'Esthétique Cérébriste* (1920), Canudo refers to Stravinsky's *Sacre du Printemps*, a piece brought to glory by Nijinsky in 1913, after the scandal of *L'Après-midi d'un Faune* of 1912, a ballet based on Stravinsky's setting of a poem by Mallarmé. Italian audiences welcomed both the supple Nijinsky and the slender ballerina Ida Rubinstein. These two dancers became so successful that Febo Mari directed himself in the film *Il Fauno* (1917), in which the protagonist of the ballet becomes the hero of a woman's romantic fantasy. Meanwhile, Rubinstein left dance to become an actress in D'Annunzio's play *Le Martyre de Saint Sébastien* (1911). Another example of cooperation between D'Annunzio and Rubinstein is *La Pisanella* (1914), a mystery play with music by Debussy, sets by Bakst, and a presentation by Canudo. Eager to promote his insights in relation to different art forms, the critic also devoted a special issue of *Montjoie* (1914), his avant-garde magazine, to the dancing styles of Rubinstein and Saint-Point.[36]

Responsible for having opened many doors in the high society of Paris and in literary circles, Saint-Point, too, benefited professionally from her union with Canudo. This egalitarian exchange was possible because she was the granddaughter of the French writer Alphonse de Lamartine (1790–1869). Born in Lyon in 1875, Valentine's full name was Anna Jeanne Valentine Marianne Desglans de Cessiat-Vercell. By 1904 she was already going through her second divorce and modeling for Alphonse Mucha and Auguste Rodin. It was also in 1904 that she and Canudo began their "free" relationship, thus discarding in one blow all bourgeois conventions. Encouraged by Canudo, Saint-Point produced work as a visual artist, poet, novelist, and essayist. By 1913 she presented herself as a dance theorist and delivered her first lecture, "Métachorie," about a new kind of experimental choreography. During the summer of 1916, Saint-Point was in Spain with a group of artists who avoided the war by taking on false identities. From there, she decided to travel to New York, where she performed her "métachorie" at the Metropolitan Opera House in 1917. While she served as a nurse during World War I, Canudo fought on the front lines and received the serious wounds that led to his death in Paris in 1923.[37]

The result of Saint-Point and Canudo's anticonventional nine-year involvement can be read in the light of the Italian critic's awareness of the debate on gender roles. In fact, his fiction and nonfiction bibliographies include words such as *androgynous* and *metamorphosis*.[38] Canudo used both these terms independently of the diva film's concern with a reconfiguration of the female image. This is indeed the case, because, at the time, these two words—*metamorphosis* and *androgyny*—were symptomatic of a general interest in experimenting with new models of subjectivity and involvement between men and women.

Canudo was neither a coherent nor a rigorous thinker. Within Italian culture, however, he stands out as an unusual figure in the history of the fin de siècle. He was one of the few people who managed to cultivate contacts with both D'Annunzio and Marinetti. These two celebrities, extremely competitive and self-centered men of letters, appealed to different constituencies: Marinetti was the spokesman of the futurist avant-garde, whereas D'Annunzio upheld the classical values of antiquity and the Renaissance, albeit as

Gabriele D'Annunzio. Author's collection.

Filippo Tommaso Marinetti. Author's collection.

revisited through an exacerbated and contemporary symbolist sensibility.

Saint-Point sent many of her books to D'Annunzio, and also kept herself informed about Marinetti's statements. However, she disagreed with one particular sentence in Marinetti's founding declaration of intent, published in 1909 in *Le Figaro:* the phrase that expressed contempt for women.[39] As a result, in 1912 she produced the *Manifesto of Futurist Woman* and launched a feminist agenda. Only one year later she declared, "Lust is a force," possibly echoing the Bergsonian concept of élan vital, until she became even more controversial for her *Futurist Manifesto of Lust* (1913). Unfortunately, neither manifesto moved beyond an androgynous iconography and a nationalist, bellicose rhetoric. More research might be necessary to evaluate Saint-Point's work as a whole because what has survived is problematic.

At this stage, it is interesting to note that both she and Canudo used the term *cérébriste.* In a text titled "My Choreographic Beginnings," Saint-Point relies on the word *cerebral* to mean "modern."[40] By vulgarizing Bergson's opposition of intuition and intelligence with the term *cerebrismo,* Canudo advocated the integration of the sensual and the cerebral, the instinctive level with the intellectual, intuition with thought. On February 9, 1914, *Le Figaro* published Canudo's *Il Manifesto dell'Arte Cerebrista,* whose program supported any artistic expression that would simultaneously incite thought and kindle the senses. But there is even more to *cerebrismo,* since one of the great topics of the period was the construction of the new man and the new woman through the invention of a new vocabulary of feelings, ideas, and attitudes. Again, this plan of radical reinvention can be linked to Bergson's belief about the originality and creativity of the deep self. Both these modern creatures—man and woman—were supposed to be born out of unprecedented combinations and calibrations of masculine as well as feminine features—a perfect marriage of intuition and intellect for both, but in different ways. And since, according to the popular and misogynistic opinion, "woman" was all about emotion, whereas "man" embodied only ratiocination, Canudo's *cerebrismo* played with still undecided dosages of gender-specific traits in the new context of modern life.[41]

To be sure, well beyond the circles of Canudo and Saint-Point, the era of futurist manifestos and diva films was obsessed with the vocabulary of sensations and with a cinema made of images about internal states and invisible transformations. The most important words during the period of the diva film were *isterico* (hysterical), *nevrosico* (neurotic), *cerebrale* (cerebral), and *lussuria* (lust). The popularity of this terminology can be inferred from reading profiles of various divas as well as reviews of their melodramas in the film trade journals.[42] Lyda Borelli and Diana Karenne were officially *cerebrali* divas, which meant that they were women with brains, but not in the sense of intellectual power—a state that, according to Lombroso, would have masculinized them.[43] *Cerebrale* here meant that these actresses had such an inner life of their own, such a sense of spirituality, that they were superior not only to the average woman, but also to the average man. On the other hand, for the talented male, and especially for Lombroso's man of genius, *lussuria* was automatically intertwined with *cerebrale*, for he was the only living being entitled to a complete fusion of the demands of the body and the ambitions of the brain, which was at other times referred to as "soul" or "spirit," in the intellectual and religious sense of these words.

Within this context of different levels of sensations describing competing levels of emancipation, it was therefore extremely daring for diva Diana Karenne to define herself as a woman *cerebrale*, as a performer with a bleeding soul, and as a heart filtered by the brain. From a profile of Karenne in *Penombra:* "Among actresses she admires Asta Nielsen. She is aware of the profound difference that exists between Nielsen and herself. The former is mostly an intuitive performer, but she plans to establish herself through her reputation as a 'cerebrale'... 'In my poetry my heart bleeds through the filter of my brain.'"[44] It is telling that in Karenne's self-awareness of her competition with Nielsen, lust does not even come into the picture. Instead of lust, suffering, with plenty of Catholic iconography, informs Karenne's statement about the relations between heart and brain. Even Borelli, equally famous for her spiritual aura in the register of the *cerebrale*, never went so far as Karenne in claiming for herself the explosive combination of soul and blood, spirit and heart.

Cerebrismo, however, does not fully account for all of Canudo's orientalist vocation. The Italian critic had been trained in Asian languages at the universities of Florence and Rome, so he had a wide range of intellectual and artistic interests. He was genuinely curious about theosophy and comparative religions; his studies included both Lutheran beliefs and Nietzsche's interest in Zarathustra. But how to bridge the gap between the fabled Orient and Italian culture? Lust in exotic, medieval, and gothic settings seemed to be

Diana Karenne. Author's collection.

(left) Lyda Borelli. Author's collection.

the answer. Canudo organized regular readings of Dante in Paris. In addition, the literary taste of Canudo's circle was scattered enough to support and applaud a wide range of texts, from Dante's *Divine Comedy* to Poe's *Tales of the Grotesque and Arabesque* (1840), which comes up again and again in Gallone's *Malombra.* In his *Inferno,* Dante wrote about lust in relation to two lovers, Paolo and Francesca, united and seduced by the reading of a book. Edgar Allan Poe, instead, dealt with the power of invisible forces. Accounts of medieval sinners, such as Paolo and Francesca in Dante's hell, and nineteenth-century horror stories with haunted houses satisfied a widespread curiosity about psychic powers inhabiting a space halfway between art and science. And the cinema, of course, shared this kind of ambiguous placement in the popular imagination of the period.

Dante, Poe, and the diva film served the same taste for sensationalism, melodrama, high culture, and nostalgia. Just like Canudo, Marinetti loved Dante and Poe, and D'Annunzio decorated his mansion, Il Vittoriale, along the lines of Poe's sensibility in "The Fall of the House of Usher" (1839). To complete this brief sketch of persons and trends, even the obscure French philosopher René Guénon, author of a book titled *L'Ésotérisme de Dante* (1912), belonged to Canudo's circle.[45] Guénon not only participated in Canudo's public readings of Dante, but also later became a mentor to Saint-Point, in Egypt. This tireless French woman moved to Cairo in 1924, following Canudo's death, in 1923. She had traveled to Morocco in 1916, and later converted to Islam, taking the new name Rawhiya Nour-el-Dine ("Spiritual Light of Religion"). In Egypt, she continued her intellectual and journalistic activity until she became a proponent of Islamic nationalism against the English and the French colonial powers.[46]

In comparison with the Italian film diva, Saint-Point enjoyed many more freedoms and successes, for she became the diva of Canudo's salon, even though, like him, she remained a marginal figure eager to be at the center of pivotal events and crucial circles. Like Canudo and the film diva, Saint-Point kept looking for some higher cause or noble ideal in art and life, but never reached a condition of peace and fulfillment. Knowing that she was the only French woman among the futurists; that her distinguished literary lineage opened doors but also stirred criticism of her anticonformist ways, one is likely to ask who was the true Saint-Point. Did she pay a price? Was she a happy and reckless twentieth-century Salome, turning orientalism into a permanent way of life and leaving behind a series of broken hearts and dead lovers? Or, considering her restless production of literary pieces—novels, lectures, pamphlets, manifestoes—and experiments in dance, the visual arts, religious philosophy, and colonial politics, was she limited to a small circle of real friends while generally struggling to make her own ideas count? Were her ideas really major for her time? It is very difficult to tell, but she certainly stands out as one of the most energetic socialites of her period.

The same kind of intellectual restlessness and search for spirituality and notoriety will be the topic of the following chapter, "Wings of Desire," which deals with Italian women and actresses turning to airplanes, fashion, and circus stunts to rise above social conventions and stereotypes based on gender roles.

Wings of Desire

AVIATION, FASHION, CIRCUS STUNTS

The first Italian airplane flew in 1908, when the cinema had just taken off; together the airplane and the cinema redefined the boundaries of the visible and, consequently, these two media questioned who was looking.[1] Both media, one for transportation, the other for communication, accommodated the possibility of living beyond one's body, in defiance of gravity and history. Italy excelled in the design of airplanes, just as it did in that of racing cars. The famous brand names, Ferrari and Fiat, found their aerial counterparts in the Savoia-Marchetti, the Macchi, and the Monfalconi.[2] The analogy, however, between earthbound and airborne vehicles stops at the cult of elegant design. The perceptual model conjured by the airplane was even more unsettling than the one involved in terrestrial transportation. To be sure, the train, like the cinema, was about time passing and movement through space, but the airplane and the cinema together showed the possibility of ascending higher and higher, to the point of making everything look small. The invention of the airplane marked the twinning of modern technology with visual vertigo.

In line with the futurists' glorification of machines, flying took on cosmic and visionary connotations that were more appropriate for science fiction than for military or commercial applications. In Pirandello's *Shoot!* this quasi-divine version of technology emerges through the social privileges enjoyed by a professor of astronomy. His last name is Zeme, a strange variation on *seme* or *seed*. In keeping with Pirandello's taste for the combination of opposites, Professor Zeme, who runs an astronomical observatory, is an old man with a name that sounds like the beginning of a plant buried in the earth.[3] Furthermore, in *Shoot!* Pirandello's irony about flying justifies the name of Fantappiè, not far from *fantascienza,* the Italian word for science fiction. He is the comedian who stars in innumerable short adventure films for a production house called Kosmograph, where the *cinematographe* sounds like a program for rewriting the cosmos. To be sure, Fantappiè is torn between holding his feet to the earth and his desire to go to the moon by interpreting a new film.[4]

This redesigning of an airborne body through the mobilization of the eye and the defiance of weight was not only a theme of the art nouveau style, but also an agenda consonant with the reshaping of the self sought by men and women at the beginning of a new century. By taking humans into the heavens, the airplane enabled male pilots to feel godlike, but it also showed women what it could be like to leave the *man* of *hu-man* below, on the earth. Yet any discussion of aerial motifs in turn-of-the-century Italy must begin with two self-made, precinematic stars: F. T. Marinetti, the leader of the futurist avant-garde, and Gabriele D'Annunzio, the major figure of Italian literary symbolism. Shortly before the outbreak of World War I, the airplane found two major advocates in Marinetti and D'Annunzio, who wielded immense influence in both Italian intellectual life and the popular media. If stardom can be said to have existed before its establishment in the cinema, Marinetti and D'Annunzio held a monopoly on it. Everything they said or did was always an event, a scandal, a statement.

The airplane fad was only one among many passionate interests cultivated by these two eclectic personalities. Indeed, they were eclectic to the point of self-contradiction. To begin with, the linear optimism of some of Marinetti's futurist statements was in keeping with automobile races and at odds with the airplane's disappearance behind the clouds; furthermore, the airplane, tied as it was to modern technology, clashed with D'Annunzio's love of monuments and ruins. Yet both cinema and the airplane were too new and too exciting to be ignored.

Marinetti's and D'Annunzio's early support of the airplane not only showed their eagerness to be ahead of the very latest trend but also heightened their public image as men of action. Thus, they flew or wrote about flying even before the outbreak of the Libyan campaign of 1911–1912, Italy's first colonial adventure in North Africa. It was this conflict that made the rest of the world realize that the airplane was here to stay as a weapon of war. Even before the Libyan campaign, Marinetti had linked aviation to masculinity. The protagonist of his *Mafarka the Futurist: An African Novel* (1909) is a pilot who rapes the wind and feels a terrible hate for the earth below.[5] Inasmuch as woman was despised by futurism, she was deeply envied. Mafarka's behavior, for instance, exemplifies the ultimate procreative male fantasy: after landing, he copulates with a chair, and fathers a mechanical son.

Instead of taking the aggressive sexual stance of Marinetti's aero-futurism, D'Annunzio held on to moonlight, seduction, intrigue, and love letters. D'Annunzio peopled his novels with languid androgynous women and effete male aristocrats. But he was also a daring aviator. On January 16, 1916, during World War I, the poet was flying toward the Italian city of Trieste, which was being fought over by the Austrians and the Italians. All of a sudden he was forced to make a dangerous sea landing near the beaches of Grado. Such a traumatic experience did not keep him away from airplanes. On August 9, 1918, D'Annunzio climbed into the cockpit once more. He flew from Venice to Vienna, the capital of the Austro-Hungarian Empire, dropping along the way thousands of leaflets that called for the liberation of Trieste.

While Marinetti achieved a strange mixture of disembodiment into vision and the hypermasculinization of military technology, D'Annunzio managed to combine the amorous Don Giovanni with the intrepid hero, the modern Icarus with the patriot, the aristocratic dandy with the tough leader of a commando action. In 1919, D'Annunzio went up into the sky again and conquered Fiume, a city near Trieste that is now in Slovenia. Following this success, D'Annunzio drafted a new legislation for the area, the Carta del Carnaro; one of his major initiatives had to do with granting women the right to vote. A few years later, in 1923, Benito Mussolini was so impressed by D'Annunzio's two aerial feats that he gave the poet a personal hydroplane as a gift.[6]

Gabriele D'Annunzio and a young woman. Author's collection.

Aerial bombing in Libya. Author's collection.

D'Annunzio's favorite pseudonym was "Ariel," from the character in Shakespeare's *The Tempest* (1610–1611), and he was obsessed with flying beings in general. When the poet in a clumsy moment fell from a window at the Vittoriale, he humorously labeled the episode "*volo d'arcangelo*" ("angel's flight").[7] Flying, for D'Annunzio, involved quite a bit of military heroism, but it was also, and perhaps above all, a poetic enterprise. After losing one eye in 1916, during his forced landing, the poet started to speak of his third eye, as if the physical injury had opened the door to a sixth sense. D'Annunzio's fascination with the irrational, his love of perfumes, and his experimentation with drugs could not be further from Mafarka's high-tech monolithic machismo among the clouds.[8]

But what is most important about these two writers' love for the airplane is that this new invention was made of death and exhilaration. Perhaps they put on wings, believing that self-destruction might become the first step toward rebirth. Unfortunately, this regenerative view of military technology, including a violent use of the airplane, fueled enthusiasm for World War I. Considering the Mediterranean context in which Italy was linked to North Africa through Libya, and to Greece through Rome, Marinetti's and D'Annunzio's allegiance to the airplane suggests a rewriting of the Icarus myth. This ancient Greek tale is about a father, Daedalus the inventor, and his son, Icarus the explorer. The story is well-known, except for the ending that concerns Daedalus: after Icarus crashes into the sea because he flew too close to the sun and melted the wax that held his wings together, Daedalus—the architect of the labyrinth for the Minotaur—flies safely to Sicily on his own set of wings and is received kindly by the king.[9] While Icarus's wings are easily comparable to the airplane, his death hardly fits the fantasy of rebirth behind Marinetti's all-seeing futurist flier and D'Annunzio's dissolution of visual language into sound effects of cosmic import. These two writers' passion for the airplane makes sense only if Icarus does not really die and if Daedalus, who lands in Sicily, is not the father but a new Icarus—a mechanical futurist man, in Marinetti's case, and a refined aesthete, were he to embrace D'Annunzio's ways. In fact, the poet's longing for all sorts of male alter egos was expressed through the androgynous female heroines of his novels.

Women in Flight

In the wake of Marinetti's and D'Annunzio's highly publicized experiences with the airplane, Italian men and women got involved to varying degrees with both aspects of the airplane's appeal: first, the airplane as a weapon for military action; second, the airplane as a fantasy of imaginative freedom. More specifically, in the days of the Libyan campaign, shortly before World War I broke out in Italy, in 1915, Marinetti and D'Annunzio were not the first or the only celebrities roaming the skies. In the 5 February 1911 issue of *La Donna*, a women's magazine published in Turin, the theater actress Lyda Borelli appears in a lavish front-page spread. Having been celebrated for her success in Oscar Wilde's *Salomè* (1910), Borelli appears in exotic garb. In a little photograph on a subsequent page, she is also shown as the only female passenger in a hot-air balloon. The caption below the image reads: "In love with strong emotions, after the flights of fancy, Lyda Borelli has decided to try the fantasy of flight, and she came back most enthusiastic from her nocturnal ascension."[10]

The photograph from *La Donna* of Borelli in a hot-air balloon makes it clear that the theater actress is the catalyst that puts to work the ten gentlemen standing around her. To a much greater extent than the hot-air balloon, the airplane could twist and turn and thus revolutionize time and space, turning a linear path into a marvelous arabesque with loops and curves. What was most significant about the airplane fad, however, was not its cinematic mobilization of the point of view, but rather the secret it kept hiding underneath its wings. In fact, the diva and the airplane share a whole set of affinities. The diva even seemed to live according to this new technology's extremes: she could crash, killing the enemy at the cost of killing herself; or she could fly beyond the constraints of her own body into a utopian realm. The airplane's ability to move between ground and sky matched the diva's oscillation between historical change and personal ruin. This parallel suggests that a newly born technology could house an older cultural type by way of a metaphorical replacement or an unexpected analogy.

The combination of old and new transpired through the ambivalent and simultaneous backward and forward orientation of leaves and flowers in the art nouveau style. It is the curve that interests me in the construction of the film diva as a cultural type. The curve, directionally a mixed form par excellence, can split itself between the avant-garde and the backlash. Thus, the curve also echoes cinema's blurring of the boundaries between high culture and popular entertainment. This

Francesca Bertini (film source unknown). Courtesy Cineteca Nazionale, Rome.

Katsushika Hokusai, *Woman Being Violated by an Octopus* (1814). Print from *Kinoe no Komatsu* (1820; Young Pines) album (OA+.0.109). British Museum, London. © Copyright the Trustees of the British Museum.

Publicity for the film *Ivonne* (1915), starring Francesca Bertini. Author's collection.

Cover of *Cines* review (1912). Author's collection.

Mario Roncoroni's *Filibus* (1915). Courtesy Nederlands Filmmuseum, Amsterdam.

A poster for *L'Amazzone Mascherata* (1914; The Masked Equestrienne). Courtesy Nederlands Filmmuseum, Amsterdam.

Scene from *Sulla via dell'Oro* (1913; On the Golden Road). Courtesy Nederlands Filmmuseum, Amsterdam.

Scene from *Sulla via dell'Oro* (1913; On the Golden Road). Courtesy Nederlands Filmmuseum, Amsterdam.

Lyda Borelli in *Il Fior di Male* (1915). Courtesy Nederlands Filmmuseum, Amsterdam, and Ripley's Film, Italy.

Poster for Mario Roncoroni's *Filibus* (1915). Courtesy Nederlands Filmmuseum, Amsterdam.

Nino Oxilia's *Sangue Bleu* (1914; Blue Blood). Courtesy Nederlands Filmmuseum, Amsterdam.

mixing of directions and levels can be assessed through two complementary processes at work in art nouveau itself: on the one hand, the raising of minor arts to aesthetic ranking; on the other, the serializations and consequent lowering of icons from high culture into clichés for popular consumption.

Despite the serpentine line connecting the film diva to the airplane as the symbol of space and time intertwined, the role of a revived, successful Icarus remained a male prerogative. Women could not fit into the Icarus myth with the same degree of satisfaction, because this tale's oedipal genealogy goes from father to son, not from mother to daughter. Furthermore, the problem was not just with storytelling, but with history itself. With the convulsions of hysteria keeping women on the margins of history, mothers and daughters could hardly find a good place for themselves within a linear and teleological view of the historical process.[11] As a result of this double difficulty with the time lines of both history and storytelling, women, or at least some of them, were perhaps dreaming of bending the rules into a new way of living when they looked at aerial twists on-screen. In response to all sorts of skywriting, female viewers might have been seeking a redefinition of femininity that went beyond the gender-biased structures of the Icarus myth. And it was especially by going to the cinema or to the airfield that they expressed their longing for the mobility of the aerial arabesque, the empty openness of the sky, and the freedom of flight.

In comparison with their European colleagues, Italian women climbed more slowly into the cockpit. It was not until the 1930s that the airplane became accessible to many of them. Even then, female fliers were usually aristocrats, intellectuals, or artists. (Although a metaphorical view of aviation flourished among women in general, the airplane fad was primarily a pastime for the upper classes.) For the record, the first Italian woman to earn a license as a civil pilot was Rosina Ferrario, in 1913. Yet her achievement was so isolated that in 1928 the *Almanacco della Donna Italiana* forgot to mention Ferrario and mistakenly assigned the achievement to Clelia Ferla, who flew for the first time fifteen years after Ferrario. In the wake of these two pioneers, Princess Miriam Potenziani, Contessa Bonmartini, Contessa Di Sanbuy, and the Marchesa Carina Negroe Di Cambiaso went up into the air, whether alone or with a male partner is not clear.[12]

Moving from the historical record to the cinematic screen, we encounter the Baroness Troixmonde, or Filibus, the female air pirate played by a little-known actress, Cristina Ruspoli, in the adventure film *Filibus* (1915), directed by Mario Roncoroni. She is an imaginative criminal who lives in a dirigible filled with silent faceless male assistants in tight black skin suits. At ease with all kinds of technological gadgets, including a heliograph (a sort of solar-powered telegraph), Filibus engages in four major activities: observing the whereabouts of her enemy, Detective Hardy, who is scheming against her on the earth below; traveling between the ground and the sky inside an elevator that looks like a moving can; operating ground technology to keep in touch with the dirigible hidden among the clouds; and swiftly assuming new identities by putting on different sets of clothing.

Whenever she is not wearing one of her disguises, such as the sober tuxedo of "the dandy Count de La Brieve," Filibus appears with all the feminine accoutrements of her aristocratic class, including a large brimmed hat. This accessory not only quivers in the

Cristina Ruspoli as Baroness Troixmonde in Mario Roncoroni's *Filibus* (1915). Courtesy Nederlands Filmmuseum, Amsterdam.

wind, but is also ornately trimmed with feathers—an elegant reminder of her avian "underground" activities. Even though this female pirate is competent on land and in the sky, and at home in the worlds of fashion and technology, she never manages to drive her zeppelin household to a destination that belongs only to her. In a sense, Filibus enjoys Daedalus's technological ingenuity, but she never lands in Sicily.

In real life, if an airplane was not easily available, any kind of reference to flying, even through fashion, was a statement of emancipation for the aristocratic Italian woman. In Alberto Degli Abbati's *La Memoria dell'Altro* (1913), the diva Lyda Borelli is a famous aviatrix whose flight is an endless source of fascination for the camera. With her supple acting style, wavy blonde hair, and liquid hand gestures, Borelli was considered by critics and fans alike the most D'Annunzian of all divas, the ultimate embodiment of the art nouveau arabesque.[13]

In *La Memoria dell'Altro,* the first part of the narrative deals with the success and courage of Lyda as a female pilot. Later on, this positive persona is set against another portrait of Lyda—as a woman suffering and in isolation because she loves a married man, Mario. It is as if the diva were interpreting two different characters through one role: no better example could be found of how the new woman of modernity could live next to the mater dolorosa of Catholic iconography. To be sure, Lyda's commitment to Mario is "everlasting," so that it comes to

Filibus's zeppelin, in Mario Roncoroni's *Filibus* (1915). Courtesy Nederlands Filmmuseum, Amsterdam.

resemble a blood pact, a mother's attachment to her son.

La Memoria opens with a sequence at an airfield. As soon as she lands, a group of admiring men surrounds the beautiful Lyda, who is wearing pants and a pilot's beret. Lyda's outfit recalls Pierrot's *jupe-culotte,* the first kind of loose pants available to city women for daily wear. According to the historian Michela De Giorgio, the first Italian woman to wear pants in public appeared in Piazza San Carlo, Turin, in 1911. Of course, she caused an amazing stir. Apparently, a few men addressed the woman so rudely that she was obliged to leave the street.[14]

A few days later, in Florence, Lyda Borelli was also photographed in a jupe-culotte; her choice of garment turned a social transgression into a trendsetting gesture.[15] This was, indeed, the power of the diva: in *La Memoria dell'Altro,* her character, also named "Lyda," chooses self-annihilation after her beloved Mario's death. In real life, however, the actress could get away with all sorts of eccentricities. The aviatrix's jupe-culotte also required a thin figure; therefore, for the first time, thousands of Italian women went on diets.

It was as if the cinema needed Borelli's special aura of celebrity to justify women's association not only with pants and thinness, but also with flying. Nevertheless the diva's avian identity was characterized by some major limitations. The aviatrix, for instance, became visible only when her feet were on the earth. This limited representation of the female pilot at the controls was not exclusively due to technological limitations. It is true that in 1913 the film technology necessary to shoot someone in an airplane from another airplane was not readily available. Cameras were still heavy and awkward to handle. This is also why Roncoroni's *Filibus* depends so much on miniature models to depict landscape overviews, dirigibles, and hot-air balloons. But besides these technological constraints, Borelli's grounding contains a hidden agenda: to delineate a woman's proper place, namely, either in front of a mirror or in the passenger's seat. This approach was inflected not only by gender but also by class. When the aviatrix leaves the airfield, she sits in the back of a car driven by a chauffeur.

It is only before her flight that the camera dwells on Borelli's dressing up. She carefully positions a pilot's beret on her head. The actress's precise little movements suggest her concern about continuing to look feminine despite her unusual headgear. Thus, the new woman could be born only through male clothing, whereas the way to construct her image from a female point of view remained as vague as a breath of fresh air.

Despite the ideological limitations built into the character of Borelli's aviatrix, the partnership of airplanes and women in film is too anticonformist to stop at just one episode. Here is an additional example in which the costuming for an aerial dance about the cinema suggests that freedom thrives inside the metaphors of women's imagination, even though they may not have access to the technology itself. My description of Giannina Censi's dance costume, which contains allusions to the cinematic apparatus as well as to airplanes, is based on several black-and-white photographs published by Claudia Salaris in her volume on aviation and futurism.[16] In 1917, Marinetti wrote out directions for a performance entitled *Danza dell'Aviatrice* (The Aviatrix's Dance). In line with Marinetti's original approach, Censi danced on a brightly colored map of the world; on her bosom she wore a huge celluloid propeller, supposedly shaped like a flower to signify her gender, but also resembling a reel of film mounted on her projector-like body. On her head, Censi wore a white hat shaped like a monoplane. No photographic record exists of Censi performing Marinetti's 1917 choreography. In Claudia Salaris's book, however, the photographs of Censi dancing a comparable piece in 1931 suggest fluidity, especially when the dancer stretches her arm outward in a straight but unaggressive line—a line that wants to be a wing instead of an arrow. The 1931 photographs indicate that Censi emphasized shape-shifting and plasticity rather than the virile penetration of soft clouds at sunset, which was the way Marinetti imagined the 1917 piece. Furthermore, in Censi's performance of 1931, the wing motif replaces Marinetti's 1917 airplane with its bellyful of bombs. This last example illustrates a female dancer's power to move beyond Marinetti's view of aviation as a masculine monopoly or an expression of virility and violence.

Yet another telling anecdote concerns Diana Karenne, who sought D'Annunzio's cooperation in order to take off into the sky of fantasy.[17] In 1918, as the representative of the Lega Aerea Nazionale (National Air League), an organization interested in producing a film about the heroism of Italian pilots, the diva Diana Karenne traveled to D'Annunzio's residence, Il Vittoriale, in Gardone Riviera, to plan such a project. Around that time, the poet was approaching the climax of his involvement with the airplane. Karenne's arrival was preceded by a suggestive telegram: "My soul is dreaming of becoming one of

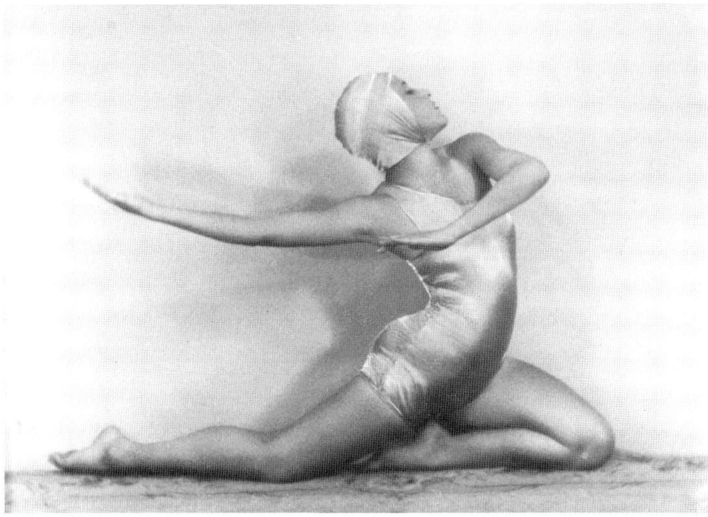

Giannina Censi in *Danza dell'Aviatrice* (1931). Courtesy MART, Rovereto.

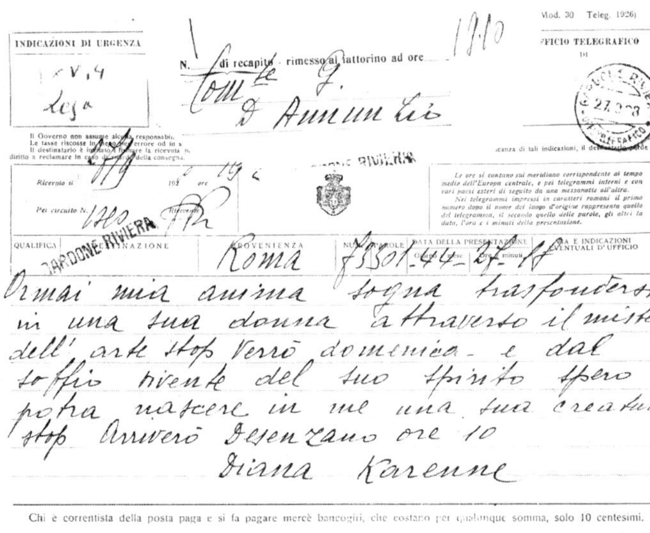

INDICAZIONI DI URGENZA

Com.te G. D'Annunzio

Roma

Ormai mia anima sogna trasfondersi in una sua donna attraverso il mistero dell'arte stop Verrò domenica e dal soffio vivente del suo spirito spero potrà nascere in me una sua creatura stop Arriverò Desenzano ore 10
Diana Karenne

Chi è correntista della posta paga e si fa pagare mercè bancogiri, che costano per qualunque somma, solo 10 centesimi.

(bottom) Telegram from Diana Karenne to Gabriele D'Annunzio, 1918. Courtesy Il Vittoriale, Gardone Riviera.

your women through the mystery of art STOP shall arrive on Sunday. From the living breath of your spirit I hope one of your [literary] creatures can be born in me STOP shall arrive in Desenzano at 10."[18]

Here Karenne wishes to be reborn as a D'Annunzian fictional heroine in a tale of wings, technology, and erotic mystery. More important are the larger questions raised by this episode: What happens when the diva Diana Karenne identifies with the sky diva of the movies and aspires to become an aviatrix in a new film? Will she function as a fantasy icon for men, for women, or for both? Karenne's telegram seems to declare that her crossing over into the new woman of modernity will depend on how the dandy D'Annunzio creates ambiguous images of femininity in his literary work. It is as if Karenne, in real life, were stepping into the clothes of the historical spectators mesmerized by the D'Annunzian features of the film diva Borelli in *La Memoria dell'Altro.* To find alternative avenues of expression for her desire, a woman (Karenne) identifies with a man (D'Annunzio), who, in turn, is attracted to androgynous heroines in order to reinvent himself as a male artist. Daedalus's labyrinth could hardly be more convoluted than Karenne's romantic connection with flight through D'Annunzio. In a sense, he is Daedalus, the architect, and she is Ariadne, following the thread toward freedom via either *divismo* or fashion.

Since both Marinetti and D'Annunzio either marginalized or used women to spur male creativity, the question remains: which one of these two artists would have been more tolerable to fly with? Probably D'Annunzio, since Marinetti was more rigid in the matter of gender roles, more concerned with virility and less with androgyny. In *La Memoria dell'Altro,* Borelli's outfitting herself in men's clothes to pilot a plane does not oblige spectators to give up heterosexual norms. Yet it enables them to shed the clothing of rigid stereotypes and perhaps to take on D'Annunzio's outlook on gender roles. With the film diva, crossing over is not an intolerable transgression, because it immediately becomes an aesthetic choice, an avant-garde position, a fashion statement that receives its seal of approval from highbrow literary culture.

Flying in the Circus

Flying was not just an expensive pastime for the jet set of the day, a pack of socialites who crowded the balls and horse races, airfields and art openings. Flying, as performing in the air, was also a popular form of entertainment in the circus and in silent-film comedy. Borelli in flight was not visible, but she posed, so to speak, in pilot's clothing before taking off and after landing. By contrast, in silent-film comedy and in the circus, the audience could actually admire female acrobats flipping in the air or performing stunts that required them to leap around.

Between 1910 and 1920, many Italian aristocrats were involved in the movies, but they rarely belonged to the world of the circus. This popular, lower-class space of live performance was traditionally reserved for nomadic mountebanks. An exception to this class division in regard to the act of flying was Astrea, a female athlete born in Vicenza and formerly known as Countess Barbieri. A stage name with cosmic implications, Astrea had also been an alias for Elizabeth I during the English Renaissance.[19] Little is known about Barbieri except that she was so protective of her real name that she narrowed it down to a mysterious "Countess B." Although the title "Countess" lingered on in her private life, the way Astrea looked on-screen—huge and grotesque—undeniably brought to mind circus freaks. And yet through an intriguing turn of events, stooping so low in social class for the sake of a professional adventure in film became Astrea's ticket to stardom. Astrea was first discovered by the French comedian Ferdinand Guillaume (1887–1977). With him in the role of Birillo, she starred in four well-known action-comedies: *I Creatori dell'Impossibile* (1921; The Creators of the Impossible), *Justitia* (1919), *La Riscossa delle Maschere* (1919; The Masks' Counterattack), and *L'Ultima Avventura* (1920; The Last Adventure). The gigantic Astrea and her small partner, shrewd and goofy, achieved success by playing off each other's sizes and by engaging in picaresque adventures across the world—two traits that are reminiscent of Don Quixote and Sancho Panza.

It is most interesting that the aerial

Astrea. Author's collection.

Poster for Astrea's *Justitia* (1919). Author's collection.

metaphor at work in Astrea's name can be stretched to include her gigantic look as well as the miniature size of Valentina Frascaroli, another star of the comic genre whose screen name was "La Farfalletta" (Little Butterfly). Frascaroli stands out as a minor star in the context of the adventure film. Furthermore, the parallel between Astrea and Farfalletta not only involves airy names, but also includes a similar generic placement in film comedy. Just as the gigantic Astrea paired up with Birillo, the minuscule Farfalletta developed her screen career next to André Deed (1884–1938). The male partners of both actresses were clownish creatures rather than good-looking men. In addition, Farfalletta was so small that she appeared childlike and unable to claim a woman's sexuality. By contrast, Astrea's ballooning figure suggested the stereotype of the overwhelming mother, one who could never lose weight and therefore become an appealing wife or a seductive mistress.

Besides Astrea, other athletic women started in the circus and went on to star on Italian screens. Taking the new name of "Sansonette" for the screen, Linda Albertini was originally a star of the circus, "an amazon of the air, and a dancer of the prairie." Along with her Danish colleague Emilie Samson, who specialized in airplane stunts, Sansonette excelled in airborne acrobatics involving the trapeze, ropes, horses, and all sorts of flying vehicles. Finally, the aerial motif informed the career of Gisaliana Doria, whose films about war and aviation turned her into

Valentina Frascaroli ("La Farfalletta"). Author's collection.

an icon of courage and helped her become the female cinematic version of the heroic Italian pilot Francesco Baracca.[20] In 1914 the engineer Gianni Caproni built the first of eighty-nine bombers to be deployed in World War I. Five years later, Gisaliana Doria starred in the first Italian war film with a female heroine, *Il Pilota del Caproni n.5* (1919).

Abstraction and Disfiguration

The iconography of physical courage stretching from the muscle-bound female star to the arabesque-like, graceful persona of Borelli seems to indicate that these women of the air wanted to fly away from the confinements of a passive and domestic identity. In this respect, the diva joined ranks with Sansonette and her sisters: they all stepped outside the conventional roles of obedient wife and timid daughter. It is also true, however, that in comparison with Borelli's androgynous oscillation between nervous but sensual, and muscular but spiritual, the strong women of Italian silent cinema are by far more statuesque and unidimensional icons of national health. Thus, when placed next to Karenne or Borelli, the airplane endows female desire with wings of self-expression, or at least with the possibility of it. By contrast, for Sansonette, Farfalletta, and Astrea, flying is more about dexterity, spectacle, and entertainment. When Sansonette flies all the way to the top on her trapeze, her trajectory downward is both reassuring and predictable. By contrast, when Borelli disappears in the sky, the camera cannot show much, but can only wonder about an unknown metamorphosis taking place below the level of clothing or beyond the female body, but definitely behind the clouds.

Both Borelli and Astrea were trangressive women, but whereas the former's flight was an aesthetic gesture, the latter's jumps degraded her femininity. Astrea embodied the disfiguring side of flying: grotesque and gynandrous, her oversized body bounced over enemies and dangers. As visual forms, the arabesque and the grotesque are comparable in that they perpetuate narrow views of femininity, for they demand either the complete denial of the sexual body or its exclusive use for reproduction. These visual forms—nonfigurative and disfiguring, respectively—might have become popular because of the imaginative possibilities they released in whatever realm they appeared: in the circus, on the movie screen, and in the world of fashion.

Linda Albertini ("Sansonette") performing in the circus. Author's collection.

The semantic asymmetry between the diva and the female athlete in relation to the theme of flying stems from the fact that the diva belongs to the unconscious, to the boudoir, to a vertically oriented oxymoron of simultaneously futuristic and archaic emotional experiences. In contrast to the diva's backstage location, Astrea and Sansonette happily occupy the façade of family life and national identity. They mobilize and energize the domestic psyche. Yet they do so by holding on to a horizontal axis of stability that reinforces a linear teleology, a historical trajectory compatible only with improvements and successes. Unlike these two cartoon-like strong women, the diva is a much more contradictory catalyst of repressed desires and an agent of destruction aimed at herself and at the status quo.[21]

Were we to narrow the comparison between Lyda and Astrea and consider only the function of clothing and the analogy between the art nouveau arabesque and Borelli's protean body, we would gain a much clearer understanding of the changing gender roles at the beginning of the twentieth century. Through these limits of representation it is possible to infer what the audiences of the day imagined behind and beyond the moving visual forms they saw on-screen. The comparison between Lyda with Astrea also makes us wonder whether the female athlete is in any way like the male transvestite. Astrea is not a successful example of transsexuality, for the layering of female clothing on a successful male transvestite is usually meant to tone down the masculine contours of his muscles. Astrea's enlarged size does make her look like a female Maciste, the strong-man protagonist of innumerable Italian action and adventure films. Yet her large hips and beautiful face unmistakably prove that she is a gorgeous oversize woman. On the other hand, Borelli's appearance as a male pilot is an appealing icon, an erotic teaser, as long as her metamorphosis stops at the clothes. If her female body were changed by her masculine outfit, or, to twist the proverb, if her clothes made her a man, the diva's playful androgyny would degenerate into monstrous hermaphroditism—an aberrant mixture deep inside instead of an intriguing layering on top.

When seen alone, Astrea is a large but striking woman. And yet there is something grotesque about muscular Astrea towering over little Birillo. There they are: two freaks, two bodies engaged in a comedy of errors made by Mother Nature. She always wears the same male outfit—baggy pants, loose shirt, and a wide-brimmed hat—and there is nothing else she can do: Astrea is just too big for a normal woman. Likewise, her tiny man, Birillo, is no dandy; he has lost his male status and has been reduced to either a child or a dwarf. This is why "androgyny" is too aristocratic a term for Astrea. By contrast, she is an example of "gynandry," a word pointing to the populist reconciliation of high and low social classes.[22] In this respect, Astrea's oversize body is a way of masking divisions that are difficult to bridge in a small, newly born nation.

It is also true that the grotesque, in the history of art, can be a manifestation of weightlessness; thus Astrea's oversized body engages in leaps and bounds and defies the law of gravity that should apply to a naturalistic space.[23] But her victory over the pull of the earth is not an event staged in the utopian and rule-free space of nowhere. Rather, her stunts are a temporary and extreme performance to straighten out a society that is undergoing radical change.[24] Within this changing world, stable binary oppositions—male and female, heavy and light—risk turning into stunt-like reversals of values and roles. While she takes one risk after another, Astrea operates within a picture that remains safely figurative—that is, stable and anthropocentric—and does not dissolve into the blank slate of abstraction and revolution.

It is as if the action cinema to which Astrea belongs were made of topsy-turvy moving pictures in which the potential for abstraction begins to show, but is nevertheless pulled down by this superwoman who is in charge of maintaining the status quo. It is this sort of denial within the image itself that makes her figure look incongruously large. In other words, the size of her body overbears the architecture shown in the film—namely, the small portions of roofs and chimneys that are set against the open sky—as she chases the evildoers, jumping into the air and leaping from one building to the next. This discrepancy in scale between the protagonist's size and the sets suggests that the fundamental rule of anthropocentric painting—man is the measure of all things—is being distorted, but not overcome, by a woman. On the contrary, Astrea's body bears witness to the deformation of appearance in store for women who dare to leave their social class and domestic space, as Countess B. left her Venetian palace. Paradoxically, Astrea's large size is about the relapse into an image of traditional female reproduction, combined with the social stigma of monstrosity.

If androgyny means more than one gender, to the point of promising a quasi-magic, fluid persona, an arabesque-like body shape, then Borelli embodies an androgynous ideal of bipolarity. This ideal could be adopted by men and women alike as long as they remained within a privileged milieu. In contrast to androgyny's "more than one," gynandry is not about sliding out of one's own mold to become someone else. Rather, it stands for an abnormal male element weighing heavily inside a normative female vessel. When seen as a punitive pregnancy without delivery, gynandry is not only a populist solution rooted within a working-class stereotype, but also, psychoanalytically, a sort of *Oedipus interruptus* that risks breaking the metonymic chain between father and son.

Where men and women are concerned, the semiotic transferability of androgyny is broader than the semantic adjustment of aviation: it is easier for women to dress like male pilots than to actually fly. By putting on modern clothes, the women of the diva's period displayed their desire for inner change as well. This dynamic of an exceptional surface replacing a continuum-in-depth speaks to the association of the vertical line with modernity through its most famous icon, the American skyscraper, so vehemently celebrated by the futurist Fortunato Depero.[25] Whereas women can translate themselves into the clothing of masculinity, men follow an imperative not to cross-dress, for such a transgression would irreversibly destroy their masculine appearance. Yet in comparison with women, men have a greater chance to experience flying in the first person, as pilots. It is ironic, however, that androgyny applied to transportation is more transitional—that is, reversible—for women than for men, because women, who are the most transitional in their fashions, are also less mobile in society. And mobility is at the heart of the airplane and the cinema.

On the other hand, the slimming down of the androgynous body is closer to an antianthropomorphic abstract mode than to the Lombrosian, eugenic, procreational expansion of female form achieved through Astrea's gynandry.[26] The latter is a form of biological

The androgynous look in the paintings of Romaine Brooks. Romaine Brooks, *Self-Portrait* (1923). Oil on canvas, 46¹/₄ × 26⁷/₈ in. (117.5 × 68.3 cm.). Smithsonian American Art Museum, Washington, D.C. Photo: Smithsonian American Art Museum, Washington, D.C./Art Resource, N.Y.

reproduction outside industrial production, a reminder of women's ability to give birth by housing another body inside their own. Androgyny is more about suggestions, intuitions, leaps, layers, and hints. Astrea's gynandry, by contrast, celebrates physical might, thus it stands for the massive accumulation of force, expansion, serialization, and incorporation. As a visual form, androgyny would look odd in a populist or colonial or family narrative, in which the emphasis would be on rigid sexual, class, and racial roles. In conjunction with flying, androgyny means leaving one's own heavy shape on the earth in order to experience a metaphysical transition or corporeal transfiguration, to the extreme of masochistic self-effacement and to the point of veering toward the divine. Such a process of self-evacuation is antithetical to gynandry's embodiment. And, in the context of Catholic Italian culture, what could be the cultural model of this bodiless, nonsequential, anti-oedipal leap into abstraction?

Within the Italian visual culture of the silent period, the strongest term of reference available to the more or less androgynous and arabesque-like film diva was the mystical iconography of the baroque. The undulating silhouette-in-jouissance of Bernini's Saint Teresa matched the serpentine line of the art nouveau arabesque as well as the convulsions of the diva's hysterical acting style. In his compilation film *Lyrical Nitrate* (1991), Dutch filmmaker Peter Delpeut manipulates the speed of Borelli's acting style in *Malombra* so that he is able to show with great precision the process of a physical upheaval, which Bernini's sculpture conveys through the draped cloth. It is also interesting to note that a religious subtext of self-denial informs journalist Ester Danesi-Traversari's account of her first flight over Rome. Publishing her impressions in the pages of *La Donna* (1921), she wrote: "Everything seems incredibly small, forsaken, lost during our physical elevation, which nearly resembles a spiritual one. This is perhaps what death is like, death which is always near all of us, but we do not feel it, vibrating as we are from this unparalleled joy of flying."[27]

The Virgin Mary's holy body gets to fly because it is asexual and hence angelic. In this case, masochism as mysticism wins over the fulfillment of sexual desire. It also defeats the dream of flying that Sigmund Freud associated with the discovery of sexuality in the dream work.[28] Danesi-Traversari's remarks are mostly introspective, and she only briefly touches on why the landscape engages her. Even then, her words are more metaphorical than accurate: the smallness of things down there reminds her of how frail mankind is, and her joy, in the end, is like that of a soul traveling toward paradise. In conclusion, the airplane functioned within film culture like a palimpsest object: the film diva was hidden behind its extremes of freedom and death, and Saint Theresa was hidden behind the diva's extremes of self-destruction and love everlasting.

While it is certainly true that the film diva as a cultural type appropriates her outward-directed destructive force from the northern European femme fatale of the nineteenth century, it is also important to remember that crashing during flight could be seen as an odd demonstration of will to power, though one with a negative, masochistic overtone. And in some cases the will to power stored in the airplane fad was an opportunity for the new woman of modernity to express her enjoyment of life and her self-consciousness about a negative agency—a form of active subjectivity notwithstanding. This kind of willful memento mori can be found in Sibilla Aleramo's "Il Mio Primo Viaggio Aereo" (1925). Aleramo, one of the most famous and openly feminist writers in early twentieth-century Italy, described a flight she made in 1920 from Le Bourget airfield, near Paris, to Croydon, a borough of London:

Only three passengers on board: we were three women. . . . The world. Light areas, dark areas. Subdivisions and quasi-childish, elementary categories. Even time is suspended. Light, a huge light. Behind me the pilot, who knows the invisible way. The ship bounces up and down and has its own jarring song, as if it were giving rhythm to whatever we bring into space, our powers and our frailties. . . . The cruel life, life overflowing with bitterness, where justice and transcendence exist, yes, but too often they are veiled by our tears and

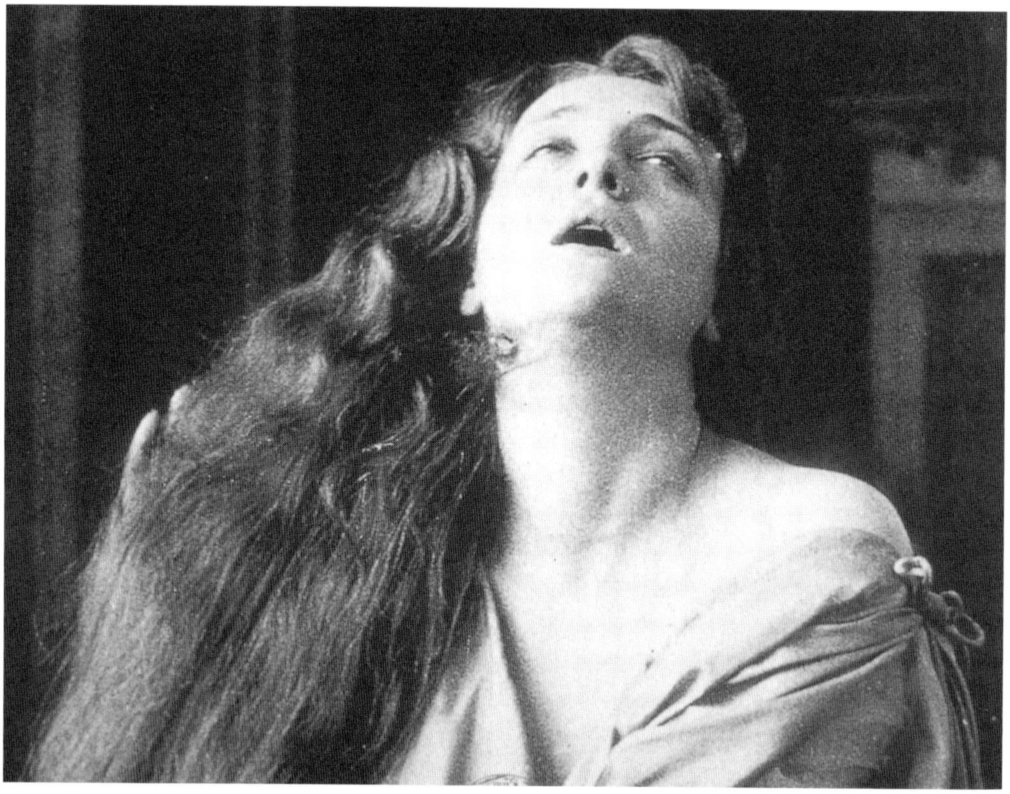

Lyda Borelli in Carmine Gallone's *Malombra* (1917). Courtesy Cineteca di Bologna.

by our fatigues, life on that day, up in the sky, a thing made of air, something that a trifle could have blown away, scatter in the happy, azure mists, without regrets, life was something tenuous but imbued with an infinite grace. . . . Thus, if we cannot be sure about anything, if the most beautiful things, which have just happened, can look like ephemeral figments of the imagination, why should we worry about tomorrow's countenance?[29]

In contrast to Danesi-Traversari's inward gaze and somewhat mournful tone, Aleramo actively enjoys her ephemeral and minimalist landscape. The feminist Italian writer wants to rise above the mundane details of a life based on subordination. She shuns Danesi-Traversari's language of finitude and sublimation and instead celebrates lightness as a form of infinite freedom, seen as the mobile and film-like view of things passing.

Metaphor and Metonymy

The deployment of mysticism as a model of femininity suggests that Italian women struggled to move forward while they dreamt of flying upward.[30] From the point of view of social emancipation, their choice was not much of a choice. In fact, the visual forms available at the time—the grotesque and the arabesque—spelled out two options: either femininity was a nonhuman, almost bestial identity, or it was a flight to a religious heaven, a sort of saintly death.[31] Significantly, the film diva's avoidance of gynandry as figurative enlargement, along with her choice of an-

Gian Lorenzo Bernini, *Ecstasy of Saint Teresa* (1645–1652). Cornaro Chapel, Santa Maria della Vittoria, Rome.
Photo: Scala/Art Resource, N.Y.

drogyny as extreme downsizing, was based on a negative economy of metaphorical replacement through loss, absence, and lightness rather than on a positive, lawful regime of metonymical appropriation through gain, accumulation, and conquest.[32]

To be sure, the oedipal subtext of the tale of Icarus and Daedalus, just like the airplane as seen by Marinetti and D'Annunzio, was a metonymical way of mastering time and space and of claiming a masculine monopoly on modernity. Of course, the metonymic chain includes the airplane, which was an extension of the cinematic mobilization of looking. But, because of her operatic and consequently premodern roots, the diva's iconography of flying was neither compatible with modernist technological metaphors nor applicable to metonymies about twentieth-century industrialization. Borelli's jupe-culotte in *La Memoria dell'Altro,* for instance, was an extension of the male pilot's outfit brought to the female body, but it became fashionable because it also recalled the traditional Pierrot costume from the premodern days of the commedia dell'arte. The jupe-culotte established itself as an acceptable garment for women's daily wear, and not just for female pilots, because it was the most skirt-like pair of pants conceivable at the time. This argument finds confirmation in *L'Histoire d'un Pierrot* (1914), a story with a subtext of lesbian love between Leda Gys (as Lisette) and Francesca Bertini in the title role, elegantly wearing the jupe-culotte. Except for the death of Lisette's beloved bird, there is no other avian reference in this pantomime staged in a timeless arcadian setting. The bird, however, plays a crucial role in the narrative, for its death marks the crisis in the marriage of Lisette and Pierrot. Hence, the bird can be seen as a veiled metaphor of sexual flight splitting the two characters.

On the whole, the theme of femininity in flight amounted to an utterly antitechnological, quasi-therapeutic imagery of veils, feathers, and butterflies, of the winged sphinx and the rising phoenix. Even in Gustave Moreau's famous painting of Salome (1876), a major source of inspiration for the cruel femme fatale, she has a pair of little wings attached to her feet as she dances on tiptoe for Herod (see page 80). The following example about the reinscription of aerial iconography into a premodern register is meant to further demonstrate the continuity of aerial imagery from orientalist fin de siècle painting to early Italian cinema. Toward the end of Giovanni Pastrone's *Tigre Reale,* Countess Natka (Pina Menichelli) lies dead. While her lover mourns the beautiful Russian aristocrat, a huge fire breaks out in the Grand Hotel, where the couple was having their secret and final tryst. The flames invade the screen, and for a while everything seems lost; the flames seem to predict the lovers' condemnation to hell. And yet a utopian fantasy of romantic love prevails at the end. It becomes clear that, just like Shakespeare's Juliet, the diva only appeared to be dead—the effect of a special drug. Reborn like a phoenix, the bird of eternal youth, she rises again and embraces her mate.

This premodern, fantastic approach, of course, ranges from the arabesque to the grotesque extreme. Pina Menichelli's bizarre owl-like headdress in Pastrone's *Il Fuoco* (1915) and Ida Rubinstein's vulture-like motions as Basiliola in *La Nave* (1921) show how the arabesque of birds flying out into the freedom of an abstract design can turn into the grotesque incorporation of birdlike features, expressed by the strikingly elongated body of

Drawing for Baldassarre Negroni's *Histoire d'un Pierrot* (1914), with Francesca Bertini and Leda Gys. Author's collection.

(right) Leda Gys. Author's collection.

Basiliola, the ultimate superthin vamp and killer of men. Likewise, Menichelli, in *Il Fuoco*, seems to emerge out of the bushes like a predatory bird. In *La Nave*—a monotone and nationalistic tirade directed by D'Annunzio's son, Gabriellino—Rubinstein, the famous Russian dancer, is all beak and bony arms and legs, her body as angular as the arrows she uses to kill a group of scantily clad, sexy male prisoners trapped inside a pit. Their frenzied gestures are competitive and attention seeking. The prisoners' behavior suggests that they both welcome Basiliola's cruelty and beg her for mercy. The sadomasochistic subtext of this scene echoes Rubinstein's famous performance in *Le Martyre de Saint Sébastien* (1911), incidental music by Claude Debussy, a text in which the arrow is an instrument of both pleasure and pain.

In the sequential, teleological increase of metonymy, the airplane is only one element in a long list of new, interrelated inventions, including the cinema. Metaphor, instead, requires the erasure of one image (woman, for example), which is in turn replaced by or transformed into another (the butterfly). The butterfly stands for the flight into a new sense of self. Here, the butterfly is an alternative to or substitute for the airplane because the new technology is not easily accessible to women. This is to not say that metaphor and metonymy are unrelated, but metaphor emphasizes a mental twist conducive to metamorphosis at the expense, if need be, of logical, consecutive development; metonymy underscores a historically grounded linear movement from one stage to the next. Veils, feathers, and butterflies do not mark a logical

Romaine Brooks, *Esquisse d'Ida Rubenstein* (1912). Smithsonian American Art Museum, Washington, D.C. Photo: Smithsonian American Art Museum, Washington, D.C./Art Resource, N.Y.

progression from one stage to the next; they are only exchangeable and equivalent aerial images. With metaphor, imaginative, analogical associations win out over the causal, rational links of metonymy. In a word, premodern iconography fulfills wishes for achievements that are still unattainable, even in the modern present.

One very complex antimodern or premodern example of aerial imagery used as a metaphor for children's toys occurs in Carmine Gallone's *Maman Poupée* (1919), starring his wife, the diva Soava Gallone. In this film, the diva plays an unhappily married woman who draws comfort from her children's miniature world of little houses, streets, rivers, lakes, and villages. By mimicking a human universe, the miniature scale of the toys is also the way things look from the pilot's cockpit as the airplane surveys the land below. As long as the modern technology of flight is linked to childhood and the imaginative power of a children's garden party, Maman Poupée enjoys the aerial point of view. In Gallone's *Maman Poupée,* the toylike, miniature village is replaced by the real size of people and things when the observer's feet are on the ground. Yet this abrupt return to a human scale happens exactly when Maman Poupée spells out her predicament as an unhappy wife caught in the drudgery of domesticity. She becomes a moving life-size doll. An old-fashioned technology often used or depicted by artists from the sixteenth to the eighteenth century, the automaton as a sort of sculpture in motion fits Maman Poupée, who turns into a metaphor of overwhelming private despair. By contrast, her previous aerial point of view of the children's miniature world stands for a utopian, but only temporary, space of innocence and play.[33]

In *Maman Poupée,* Gallone's iconography is doubly misogynistic because the airplane is a positive image but an unviable one for an adult woman, and because the automaton is an outdated technology that discloses the wife's problems in her present life. In either case, whether in scenes taking the aerial point of view or in the automaton sequence, Gallone's approach is metaphorical and associational, poetic rather than expository. It is as if the director's choice of iconography, whether futuristic or premodern, is at odds with the possibility of linear narration. By virtue of the chiasmatic structure of her negative associations with technology, Maman Poupée's predicament indicates that both the future and the past are arrayed against the female protagonist in the present.

The diva film's metaphorical rerouting of the future into the past, however, is a two-way street that can also become a bypass around modernity as present history for the sake of a postmodern visionary approach. This is why a scenario of postmodern utopian rebirth through premodern imagery appears at the end of Nino Oxilia's *Rapsodia Satanica*. At the end of this film, Borelli imitates the famous American dancer Loie Fuller. She wears a long loose-fitting dress made of gauzy material with wing-like sleeves. Instead of looking like a phoenix, she brings to mind a newly born butterfly emerging out of a constricting cocoon. A small figure in the distant background, she walks through the huge door of her villa. Framed by the camera from below, Borelli's size gradually increases as she moves forward toward the beginning of a new day, a new identity beyond history. She has regenerated herself into a third being, an alternative to the previous two stereotypes: the evil seducer who is young, sexual, and dangerous, and the aging diva who is grotesque and full of anger at her inability to defy time. Here Borelli is no longer a stereotype. She is not just "woman" any more, but has become a person in full—and also a paradox, a person with no body, no weight.[34]

What can studying the silent film diva in the light of the new woman and the airplane teach us about the history of visual forms such as the arabesque and the grotesque—some of them leaning toward metaphor, others toward metonymy—and their relation to processes of historical change? In this essay, the curve of art nouveau, of the airplane, of the diva's acting style is nothing but a form of replacement, an imaginative twist of mind usually called metaphor, a looping outline of substitutions set against the step-by-step sequence of metonymies, of chronologies, and of stories in search of a final goal for the male hero. The curve as metaphor is the only possible revitalizing and rewriting force of the Icarus myth, for the wing itself curves during flight. A new Icarus replaces the young dead son and the wise old father, thus enabling the airplane's popular success among men and women at the turn of the century. And this new Icarus, neither father nor son, is also the secret airborne messenger of women's hopes for the future, for a time of new roles outside the realm of the patriarchal family and oedipal genealogies.

Historical changes in gender roles are hardly ever exclusively linear, generational, or oedipal—or metonymical in a visual sense. That is, they rarely happen as a singular, direct transit from old to new. Rather, linear change is often mixed with transformations and transfigurations, so that the figurative element, or the normative unit of measure, is taken over by abstraction or by some kind of antilinear rerouting to the point that space and time become interchangeable. This rerouting, then, is made of replacement images or metaphors, together with development images or metonymies. But the replacement image is more powerful than any other image, for it is about the disintegration of earthbound labyrinths, and it enjoys the utopian circularity of the so-called heavenly spheres. In other words, it is comparable to the metaphysical presence of an absence, and as such, it is like an ephemeral, extracorporeal leap forward into a lingering shadow left behind by the past.

Notwithstanding the imaginative power of metaphors, the vertical air-bound yearning of the modern Italian experience found in the

Lyda Borelli's dance of the veils in Nino Oxilia's *Rapsodia Satanica* (1917). Courtesy Cineteca di Bologna.

diva's curvilinear acting style is only the initial stage of a much longer and more difficult liberating process that was not to take place in its entirety. In comparison with the futurists' visionary leap into some kind of reinvented cosmos, Asta Nielsen's use of the vertical line in her acting style endowed the female image on-screen with depth and interiority at the basic level of daily life. Furthermore, the Danish film star did so in ways so explicit and profound that the Italian diva's shifty silhouette could only invoke but never match Nielsen's psychological intensity. In the diva film, because of a confusion with mystical upheaval and utopian yearnings, the theme of verticality lost its élan vital, yet it acquired a radicalism more in tune with a regressive loss of self into suffering and anger.

History and Analysis

Acting

PROSTITUTION, VERTIGO, CLOSE-UP

The most famous supporter of the equations across acting, deception, and femininity was Cesare Lombroso, who wrote: "Women have something close to what might be called an instinct for lying. Caught at something unexpected, they start concocting a lie. . . . Their first move, even when they are not guilty, is to dissimulate. This is so organic that they are unaware of it, and they are never able to be entirely sincere. Unconsciously, all are a little false."[1]

Before linking prostitution with acting, it is crucial to mention that brothels were legal in Italy until 1958.[2] France outlawed prostitution in 1946, England in the 1880s, and the United States in the 1910s. In the wake of the widespread prejudice that femininity amounted to an arsenal of acting-based deceptions, several film training schools made money from women eager to access the new industry and to develop some legitimate credentials. These schools promised professional training while reassuring the female applicants of the institutions' morality. Yet the advertisements did all this in a language that was so ambiguous and laden with innuendo that one wonders who was really behind these flourishing businesses. Did these schools employ truly devoted teachers who could offer modern women a career path, or were these teachers nothing but white-slave traders in disguise, ready to take advantage of naïve and ambitious girls?[3]

As early as 1896, prostitution and sexually transmitted diseases were considered the key factor in weakening and leading adult Italian males astray. This argument was even used to explain the Italians' defeat at Adwa. Historian Mary Gibson demonstrates that around 1915, *prostitute* was a misleading label. More often than not, the so-called streetwalker was simply an unaccompanied woman taking a walk on a street or, worse, someone obliged to live in the street for lack of a better alternative. Many women labeled prostitutes in the official records were simply unemployed or homeless. Of course, these same women were well on their way to becoming real prostitutes, permanently or temporarily. Some would also alternate domestic service in middle-class families with prostitution.[4]

In *La Storia di Una Donna,* for example, Pina Menichelli plays an orphan girl who is the paid companion of an old lady whose son leads a life of debauchery and womanizing. Slowly but surely, he seduces the naïve orphan. Persuaded that he will marry her, she becomes pregnant. This kind of situation happened most frequently in diva films and in daily life. Gibson, for example, points out that by 1906 premarital sex was common in northern Italy among the lower classes.[5] In *La*

Storia di Una Donna, the old lady throws the young woman out upon discovering her pregnancy, while the son starts courting a wealthier family friend with his mother's approval. After delivering her baby in a convent, the young orphan ends up on the city streets with no job and no home. Seeing her alone for too long a time, the police are about to register Menichelli as a prostitute. All of a sudden, a well-dressed gentleman takes the lost soul under his protection with the full approval of the police. Later on, the honorable protector and his shady friends become Menichelli's pimps, and the diva turns into a cynical and fashionable courtesan.[6]

Romance in the diva film seems to be unthinkable outside women's ability to bear children. Prostitution is often held responsible for the large number of out-of-wedlock children who are abandoned to their fate on the threshold of a church or handed over to peasant families in the remote countryside. In his study of the birthrate in early-twentieth-century Italy, the cultural historian Carl Ipsen has researched children born out of wedlock, orphanages, and all sorts of administrative abuses in the area around Naples.[7] To choose not to have any children at all was as sinful as producing children out of wedlock. Eager to condemn married and single women who rejected their biological role, the symbolist painter Giovanni Segantini (1858–1899) produced *Le Cattive Madri* (1894; *The Bad Mothers*).

As we learn from Reinhold Heller: "These pictures might be interpreted as a warning to the 'new' woman, desiring an independent life, freed from the shackles of marriage and motherhood. The theme of the wicked mothers is borrowed from an Indian poem, *Pangiavahli,* introduced into Europe by German philosopher Schopenhauer and translated into Italian by Puccini's librettist, Luigi Illica. The passage illustrated by Segantini tells of punishment inflicted on women who deny their biological role of motherhood."[8]

The parallel between prostitution and acting goes well beyond the obligation of the theatrical performer and the streetwalker to lead a nomadic life, with no permanent address. According to the Lombrosian Salvatore Ottolenghi in *The Sensitivity of Women* (1896), prostitutes were supposed to be coldhearted creatures with no maternal feelings. Their acting skills were so overdeveloped that they were considered incapable of any authentic emotion.[9] This lack of affect also explains why Ottolenghi argued that prostitutes had a special tolerance for a life of hardship and physical pain. In clear defiance of criminal anthropology's scientific authority, the diva film is much more sensitive to women's plight, and it does not hesitate to show and even display that prostitutes, as well as homeless women, have haunting memories and complex feelings about their male lovers and their offspring.

A working-class woman was likely to become a prostitute if she had no job. A middle-class woman, who did not have to work but could choose to do so in any case, was looked upon as someone overly eager to meet a man and share his space. This cluster of contradictory connotations about personal independence and working, leaving home and compromising one's reputation, becomes the topic of an entire sequence in *La Memoria dell'Altro.* In this film, Lyda, who has sold the last dress remaining from her days of wealth and glamour, dances in a bar. The outrage of such a reference to prostitution is softened when it becomes clear that an honorable intention is behind Lyda's debasement: she needs to make money to pay for medicine for her sick lover. The film spectators, like the customers of the

Giovanni Segantini, *Le Cattive Madri* (1894; *The Bad Mothers*). Oesterreichische Galerie, Vienna. Photo: Erich Lessing/Art Resource, N.Y.

bar, can put their consciences at ease. They look at a sexual dance, but can reassure themselves that it is a wife, or a mistress, who prostitutes herself for a noble cause. This reading is confirmed by the costume Lyda wears during her performance. She is no exotic Salome, but wears a kitchen apron on top of a simple black dress. It is left to the viewer to decide whether this modest clothing is meant to underline her wife-like identity or to evoke the commonly held view that workingwomen are like prostitutes.

The Italian historian Gloria Chianese reminds us that if acting was the profession closest to prostitution, teaching was not far behind; the first generation of female schoolteachers, at the turn of the century, were gossiped about because their work was considered a form of social downfall. Chianese remarks, "Female teachers received notoriously low salaries, often less than those of working-class women. According to authorities, education was a double-edged sword, for reading as well as ignorance could lead to vice."[10]

Francesca Bertini in *Sangue Bleu* (1914; Blue Blood, directed by Nino Oxilia) cooperates with a mime until she slides from the world of philanthropic acting to that of high-class prostitution. A crucial moment in the narrative concerns a parade of posters advertising Countess Mira's performance in the local theater. The procession of images goes by in the street just as Mira runs into the daughter whose legal custody she has lost to her adulterous husband. The young girl nearly recognizes her mother. But Mira quickly covers her face with a black veil and ducks out of the street. This episode not only points to women's condition in modern Italy, but also to the negative reputation of mechanically reproduced images. In "The Poster in Fin-de-Siècle Paris: 'That Mobile and Degenerate Art,'" Marcus Verhagen writes: "The poster was a corrupting presence in the modern environment. . . . It reflected the frenzied pace of urban life, to which it gave an edge of madness as it assaulted city dwellers with a barrage of unsolicited messages. . . . It fueled every desire and ambition and so contributed to the degeneracy of the urban population. Crowds were easily moved by it, as were women and children. . . . The poster was fundamentally pornographic."[11]

By linking a woman's demise to mechanical reproduction, *Sangue Bleu* illustrates the prejudice that beset any aspiring young actress. All these examples from diva films articulate the contradictory roles that a woman may have to embrace during the course of her life. By binding together the prostitute and the actress, as well as the single mother and the prostitute, the diva film spells out to what extent femininity was unthinkable outside artificiality and commerce. On the other hand, by arguing that womanhood is based on the maternal instinct, these films can also reduce femininity to biology. A problem arises when the prostitute is also a mother, as is Lyda Borelli in *Il Fior di Male.* Borelli's double-edged acting style in *Il Fior di Male* is brilliant, for she can combine artificial manners with moments of sincere pathos in ways that Bertini and Menichelli cannot sustain for long without losing the balance between the critical awareness of the cliché and the emotional investment of experiencing it anew. In Borelli's case, Lyda, a prostitute spending time alone by the seashore, walks to a nearby religious tabernacle. Her little geisha-like steps, performed on quite noticeable high-heeled shoes, underline the connection between orientalism, immorality, and feudal walking shoes. On the other hand, Borelli's drooping posture, her thin silhouette, and the precarious equilibrium of each step underline the physical and mental struggle of a woman with no means, on her own, and at the mercy of others.

To sum up, the discourse about prostitution was symptomatic of the bad reputation hanging over the acting career. Lombroso's double equivalence of acting as a form of prostitution and prostitution as a form of acting conveyed deeply rooted fears about an economic and social order that was changing too fast, especially in regard to the new professional roles available to women. Because she received money from the film industry, the actress was a sort of prostitute who had no authentic emotions. By receiving money from anonymous clients, the prostitute was the lowest kind of actress; she, too pretended to have sensations, and she could reproduce them on command to please her customers about their masculine prowess. This logic of performance and consumption was not too far from the serialization of melodramatic sentiment upon which the diva film counted for its mass appeal.

Bernhardt and Duse: The Rivals

So encrusted with glamour and power is the word *diva* in English that its Italian facet of mater dolorosa is hard to believe. Even more difficult to grasp are the ways in which the Italian diva situated herself in relation to two prima donnas of the theater: Sarah Bernhardt and Eleonora Duse. In comparison with Duse and Denmark's Asta Nielsen, Bernhardt was the oldest star of the theater. Actually she was the inventor of stardom, in the sense that she promoted her name from the stage to every nook and cranny of society, and she did so single-handedly, in a way that anticipated Hollywood's promotion of celebrities. Trained very carefully at the Comédie Française, she developed an acting style characterized by the spiraling use of her whole body, a melodious voice, and a tripartite technique (saying, doing, showing) to produce emotions. Art historian Carol Ockman equates Bernhardt with the serpentine because the spiral's crescendo and decrescendo shapes all of Bernhardt's gestures.[12] This is also why artist Georges Jules Victor Clairin (1843–1919) portrayed Bernhardt's slim figure spiraling from her feet to an incredibly thin waist in the upper half of his portrait of the actress. The overall effect is one of upward-moving energy, power, and youthfulness. Although Ockman dwells on Sarah's morbid taste for death, her basic acting vector—the upward-spinning spiral—is adjustable to Hollywood's teleological view of history as a positive, forward-moving trajectory accumulating climax first and then thinning out into an improved yet cathartic resolution in relation to a previous state.

For her time, without a doubt, Bernhardt was modern. She fought against anti-Semitism, and she masterminded her own career. She had no fear of displaying in public her lesbian orientations, and there was no anticonventional act she was not eager to perform. After the amputation of her leg, she had the ingenuity to design a moving contraption that allowed her hide her handicap, slide around the stage, and continue her acting career. She did not hesitate to link her name to bouillon cubes as well as to lofty causes, as long as the publicity was constant. Her energy, resourcefulness, self-confidence, and courage turned her into an inspiration for all modern women. On the other hand, Bernhardt's acting style was based on a model of emotional buildup, which matched a melodramatic model of representation popular during the nineteenth century. Bernhardt infused melodramatic energy into the well-made play. The latter is a complex yet organic text with enough major and minor characters to strike a good balance between psychological depth and social stereotypes, narrative predictability and structural surprises, fatal coincidences and persuasive closure at the end. One of the masters of the thrill-and-chill genre was the French writer Victorien Sardou (1831–1908). He became a close friend of Bernhardt's and his theatrical-novelistic repertoire provided many subjects for diva films. The association between Bernhardt and the well-made play grounds the actress in the nineteenth century, while it also helps us understand that her scandalous choices in real life were even more innovative than her acting style. At any rate, the actress was quick to embrace the new, and this is why she also worked in short films at the end of her career.

It is well known that there was a legendary rivalry between Sarah Bernhardt and Eleonora Duse, who was younger than her French colleague. There also seems to be a critical consensus that, for the theater of her day, Duse's acting style was more modern than Bernhardt's spiral. Indeed, if the serpentine was the French actress's trademark, one would have to say that the horizontal line became Duse's signature. This approach linked Duse's acting from the stage to her performance on the screen. Although Duse's horizontal vector in the theater challenged the hierarchical conventions of high drama, with its major and minor characters, in film the dimension of horizontality did not work as well, perhaps because the theater is based on the real presence of the performers' bodies, whereas in film everything—mechanical as well as psychological—is about perception and projection. This is also why the vertical line addresses much better the intensity of something absent or imagined in comparison with the horizontal vector's reassuring function that everything—there—is really there, concrete and solid.

Although he was thinking about photodynamism, this overlap of projection and

Georges Clairin, *Sarah Bernhardt* (1876). 98.4 × 78.7 in. (250 x 200 cm). Inv. 744. Musée de Petit Palais, Paris. Photo: Bridgeman-Giraudon/Art Resource, N.Y.

verticality was discussed by Anton Giulio Bragaglia, in words that intelligently tie the cinema to the unconscious: "The revelation contained inside the unconscious, namely, that the vertigo is part and parcel of photodynamic vision; and the vertigo . . . contains the primitive and confused form of motion."[13]

In English *vertigo* and *verticality* mean two different things, but the point here is that the cinema invokes a loss of spectatorial control intertwined with the corporeal elusiveness of the performer's body. This double absence is vertigo, and a vertiginous experience involves imagined motion due to an actual fear of heights. To return to the comparison between acting styles, in contrast to Bernhardt's roller-coaster-like trajectory, Duse's horizontality had the impact of a twentieth-century avant-garde choice. Set against the history of modernism in the arts, Duse's flattening of Bernhardt's serpentine can be said to be comparable to John Cage's use of silence in music to question our understanding of what is empty or full, what speaks and what is mute yet eloquent. In Duse's only film, *Cenere* (1916; *Ashes*), the horizontal line underlines her mater dolorosa's passive and painful stance of acceptance. Theater historian Cesare Molinari argues that it was precisely Duse's understated stage acting that made her look much more powerful and deeper than the flamboyant Bernhardt.[14] In fact, within the boundaries of the stage, where the performer must dissolve the body into another living self, Duse's self-effacing and minimalist technique was especially effective in allowing the character to emerge out of small or humble details.

It seems that instead of adapting the same acting formula for all her characters, as Bernhardt did, Duse practiced hours and hours of exhausting autosuggestion in complete loneliness, thus fixating on each role, every time, until she drained herself to exhaustion. Bernhardt projected the image of a powerful woman who was always surrounded by an entourage. By contrast, Duse left behind a perfectionist persona; she was physically frail and mentally restless. Finally, both actresses were sensitive to women's issues and aware of the fact that gender roles were in transition. Bernhardt cross-dressed to perform, whereas Duse did not. On the other hand, the Italian actress started a library and a residence for women involved in the theater in Rome, turning Ibsen's feminism into a long-term personal and professional flag.

Cenere

While it is difficult to imagine Duse live on stage, the cinema enables us to see her at work and in motion. Unfortunately, *Cenere* was not a success. After seven years off the stage, during which she continued to have trouble finding the right parts for her subtle sense of drama, in 1917 Duse decided to work with Febo Mari, using a screenplay based on an adaptation of Grazia Deledda's short novel *Cenere*. According to Cesare Molinari, at this point Duse was also emerging out of a negative professional experience with D'Annunzio, with whom she had been romantically involved for some time and with whom she had planned the development of a theater of the future. After investing a lot of her own money in her own production of D'Annunzio's *La Città Morta* (1898; *The Dead City*), Duse had to face not only a lukewarm reception by the public, but also a sense of loss concerning her impact onstage. Though the actress would choose the least obvious moments to step into the action, it was well known that once she was in front of her public, the intensity of her presence was undeniable. By contrast, in her work with D'Annunzio, Molinari argues, the architectural aspect of the staging became so dominant that the dramatic edge of the entire performance suffered. Duse herself, for example, looked more like a passive hieroglyph inside a larger picture than a living source of action, thought, and feeling.[15]

Cenere spells out the concept of the memento mori that subtends the melancholia of the diva film's visual style. Furthermore, the modest connotations attached to the theme of human finitude underscore how Duse, in clear contrast to Bernhardt's specialization of spectacular death scenes, would typically avoid high-pitched situations for the sake of muffled but nonetheless devastating outcomes.

After shooting *Cenere*, the actress played with the idea of making a couple of films about famous female saints, such as Saint Catherine of Siena (1347–1380) and Saint Angela of Foligno (1248–1309), without, however, reaching any practical result. Still, Duse's filmic orientation toward the lives of female saints is worth mentioning. This direction parallels the mystical component of the diva film as a genre. Duse's fascination with the lives of saints seems to me symptomatic of her uneasiness with the filmic image itself. Unable to separate film from photography as Ricciotto Canudo did, Duse was trying to elevate cinema's mechanical and scientific reputation by combining religion with painting, spirituality with high culture.

Did Eleonora Duse believe in the cinema? The answer is yes and no. William Weaver reports that during World War I she had become an avid moviegoer; she was aware of American theorist Vachel Lindsay's *The Art of the Moving Picture* (1915); she had rejected an invitation by D. W. Griffith to work in Los Angeles; and she had seen Francesca Bertini perform in the filmic version of Sardou's *Odette* (1916), directed by Giuseppe de Liguoro with Alfredo De Antoni, Olga Benetti, and Carlo Benetti.[16] On the other hand, in a letter to Giovanni Papini—probably from the war years but undated, as are nearly all of her letters—Duse writes about looking for the right text for a screen debut. Even before she settled on *Cenere*, her tone was somewhat negative, yet resigned to the march of time and to the unavoidable necessity to confront the new medium:

> *Do you have any time for me? Here, I dare to send you that book which perhaps you do not happen to have handy today. Look at it, page thirty-nine. Every word that says, it sees as well. Sea, silence, movement, and an infinite variety of framings and states of mind. In art, it is impossible to reach the shore other than through these very means. And that monster of the cinema can capture for just an instant something so ephemeral, a palpitation nobody sees and nobody hears, but, which is the key, to make the glass plate move—that palpitation over there, that is the only thing which is truly about us, inevitably ours, because it is about life and life is about that. "Life is not cinema."*
>
> *Of course I know this, but, on the other hand . . .*
>
> *Please let us look at this together. Do not take my courage away as far as going toward that cold [eye] but, it is light after all, how is it, please explain it to me, that the soul (nearly) comes down if for a moment we see it?! Reproduced, one way or another, in front of us, nearly detached from its timeless anguish?*[17]

In her letter to Papini, the actress gives away the real reason for her fears about the cinema: the "cold light" stands for the camera performing a close-up. And Duse profoundly disliked the close-up, keen as she was on an indirect yet passionate representation of inner life.[18] Duse visited the chaotic Cines studios in Rome, but eventually signed with Arturo Ambrosio from Turin. Duse went back to study Giotto's paintings because she envisioned herself acting in a series of *tableaux vivants* evoking that painter's horizontal and simple compositions. Since *Cenere* was set in the area around Nuoro, Deledda's native town, on the remote and primitive island of Sardinia, Duse, with her usual sense of diligence, read the work of ethnographer Francesco Orano about Sardinian folklore. It is also true, however, that since World War I was going on and Duse was afraid of enemy submarines, she never sailed to Sardinia. As a result, *Cenere* was shot in Tuscany, Liguria, and Piedmont. Despite adjustments for the mountainous landscape, there are ways in which the ethnographic style of Deledda's *Cenere* stays on in Mari's filmic version. Most importantly, the use of objects in the film echoes the class and gender issues of the diva's genre.

To begin with, Duse, along with various extras in regional costumes, adopts peasant garb—to the extent that, at one point, she throws a shawl over her head with the mindless ease of a local woman who does this automatically every time she goes out. She also gives her son a local amulet, called a *rezzetta,* to protect him from danger. By preferring the long shot, Duse turned the few up-close medium shots of her worn-out unmade-up facial features into stunning moments of introspective power. Again, her dislike of the up-close medium shots was not based on vanity, but on her reservations about the cinema's surgical power.[19] While she is looking at her son, her grey hair and shining eyes convey the intensity of a mother's love with such extreme sobriety that Febo Mari's acting, by comparison, looks old-fashioned and artificial.

Cenere relates to the women's issues explored by the diva film also because Deledda's story deals with pregnancy out of wedlock. *Cenere* is about a family triangle: Rosalia (Duse), an unmarried woman who gives birth to a son and is ostracized by the community; Anania (Febo Mari), the young son whom Rosalia decides to give to her former lover so that the child might have a better future; and Margherita (Misa Mordeglia Mari), Anania's school friend. She becomes his mate for life, but she also prevents him from giving shelter to his old and destitute mother. From this partial plot summary, it is easy to see that the triangle is hardly a threesome, since the screen time given to Margherita is minimal. More significant is the theme of a weak young son in comparison with a hardly visible but strong father, shown only once, as a laborer pushing a circular machine to grind olives. The combination of an overwhelming and anguished maternal figure with a son living in the shadow of a brutish male parent fits right into the diva-film genre.

From this tragic plot structure, additional tropes of the diva film stand out. The theme of a rivalry between two women, Rosalia and Margherita, is in line with the genre; the younger woman's becoming a sort of new, surrogate mother, from whom Anania seeks guidance, also reconfirms the strange dynamics of power and subordination involved in the type of the mater dolorosa combined with a weak son. In agreement with this trope of feminization of the male protagonist, Anania suffers deeply from the trauma of having been separated from his mother at an early age. His sensitive and intuitive nature makes him prone to hallucinations, forebodings, and inklings of all sorts about Rosalia. In her son's imagination, she appears like a dark shadow climbing the wall below his open window, a *mal ombra* stretching out her hands, her fingers and arms monstrously lengthened by the angle of the sunlight beating harshly on the rough stones. The strange telepathy depicted through the intercutting between mother and son is comparable to a key scene in F. W. Murnau's famous *Nosferatu* (1922). There, the vampire's shadow, longing for a soul mate, is intercut with shots of Ellen stretching her arms forward into the night.

In comparison with the affectionate but asexual interaction between Anania and Margherita, the bond between Rosalia and Anania has a level of intensity more appropriate to a love story than to a family reunion. Without a doubt, in *Cenere,* Duse is repeating the melodramatic cliché of innumerable diva films written by much less prestigious authors than Grazia Deledda, who was awarded the Nobel Prize in 1926. It is also true, however, that Duse in *Cenere* is simply Duse, once again at her best in her self-absorbed and absorbing theatrical approach. Yet she is displaced in relation to the constitutive specificity of the new medium. In fact, the theater is about making the actor absent for the sake of the character, yet allowing these two beings to inhabit one body together. At first sight it would seem that the theater is a medium in which this duality leads to depth. The cinema by contrast is a medium doomed to a certain superficiality, with neither body nor depth, because both actor and character are only shadows. Especially at that time, the cinema was considered to be either the art of movement, exteriority, and superficial change, or the art of ghosts, the medium of the living dead, and of occult powers.

As literary historian Kristen Grimes has brilliantly explained, the horizontal organization of the shots allows mother and son to share the same space while it also covers over the depth of their estrangement. On the one hand, Duse's horizontal style of acting underlines a space that cements the community. On the other hand, her flattening stance intersects with a vertical line, either when it is necessary to underline class differences between her and her son or when her ejection by her son becomes Christian martyrdom. At the end of *Cenere,* the dark shadow of Rosalia's coffin forms a cross with the vertical street leading to the graveyard. A comparable indication that the vertical line is something alien to Rosalia: at the beginning of *Cenere,* Rosalia sits on a wall that runs parallel to the frame, and holds the child in her arms. A river flows behind the wall. Together, stone and water reinforce the parallel lines of mother and son running along the picture plane. This use of the performers' bodies in space shows two lives that unfold in parallel. However, once Rosalia has come to her decision, she holds the child up above herself and the wall, thus signaling that the achievement of upward social mobility for the son requires separation from her.[20]

Just as horizontality underlines the passage of time without significant changes at the level of class structure, clothing is used to signify how Rosalia's personal situation worsens instead of improving. In her excellent reading of *Cenere,* Grimes notes that despite the village community appearing to be based on closeness and support, Rosalia is dishonored forever by her pregnancy. Always isolated, she looks like an outcast, doomed to suffer for her sin and to perish over time. The second part of the film begins with the following intertitle: "In the following years Rosalia starved and lived in misery." Grimes continues:

We see Rosalia's s face for the first time: *she is old and dressed completely in black. In the opening*

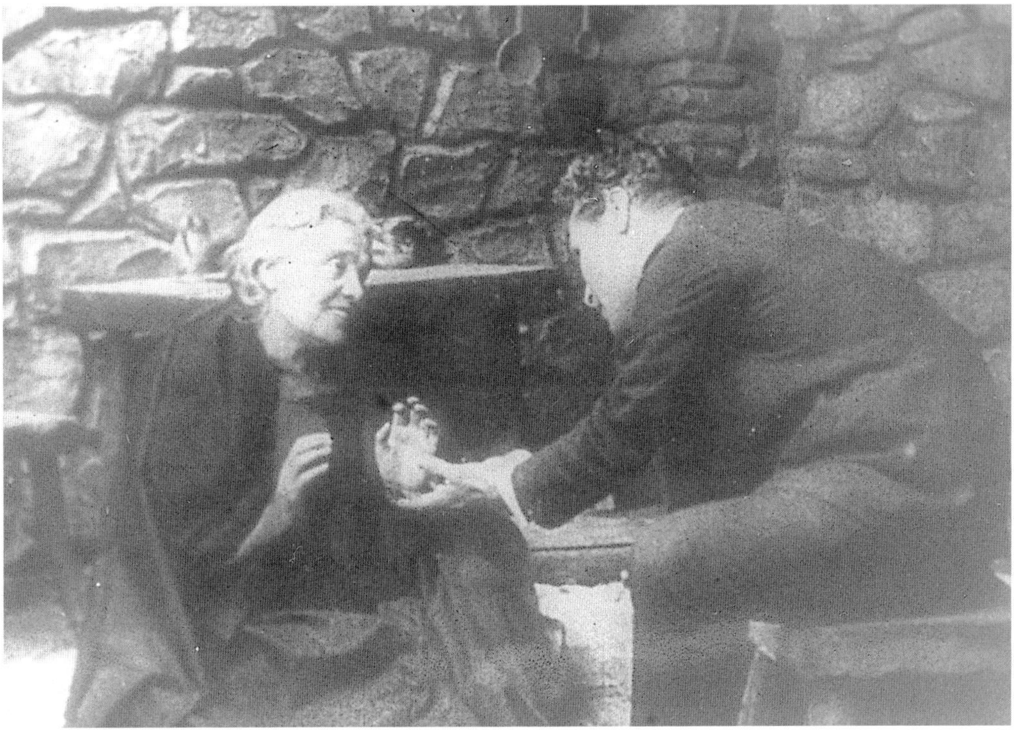

Eleonora Duse in Febo Mari's *Cenere* (1917). Courtesy Cineteca Nazionale, Rome.

scene she had worn a white kerchief on her head. Now this kerchief is replaced by a dark cape. The low angle shot from Rosalia's perspective underscores her humble status. She sits alone on the ground against a stone wall. This image recalls the first scene of the film when Rosalia sat upon the same wall with her little son. The deliberate change in Rosalia's physical relation to the wall indicates her deteriorated situation. Rosalia's poverty is further emphasized through an additional horizontal element; she contemplates an old badly torn stocking, stretching it out to form a line in front of her, symbolic of her worn-out condition.[21]

Mater dolorosa, mysticism, horizontality, the links between cinema and painting—all these elements throw light on the reasons why *Cenere* can be considered a diva film, even though it involves a towering figure from the theater who shied away from center-stage glamour. These same elements also account for Duse's failure in the cinema, even though her feminist and patriotic activities in real life brought her much closer to the emancipationist ideals associated with the new woman of modernity. Despite the ups and downs of her career, Duse became a legend, but her acting required the physical proximity of a live audience and the use of real time.

Miming and Camp

Since Lyda Borelli was the oldest of the major film divas, it is not surprising that she was the one most influenced by Duse's acting style. As a matter of fact, they even performed together onstage in 1905.[22] Theater historian Jolanda Hawkins remarks: "In one year Italy was besieged by the chattering buzz of the Dusettes, who scratched their heads, bit their fingers, kicked their legs about, pirouetted, hoping to assimilate her [Duse's] power of revelation, by foolish counterfeits of external attitudes."[23]

Even Lucio D'Ambra's strange oxymoron for his charming little film about a daughter's rebellion and a woman's creativity, *L'Illustre Attrice Cicala Formica* (1920; The Illustrious Actress Cicada Ant), with Lia Formia, can be used to understand the ways in which public opinion perceived—sometimes together, sometimes separately—Duse's and Borelli's overlapping repertoires of gestures. Duse was the silent worker—D'Ambra's *formica* (ant), so to speak—the publicity-shy actress, the laborious professional who rejected fancy backstage visitors. Borelli, instead, was comparable to the cicada. The younger actress amplified and complicated Duse's technique into a much faster and more fluid style in which microgestures followed one another continually, at amazing speed. Thus, Borelli's acting style came to resemble how the cicada's voice lulls the mind into reverie during long hot summer afternoons.

Lia Formia. Author's collection.

In the aftermath of the "Dusettes" came the verb *borelleggiare,* that is, to imitate Borelli in real life. Film critic Antonio Baldini cites the 1917 edition of Alfredo Panzini's *Dizionario Moderno* to explain the term: "Young women fussing and moping around, in the manner of the beautiful Lyda Borelli's gratuitous and aestheticizing poses. Borelli, in turn, developed her range of attitudes out of Duse's acting style. Borelli's and Duse's two feminine ways of being frivolous and graceful have disappeared with the increasing masculinization of women."[24]

In contrast to Duse, who had a passion for simplicity and spirituality in painting, Borelli injected more erotic allusions into her style. Art historian Robert de la Sizeranne explains the links with Pre-Raphaelite painting: "Heads seem to bend just a little too much, in order to meditate; the arms twist themselves sometimes more subtly than is necessary, in order to produce an unexpected gesture; to draw new expressions out of the human body, they look like the branches of fruit trees obliged to take on strange poses along their supporting fences. The desire to intensify the most minute of feelings sometimes becomes an obsession."[25]

Another way that Borelli called attention to the elusive nature of female sexuality was by modeling her motions on the discontinuous prose of D'Annunzio. In his novel *Forse Che Sí, Forse Che No,* for example, the writer plays with words in such a way that the moving female body inside the clothes produces an impression of androgyny: "Her body, too, was deceiving, nearly duplicitous, as if it had been simulated and disclosed within an ongoing tale. Now she would go up, step by step, with such supple movements that they seemed to lengthen her legs, slim her hips, thin out her waist; she was slim, slender, as fast as a young boy trained to race."[26]

For Borelli, acting was clearly a tightrope-walking act between naturalism and expressionism, and this thin balance degenerated into the grotesque only in her most operatic moments of desperation. A case in point is Marina's consumption of a meal before killing Silla at the end of *Malombra.* Borelli's facial expressions disfigure her as she uses a knife like a weapon and her gaze is lost in the void. Baldini is correct in calling Borelli's moves "frivolous" and in describing Duse as "graceful," since the younger actress was eager to underline her cultural sources. By contrast, Duse's approach was based on thinning out the melodrama while intensifying the dilemmas affecting a being whose vulnerable condition was based on having been born a woman.

Borelli's premeditated use of clichés, however, defies the idea of a shallow beauty eager only to look cultured, elegant, or alluring. At the very beginning of *Il Fior di Male,* for instance, Borelli holds an adorable cat in her lap while she points her most feline expression toward the camera. Here, the actress is miming the Egyptian sphinx while drowning this famous icon of elusive femininity in the banality of a domestic space shared with a pet. It is not an exaggeration to say that Borelli is engaging in a camp deconstruction of the cliché. The sphinx-like pose was used by women to poke fun at men's dead-end interrogation of female desire and the female mind. Besides Borelli's, two additional, truly amusing examples come to mind: an image of Ida Rubinstein as she appeared in the ballet *Scheherazade,* and a reenactment of the sphinx performed by the American wife, Mary, of the painter Franz von Stuck (1863–1928). This decadent-symbolist artist made a fortune by depicting women as threatening, bestial creatures. The idea that von Stuck's homely Mary from the New World poses in the nude and mimics her husband's misogynistic clichés is hilarious and liberating, to say the least. In short, miming a sphinx-like pose in Borelli's day was already an ironic form of camp instead of a naïve act of kitsch imitation.

It is easy to discuss Borelli's acting because most of her films from 1913 to 1918 have survived. By contrast, it is practically impossible to say anything specific and deep about Pina Menichelli's style. Most of her films, a large number of titles from 1912 to 1923, have perished or have not yet been recuperated. We can note only that thanks to Salvador Dali's famous quote, Menichelli acquired a diabolical reputation: "In those days characterized by such a violent eroticism, palms and magnolias were bitten off and devoured by these women whose frail and sickly look did not rule out corporeal shapes thriving on a feverish and precocious youth."[27]

In addition, Menichelli worked with an impressive number of strong directorial personalities (Oxilia, Genina, Ruggeri, Guazzoni, Martoglio, Palermi, Negroni), who are likely to have influenced her performance just as much as she may have directed her male directors into new paths. Borelli's work is most famous for its see-through structure or lace-like glimpses of spirituality and coyness, dreamy eroticism and physical loss of control. Were we to compare Menichelli with Bertini, whose acting style falls somewhere between

Ida Rubenstein in *Scheherazade* [*MGZEA #3]. Jerome Robbins Dance Division, New York Public Library for the Performing Arts. Astor, Lenox, and Tilden Foundations. Photo: Druet.

the aristocratic and populist registers, the former might emerge as the strongest tongue-in-cheek comedienne of the three major divas. But this argument would require an in-depth recovery of Menichelli's lost films.

In the end, no actress and no critic would ever question the technical and psychological superiority of Asta Nielsen's acting. She was not only more modern, but her work was also different from the Italian approach based on plasticity. To be sure, the general acting style of Italian divismo was based on the curve, while the Danish star avoided this aspect of art nouveau. Instead, she chose to articulate the twentieth-century sensibility through verticality, namely, vertigo about the never-ending and ever-moving continent of a woman's interiority.

Asta Nielsen and the Vertical Line

Like Bernhardt and Duse, Asta Nielsen was trained in the theater, but in clear contrast to those colleagues, she was the only prima donna in Europe who incorporated into her acting technique a deep understanding of cinematic specificity in conjunction with an explicit feminist consciousness. As a theater actress, Nielsen was strong enough not to let herself be intimidated by the camera's mechanical recording eye and the editor's cuts. As a film actress, she brought to the camera such a strong sense of presence that she was able to let her movements speak through her self-crafted on-screen image and dominate the fragmentation of each cut on the editing table. Instead of losing herself in these pieces,

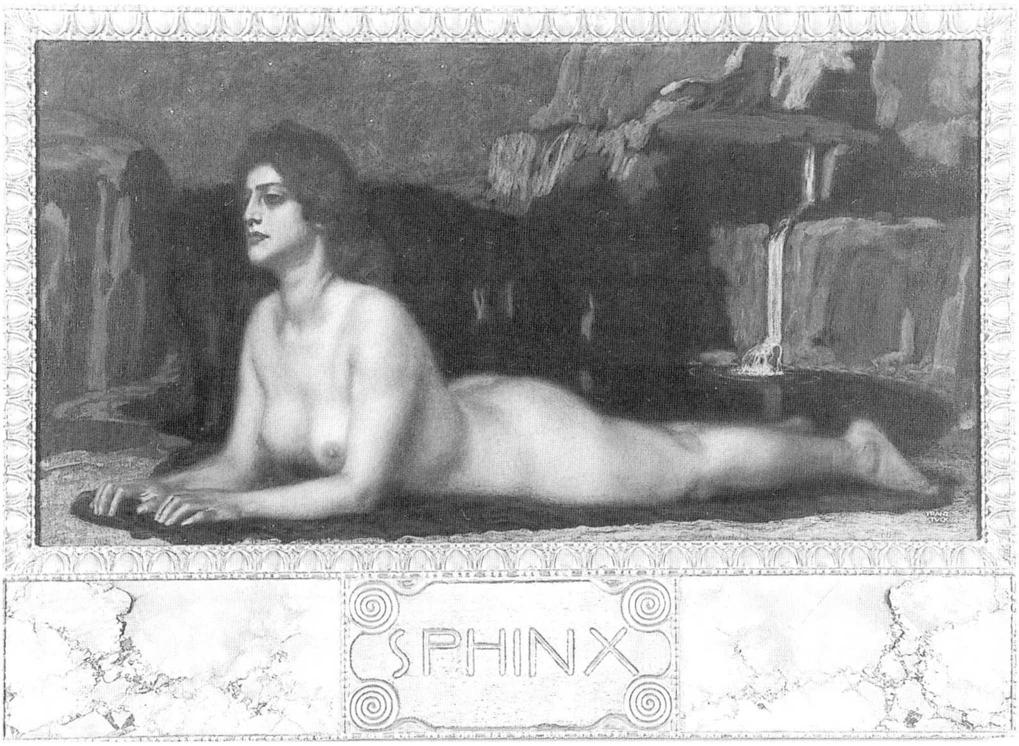

Franz von Stuck, *Sphinx*, with Mary von Stuck (1904). Oil on canvas, 32.7 × 61.6 in. (83 × 156.6 cm.). On loan from the Federal Republic of Germany. Hessisches Landesmuseum, Darmstadt.

Nielsen used the continuous vertical line of her body to articulate her characters' inner selves. She understood that in film the most important issue for a performer is to make visible the invisible, even though the medium may seem to work better on external reality than on internal states. Hallucinations, dreams, flashbacks—all the operations of the mind can be powerfully rendered through film, but precisely because the screen is comparable to an extension of the viewer's brain, it takes almost nothing to tip the balance between inside and outside the wrong way, leaving only a fall into artificiality or excess.

Which spatial dimension would be most suited for acting in film? The horizontal vector may seem to be about equality, and the vertical may invoke ideas of domination and subjection, but horizontality is also linked to measurable and controllable space and to gravitationally bound movement on the earth. By contrast, the vertical line has no beginning and no end. It is suggestive of the unknown above and below human experience, the heaven of utopian visions and the whirlpool of the unreachable unconscious. The clouds above and the instincts below escape stable shapes and change in ways that are not far from the ever-shifting flow of images in the cinema. In other words, there is something about the vertical line that points toward the abyss of human nature, while its direction toward the sky may signify elevation, rebellion, and abstraction. But why is the vertical line so profoundly cinematic?

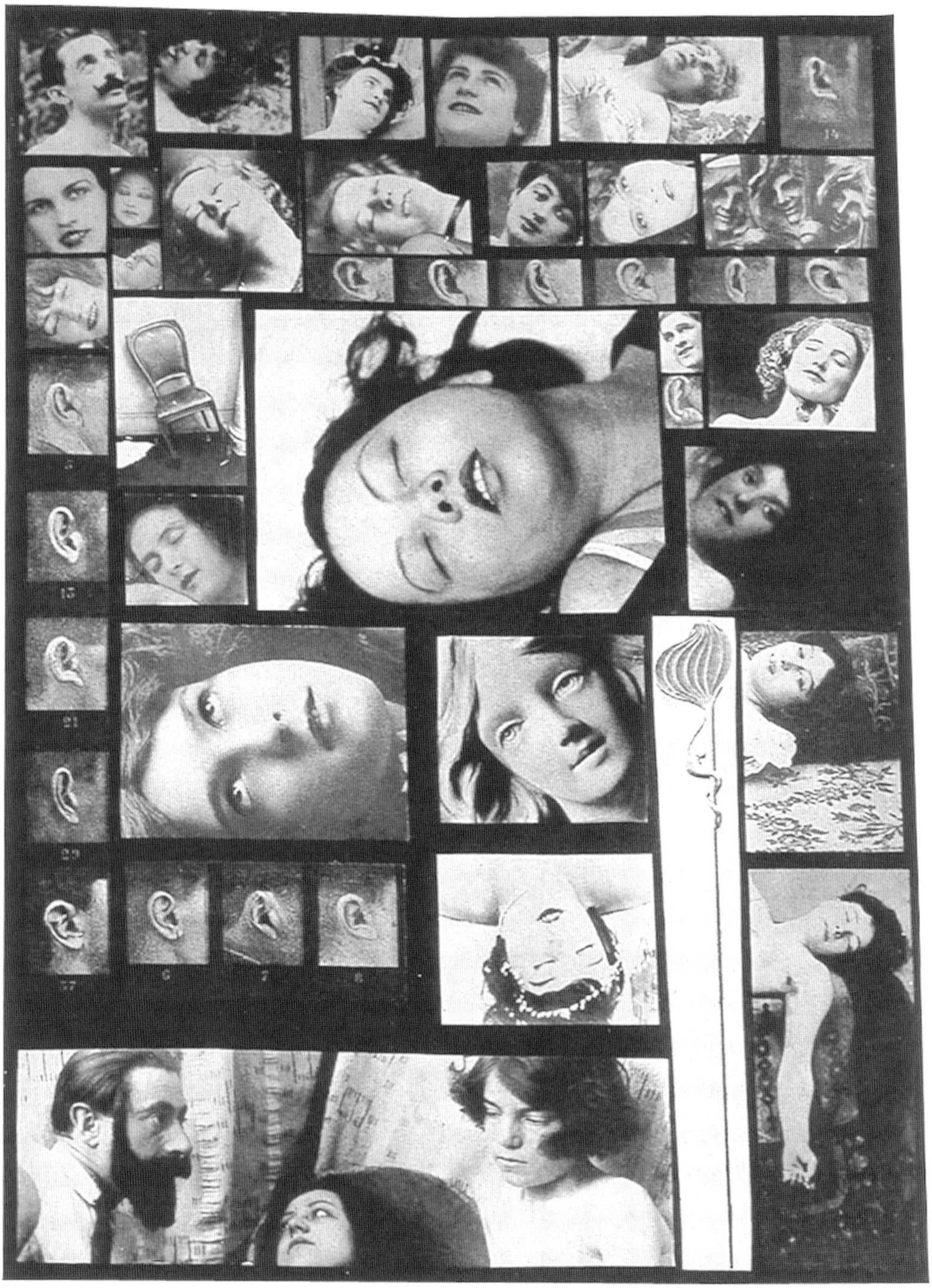

Salvador Dali, *Phenomenon of Ecstasy* (1933). Photo collage. © 2006 Salvador Dali, Gala-Salvador Dali Foundation/Artists Rights Society (ARS), N.Y.

To be sure, in his *Un Pioniere del Cinema Scientifico: Roberto Omegna, 1876–1948* (A Pioneer of Scientific Cinema), film historian and filmmaker Virgilio Tosi compares the screen to a white sheet hanging so as to underline height, while width remains unmentioned.[28] Furthermore, in a 1930 letter to Marinetti, written from New York, the futurist designer Fortunato Depero underscores the association of verticality and fast-moving urbanism: "The psychological vertigo is daily rhythm."[29] Finally, as we learn from Papini's rethinking of Bergson in "Philosophy of the Cinematograph," despite its industrial, Tayloristic, and scientific uses, cinema belongs more to mental projection and imagination than to a metonymical and quantitative logic.[30] Its specificity is about being poetic, visceral, erratic, solipsistic, but also in touch with the masses. In other words, the vertigo fits cinema's irrational and collective vocation.

Pina Menichelli in Amleto Palermi's *L'Età Critica* (1909). Author's collection.

Yet the link between verticality and the close-up is what matters most, were we to fully understand Asta Nielsen's acting style. By combining a gigantic and a miniature scale in an oxymoronic arrangement, the close-up itself indicates that cinema is, on the one hand, a human invention for accessing realms alien to the human eye and for making us feel empowered through a technological eye. On the other hand, the cinema also delivers to us an image of how the cosmos sees us down below: small modern beings rushing around with hardly any sense of direction. But there is even more to how the vertical line operates between a way of looking that reverses itself between the microscopic and the cosmic, the human and the alien. This is the case because the rise of the vertical line in acting through Nielsen marked the shift from a nineteenth-century, teleological, optimistic sensibility to a twentieth-century desire for risk, accident, chance, and speed. Meanwhile, modernity's exhilaration undermined faith in objectivity, rationality, predictability, and linear cognition. And this definition of modernity as taking a gamble with one's own destiny, as embracing the vertigo of something or someone unknown, is a precise plot summary of Nielsen's *Afgrunden* (1910; *The Abyss*).

Regardless of these metacinematic speculations, Nielsen publicized her love of verticality by wearing dresses with vertical stripes so frequently that the vertigo of modern life based on speed and desire became her personal fashion trademark.[31] In contrast to the clichés of the nineteenth-century vamp, Nielsen rejected literary and pictorial acting models and became the first actress to develop a clear equivalence on-screen between female desire and simple movement. Her desire for self-fulfillment as a woman had the force of a punch, but one seeking pleasure, communication, and intimacy instead of aggression, humiliation, and power. This is why Nielsen is, by far, more original than the Italian diva, who was obliged to remain tied to the clichés proliferating in the visual culture of art nouveau. In the end, Nielsen's acting was both so personal and so compatible with cinema that her performance style became competitive with the cinema itself. Nielsen's talent to combine the execution of any trite movement with an inner sense of herself as a sexual being can be better understood as soon as one looks at the situation of women in Danish culture and at her career trajectory.

Born in 1881 into a working-class family (her father was a coppersmith and Asta worked in a bakery), Nielsen grew up in a society open to increasing rights for women. In 1871, the Danish Society for Women was founded, its primary purpose being to obtain the vote. In 1875, women were admitted to the university. In 1915, Danish women gained full suffrage. As Danish film historian Marguerite Engberg puts it: "This lengthy struggle for equality undoubtedly influenced Nielsen's artistic development and inspired her to portray modern, independent women."[32] In fact, shortly after completing her education, Nielsen chose to raise her child alone as an unmarried mother while she pursued her theatrical career. Very little, however, is known about Asta's daughter, who is barely discussed in Nielsen's famous autobiography, *Den Tiende Muse* (The Silent Muse), published in Copenhagen in 1945.

Motion pictures first appeared in Copenhagen when Nielsen was fourteen. By the time she was eight, she had decided she wanted to become an actress. At age twelve, she gained admission to the school of the Royal Theater of Copenhagen. This same institution had seen the premiere of Henrik Ibsen's *A Doll's House* in 1879. Nielsen's first theatrical steps were not easy, partly because of her androgynous voice and also because of her svelte brunette appearance at a time when stage prima donnas either were blond or tended to look matronly.

Because of her attachment to Ibsen, she was very close to Duse's famous repertoire, and she became known as "the Duse of the North." After traveling in Scandinavia between 1902 and 1908, in a mixed atmosphere of economic uncertainty and professional stagnation, somewhat by accident Nielsen and her soon-to-be husband, the set designer Urban Gad, began to develop a film project. It is worth noting that Gad had never worked in film before, but had some training as a painter. He was the son of Emma Gad, a famous Danish feminist writer and socialite. For these two ambitious theater artists, Gad and Nielsen, this turn to cinema was a choice based on an economic and a creative impasse. And they were not sure about what they were doing. Danish film historian Caspar Tyberg notes that Nielsen expressed strong doubts about the cinema as an art form when the writer Thomas Krag first approached her about it in 1909.[33]

When Gad and Nielsen went into filmmaking, Nielsen's theatrical career was on the line, and she needed a groundbreaking performance more than ever. They made the thirty-seven-minute *Afgrunden* (*The Abyss*), which became an international success and received coverage in all the Italian film trade journals. The making of the film was punctuated by one quarrel after another between Gad and Alfred Lind, the cameraman and the only member of the group with previous filmmaking experience. To make things worse, Lind did not think that Asta's acting style was suited for the camera.

Besides marking the birth of the first European film star, the year 1910 also saw the construction of theaters specifically reserved for showing movies, meaning venues (and audiences) no longer had to be shared with theater, vaudeville, or the fairgrounds. The screen now had geographical and architectural autonomy. Thus, Nielsen and Gad's joint venture coincided with the invention of a special kind of spectatorship for stardom that arose from this new kind of exhibition space.

But what was this hypothetical film viewer of circa 1910 really like, looking at *The Abyss*, a film of enormous emotional impact, long before the refinement of the close-up, the ultimate cinematic technique of psychological upheaval, spatial penetration, and temporal confusion between near and far, small and large? Possibly more research in the history of technology, and in particular of aviation and the perceptual changes brought about by photography, may disclose a connection between the refinement of the close-up in film and the popularization of the aerial point of view.

The pilot's visual range includes the curve as well as the vertigo, but it is based, first and foremost, on the experience of dominating the land below. Just as, in the close-up, it is hard to tell whether something is very large or very small, whether we are seeing well or not at all, when seen from the pilot's cockpit, huge things look like miniature models. At the same time, small ripples in the landscape, indiscernible to an earthbound viewer, become visible for the airborne observer, taking on the appearance of monumental geological formations. This confusion between near and far, big and small, explains why visible cinematic movement relies on verticality to turn a character's invisible state of mind into the corporeal registering of an emotional condition at the level of the spectator.

According to Nielsen, *The Abyss*, like her subsequent films, was carefully planned throughout the cold winter months. The shooting and actual printing was done from spring to summer. Her involvement was total. The historical record confirms that she directed, chose scripts, and wrote the intertitles. In *Die Film Primadonna* (1913, directed by Urban Gad), Nielsen plays herself, a character involved in all aspects of filmmaking. *The Abyss* was released on September 12, 1910, with a premiere at the Kosmorama theater in Copenhagen. Henceforth the cinema became the public space to go to in order to get away from the public, to be alone without feeling either abandoned or utterly excluded from the public sphere.

Male or female, the film viewer was quite different from a member of the theater audience. At the movies, men and women wanted to be touched in secret, to experience extreme intimacy with the human beings on the screen, and yet to be completely separate and isolated from anyone real or fictional. The film viewers of 1910, like those of today, perhaps were seeking intense, even dangerous, human contact from the screen while safely and contentedly watching silent images of light and motion. Right away, even as the cinema's origins coincided with Nielsen's screen debut, the rewards of film viewing were clear: to feel screen movements mobilize the heart and to witness secretly the magic transformation of love into story, of psychology into narrative. The viewers in the dark could sense their own old selves move out toward the screen and slowly change into something else, maybe even into someone they wanted to be,

Scenes from *Afgrunden* (1910; *The Abyss*), with Asta Nielsen. Courtesy Danish Film Institute, Copenhagen.

or to meet. And this idea of fantastic metamorphosis through psychological identification, of transformation into an impossible other, is also a basic definition of cinematic stardom.

As an actress capable of using movement to affect the whole crowd, Nielsen tapped into this secret, very modern, and all-too-human desire for an intensity of feeling that only the cinema could so safely and secretly provide. As a flickering image of light, she was an alien made of shadows and electricity as well as a passing sensation of life pulsing in the dark—one that felt like a kiss, a caress, a scream, or a cry inside the mind. In fact, naturalistic acting in the theater privileged speech over the "natural language of gestures." The latter was an expressive mode that, as it was developed through Nielsen's mute eloquence, film theorist Béla Balázs found cosubstantial with the art of silent film.[34] Especially in silent-film melodramas of the twenties, the power of bodies, faces, and objects could speak more eloquently than literary or theatrical language. For Balázs, the close-up was the quintessential antiliterary, antipictorial, and utterly cinematic technique at the heart of this visual culture of abstraction and empathy. Before the development of film sound, the close-up brought out in bodies, faces, and objects a special kind of voice. It could be heard only in the film viewer's mind, in the guise of an extremely private and yet intelligible level of inner speech.[35]

In contrast to or beyond the verbal precision of the naturalistic stage acting valued in Denmark, the silent gestural approach was inaugurated through Nielsen's talent. She took ballet lessons to develop the expressiveness of her wordless range. Engberg reports that "autosuggestion" was involved in Nielsen's technique.[36] We still know very little about the thoughts of the actress and her peers who took pantomime from the stage to the screen. Yet it is clear that Nielsen spent days preparing a part and that she explicitly valued facial expression and bodily movement. Thus autosuggestion may refer to the deep internalization of a character's pattern, an incorporation into oneself of another's living body, a tricky process of self-transformation through surrendering to a different identity without a loss of self or control: "He is enthralled by *her barefoot freedom to climb over walls and balance on the barrel of a cannon.* And the more he is captivated by the sight of her, the 'truer' her expressive movements become, shaking off any aspect of calculation and becoming filled with devotion" (emphasis added).[37]

Nielsen's ability to transform movement into something as impressive as the yet-to-be-invented close-up is comparable to an actress's repetition of the same sentence with two completely different intonations. And it was precisely this particular voice timbre that the film viewer heard from the screen: a silent but unmistakable call from feelings still inhabiting the unconscious. Significantly, in *The Abyss,* as Nielsen walks on a cannon barrel or climbs from her bedroom window to elope with the cowboy, she is neither a vamp like the American Theda Bara nor a female daredevil like the serial queen Pearl White. And this is because her transformational take on movement is invisible, working from inside the filmic image out into the spectator's mind. This kind of acting produces emotional connections rather than figurative and physical ones. Duse understood and used this process in the theater, but could not properly adjust it to the screen.

A standard definition of the female star is a woman whose beauty or power hypnotizes her viewers into submissive worship without freezing them. But in Nielsen's case, her acting talent protected her from becoming just a seductive object to be looked at, an alluring fetish to be played with, an erotic icon to be consumed, with no personal willpower of her own to contend with. Finally, despite the undeniable visual bonds between silent images and acting movements, Nielsen achieved a strange miracle. She managed to remain simultaneously as unclichéd yet as average as anyone's internal voice or train of thoughts. For example, in *The Abyss,* when she gets off the tram and walks to the café with Knud, the two characters nearly lose their fictional images of male suitor and single female in the anonymous crowd—the same mass of people that could have just streamed out of a newsreel or a movie theater.

As the title, *The Abyss*, suggests, Nielsen falls into a vertigo of sexual desire with Rudolph, a rough cowboy working for the Fortuna circus. By performing a gaucho dance in a skintight black satin dress and twirling around Rudolph, Magda (Nielsen) rejects Knud, the vicar's decent and boring son. Back in the city after her circus escapade, Magda loses her identity as a respectable, educated, self-supporting single woman. Rudolph accidentally meets Magda again while she is working as a maid and prostitute in a beer garden. Blinded by jealousy, the cowboy drags Magda violently around the table, but during their struggle, she kills him in self-defense. The police arrest her, and the film ends somewhat openly, with a long shot of Magda being taken away.

At the time of the film's release, all critics seemed to agree that despite the distance of Nielsen's face from the camera, the final shot vibrated with a unique intensity. Therefore, using her performance in *The Abyss* as a prime example, the question is what, besides her love of vertical stripes, was the secret acting formula that Nielsen used to achieve such an emotional impact on the audience? Many film historians have referred to Nielsen's self-awareness as a professional actress and as a moving body before a static camera. It is indeed this mechanical eye with the unforgiving lens that Nielsen openly addressed by literally playing to the camera as the one and only audience member to satisfy. An anonymous reviewer of Nielsen's films wrote in the *Chicago Record* of 12 February 1925: "The camera is such a truthful instrument that only the most finished emotional acting comes out convincingly on the film."[38]

On the one hand, Nielsen viewed the cinema as the best training device for mimes: they could see their performances on-screen, analyze, correct, and improve themselves. On the other hand, Nielsen believed in complete control and rejected the use of improvisation in acting. Before analyzing in greater depth three key features of Nielsen's acting—verticality, the rejection of literary or pictorial origins, and the overcoming of boundaries imposed by social types or sexual masquerades—it is worth linking the actress as a career woman to Magda's independent character in *The Abyss*. It includes unmistakable references to women's emancipation in contemporary Danish life.

At the film's beginning, for instance, Magda is the music teacher of a young female student. Her profession refers to the fact that since 1876 the Royal Danish Academy of Music had admitted women on equal terms with men. Despite this public statement of equality, artistic careers in music or the theater were still considered slippery choices for women, and much more viable paths for men. After her music lesson, Magda meets a gentleman, Knud, during a tram ride across the city. Without any chaperone, the two end up in a café for a drink. Significantly, we see Magda paying her tab. As in many other Danish films of that period, the couple's first date establishes the story's modern urban environment. On the other hand, Magda's chance encounter with the cowboy from the circus takes place in the countryside. Yet the rural setting is only an interlude. Without doubt, *The Abyss* underlines the connection between city life, public transportation, and changing sexual mores. And the city's motion and commotion was, of course, a source of libidinal energy, one that would account for the association of modern technology with sexual desire, of movement in the street with social change, and of cinema with eros.

Even at only twenty-three minutes, *The Abyss* stands out as one of the first long fea-

Asta Nielsen in *Afgrunden* (1910; *The Abyss*). Courtesy Danish Film Institute, Copenhagen.

ture films. This increase in narrative length allowed Nielsen to develop her character's psychology through an acting style that defied the classical model of timeless, ideal poses, all equally placed on an unchanging horizontal axis. In other words, during her trajectory from stage to screen, Nielsen the perfectionist found a way to transform her painfully sustained technical control into a kind of intuitive mechanical response, equivalent to acting as if she were sleepwalking. To produce a vertical vector of performance in *The Abyss*, Nielsen relied on microscopic and precise gestures distributed up and down her slender figure. At the onset of her film career, she would determine her movements' proper scale and speed by watching herself on-screen. The screen was a mirror she used, now as a performer, now as a spectator, constantly sliding between two sides of the cinematic experience. Her acting encompassed the three separate elements of the cinematic experience: the projector, the screen, and the movie theater. The compatibility of Nielsen's vertical approach with film technology is not a surprise. Since 83 percent of *The Abyss* is in long or medium shot, the film viewer mostly saw Nielsen from head to toe, and only a few shots qualify as close-ups.[39]

Obviously, Nielsen had no idea that *The Abyss* was going to turn her into the first European star overnight. The energy released by

Scenes from *Afgrunden* (1910; *The Abyss*) and *Das Liebes-ABC* (1916; *The ABC of Love*). Courtesy Danish Film Institute, Copenhagen.

its controversial topic, therefore, stems from the actress's and the director's awareness of women's rights. As a result, two themes in *The Abyss*—the rejection of family origins and the overcoming of artistic sources—set the tone for the rest of Nielsen's film career. In contrast to Knud, for example, Magda has no parents. Nielsen continued to choose rootless roles in many other films. Thus, she is a nomadic gypsy woman in *Das Mädchen ohne Vaterland* (1912; The Girl without a Country); a young girl seducing a young man, even though the latter is scared of his father, in *Das Liebes-ABC* (1916; The ABC of Love); a seventeen-year-old daughter born five years before her parents' actual marriage and obliged to behave like a twelve-year-old to appease the community's morals, in *Engelein* (1914; The Little Angel); a single, financially independent business woman in *Die Börsenkönigin* (1916; *The Queen of the Stock Exchange*); a young woman with a sexually haunted past but no binding family ties until she marries a widower, in *Der Reigen—Ein Werdegang* (1920; *The Merry-Go-Round*); and finally, Hannah, whose weak father is unable to protect her from lapsing into vice, in *Die Sünden der Väter* (1913; literally, "The Sins of the Father," released in the United States as both *Regina* and *The Devil's Assistant*).

When these plots and roles are compared to those of Italian diva-films, the impact of the struggle for emancipation is clearly more apparent, as is the absence of the censorship regulating the Italian film industry. In *Die Sünden der Väter,* Hannah models for an emerging young painter with a powerful father figure, or mentor. This film, especially, can be read as Nielsen's manifesto against the old art of painting and, indirectly, in favor of film as a medium sufficiently new to be open to women's issues. Nielsen's stance well fits her cinema's overall antipictorial style of simple sets, ordinary clothes, and a general sparseness of décor. In this respect, the contrast with the pictorial qualities of the Italian diva film could not be stronger.

Briefly, the plot of *Die Sünden der Väter:* Marten, a young painter, finds Hannah, in a striped shirt that shows deep cleavage, entertaining clients in a pub. On the wave of his newly acquired fame, Marten chooses Hannah as his model for a portrait because she looks like the embodiment of misery. While the model poses for the artist in his studio, Marten notices that day after day Hannah's expression slowly shifts from sad to happy. Indeed, Hannah has fallen in love with Marten's gardener, Hans. Selfish and ambitious, the artist makes Hannah drink until the portrait is finished and Hans leaves Hannah, who returns to her miserable life in the pub. On the day that Hannah's portrait is officially unveiled, the young woman finds the willpower to overcome the temptation of alcohol and show up at Marten's studio. Once there, she demands her honorarium as a model. She accuses Marten of having pushed her back into alcoholism for the sake of art, and taking a knife, she defaces the portrait of her past misery. By rejecting painting, Nielsen seems to suggest that cinema is an art with a magic light of hope for women, a sort of beam of what it could be. In downplaying the literary dimension of her theatrical training, she explores how the silence of silent cinema could become a form of expression so powerful that it would impress itself in the viewers' minds with an emotional force superior to that of words.

In *The Abyss,* Nielsen's performance style downplays as much as possible any level of recognizable role playing or trite iconographic appropriation. One exception to her antimasquerading approach is evident in *The Abyss* when Magda ropes in the cowboy by using a lasso, an object that clearly belongs to the visual culture of the American Wild West. Likewise, the fringe on the hem of her outfit resembles that on an Indian squaw's garment. One wonders to what extent the Wild West iconography of *The Abyss* stirred the fashion of

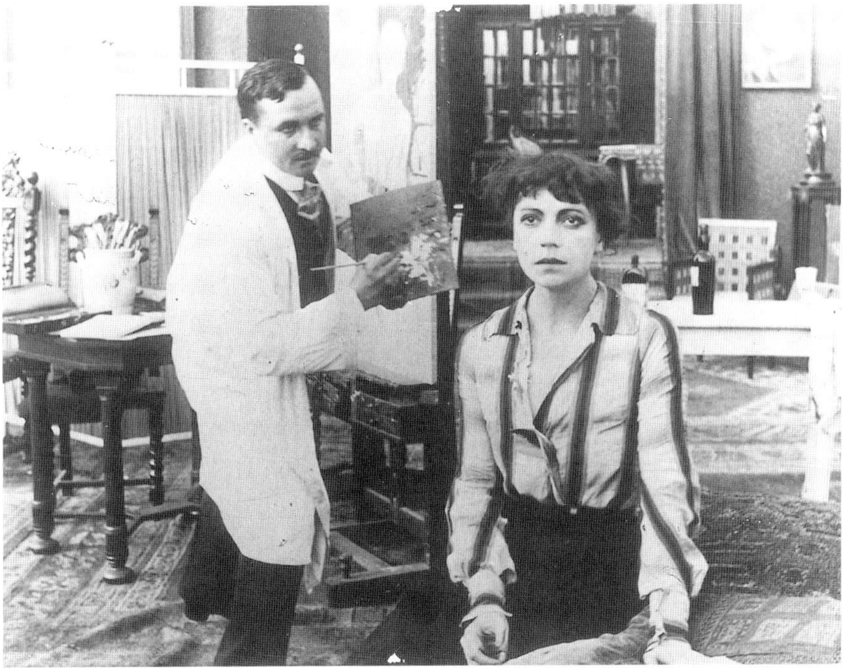

A scene from *Die Sünden der Väter* (1913; The Sins of the Father). Courtesy Danish Film Institute, Copenhagen.

gauchos, cowboys, tango dancers, and Apaches in Italian silent cinema. All these elements amounted to a whole vocabulary of open spaces, freedom, violence, transgression, and sexual desire brought back to the Old World.

Although Nielsen minimized the level of impersonation in the climactic scene of *The Abyss*, it would be erroneous to say that she rejected cross-dressing during her career. Not only did she argue that Hamlet was a woman, during the execution of the 1921 filmic adaptation, but she also refused to use Shakespeare as a canonical literary source, turning instead to an obscure Scandinavian source. She also dressed as a young man in *The ABC of Love*, just to name only one of her most successful romantic comedies.

The cowboy's rope is the only element of exotic cross-dressing used by Nielsen in *The Abyss*. Yet despite her stepping into a masculine role as the sexually aggressive suitor, Magda neither becomes a grotesque cowboy nor a destructive vamp. Magda remains Magda: all will and all subjectivity, sheer lust presenting itself on-screen through simple movement. It is amazing that Nielsen, the most self-conscious and assertive of actresses when necessary, could let go of her own self-image in front of the camera to allow its indifferent lens to record Magda's most secret urgings. Of course, the scandal and success of the film had to do with Magda's erotic dance turning the cowboy into a sexual object.

What conclusion can be reached about Nielsen's self-conscious stripping away of literary and pictorial referents from her acting? Her gaucho dance in *The Abyss* makes visible, to the point of laying bare, a woman's desire for a man. In other words, it surpasses the notorious dances of female vamps at the cabaret or the music hall, and for that matter it moves far beyond Loie Fuller's serpentine dance. To be sure, she twists and rubs her body on her male partner. But the overall result is so shocking that it turns physical sex into abstract eros, thus jolting the pejorative aura surrounding the double standard about female sexual desire. Nielsen's gaucho dance produced in the viewers' minds a literal shift from the physical to the metaphysical. Sex became only one of the forms imagination could take on its way to abstraction.

To begin with, such a rejection of origins, models, and sources prevents her from becoming a sort of letter-picture or rigid on-screen hieroglyph. Nielsen's appreciation of cinema as an art form of silence and light spares her from subordinating herself to the category of woman as static image-word. For Mary Ann Doane, the hieroglyph is both an inferior form of picture writing—too easy to determine to be taken seriously—and an alien kind of alphabet, so impenetrable, so archaic, that it emerges as both mysterious and threatening.[40] Likewise, Doane continues, the use of the female body on the Hollywood screen yielded a comparable result: on the one hand, it was an image of lack, on the other, an image of excess. Nielsen does not fit into Doane's brilliant equivalence between the hieroglyph and the image of woman in film. During *The Abyss*'s famous gaucho dance, Nielsen is lewd, but she is also completely self-assertive and spontaneous. Clearly, she is nobody's erotic projection but her own, even as she becomes everybody's erotic fantasy. Magda's dance is for and about herself, yet it also fits everybody else's longings. Thus Nielsen's acting moved across being and having, looking and being looked at, and it was so much in touch with the producing and receiving ends of the cinematic apparatus—

projector and screen—that she succeeded in extending the camera's technical range before the actual refinement of the close-up.

Interestingly enough, Nielsen spoke against the close-up and the beauty of stars in American silent films. During an interview in 1917, she declared: "Your actresses . . . often are more beautiful than talented. . . . You get the best possible out of close-ups by merely showing the face of the actor. Hands and body may be equally expressive, and may be shown quite sufficiently large upon the screen without nullifying the effect of facial expression."[41]

It is well known that the close-up is comparable to a surgical gaze that stands for voyeurism and fetishism. Yet Nielsen's acting and its close-up-like effect impresses itself in viewers' minds not with the trauma of bodily invasion, but with the unforgettable intimacy of an intuitive connection. The latter can be best understood if situated at a prelinguistic age, when the child holds onto the mother's breast and sees only her face—the child's first and most reassuring world—a universe of emotional warmth and physical tactility: all visually framed as a cinematic close-up. Likewise, the close-up promises the film viewer a certain kind of everlasting bond with the screen image, while the world outside is about alertness, interruption, shock, distraction, and loss.[42]

To sum it all up, Nielsen's acting not only suited cinema but was also completely capable of keeping pace with all aspects of its technology. Her virtuosity as a performer became the subtext of an episode from *Vordertreppe—Hintertreppe* (1915; Front Stairs, Back Stairs). In this film, Nielsen is Sabine, a cardplayer. At breakneck speed, Nielsen's broad range of gestures during a game—involving hands, mouth, eyes, smile, head motions, her bust's changing axis, elbows, fingers, and the chair she sits upon—unrolls on the screen. Some of these gestures are self-congratulatory; others are expressions of pleasure aimed at the viewer; others seem to catch the actress by surprise, as if the character, or the game, had gotten ahead of her; some are quite vulgar; and others, again, are appropriate for a lady. In some moments she exhibits a professional gambler's aggression; in others, she seems to transform the card game into a metaphysical interrogation of the human soul. Most importantly, all these different gestures come from one source—her acting. In a sense, she is playing with the intricate geography of interiority by using the card game as a tool of exploration.

Still, one may wonder against whom Nielsen is playing during this competitive game of cards. Of course, before the successful release of *The Abyss,* Nielsen's opponent was the cinema itself, the worst enemy of the theater. In the role of the cardplayer, the actress plays against what happens to the performer's live, breathing body when it turns into a series of separate takes on the editing table. There she was: by moving faster than the projector, she raced against the camera to win the game that the cinema always plays between absence and presence, acting and editing, between being present before the camera as body and subject and ending up on the screen as an insubstantial but powerful shadow. But in the end, neither Nielsen nor the cinema lost the game, for both the actress and the new technology knew how to use external movement to stir the viewers' minds to a special place between the beam of light from the projector and the flat dark screen. There the game of acting and spectatorship would become a shared dance of emotions.

Francesca Bertini

In the wake of Asta Nielsen, most Italian actresses (Diana Karenne, for example) tried to match her achievements. It was clear to all, however, that Italian Catholic culture did not allow such an emancipated view of femininity. Bertini's career can be reevaluated in the light of her efforts to negotiate between Nielsen's more open expression of sexual desire and social independence, and the conservative expectations of Italian audiences. Eager to become a film diva, Bertini had to sacrifice some degree of innovation for the sake of celebrity. Reared in Florence by a bourgeois family and having two female cousins in a convent, Elena (Taddei) Vitiello (1892–1985), born out of wedlock, was no *figlia d'arte* like Duse, nor did she receive theatrical training as Borelli did. Launched by the Neapolitan entrepreneur Giuseppe Barattolo, Francesca not only had to compete with Lyda during her career, but she also lacked an artistic origin, although she tried to turn this into an advantage. Unlike Borelli and Nielsen, both from the stage, Bertini started in the cinema, though she did some work in the theater also.

A young girl full of ambition but lacking formal education, Bertini had the good fortune to find some supportive male mentors, such as the Neapolitan writer Salvatore Di Giacomo. While pushing her to study foreign languages, he undertook to guide her artistic and intellectual development.[43] In Naples, Bertini started out working at Film d'Art, which around 1908–1911 was a branch of Pathé. Her roles for this company were based on long shots, cardboard sets, old-fashioned costumes, and simple sculpted gestures that everybody could understand and see from afar, as if they were watching an opera.

For the young Bertini, stuck in this operatic context, Nielsen's *The Abyss* came as an exciting revelation, and the actress became eager to play more emancipated and contemporary roles. If Bertini took Nielsen as a role model, Nielsen was equally well aware of how her acting technique differed from the tradition of Italian divismo. This indirect and coincidental acknowledgment can be inferred as late as 1922 from Nielsen's schizophrenic performance in *Vanina* (1922), directed by Arthur von Gerlach, produced by Union Film, and based on an 1829 short story by Stendhal.[44] Although *Vanina* was not one of Nielsen's best films, its credits include some of the most prestigious names in German expressionist cinema: the actor Paul Wegener, the writer Carl Meyer, and the set designer Walter Reimann.

In von Gerlach's production, Asta adopts a stiff style to play Vanina during the film's first half. When acting like an Italian operatic diva, she stands near a door frame and extends her arm outward toward no obvious source. This is the gesture of someone who feels persecuted by invisible forces. Here she underlines the frame's horizontal stretch and amplifies feeling until freezing it into pose. The crucial shift in Nielsen's acting style coincides with a turning point in the plot. The new Vanina can emerge out of her old monumental and paranoiac approach as soon as her tyrannical father (Paul Wegener) loses his physical strength. Only then can Vanina protect her beloved, a political rebel; express her support for the patriots' insurrection; and become a leading figure of the revolutionary movement. In line with this shift from submissive daughter to rebellious woman, Nielsen's acting style switches from operatic to naturalistic.

According to Iole Ribolzi, Bertini wanted to become the Italian Asta Nielsen, but she

A poster for *L'Amazzone Mascherata* (1914; The Masked Equestrienne). Courtesy Nederlands Filmmuseum, Amsterdam.

faced a new problem: how much emancipation and explicit eroticism would small-town Italian audiences and the local priest be comfortable with?[45] Tired of old-fashioned operatic roles, the actress left Film d'Art, and in 1913 she was working at Celio, playing the female lead in *L'Amazzone Mascherata* (1914; The Masked Amazon). Within the formula of the adventure genre, female characters were less passive than in operatic adaptations. The model was not only Asta Nielsen's *The Abyss,* but also Benjamin Christensen's stupendous *Det Hemmelighedsfulde X,* also known as both *The Mysterious X* and *Orders Under Seal* (made in 1913 and released in 1914), a spy thriller that received enthusiastic coverage in the Italian trade journals.[46] Interestingly enough, *L'Amazzone Mascherata* was directed by Baldassarre Negroni, who had already collaborated with Bertini on *L'Histoire d'un Pierrot* (1913), a pantomime that gave the actress the opportunity to try out cross-dressing, since she plays the role of the free-spirited Pierrot.

Briefly, the plot of *L'Amazzone Mascherata:* Some important military documents belonging to Count Alberto Ferrara (Alberto Collo) are stolen by Sterosky (Emilio Ghione). The latter is an international spy who operates with the help of Nadia—played by Leda Gys, another future Neapolitan diva—using a fictional Slavic name and playing the role of an American Indian in blackface. Together, Nadia and Sterosky run an equestrian circus. The poor count goes to trial and is given a life sentence. In the meantime, the count's wife, Francesca (Francesca Bertini), is absolutely certain that her husband is innocent. Thus, she decides to figure out the intrigue on her own while the innocent man languishes in jail. One clue makes Francesca suspicious of Sterosky. To learn more, she decides to become a performer specializing in acrobatic riding, donning a black mask to hide her identity. Francesca becomes a very famous stuntwoman, and her faithful male servant accompanies her everywhere and keeps an eye on the evil Sterosky. In one long scene, Francesca distracts Sterosky with her cleavage during a romantic dinner, enabling her servant to retrieve the stolen documents. Both the *amazzone mascherata* and her assistant flee Sterosky's country by train. Sterosky chases the fugitive team by motorcycle and has Francesca arrested as soon as the train reaches the frontier. Luckily, the faithful servant is able to run away with the evidence and turn it over to the police. As a result, Count Alberto is declared innocent and allowed to return to his honorable and happily married life with Francesca.

Sterosky is a sad example of anti-Semitism in early Italian cinema, but what is most important here is to underline the adjustments to the original, *The Mysterious X,* required by the Italian "remake," so to speak. These adjustments, in fact, also had an impact on Bertini's acting style, which never achieved Pearl White's athleticism, despite the opportunities provided by a chase scene and indoor equestrian performances. Christensen's plot is as convoluted as that of *L'Amazzone Mascherata,* but *The Mysterious X* makes sure to assign the role of brain to the female heroine. By contrast, in *L'Amazzone Mascherata* the male servant is the brain and the faithful wife is the body, even though the two work well together. This was a revision seemingly necessary to please the censorship board, the producers, or the Italian audience. There is insufficient documentation to figure out what were the main ideological forces shaping this film.

The year before *L'Amazzone Mascherata,* Bertini starred in a shorter but perhaps even more daring film, *La Terra Promessa* (1913; The Promised Land), again under the direction of

Baldassarre Negroni for Celio Films, but distributed outside Italy with the alternative title of *Oro e Cuore* (Gold and Heart).

Again the plot: A rich banker, William Grace (Emilio Ghione), learns that there are gold mines in Uganda, so he decides to conquer this African country and give it to his government. The State Council is against colonization, but Grace proceeds anyway by sending his representative, the engineer George Tealove, to Uganda. Six months later, Tealove cables Grace to inform him that the search for the gold mines has not been going well. Meanwhile, Betty, Tealove's girlfriend, meets Grace, who becomes her mentor and encourages her to become a successful opera singer. The first time we see Francesca Bertini in *La Terra Promessa,* she is a piano teacher, just like Asta Nielson in *The Abyss.*

Eventually, after great hardship during his mission in Uganda, Tealove returns home to discover that Betty has started a relationship with Grace. The abandoned man has a fight with Betty and, discouraged about his personal life, goes back to Uganda. It just so happen, however, that Grace decides to join Tealove for this second stage of the African mission, and together the boss and his employee succeed. The film ends with the loving reunification of Betty and George, while Grace, who donates a whole country to his government, can start his retirement.

For the moral standards of those days and in the eyes of the censorship board, *La Terra Promessa* was a daring film because it states that an unmarried woman is entitled to have a relationship with more than one man. The film also makes clear that such a woman has the right to change her mind instead of following a feudalistic code in which the loss of her virginity binds her forever to her first seducer. Asta Nielsen's influence is undeniable: Magda (in *The Abyss*) not only lives alone, but she replaces one man with another, even though she chooses badly in doing so.

In other words, while the diva film usually features a man with two women, Bertini followed Asta's example by choosing several plots in which one woman has two men. Even though Grace plays the role of Betty's fatherly mentor and supportive lover, the diva, in the end, finds a successful career along with true love with Tealove. This is perhaps why the film, at least abroad, was retitled *Oro e Cuore,* to show that the times were mature enough, as far as the perception of women was concerned, for a happy ending rather than some kind of public or private loss, as happens in *The Abyss.*

Interestingly, *La Terra Promessa* got rave reviews in Great Britain, even though an English critic naïvely reported: "We do not quite understand why it has been considered necessary to Anglicise the names of the characters, and the spectacle of the Italian marines taking over a new territory and saluting an adoption of the English flag is an incongruity that detracts from the merits of a play which is otherwise intensely interesting and superlatively well played and produced."[47]

The diplomatic relations between Italy and Great Britain on the topic of African colonialism in 1913 fall outside the range of this study, but the reference to the use of English names shows that the critic did not know that this was a self-imposed censorship practice in early Italian cinema: Betty can come across as a foreign-born, hence more emancipated, woman. Such a controversial role confirmed the risks Bertini was willing to take with her professional and public reputation. Even if the names of the characters were English, the audience knew that the players were Italian.

Bertini's career indicated that in comparison with orientalist melodrama, the adventure genre was more conducive to providing successful modern roles for women, while the 1913 advent of the long feature film led to socially self-conscious, but also darker and more conservative, diva roles. Right after working with Nino Oxilia in *Sangue Bleu,* Bertini recovered from such a traditional ending by developing the scenario for Oxilia's adventure film set in Piombino's steel mills: *Nella Fornace* (1915; In the Furnace). Under the male pseudonym "Frank Bert," the diva came up with an adventure film that was a tale of industrial espionage calling for an action-oriented woman. Since the release of this film was delayed, despite Bertini's efforts, its production history might have also been troubled. Possibly the censorship board was unwilling to tolerate a diva film without a mater dolorosa.[48]

One more episode proves Bertini's awareness of more-emancipated foreign female role models. The diva corresponded with the French writer Colette (Sidonie-Gabrielle Colette, 1873–1954), who was asked to work on the adaptation of a realist text, *La Piccola Fonte* (1906; The Little Spring), by the Neapolitan socialist Roberto Bracco (1862–1943). Unfortunately, this plan never came to anything; one wonders whether Colette's refusal was triggered by Bertini's concern about controlling the final product in such a way as to combine Colette's feminist cachet with an approach palatable to the more ideologically conservative Italian audiences. According to one of Colette's letters, Bertini wanted so much control that the French writer refused to cooperate. In the end, the diva settled for Roberto Roberti's 1917 film adaptation of Bracco's text.[49]

One final film needs to be cited in the list of Bertini's efforts to stand out as the Italian Asta Nielsen. Although in 1921 the famous diva was about to marry Count Paul Cartier, she did not turn down the opportunity to star in *Il Nodo* (1921; The Knot), a stunning film about a jealous yet adulterous husband who tries to incinerate his innocent wife during their process of separation. In short, with an approach possibly more explicit than Borelli's, Bertini seems to have done as much as she could to leave inside her work a feminist legacy without losing the favor of her audiences or running afoul of the censors.

To some extent, Borelli embraced a more cryptic style, as if she wanted to keep her emancipationist opinions inside the folds of her veils. Still, when one thinks that, in those days, female nudity was allowed only in the anatomical theater and not permitted even in art schools, the skimpily clad Borelli as Salome in 1910 was seen not only as a major male fantasy, but also as a serious transgression against the Catholic Church. It is also significant that Borelli's interpretation was one of the very first Italian Salomes; Oscar Wilde's play (1893) had originally been created for Sarah Bernhardt.[50]

Perhaps the difference between Bertini's and Borelli's ways of expressing their libertarian views about women was more a matter of degree or style than an actual contrast. Just as Bertini would settle for compromises so as not to alienate her audiences, Borelli would state her most anticonformist views between the lines or through innuendoes that are not easy to unpack. For instance, at the end of her preface for Mario Carli's *Retroscena* (1915), Borelli declares sotto voce: "Would you like to say that one can have a literary intelligence even when one lives half of the day on stage? Of course, I know that this is indeed the case. You do not need to tell me. On some things, it is best not to dwell, in order to avoid nasty

Lyda Borelli, *center,* in *La Leggenda di Santa Barbara* (1918). Courtesy Nederlands Filmmuseum, Amsterdam.

(bottom) Gustave Courbet, *Le Sommeil* (1866; *The Sleepers* or *Sleep*). Oil on canvas, 53.1 × 78.7 in. (135 × 200 cm.). Musée du Petit Palais, Paris. Photo: Erich Lessing/Art Resource, N.Y.

reactions. . . . I repeat, I must be silent."[51] In these words Borelli shares with Carli that she is well aware of her intellectual abilities, but to avoid polemics, she chooses a diplomatic silence, as if her profession, so closely associated with display, could backfire to the point of confirming Antonio Gramsci's view of her as a sexual animal.

With an appropriate awareness of contradiction and ambiguity, Gianfranco Mingozzi (b. 1932), in his documentary *L'Ultima Diva: Francesca Bertini* (1982; *The Last Diva*), offers a split view of Bertini's career: on the one hand, just as Borelli at the very beginning of *Il Fior di Male* makes fun of the Egyptian sphinx and looks at us, Bertini usually addresses the camera at the start of her films (e.g., *L'Histoire d'un Pierrot, La Terra Promessa, Il Fascino della Violenza* [1912; The Charm of Violence], *Mariute*). It is during this rupture of cinematic illusionism that Bertini shows herself stepping into a character's clothes. Thus the diva—who is in charge of the construction of images, or at least self-conscious about them—shows that she can break through not only the fourth wall, but also the stereotypes that society imposes on women's roles.

In his documentary, Mingozzi also underlines Bertini's role *en travesti* for *L'Histoire d'un Pierrot.* To this day, this is the only surviving example of a female Italian diva playing a male character. To be sure, Mingozzi's documentary also contains a passing reference to the unwritten history of lesbian liaisons in early Italian cinema, a topic that would repay further research. Likewise, a surviving shot from Cines' *L'Altro Esercito o La Leggenda di Santa Barbara* (1918; The Other Army, or The Legend of Santa Barbara), with Lyda Borelli, features three women intertwined in a state of bliss. The scene is not far from Gustave Courbet's *The Sleepers* (1866), his famous painting about female homoeroticism. Unfortunately, at the very end of *The Last Diva,* Mingozzi does not hesitate to ask Bertini to perform, once again, the most stereotypical and misogynistic of operative roles, the prima donna's suicide from Puccini's *Tosca* (1900).

By linking the two poles of Bertini's career—the elegantly feminine diva and the slender cross-dresser—Mingozzi's overview paves the way for a meditation on the curve as the central figure of uncertainty, ambiguity, and compromise in Bertini's acting style. While the curve belongs also to Borelli and Menichelli, one of its greatest applications occurs through Bertini's use of the shawl in *Assunta Spina.* The Venetian garment's flexibility is exploited for a Neapolitan story, but Bertini does it so expressively and dancingly that the regional discrepancy is not even an issue. *Assunta Spina* gave Bertini her well-deserved international success, but it also required the ultimate tightrope-walking act in the context of her agenda to become the Italian Asta Nielsen.

Based on a 1909 realist play by Salvatore Di Giacomo (1860–1934), *Assunta Spina* can be taken as a more ambiguous Neapolitan answer to the explicit scandal of *The Abyss.* This is not to say that Di Giacomo was not a progressive and liberal-minded intellectual. In fact, his decision to be a realist writer and Bertini's decision to be in a realist film were already two progressive choices, with a level of resonance comparable to the scandal that erupted when Édouard Manet made clear that Victorine Meurent was a prostitute in his painting *Olympia* (painted in 1863, first shown in 1865).

Interestingly, this French art-historical example predates early-twentieth-century Naples by approximately forty years, but this is exactly the point. Italy, and especially the cities of Naples and Palermo—rich in art, history, and culture—were poor, badly run, and very dangerous. Naples and Palermo had all the social problems that socialists like Antonio Gramsci, positivist scientists like Angelo Mosso, and criminal anthropologists like Cesare Lombroso wanted to solve. Di Giacomo was particularly aware of this dreadful situation, as were the Neapolitan philosopher Benedetto Croce and the journalist Matilde Serao, a friend of Eleonora Duse and the author of the social melodrama *Il Ventre di Napoli* (1884; The Belly of Naples), about the poorest neighborhoods. Not only did Di Giacomo title one of his first dramas *Mala Vita* (1887; Crime), but he also regularly covered crime for the local papers.[52] As a result of his reporting, he stated: "My fixation is this: Naples is a forsaken city, in the hands of incompetent, lazy and ruthless individuals.

Everything happens from breaking the rules."[53]

In keeping with Di Giacomo's passion for his city and frustration with its problems, *Assunta Spina* starts with an iconization of Bertini: Naples is Assunta, as the protagonist wears her white shawl with long fringe and stands in front of an emblematic seascape. In this particular film, the diva chooses not to show herself entering a fictional role, perhaps because her ties to Di Giacomo, and to Naples, were very strong. Hence, her identification with the city was complete, on-screen and in real life. Assunta Spina's Catholic name (Virginal Ascension–Mystical Thorn) announces that her character will be no new woman of modernity, but a regional mater dolorosa. On the one hand, the Virgin's ascension to heaven was due to her virginal body, the ultimate negation of female desire; on the other hand, the image of the thorn is a reference to mysticism, suffering, and painful sublimation. Besides these allusions to Catholicism, the film is replete with references to Neapolitan history and social problems. The famous sequence of Assunta walking alone in the flooded streets of the market as well as her becoming the manager of Raffaele's laundry both resonate with the ghost of several cholera epidemics from 1844 to 1911.[54]

One could say that in the footsteps of Di Giacomo's social consciousness, Bertini's *Assunta Spina* explores the continuity of past social evils disguised in new or updated forms. Even if Assunta Spina is a Neapolitan Catholic and no cosmopolitan suffragette, there was enough energy in Di Giacomo's story to denounce centuries-old prejudices and abuses. This is why Bertini's choice to take on the leading role, and to operate within the vernacular milieu of streetwise urchins and criminal figures, was already a daring gesture.

The sequence of Assunta walking toward the courthouse with a crowd of local extras has a genuine political force because it was shot on location with, in proto-neorealist fashion, nonprofessional actors. The image of Assunta at the center of a mass of restless and destitute individuals immediately brings to mind Pellizza Da Volpedo's famous canvas *Il Quarto Stato* (1901; The Fourth Estate), a major icon of the class struggle. Precisely because Bertini stands for the whole of Naples, the film is more about the city and, unlike Nielsen's *The Abyss*, less about a woman's need to choose the right partner. Rather, *Assunta Spina* deals with the ways that, as a figure of temporality, the female protagonist articulates Naples' descent from one feudal way to another, slightly updated and pseudo-modern one. In *Il Ventre di Napoli*, Serao writes:

> *A large portion of the population of the city lives in filth and poverty, in slums and urban caves. These are the people for whom the renewal and sanitation programme was intended, for whom 100 million lire were spent. Now, having lived through the rebuilding, these people reside just behind the new structures while they continue to die from every manner of disease. It is this fact that fills me with pain and regret. The majestic façades of the new buildings seem like a sardonic joke because they serve only to shield the eye from the squalor and canker of our city. . . . Just like before! Worse than before!*[55]

After the opening shot of the film, near the sea, a sort of timeless cliché of beauty, we see the arrival of a train, and it becomes clear that *Assunta*'s subtext is about historical change and modernization. Yet the film's conclusion is about the failure to achieve those goals. And, indeed, it makes sense to recognize that the arrival of cinema in Naples was not enough to get rid of old dysfunctions. The cinema may have raised great hopes among women and unemployed young people, but much became lost in the shift from imagination to implementation. In a sense, Di Giacomo and Bertini's project in *Assunta Spina* is to expose this lacuna.

In my view, *Assunta Spina* is silent cinema's counterpart to *Il Gattopardo* (1959; *The Leopard*), by Giuseppe Tomasi Di Lampedusa (1896–1957), which Luchino Visconti brought to the screen in 1963 in a version starring Burt Lancaster, Claudia Cardinale, and Alain Delon. In this renowned historical novel, Prince Salina is willing to see Garibaldi's revolution change everything as long as, in the end, the lower classes, even if allied with the bourgeoisie, will continue to be in the same position—at the service of the aristocracy. Along with Benedetto Croce, Giuseppe Ceci, and Mariano D'Ayala, Di Giacomo had contributed to an anthology titled *La Rivoluzione Napoletana del 1799* (1899). This pictorial album was conceived as a collection of historical entries and illustrations covering the failed Neapolitan revolution in the wake of the successful one in France, in 1789. And as we learn from Gramsci, such a sad outcome echoed the shortcomings of Garibaldi's mission to Sicily in 1860: its revolutionary and popular upheaval was stifled by the Piedmontese monarchy, fearful of popular insurrections.

Interestingly, Di Giacomo also published a book on prostitution in Naples, *La Prostituzione in Napoli nei Secoli 15, 16, e 17* (1899). Although this treatise did not deal with the present, both Di Giacomo and Bertini were aware of professional women's rise in social prominence in the years just before World War I. Despite improvement in women's status, the mores of private life in Naples were still medieval. And Di Giacomo's fiction explores precisely how the fear of modern changes went together with Assunta's surrender to promiscuity. But what were Assunta's options when choosing among the men in her life?

Michele, a butcher, arrives by train; dressed like a bourgeois, he wins the approval of Assunta's father, a modest man living in a suburb of Naples. The father is eager to give his daughter to Michele, a good suitor because he owns his own butcher shop plus a laundry nearby. At the end of a brief scene with Assunta and her father walking together in a park after Michele's departure, the old man gives his daughter a few coins. It is a small detail that implies, notwithstanding the lack of intertitles, that marrying Michele will mean a financial improvement for both Assunta and her father, who are obliged to pinch pennies. It would be difficult to imagine someone owning two businesses in a crowded low-income neighborhood without the

approval of the *camorra*, namely, the Neapolitan Mafia, which still exists today. In fact, Michele is now a neighborhood boss. Michele's two stores spell out the key ailments of Serao's "Neapolitan belly": violence, represented by the butcher, and cholera, which the laundry is a weak defense against, since the disease may have been spread through improperly laundered bedsheets.[56]

Assunta's other option is Raffaele, a much less established type than Michele, as indicated by the hat he wears. He is one of the many unemployed locals living off petty or major crimes, as well as the author of an anonymous letter about Assunta's unreliable behavior with men. The third man in Assunta's life is the court clerk, Federico Funelli, a Don Giovanni to whom Assunta sells herself because he has the power to prevent

Michele from ending up in a jail far from Naples. Again, this geographical detail may seem insignificant, but it is absolutely crucial because it encapsulates the idea that spatial separation, just like historical change, is too painful to handle, hence a compromise involving sex is a preferable solution.

Instead of drawing a clear line between past and present, in the manner of an irreversible and successful revolution, Assunta chooses not to forget Michele, who has scarred her for life with a butcher knife. Just as her scar will remain on her face forever, her memories of his love for her are permanent. With her stubborn mixing of the past with the present, Bertini's character stands for both Naples and Italy. Assunta is unable to break away from Michele, just as she is unable to forget Raffaele. Likewise, Naples is unable to eliminate the camorra in the transition from feudalism to modernity, and even postmodernity. By the end of the film, she is all the more helpless because she feels overwhelmed by the prospect of a cut-and-dried separation from Federico, who has become bored with her.

While the transfer from the father's suburb to the laundry in town is tolerable because the distance is short, the possibility of a definitive separation with anyone is mindboggling. No matter what, everybody must be intertwined with everybody else; Assunta is weary of turning over a new leaf, despite the fact that she lives surrounded by the white sheets of the laundry. Although a fresh piece of bedding may be read as the image of a new start, the conclusion of *Assunta Spina* is a perverse revision of the tragic end of *The Abyss*. Michele kills Federico in a jealous rage and runs out the door. Assunta then succeeds in persuading the *carabinieri* that she is the only culprit. Unlike Nielsen's Magda, who does kill Rudolph, Bertini plays a sacrificial role without ever taking any action, only reacting to protect someone else, the way a mother would with a bad child. Bertini is a mater dolorosa, whereas Nielsen is a strong-minded woman whose chosen partner is unworthy of her generosity and destructive of her future.

Bertini's use of her shawl when she moves between Raffaele and Michele gives full evidence of the wavy, curvilinear acting style that also applies to Borelli and Menichelli, in clear contrast to Nielsen's vertical and Duse's horizontal approaches. The diva's curve is also different from Bernhardt's serpentine because it never chooses the upward direction once and for all. This is not to say that Bertini does not cite Nielsen directly in *Assunta Spina*. In fact, during a scene with Michele and her father, Assunta uses the tablecloth to wipe her mouth and also starts eating before her guest sits down. Such rude behavior was exploited by Nielsen to convey the verticality of high and low classes, but in Bertini's case the routine simply demonstrates that the actress can play the elegant suffering lady in *Sangue Bleu* and the uneducated city girl in *Assunta Spina*. Interestingly, during the meal scene, Assunta already behaves like a maternal figure, since she cooks for both her widowed father and her suitor.

But there is even more to my reading of *Assunta Spina* in light of *The Abyss*. In his monograph on Salvatore Di Giacomo, Franco Schlitzer reports that the Neapolitan writer trusted and admired Bertini's intelligence so much that he gave her carte blanche in adapting his text for film. Schlitzer adds that Bertini's decision-making power was made possible also because the director, Gustavo Serena, knew that this was Di Giacomo's preference.[57] Weighing *Assunta Spina*'s self-punitive ending against Bertini's directorial agency raises a couple of questions. Is Assunta a mater dolorosa because Bertini wants to call attention to social evils in Naples? Or is it because Bertini does not want to alienate her audience, since she had already made one anticonformist move by choosing Di Giacomo as a literary source? My answer is that Bertini probably had both these reasons in mind as she tried as much as possible to suggest Nielsen's acting style and to point out the profound cultural differences between Assunta and Magda.

Was Bertini aware of the limitations, for diva roles, of an acting style based on the curve? I think so, because she deployed an intriguing double-edged technique in *Il Processo Clémenceau* (1917; *The Clemenceau Affair*). With the exception of a few crucial and stunning scenes, this is a long, heavy film whose sporadic and elliptical intertitles allow Bertini to play Iza Dobronowska as simultaneously frivolous, which her murderous husband accuses her of being, and thoughtful, which the emancipated new woman in the audience knows her to be. The film itself is divided into two parts: the first devoted to Iza as a girl, and the second to her as a woman. The deconstructionist moments at the level of acting are too frequent to be accidental. The textual organization of this film is both so schizophrenic and so symmetrical that the history of its prints, variations, and possible versions with intertitles in different languages is not in and of itself enough to explain so many textual rhymes set against so many oppositional statements.

To begin with, the film's narrative unfolds inside a flashback channeled through a personal memoir. Pierre Clemenceau, the writer of the memoir, is a sculptor who, thanks to Iza's beauty and family money, has become famous and rich. The purpose of his memoir is to link Bertini's acting to the idea that she is interested only in buying clothes, does not care about her child, runs after a Russian aristocrat, sleeps with her husband's best friend, and is rude to her mother-in-law. But this version of Iza belongs only to Pierre's memoir. In fact, the spectator sees such a blatant discrepancy between Bertini's behavior and the intertitles that one could say that the diva's acting on screen visually defies her persecutor's writing. For instance, when Constantino Ruiz, Pierre's best friend, tries to seduce Iza, Bertini's face wears a grimace of disgust. Bertini's odd use of her face not only dates back to theatrical acting before the diffusion of the close-up, but is also meant to deny Pierre's allegations in his memoir about his wife's promiscuity. Bertini's face says the opposite of what he writes.

The schizophrenic nature of the filmic text—split as it is between his written story and her body language—also emerges from two opposite takes on the politics of Iza's father. At first, the intertitle says that he was a Bolshevik; later on, another intertitle declares he was a supporter of the czar. In the end, the second explanation prevails: a third intertitle explains that Iza has inherited money from her aristocratic family, the same money she spends on herself, her family, and Pierre's maintenance, since he has no money of his own.

One more moment of contradiction in the film concerns the use of Bertini's naked body in Pierre's sculpture. When his chisel carves a male or a female nude, the level of idealization of the human body functions as a sort of invisible skin-dress that binds traditional stereotypes of masculinity and femininity even more tightly into static and predictable gender roles. This reading of the sexual politics of sculpture between Pierre and Iza is somewhat shaken during their honeymoon.

In a rare sequence shot en plein air, Pierre and Iza spend the day frolicking in the countryside. Eager to get rid of him and have more freedom of movement, she sends him off on a bizarre errand: to bring back fresh milk inside a silver cup.

As soon as Pierre is offscreen, Iza decides to take off her clothes and go swimming alone in the nearby river. When Pierre returns to the riverbank and Iza emerges from the water, a white sheet in the guise of a sculpted drapery wraps her body and turns her into a sort of odd moving statue. Due to censorship's rules, Bertini's nude body is contained inside a white sheet. Thus, her image strikes a note of contrast with the ever-rippling water. This contrast echoes the tension between an old and a new medium, sculpture and cinema, as well as between Pierre's idealized images of femininity and Iza's eagerness for motion.

In addition, this episode spells out the rift between the newlyweds, for her naturalistic style—especially when she is alone—clashes against his artificial manner. As a couple, they look grotesque and incongruous, like a silver cup in the middle of a green pasture. Whereas the swimming episode stresses Bertini's wish for freedom, the final point here is that being outdoors with a sculptor feels like posing for some kind of mythological scene inside his studio.

Though Pierre accuses Iza of not loving her child, a subsequent episode shows mother and infant playing freely and joyfully by themselves in the grass. During the outdoor sequence, not only does Bertini's acting style change, but the film itself also switches from a contrived, fictional melodrama to a clumsy home movie with an improvised flavor. All décor and posing seem to go out of the film, and the frames accelerate oddly, as if shot with a handheld camera or edited into a series of jump cuts, long before these techniques had been developed.

Once again running on the grass, Bertini looks as if she is eager to run out of her own trite diva film. One may wonder whether this loss of technological control and the breach of the narrative's seamless flow may be problems related to the long-neglected print itself. I contend that this odd moment may be intentional rather than entirely accidental because there is one final episode that puts a scenario of freedom in a heavily theatrical environment.

Iza and Serghiei, the man who truly loves her, walk out of his beautiful villa. Of course, the romance between the two cannot take off: Pierre was Iza's first lover, and just as in *Assunta Spina,* change is denied. Choosing be tween two men would empower Iza too much, and it would be humiliating for Pierre to be rejected. Together, Serghiei and Iza stop inside an artificial grotto. There, a little pond contains a school of fish freely swimming around. The long iris shot in close-up on this surprising image of fluidity and sparkling light is spellbinding. As Iza and Serghiei wordlessly observe the fish, the viewer cannot help but think that they have discovered their potential treasure trove of happiness. As lovers, they will hardly ever match the fishes' free motion, since both their lives are restricted by psychological and social constraints. On the other hand, when Iza and her child run on the grass, a flock of geese walking into the film unexpectedly foreshadows the school of fish in the episode with Serghiei. This analogy alone proves there must have been some planning that would allow the geese to rhyme metaphorically with the fish.

Besides undoing Pierre's written sentences through her acting, Bertini takes us beyond language. After an accidental meeting with her child and Pierre in the park, Bertini returns home alone, an outcast because of her reputation as a wanton woman. The separation of mother and child inspires Iza to sing an aria—a piece of music with lyrical and introspective qualities, usually performed solo.[58] Stunningly dressed in a long soft white coat and wearing a wide-brimmed hat, Bertini offers herself to the viewer's eye by opening the furry quivering collar around her throat. The camera lingers in close-up on her necklace of white pearls in a way that resembles a gentle caress more than a voyeuristic gaze. Most importantly, Bertini's theatrical gesture of opening the collar and disclosing what the coat hides underneath is an erotic moment that involves neither submission nor objectification as part of a male fantasy. On the contrary, Bertini's gesture displays a willingness to share her pain, her beauty, and her imaginary solo singing voice with others.

In the end, Bertini's lyrical yet simple moments of innate, spiritual elegance exemplify and summarize the contribution the Italian diva as a mater dolorosa made to the international history of female stardom. It is astonishing that without having discussed these particular scenes during our joint research, Dutch filmmaker Peter Delpeut included not only Bertini's aria from *Il Processo Clémenceau* in his archival compilation *Diva Dolorosa* (1999), but also a sequence from *La Piovra,* another melodrama about child custody. In it, Bertini walks into her child's empty room; the festive wallpaper with rows of little baby ducks speaks of a happy childhood that will never go on, since the son has recently died. It is as if, during Delpeut's work, these two sequences silently attracted each other.

In fact, at the time of our research trip across Italy in 1998, when I was preparing this book and Delpeut was selecting clips for his film, I was not aware of the legal edge shaping the diva film as a genre. It was only years later, during the course of my close examination of the films and of the history of that period, that I realized these images were about the legal rights of women struggling in situations of financial and social marginality as mothers, wives, and lovers. Thus, I choose Francesca Bertini, who, notwithstanding a series of balancing acts, tried to reconcile her artistic admiration for Asta Nielsen with her successful career in Italy. After all, she worked for many years—even longer than Borelli and Menichelli—with so many different creative personalities and in so many films that, in order to survive, she inevitably had to accept the complications of her context, the expectations of her colleagues, and the prejudices of her contemporaries. And she probably did the best she could to change unjust laws.

CHAPTER 6

Modern Woman

MINOR STARS AND THE SHORT FILM

To understand why the diva is an anomalous example of female stardom in film, it is necessary to be familiar with the situation of Italian women at the beginning of the twentieth century. The first leader of the emancipation movement was the Milanese aristocrat Anna Maria Mozzoni (1837–1920). During her unconventional life, she was a single mother who embraced socialism despite her class origins. In 1881 she organized the Lega Promotrice degli Interessi Femminili (League for the Promotion of Women's Interests). She allied herself with Countess Gabriella Spalletti Rasponi, a philanthropist and founder, in 1903, of the Consiglio delle Donne Italiane (Italian Women's Council), and began to work for women's right to vote. Mozzoni's efforts came up against a thick wall of resistance and a general sense of internal disorganization. At the same time, feminism was the topic of the moment, and the urgency of these issues was strong enough that entire books about women's rights were published.[1]

In 1911, Giuseppe Lelio Arrighi, a specialist in the philosophy of science, published *La Storia del Femminismo* (The History of Feminism). Eager to find role models for the Italian new woman, Arrighi looks to France and chooses Madame Tallien, an embodiment of individual rights. Well aware that Italian history was characterized by the absence of a revolutionary experience comparable to that of the French in 1789,[2] Arrighi concludes that women's issues would have achieved faster and better resolution if nineteenth-century radicals had drawn energy from the subversive and underground origins of the early Christian groups.[3] This argument was an attempt to compensate for the fact that the debate on the female vote had further deepened the tensions between socialists and Catholics, without any concrete result. Nevertheless, Arrighi's book addressed the right topics at the right time. Only one year later, in 1912, all literate males of at least twenty-one years of age who had completed their military service were granted the right to vote. This new law expanded the voting pool from 9.5 percent to 24 percent of the population.[4]

Doubts concerning the vote for women were kindled by the socialist party, which feared the conservative influence of priests on female worshipers.[5] Women were considered susceptible to religion and novelettes, and were also said to suffer from nervous weakness. So ingrained were these prejudices that some prominent intellectuals did not always support feminism, even though they were aware of new laws in England and the United States.[6] The Neapolitan writer and journalist Matilde Serao (also known as Contessa

Lara), for instance, opposed voting rights for women. On the other hand, despite her conservative views on suffrage, Serao made daring personal choices. In 1904 she left her husband and colleague, Edoardo Scarfoglio, to live with another man.

A journalist for *Il Mattino* and later *Il Giorno,* as well as a socialite who seemed to know everybody who counted, Serao wrote on a wide number of political as well as frivolous topics, including etiquette. In a piece entitled "The Cigarette: Can Women Smoke?" Serao's answer was yes, they could, but after all, it was best not to.[7] In *Il Processo Clémenceau,* Francesca Bertini, in the role of young Iza Dobronowska, freely smokes when she begins to flirt with an older but little-known artist. Although he is the one who seduces her, her smoking shows that she, too, is willing to go in the wrong direction. In one of the posters for *Ivonne, La Bella della Danza Brutale* (1914; Yvonne, The Beauty in the Brutal Dance), Bertini, using the cigarette as a marker of transgression, flaunts this controversial prop to signal her defiance.

Besides the issue of so-called universal suffrage, which in Italy did not include women until 1945, one should keep in mind that, in those days, a woman was not allowed to subscribe to a newspaper or to engage in charity work without her husband's authorization. To put it simply, women did not exist at all as legal subjects with rights and duties, yet they could be sentenced in a court of law, especially when they were found guilty of adultery. The double standard in matters of marriage and loyalty was so extreme that men suffered hardly any punishment if they were unfaithful to their wives. Women had no right to investigate paternal identity when they became pregnant. When men were involved in dispute over a love triangle, the so-called *delitto d'onore* (crime of honor) was automatically acquitted in court; by contrast, female adultery was punished by law. And, finally, married women could not inherit property without their husband's consent.[8]

Slowly but surely women were able to improve their lot and achieve some independence in the years before and during World War I. Until then, textile factories for silk and hemp in the north had been the largest and best available sources of female employment. Yet according to Luigi Dal Pane, Italian industrialization was no major revolution because small family businesses rarely grew into huge factories.[9] Hence the absorption of female labor was limited. Unemployed women could choose domestic service, twelve-hour workdays in the countryside, or prostitution.[10]

Historian Gloria Chianese remarks that the number of women who worked on assembly lines to sustain the war effort went from 23,000 in 1915 to 89,000 in 1916, and to 175,000 in 1918. Between 1911 and 1917, the number of women attending middle school rose from 0.4 to 0.6 percent.[11] Mary Gibson reports that at the turn of the century, the illiteracy rate for women exceeded by 10 to 15 percentage points the rate for men; the illiteracy rate for women ran from a low of 22 percent in Turin, in the Piedmont, to a high of 68 percent in Palermo, Sicily.[12]

Basic education was in principle mandatory and was supported by the Italian state until a child was twelve years of age. While this major reform was approved in 1904 to fight one of the highest illiteracy rates in Western Europe, the reality was that young girls hardly ever went to school, and if they did, they rarely managed to receive more than a few years of elementary instruction. On the other hand, by 1910 the teaching profession included 62,000 women and 35,000 men, al-

Publicity for the film *Ivonne* (1915), starring Francesca Bertini. Author's collection.

Pina Menichelli smoking in Eugenio Perego's *La Storia di Una Donna* (1920). Courtesy Cineteca di Bologna.

lowing an unprecedented number of women to achieve for the first time a professional role that was visible in the public sphere.[13] It is also true, however, that the teaching profession quickly became so dominated by women that the school system began to feel like a sort of gilded ghetto.

Gibson also cites demographic historian Carlo Cipolla, who proved that the average age of women at first marriage was twenty-four in 1871, an index that remained stable until 1951.[14] By the end of World War I, women made up 22 percent of the overall labor force. Thus, in 1919 the proposed Sacchi Law called into question the so-called Giolitti Clause, according to which women were not citizens in the eyes of the state. The proposed law argued for the end of paternal authority and the end of a woman's need to have her husband's authorization to participate in public activi-

Scenes from *Sulla via dell'Oro* (1913; Looking for Gold). Courtesy Nederlands Filmmuseum, Amsterdam.

ties; it gave women the right to run their own properties, ensured their right to divorce, and offered them professional recognition in a legal sense. Unfortunately, this proposal never became a law, for it ran up against the rising power of Fascism in 1922.[15]

From 1913 onward, major divas starring in the expensive long feature films acquired international notoriety. Less prominent actresses, or minor stars, remained primarily successful on domestic screens in shorter productions. The minor star–short film combination features a rich list of obscure names: Gigetta Morano, Lia Formia, Fernanda Negri-Pouget, Cristina Ruspoli, Valentina Frascaroli, Lydia Quaranta, Berta Nelson, Suzanne Armelle, and Clementina Gay. Some of these performers grew into expert professionals, either by linking themselves to a specific director—the duo Lia Formia and

Lucio D'Ambra, for example—or by specializing in a variety of roles appropriate for contemporary dramas, action and adventure films, social satires, comedies, and short films about female fantasies.

Minor female stars are extremely useful in charting the unexplored territory between the history of Italian feminism and the stylistic traits of the diva film.[16] It is puzzling, for instance, that the teaching profession does not seem to appear frequently in the short contemporary dramas. It is even more intriguing that in the action-woman film, minor stars appear to engage in professional roles that were quite uncommon in real life. But, of course, these generalizations are based only on what I have been able to see firsthand and what I have been able to read and infer.

More specifically, think of Fernanda Negri-Pouget in *Nelly La Domatrice* (1912; Nelly the Lion Tamer) or Berta Nelson in *Vittoria o Morte*. In the latter, the main actress plays a sort of secret agent. After being duped by a manipulative suitor, Blanche (Berta Nelson) sheds her identity as a quiet daughter and displays an amazing range of skills while chasing an evil man over air, land, and water. The climax of *Vittoria o Morte* occurs when Blanche, in pursuit of an international spy, jumps from an airplane in flight onto a ship, all while

Pearl White (as Evelyn Ereth) in *The Black Secret* (1919–1920), a Pathé serial in fifteen episodes, directed by George B. Seitz. Photo: Photofest, New York.

wearing a long skirt and high heels. Indeed, as we learn from Pierre Sorlin, national security is a theme that frequently appeared in the silent cinema of Europe, and not just in Italy, especially before and after World War I.[17]

Women, Sports, Motion, Idleness

Because the diva film shows women practicing sports, smoking, and struggling for child custody, it is fair to say that this genre exhibits an explicit and self-conscious link between the on-screen diva and Italian women off-screen, striving to be modern. In addition, the contrast between cinematic definitions of domesticity and the daring women played by minor stars in contemporary short dramas paved the way for the birth of the diva as a cultural type and as a star, and of the diva film as a genre. Most interestingly, the dynamic and courageous modern-woman type played by minor female stars preceded the arrival in Italy of Pearl White, the ultimate American serial queen, who was involved in action, detective, outdoor, and adventure plots.[18] The fact that the Italian modern-woman type in a short film preceded both the diva's rise and Pearl White's Italian reception indicates that a huge spotlight was pointed toward women's issues in Italian society before World War I.

To begin with, Pearl White's name appeared in *La Vita Cinematografica*, a major industry publication published in Turin, in 1914, the same year of her launch in America.[19] By publishing articles in 1914 about the "Hollywood invasion," *La Vita Cinematografica* demonstrated that Pearl White's name had already become known internationally. Yet it is crucial to remember that Pearl White's American films began flooding Italy only in 1917. Until then, as film historian Riccardo Redi explains, American distribution had to go through London to reach the peninsula's screens.[20] In *La Vita Cinematografica*, again, a sizable contingent of American actresses were discussed around 1918: for instance, the names of Mae Marsh and Mary Corwin appeared over and over again, issue after issue. By 1928 the list of American stars was so long that it is nearly impossible to keep track. What counts is that the picture gallery of Italian female stardom seemed wiped out by the triumph of innumerable young American faces: Colleen Moore, Corinne Griffiths, Phyllis Haver, Myrna Loy. Divismo was dead and dead again.

In 1917, Pearl White exploded onto screens in Italy and France. In his 1921 review of *A Virgin Paradise*, Ricciotto Canudo spells the New World's narrative ingredients: "sport, landscapes, adventures, tough people."[21] Europeans saw in the American female the best example of independent thinking and fun-loving behavior. Displays of humor and lightheartedness by Italian female characters on film were rare, perhaps even alien to the European decadent-symbolist sensibility. By contrast, the Gibson girl from America pokes fun at Mr. Pipp, a clumsy old fellow. Just before Pearl White's 1917 arrival, the Italian female heroine of the modern-woman short film was already being modeled on the international reputation of her emancipated American counterpart, and this more action-oriented genre stayed on through and beyond 1913, the diva's birth year. For example, Augusto Genina's charming *La Signorina Ciclone* (1916; Miss Hurricane), with Suzanne Armelle as Miss Fluffy Ruffles, resembles a Hollywood musical: the freewheeling energy of an all-male chorus line surrounds the restless protagonist, who tells everybody what to do.

She has seven cats, a black servant, and she has seven suitors (with seven dogs) praising

Suzanne Armelle (as Miss Fluffy Ruffles) and friends in Augusto Genina's *La Signorina Ciclone* (1916; Miss Hurricane). Courtesy Cineteca di Bologna.

(*right*) Astrea. Author's collection.

her all day long, regardless of her tantrums at the Bal Tabarin and her arrogance in rejecting all her adoring fellow countrymen, Fluffy Ruffles in the end makes a good wife for the helpless intellectual and cosmopolitan Claudio Barsac. The handsome Claudio is erroneously accused of a crime. He has no alibi and no money. Not only does Fluffy prove his innocence and save him from jail, but she is also the American millionairess who will solve all his financial problems.

The American model of femininity meant action, sport, and courage, so the publication of Edmondo De Amicis's novelette *Amore e Ginnastica* (1892; Love and Gymnastics) was well received by an audience of Anglophiles. Still, the combination of love and physical exercise in De Amicis's title requires a brief contextualization. De Amicis was a close friend of Cesare Lombroso. Early in his career, Lombroso dealt with all kinds of diseases and deformities caused by malnutrition, environment, and intermarriage in the poor regions of southern and rural Italy. National health was the topic of the moment, and as early as 1878 the De Santis Law had already introduced mandatory athletic exercise into the school system.[22]

De Amicis's *Amore e Ginnastica* tells the story of a would-be priest and a physical education teacher working in a junior high school. The use of these two protagonists is well thought out: it allows the writer to make fun of Catholicism without being overly critical. In this charming novelette set in Turin, De Amicis also underlines the rising popularity of Lombrosian theories of the improvement of the Italian race—the very same ideas that will later contribute to the Nazi cult of the perfect Aryan body.

Lyda Borelli in Carmine Gallone's *Malombra* (1917). Courtesy Cineteca di Bologna.

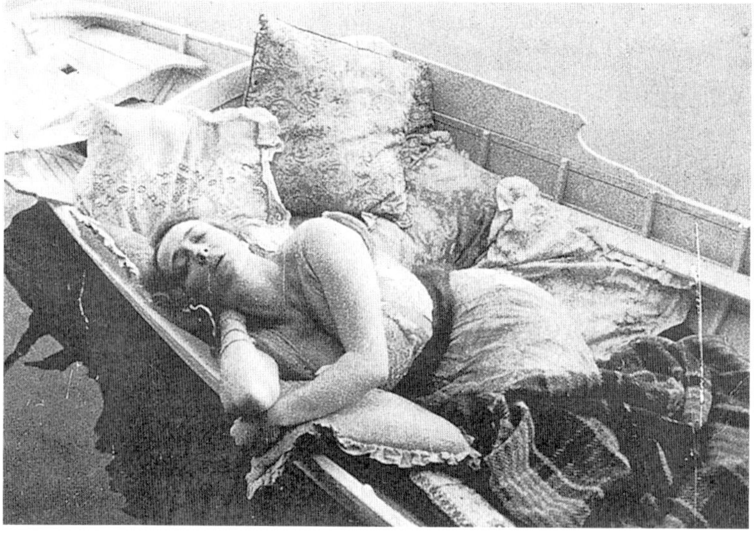

Lyda Borelli in Carmine Gallone's *Malombra* (1917). Courtesy Cineteca di Bologna.

While Pearl White had a simple psychology of her own, the Italian modern-woman short film degenerated into acrobatic spectacles based on sheer physical prowess. In comparison with her Italian colleagues, Pearl White, in *The Perils of Pauline* (1914), achieves a stronger balance between doing and thinking, thinking and choosing. By contrast, Astrea, with the freakish physique of a giant, became the most predictable and simple-minded of all minor stars. In *Justitia* (1919), Astrea does not hesitate to appear in elegant outfits the moment after grabbing a male criminal by the throat. Her large size turned the modern Italian woman into a powerful and reassuring keeper of public order.

In diva films, the female protagonists stand out for their exasperating inactivity and hopeless sense of boredom. Borelli's Marina, in Carmine Gallone's *Malombra* (1917), drives herself insane because she has nothing to do all day except read Poe's tales and take walks along the lake. The only time she changes this routine is when she goes on a hike, during which she rejects one of her suitors. It is significant that for this gesture of defiance, Borelli uses a little parasol to literally push the gentleman away. At the time, this particular accessory was called a Loie Fuller, probably because the sections of fabric supported by the ribs of the umbrella were reminiscent of the dancer's veils mounted on sticks.[23] In spite of Borelli's vigorous rejection of the suitor, Marina looks more like a store mannequin than a sportswoman. She tiptoes carefully from rock to rock because she has on a pair of shoes with tapering heels. And the only concession to physical activity is that she wears a tailleur, a matching jacket-and-skirt outfit that became popular during World War I, when women became more active and gave up the corset and the petticoat.[24]

Pina Menichelli in *La Storia di Una Donna* lounges from sofa to sofa because she is a kept woman. In *La Donna Nuda,* Borelli is a painter's model, and this profession, by definition, was linked to immobility. In *Il Processo Clémenceau,* Pierre falls in love with Francesca Bertini's Iza when he first sees her lying asleep on a sofa during a ball. At the very beginning of *La Piovra,* Bertini appears with a tennis racquet in her hand, running across the lawn. In the next shot, she wears a zippy-looking, horizontally striped outfit as she sits by a mountain lake. Yet after this dynamic, youthful start, she sinks into an immobilizing marriage with the jealous Count de Surville.

As the historian Michela De Giorgio reports:"In Rome, on May 5, 1892, in the hall of

Poster for Mario Roncoroni's *Filibus* (1915). Courtesy Nederlands Filmmuseum, Amsterdam.

the Roman College, Angelo Mosso spoke passionately to Queen Margherita and to the members of the Association for Women's Education: ' . . . We must stop them on the downward and fatal slide toward hysteria, we must take them away from society's artificial emotions and stop any reading that upsets or wears out the nervous system.'"[25] A Turinese physiologist and a disciple of Étienne-Jules Marey (1830–1904), Angelo Mosso (1846–1910) here identifies the major cause of women's unhappiness: inactivity due to the lack of professional and social outlets. Of course, Mosso could have explicitly attacked the negative effects of technology, city life, and industrialization on women's delicate nervous system. But he did not. Besides believing in physical activity, Mosso trusted technology, and he himself conducted motion studies; he later became famous for developing a machine to measure mental energy, or brain waves. Perhaps this is why the object of Mosso's indictment is the infamous novelette, a sort of poison for the female reader.

The Construction of the Diva Film

As we learn from Aldo Bernardini, the long film traveled from Denmark to Italy.[26] As detailed in the previous chapter, the first example of a Danish long film was the thirty-seven-minute *Afgrunden* (1910; *The Abyss*), by Urban Gad, which turned Asta Nielsen into the first European star. From 1910 onward, the Italian film industry produced long films in all kinds of genres, but it was really Mario Caserini's *Ma l'Amor Mio Non Muore* (1913; *Everlasting Love*), with Lyda Borelli, which, at seventy-nine minutes, stands out as the first diva film. In *Everlasting Love*, Borelli is an actress in real life playing a theatre actress who performs Film d'Art kinds of roles, ranging from Salome to Carmen. Within this contamination of film by theatre, *Everlasting Love* also borrows the themes of national security and espionage from the adventure genre. Borelli, however, does not turn into minor star Berta Nelson's successful Italian version of Mata Hari. More beautiful than adventurous, Borelli's character becomes a dancer and singer called Diana Cadouleur.

In the short film *Vittoria o Morte*, there are no doubts about Blanche's good faith and loyalty to her father, who is an important military figure. After knocking Blanche out with drugs hidden in a bunch of flowers, the enemy spy steals a small case containing confidential materials from her house. This theft offers Blanche an opportunity to prove herself and save her father's career, which, of course, she does. By contrast, in *Everlasting Love*, after the enemy spy steals military documents, Elsa Holbein (Borelli) is obliged to leave her father's house forever, becoming homeless and wandering the streets until she starts her performing career. This is only the first of her tribulations and adventures. The climax of Elsa's loneliness is staged in a railway station, the ultimate site of anonymity, mobility, and promiscuity—a location analogous to the movie theater, with its mixed audiences, ever-changing intertitles, and moving images on the screen. Elsa sits near the train track while she writes a letter. Behind her, a lonely man with a bottle of wine sits and drinks idly. The desolate, transitional, urban landscape of the railway station underlines the demise of her father's career in the military and her own precarious situation.

In *Vittoria o Morte* Blanche returns safely to the paternal house, but in *Everlasting Love*, only Diana's lover, Prince Maximilian, goes back home. After a passionate romance with Diana

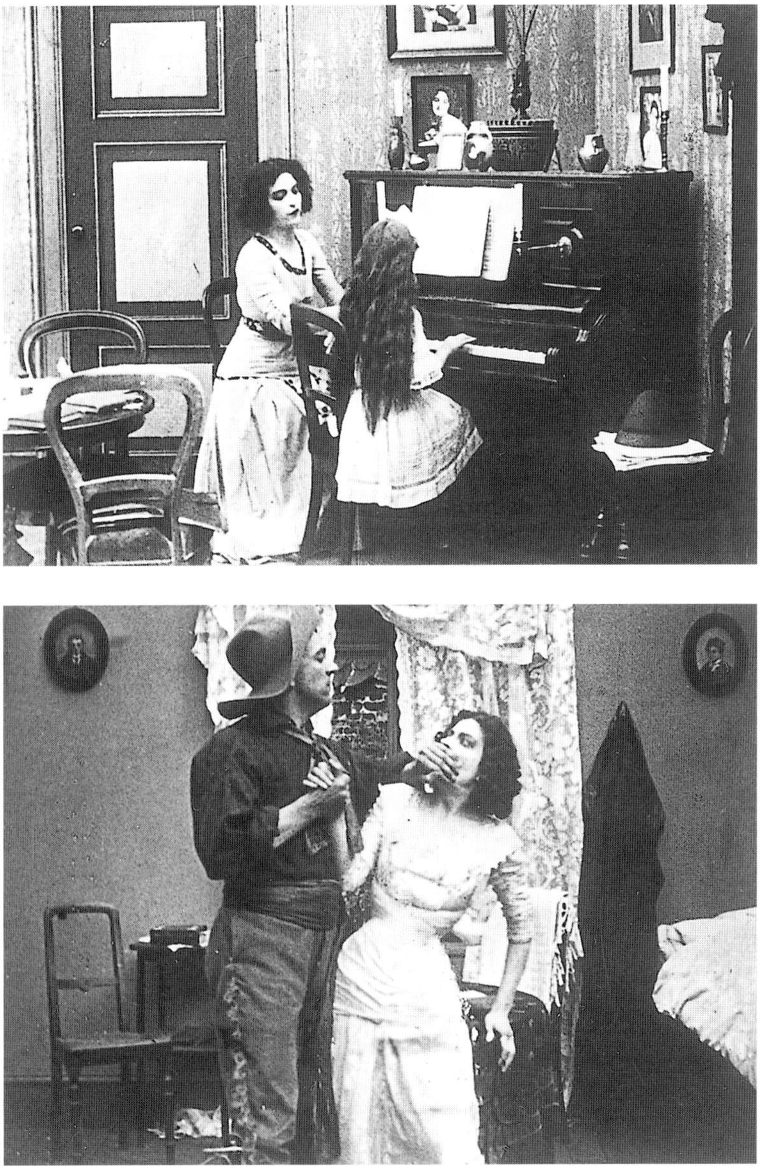

Asta Nielsen in Urban Gad's *Afgrunden* (1910; *The Abyss*). Courtesy Danish Film Institute, Copenhagen.

on the Riviera, the dashing aristocrat is obliged by his father to leave the foreign woman with the bad reputation. Desperate, Diana swallows poison and dies onstage, mixing fiction with reality: she is playing Marguerite's death scene from *La Dame aux Camélias* when the poison takes effect. Aware of Diana's suicide, Maximilian rushes onstage but does not interrupt the performance, for he is obliged to step into Armand's shoes while he holds in his arms the agonizing woman. Life must imitate art. In this particular case, the perfect collusion between theater and life confirms the cliché of the mater dolorosa, the woman who forever suffers in order to release her lover from any responsibility.

However, precisely because art was taken to be enmeshed with daily behavior, there is no reason why other episodes from diva films with an emancipationist thrust may not have been taken just as seriously by the audience. In comparison with the wholesome atmosphere of *Vittoria o Morte,* Caserini's film is a hothouse of steamy melodrama and feverish emotion. There is dishonor and betrayal; sacred love meets profane passion (Diana and Maximilian meet in a church!); horseback riding and Borelli's handling of a riding crop add a touch of female despotism to the story. Meanwhile the convalescent prince, looking lonely and romantic, turns into a figure of fantasy for every telephone operator, seamstress, typist, and shopgirl sitting at the movies.

Most importantly, courage belongs to a woman in *Vittoria o Morte,* but pleasure is brief and linked to water and motion in *Everlasting Love.* It lasts for only the span of a swift boat ride for the two lovers, who hold each other passionately and look backward toward the camera instead of forward toward their future. Their faces turn toward fiction and loss, rather than hope and reality, reminding us that suffering is endless in *Everlasting Love.* General Holbein commits suicide by gunshot; Elsa is relentlessly persecuted by the evil spy Sthar, whose tentacles extend to all centers of power; and finally, Diana's stage career is one long humiliation. Implicitly linked to prostitution, this mercantile aspect of her career is not shown, but is suggested by having crowds of tuxedoed men congregate in her dressing room.

In *Everlasting Love,* Lyda Borelli, forsaken by God, country, and family, becomes the living arabesque of art nouveau culture: she is the mass ornament of a whole epoch twisting itself in the grip of change. After the release of Caserini's film, the critics agreed that she blended elegance with eroticism, beauty with melancholia. In her history of Italian silent cinema, Maria Adriana Prolo writes: "In Caserini's *Everlasting Love* . . . what is most important is the modern *montage,* the use of close-ups, and the sets, which for the first time in film function in a mise-en-abyme arrangement" (emphasis added).[27]

Prolo's use of the word *montaggio,* in the sense of editing, is a bit premature because the autonomous tableau is still the fundamental narrative unit of this film. There is at least one long close-up of Borelli as she sits by the piano, but she looks much better in long shot. The more distant she is from the camera, the thinner her carefully arranged silhouette looks. Furthermore, the medium shot works best for capturing the fluid restlessness of her acting, which is characterized by a continuous change of registers and a constant shift from one role or attitude to another. She is all motion; her gestures use a miniature scale that is visible but not emphatic, precise and yet strangely overwrought. In the close-ups, the artificial lighting is too direct and homogeneous, so that her arms look swollen and her face slightly tired.

Notwithstanding Prolo's celebratory tone, what was new was that the single tableau functioned inside a network of multiple and powerful binary oppositions: good and evil, male and female, outside and inside, looking and being looked at. As soon as the film begins, for example, it is clear that the space near the piano in General Holbein's house belongs to Elsa, his daughter. By contrast, the area around the father's desk is a male preserve.

Toward the end of his film, Caserini duplicates but also fragments Borelli's silhouette across several contiguous mirrors that intercept areas of the room behind the static camera's eye. This echoing of the single figure across multiple surfaces makes the space look larger and more dynamic, while the deconstruction of her figure into a double profile in two adjacent mirrors spells out the contradictions of Elsa-Diana's modern identity. Just as in a cubist painting, the pieces of her life either do not fit together or are scattered here and there. In fact, the sequencing of the diva's body from mirror to mirror may underline multiple forms of entrapment: the father, the family, the social life, the society, the career, the international situation. Without a doubt, Diana's suicide is an act of masochism, but the multiplication of her image is so stunning that the camera looks as if it is moving even though it is not, and the victim appears incredibly powerful solely because of the repetition of her fragmented image. In a sense, the expression *mater dolorosa* is a strange oxymoron of family authority and social subordination.

Diana's suicide is part of an offscreen legend: Caserini, a humble man of the cinema, is filming Borelli, the great diva of the stage, who rose to fame in 1910 with her sensual Salome. The film they are making together, *Everlasting Love*, is hardly an original text, but rather a compilation of different stages of early Italian film woven together with different phases of Borelli's career: it moves from Berta Nelson's Blanche to Borelli's Elsa, from action-girl to Salome, and finally to Caserini's dying swan: dressed all in white, with pleats, folds, and ruffles of various sizes animating the outfit's sleeves, skirt, collar, and overlaid hems. Thanks to all this draping, Borelli fills the frame like a sort of endless yet monstrous creature.

Caserini's interweaving of space and time through the use of mirrors struck Prolo as a form of stylistic innovation, but the art historian Giovanni Lista argues that this conjugation in the plural of a singular element was commonly practiced by photographers in public squares and fairgrounds:

> *The itinerant photographers of the time who worked at the fairs and amusement parks made portraits that were composed of "multiple photographs achieved by the use of mirrors placed at an angle behind the sitter." A decade later, other avant-garde artists would pose for this kind of photograph. Duchamp, Picabia and Witkiewicz, for example, all composed very similar self-multiportraits. Basically this method of photography consisted of a multiplication of images of the subject, a technique used in famous paintings such as Lorenzo Lotto's* Triplo Ritratto di Orefice *(Triple Portrait of a Goldsmith) and Van Dyck's* Ritratto di Carlo in Tre Posizioni *(Portrait of Charles in Three Positions).*[28]

Even if the conceit is old, what is new here is that Caserini applied this awareness of the complexity of the self to a female film character played by a major actress from the theater. It is precisely this emphasis on the visual complications of Elsa-Diana's multifaceted image that acknowledges Borelli's official birth into film stardom. The diva is born at the very moment of her death. The ending of the film can be read as a reflection on the role that filmic stardom fulfills, caught as it is in the tension between something finite and something everlasting. Half knowingly, Caserini is already tapping into a metacinematic register of temporal metaphors. In fact, this collusion of dying minor star-character—the general's daughter—and emerging long-film diva—the singer on stage—summarizes the transition from urban modern woman to operatic prima donna in film.

The question, however, still remains of how a trite photographic technique could be deemed appropriate not only to move the diva Borelli from the theater to the screen, but also to distinguish her from a less prestigious star like Berta Nelson. Once again Lista helps with the answer by explaining that this particular photographic approach was considered to be appropriate even for important painters like Umberto Boccioni.[29] He approved of it precisely because this plural effect went against the technological specificity of photography itself. The latter was a medium considered limited to the single moment. To be sure, Boccioni used photography extensively to promote his career, but he always stressed that the camera was inferior to painting as he did so.

One particular shot of *Everlasting Love* demonstrates that the filmmaker was addressing a public whose demands for identification are more and more challenging and multidimensional. This new public was eager for narratives that were comparable one to the other, but also different each time. The birth of the diva was not only the beginning of female stardom in early Italian cinema, but also the construction of a new genre, the diva film. This extremely self-conscious text contains a turning point, and this is confirmed by the inscription of the figure of the spectator within *Everlasting Love.*

During Diana's performance as Carmen, Caserini's camera frames Prince Maximilian from behind. He sits alone inside his theater box, a faceless black silhouette voyeuristically consuming a flickering microscopic image in the far background of the shot. Borelli's minuscule figure has been made to look like the earliest example of a motion picture, which was available to only one spectator at a time inside Edison's kinetoscope (1888). This apparatus functioned as a private peepshow rather than a form of mass entertainment. Borelli is hardly recognizable, and Caserini's tunnel view of a female performer seals the start of a generic trajectory. But the gaze that fuels the genre belongs to the man. And yet the spectator is only a flat black shadow, unable to fully control the impact of the image he is looking at. Likewise, the diva became a tremendous term of reference for female spectators.

The argument in favor of *Everlasting Love*'s self-reflexivity is strengthened by Caserini's own views on the cinema and his outspoken position in the industry. In 1912, during a film conference in Rome on censorship and cinema's reputation, Caserini stated that the cinema was morally and aesthetically on a par with the theater. It seems that Caserini even tried to be chosen to direct Borelli in *Rapsodia Satanica.* Despite Caserini's efforts, Cines chose Nino Oxilia, Caserini's biggest rival. Oxilia's premature death during World War I, however, allowed Caserini to become involved with this important film during the very last stages of production, just before *Rapsodia*'s delayed release, in 1917.

The Short and the Long Film: Female Fantasies

To return to the shift from the short to the long film, theatrical methods were alive and well in diva films: the actors use the sides of the frame as if they were theatrical wings. In many cases, doors, windows, thick curtains, and thresholds frame the divas. By contrast, in the minor-star films, doors, windows, entrances, and steps have a more informational or rerouting function in the narrative and a much less theatrical or displaying function in relation to the star's body.

Unlike the modest short film with minor stars, the diva-film gave costumes a central role, since the analysis of identity was developed through one sartorial change after another. For minor stars, the wardrobe was limited and mostly contemporary. The modern woman was often a middle-class youngster dressed like an ordinary person, but the minor star had a stronger sense of initiative than the average female viewer. In Caserini's *Nelly La Domatrice,* for example, Fernanda Negri-Pouget is so brave that she treats her lion as if it were a pet; she confides the troubles of her heart to it. Unfortunately, her judgment in men is utterly superficial, for she marries an aristocrat who gallantly retrieved the handkerchief she threw in the lion's cage. After a few years with the evil aristocrat, Nelly decides to go back to her former lover, a simple member of her old circus troupe. The lesson to be learned: when you are already financially independent, do not behave like a self-centered creature. Choose a man according to your heart, and not by his wallet or his social status.

Despite the changing status of professional female identity on- and offscreen before and after World War I, it was perhaps even harder to become a female filmmaker than to succeed as an actress. Lucio D'Ambra's *L'Illustre Attrice Cicala Formica* (1920; The Illustrious Actress Cicada Ant) explores precisely this situation in the context of family life. The film is a lovely, humorous, and action-packed spoof about a young woman (Lia Formia) who wants to be both a director and a diva. Following her instructions, Lia's family dons togas and gesticulates in Roman fashion. The young director's newfound aura, however, is challenged by the arrival of a group of old men. This honorary committee awards a prize to Lia's father, a pillar of the community on the edge of retirement but unwilling to give up his place in the spotlight. The narrative, therefore, splits into a double plot involving the father's award ceremony and the shooting of the daughter's film. This competition between an old male *divo* and a young female diva discloses how the problem of women's emancipation was not only based on social and legal issues, but also deeply rooted in the structure of the Italian family.

When the day arrives for the premiere screening of the diva film, the whole family, an enthusiastic and anxious audience, turns out to see it. The projection begins amidst general laughter, and it soon becomes clear that there is something wrong with the film reel. The world and its inhabitants are all rapidly moving backward. Even though this film in reverse is a technical slipup instead of an experimental technique, it does suggest how unsettling a young daughter's ambition can be for those around her. In the end, the projection takes place correctly, but Formia's cinematic career is already drawing to a close. The patriarchal hierarchy is quickly reestablished in the last scene when the father admonishes his young daughter and reminds her that her proper role in life is to mend socks.

Despite the sad ending of *L'Illustre Attrice Cicala Formica,* the film stands out for its energy and irreverent handling of authority. The characters are all one-dimensional caricatures, but they are never drawn with cruelty. Each family member is individually introduced, and each characterization retains a certain freshness. At the same time, each family member is also presented as bordering on the grotesque, but never bizarre or monstrous. Thus, the viewer becomes aware early on that a typical Italian middle-class family can also look like the oddest possible group of people. Strangeness thrives at the heart of normalcy. Despite the punishment from her father at the end, the young diva demonstrates amazing organizational abilities.

Cinema was perceived to be a medium new and flexible enough to accommodate the representation of women breaking the rules and going unpunished, especially if the narrative framework was comedic or fantastic. It is undeniable that Febo Mari's *Il Fauno* (1917) contains a narrative nucleus based on sheer female erotic desire, presented through the self-conscious analogy between a woman's dream and the projection of a film. In this particular case, a woman's imagination brings to life the sculpture of a faun. Famous for his elegant persona, Febo Mari in the role of the faun is a product of a woman's imagination. The faun allows Fede (Faithful, played by [Antonietta] Ninetta Mordeglia, Mari's wife), the loyal companion of an adulterous sculptor, to dream of utopian love in the countryside. The selfish sculptor leaves Fede home alone to go to a tabarin in the city, where he gambles and flirts with Femmina (Elena Makowska). Through the fictional name Femmina (Female), the diva's character is limited to the stereotype of the femme fatale. Eventually Femmina, a wealthy princess, purchases the sculpted faun; Fede is too poor to buy it from her. To try to get her beloved faun back, she goes to the femme fatale's lawyer to discuss the situation. The price to be paid, it turns out, would be an affair with the old man, who then would persuade the wealthy princess to give up the statue. But Fede refuses to go down this route. The opposition of these two names, Fede and Femmina, leads to a series of tentative interpretations: on the one hand, Fede is like a wife who leads a boring life at home. On the other hand, Femmina is the modern woman because she is financially independent.

In Mari's *Il Fauno,* the cinema has the power to take a myth about male creativity and turn it upside down. Because it is a traditional art form, sculpture is associated with masculinity, but also with cold marble. By contrast, sculpture in motion—the living faun—is a paraphrase of the cinema, which originates out of a woman's mind. And a woman's imagination is as mobile and vivifying as the flames of the fireplace next to which Fede falls asleep to dream of her romance with the living faun. As soon as Fede and Femmina begin to fight for possession of the statue, the sculptor must destroy his own creation. This narrative development is crucial. In sculpting the faun, the sculptor produced an imaginary portrait of the ideal lover from a woman's point of view, although he could never live up to this model. Even his lover, Femmina, observes that the statue of the faun exercises an unusual attraction for her, thus suggesting that she is more interested in it than in the sculptor. Unable to become what he has created, the sculptor has no choice but to destroy the sculpture. The faun statue not only becomes an object of contention between two women, but also painfully reminds the male artist of his own inadequacies.

The ending of Mari's film is an interesting example of conscious male self-criticism in the panorama of early Italian cinema, outside the comedy genre.

As the sculptor grows more superficial and corrupt, the faun demonstrates greater awareness of, and ambivalence about, the sculptor's conduct. He keeps repeating to Fede: "All men are half animals." The destruction of the faun declares the artist's inability to share his art with others, while it also perpetuates the theme of women's rivalry. But even these stereotypes of Fede as a madonna and Femmina as a whore seem to have run their course. Perhaps this is why Febo Mari associated both women with the tantalizing image of arabesque. In the case of Femmina, this

Elena Makowska. Author's collection.

Febo Mari. Author's collection.

pattern appears all over a gauzy window curtain so thin that the femme fatale, by stepping away from the window, looks as though she is being born out of the fabric's folds, like Venus emerging from the sea foam. Visually, the effect is so beautiful that, all of a sudden, we begin to like this evil character. In the case of Fede, Mari uses this pattern when she is gazing through a peephole in a door. Seeing Fede's face in close-up through this opening, masked by a lace-like arabesque, we feel as if we were getting a glimpse into an intricate but also delicate and wonderfully complex mind. Once again, this arabesque is a gratuitously beautiful image that, though difficult to read, remains unforgettable, like a cipher or a hieroglyph capable of marking the film as a woman's film forever.

Thus, by unraveling the love triangle to the point of no return, Mari's film explores a general crisis of creativity that affects men as well as women: the sculptor's art generates only competition, loss, or hate. The opposition between love in the countryside and corruption in the city suggests an antimodern stance, a nostalgia for a lost world of innocence, and a sense of paralysis in the present, since neither the aristocracy, through Femmina, nor the middle classes, through Fede, are able to get what they want. In addition, Mari's iconography in the countryside becomes complicated enough to warrant analysis.

Fede's long hair is cut and used to weave the string for the faun's bow. All of a sudden she is wearing the most modern of haircuts instead of evoking the disheveled appearance of Medusa. Just as surprising, when the faun hangs from a tree, he looks like an ape reflecting itself upside down on the surface of a pond. But this topsy-turvy and unflattering reenactment of the Narcissus myth places more stress on the loss of gravity than of masculine beauty. Weightless and free of all conventions, the upside-down image of the faun invokes the camera obscura.

Another example of female fantasy is Baldassarre Negroni's *L'Histoire d'un Pierrot* (1913), based on a musical pantomime by Mario Costa, with Francesca Bertini in the role of Pierrot and Leda Gys as Luisette. After a brief marriage to Luisette, the young and naïve Pierrot is led astray by the evil wine merchant Pochinet (Emilio Ghione). The wine merchant hopes to distract Pierrot with drinking and gambling while he tries to seduce Luisette. The story ends with the reunification of the couple after the birth of a child. Although Negroni figures in the credits as the director, he left the production of *L'Histoire d'un Pierrot* halfway through. Francesca Bertini and her close friend Ghione ended up doing most of the extant work under the supervision of Baron Alberto Fassini at Celio Film, a branch of Cines. Only eighteen years old, Bertini quickly showed that she was already a leader, hence a director, for she could both act and be in charge of an entire production team. To conclude, *L'Histoire d'un Pierrot* proposes a definition of gender roles as states of being affected by all kinds of transitional appearances. Like the faun, the Pierrot figure belongs to the register of the grotesque, in the sense that both creatures are mixtures. The faun mixes the human with the animal; the Pierrot combines the childlike with a strange butterfly look, his costume a cross between a baby's dress and an androgynous nightgown. In either case, the adoption of the grotesque register suggests that hybrid identities are a temporary stage in the renewal of the modern self.

Good and Bad, Old and New

In *Il Fauno*, gambling thrives in the city, as it does in Vincenzo Denizot's *Come una Sorella* (1912; Like A Sister). References to new technologies, namely, the cinema and the airplane, overlap with the destructive and urban female sexuality of a cabaret singer. In *Il Fauno*, the split is between an aristocratic femme fatale and a modest artist's companion. In *Come una Sorella*, the struggle of values plays itself out within one woman, Nelly, a dancer who performs like a tempting Salome in an orientalist atmosphere. Nelly's movements arouse the cinematic screen itself to the point that it is overwhelmed by vivid red flames. The same kind of tinting—a red that looks like fire mixed with blood—pervades the screen as soon as the airplane of the stunt pilot, Koslevsky, crashes to the ground, leaving him between death and life. The film's associations between excitement and destruction, modern technology and female sexuality, are undeniable, but they are resolved when the cabaret singer becomes the adoring nurse who brings her beloved pilot back to health.

By going to the movies, women spectators could compensate for, and even find the energy to overcome, all kinds of sacrifices and boredom in the fabric of their daily lives. A married woman leaves the house to go to the movies, and, of course, her jealous husband suspects that she will be meeting her secret lover there in the dark. This sets off a spiraling series of mishaps in the film *Una Tragedia al Cinematografo* (1913), an eight-minute spoof by Enrico Guazzoni and starring a hardly recognizable Pina Menichelli, two years before

Pina Menichelli in Enrico Guazzini's *Una Tragedia al Cinematografo* (1913). Courtesy Nederlands Filmmuseum, Amsterdam.

her elevation to diva status. The wife's urban *flânerie* is both problematic and unavoidable; in the wake of industrialization, a woman's acceptable orbit was enlarged to include the home, the movie theater, and the department store.

The department stores Mele, in Naples, and UPIM, in Turin, opened in 1902 and 1905, respectively. The female shopper was a requirement for an industrial economy based on consumption. To make things even more complicated, the cinematic audience included families as well as unmarried couples. In a sense, the cinema was responsible for producing unprecedented mixtures of backgrounds, intentions, and situations. This is the conclusion articulated by Monsignor Alfredo Maria Cavagna in his comments about the cinema's erosion of boundaries between morality and immorality as well as among social classes: "The peasant girl imitates the city girl; the city girl stops wearing socks to imitate the wake of the country girl. It is hard to tell who is the maid and who is the young lady of the house, especially when the latter stops wearing her hat just because the maid is also not doing it; makeup and lipstick know nothing about differences at the level of class, age, and diet; everybody is happily smoking because this is the fashion of the cinema."[30]

Menichelli's jealous husband in *Una Tragedia al Cinematografo* is not the only one to associate women and cinema with sinful behavior. Without any reference to or concern for the men sitting in the theater, the manager of the movie theater interrupts the show and asks all the women who have something to hide to leave immediately. And, indeed, they all do. Such an exodus makes it clear that the cinema, like unaccompanied women, suffered from a bad reputation.

While the ending of *Una Tragedia al Cinematografo* confirms that the dark environment of the theater lends itself to illicit flirtations, it is ironic that the independent wife is perfectly innocent. On the other hand, the husband's behavior is so extreme that he manages to disrupt a whole projection. And indeed, as soon as the screening stops, all the embarrassed or guilty men left in the theater stream out of the backdoor one by one.

Una Tragedia al Cinematografo is one of several films about women at the cinema that comment on the new medium's definition of female identity. In Vincenzo Denizot's *Maciste* (1915), a sixty-five-minute film shot under the additional supervision of Giovanni Pastrone, a young woman (Clementina Gay) goes to the Salon Ghersi in Turin to see the famous *Cabiria* (1914), starring the good-hearted and athletic Maciste. While she is admiring Maciste's muscles, she realizes that he is the only one who can save her from her uncle's financial manipulations. In this case, a financial emergency takes the attention away from sheer physical lust. So Maciste's female fan goes to Itala Film, the star's production house, and persuades him to help foil her uncle's evil machinations. Finally, the powerful giant solves all her family problems. By so doing, he behaves like a big brother or protective father, and the young woman's initial romantic attraction falls out of the narrative.

The cinema, both as a medium and a social institution, could be a woman's ally, and it could also help women by revealing men's vanity. In the ten-minute comedy *Al Cinematografo Guardate . . . e non Toccate* (1912; At the Movies, Look but Do Not Touch), the comedian Ernesto Vaser plays a nincompoop who manages to get thrown out of a movie theater after committing a series of annoying acts. He begins by harassing a married woman in the street, and even follows her into a seamstress's shop. Later he follows her into the movies, still hoping for some kind of sexual contact, but he succeeds only in getting deeper and deeper into trouble: in the darkness of the cinema, he kisses her husband by mistake, and he plays footsie with an ugly old babysitter.

Everybody goes to the movies: the cinema's entrance space includes old and young, rich and poor. Furthermore, this particular story begins with the members of a model family leaving their apartment building in Turin and going off in different directions. Yet this is not a family in crisis; instead, the family draws stability from the cinema, since they plan to meet later and go to the movies together.

While the cinema has the potential to provide healthy entertainment for all, the modern street can be chaotic and confusing. The domestic threshold is associated with gestures of mutual respect and independence, but the entrance to the Turinese movie theater, "Itala," in *Al Cinematografo Guardate . . . e non Toccate,* recalls the noise and confusion of a fairground, a sideshow, or a circus entrance. It is as if a comedy of errors were being acted outdoors before the projection of a comic short indoors. Instead of containing social disorder, the urban location of the cinema stimulates unrest as the space outside the box office becomes an improvised boxing ring for the Itala employees.

Al Cinematografo Guardate . . . e non Toccate (1912; At the Movies, Look but Do Not Touch). Courtesy Nederlands Filmmuseum, Amsterdam.

These workers include the barker in front of the movie theater as well as two other fellows who are busy folding leaflets or arranging them on a nearby stand. (One wonders whether these two Itala employees in working-class garb are distributing announcements about future movies or plot summaries and reviews concerning the spectacle of the day.) The workers blend into the scene, but Vaser stands out because he is elegantly dressed, like a wealthy and respectable bourgeois. Little does he know that the woman's corset he has stolen at the seamstress's shop hangs between his legs like a tail.

A misfit, Vaser is also unable to stand in line like everybody else and nearly forgets to buy his ticket before he steps in. Because of his absent-minded behavior and lack of concern for others, the foolish playboy provokes a fight between the dwarfish barker and the other little man in charge of the stand. Mostly carried out at the level of clothes, gestures, body types, and spatial arrangements, the commentary about class relations outside the movie theater is subtle but unmistakable.

Single women and families enter the theater in an orderly manner, and the Itala workers function like an efficient assembly line. Instead it is Vaser, the unmarried middle-class male with an inflated notion of his own social standing and sex appeal, who becomes a public threat, disrupting mass entertainment. Once inside the theater, the film within the film—namely, the comedy projected to this 1912 audience—stimulates some friendly conversation between a husband and wife.

This exchange is necessary because the early cinematic narratives were not always self-sufficient or easily understandable. The man and woman are helping each other link the intertitles to the images; the movies can be part of maintaining a good marriage.

Mariute

Edoardo Bencivenga's *Mariute* (1918) is an ideal text with which to conclude this overview of the modern Italian woman, whether she is an average moviegoer, a female athlete, a secret agent, or even a diva. To begin with, *Mariute*'s split narrative structure underlines Francesca Bertini's awareness that the diva is a cultural phenomenon caught between old and new. At the end of the film, the diva presents herself as a modern woman with political views and a sense of social responsibility. On the other hand, the center of *Mariute* is occupied by the rape of a peasant woman—also played by Bertini—during World War I.

The film opens with a medium shot of Bertini as Mariute, a peasant woman in regional costume, smiling to the audience. This self-conscious greeting precedes a whole section in which Bertini, the diva, does play "the diva," but the parody is interspersed with allusions to the actress's own professional seriousness. Perhaps Bertini could afford this tone of ironic self-empowerment because her own production house was involved in making the film.

The first half of *Mariute* resembles a documentary about film history, since the people on the screen have the same jobs as they do in real life. Gustavo Serena plays the director, who repeatedly telephones Bertini in the morning to persuade her to come to work. Livio Pavanelli and Camillo De Riso are the two male leads who are kept idle on the set by Bertini's absence. The diva gets up late in the morning. One may think that she has been entertaining male suitors all night, but this is not the case: she spent the previous evening by herself. In fact, she read all night, and she wishes to continue reading in the morning. The suggestion is that she is tired of playing frivolous roles and is looking for something with more depth and concentration. Bertini eats breakfast in bed and flirts on the telephone. We see her at her morning toilette: she graces the viewer with a view of her half-naked shoulders from behind; she does her nails; she looks at herself in the mirror; and she lounges in a kimono. Here Bertini runs through all the clichés of diva behavior: narcissism, self-indulgence, wealthy habits, and excess leisure. The sequence of actions and situations is so carefully timed that the actress calls attention to these stereotypical activities—precisely because she wants to expose the constructed nature of the icon she has become.

Bertini's fondness for studying sharply contrasts with the completely bookless mise-en-scène of another waking-up scene. In Vanna Piccini's fashion booklet *Le Elegantissime* (1922), there is a chapter called "La Giornata di Una Signora d'Oggi" (A Day in the Life of a Contemporary Woman), from which we learn everything about a typical socialite's morning routine: "It is still dark in Donna Anna's bedroom: it is ten o'clock sharp . . . and Donna Anna keeps on sleeping as if it were the middle of the night." The description continues with the aristocrat consulting her personal calendar. The social engagements for the day include both male suitors and society women: "Donna Anna goes through her calendar book: a few pages in a golden case with a little pencil mounted with a turquoise." Piccini's attention to precious and ornamental detail compensates for the thinness of substance in the "little calendar book with only a few pages."[31]

Once Bertini's morning routine is over, "The Diva's Arrival" flashes on an intertitle: Bertini reaches the set in her private carriage; a group of young girls greet her; and a reception committee is standing nearby. Clearly she is a role model for future generations. Such an iconography has an aura of solemnity more than of scandal: the diva's arrival resembles the appearance of a major political personality. She is not simply beautiful; she is authoritative. Then, as usual, the daily working routine unfolds on the shooting set. After the intertitle "Miss Francesca Bertini at Work on the Set," we see a trite example of film melodrama with all the well-known ingredients: a tense conversation between two lovers, a letter—perhaps an anonymous message, because one lover has betrayed the other—scenes in which someone faints or someone gets strangled. The shallowness of the material is apparent; neither Bencivenga nor Bertini try to hide it.

Suddenly news from the front reaches the set. After listening to the words of a former soldier (Alberto Albertini) who is now working as an actor, Bertini undergoes a sudden inner change. Once back home, she cannot sleep peacefully any longer, and begins to dream fitfully. The second half of the film is based on the diva's dream of herself as Mariute. She is a peasant woman living with her children in Friuli, in the northeast. Her husband is away fighting the Austrian enemy; her only support is the old grandfather. Bertini's dream sequence turns into a nightmare when Mariute walks back into the house disheveled and traumatized. The grandfather takes his gun from the wall and goes out seeking revenge upon the soldiers who have raped Mariute in the forest.

The intercutting technique deployed during this section of the film raises many questions. When the grandfather kills the soldiers, each shot of the grandfather firing his gun is intercut with a single frame of Mariute holding on to her children. The analogy between shot-by-shot editing and killing is worth mentioning, since it provides a definition of cinema as a weapon. The intertitle, "Revenge," encourages the audience to side with Bertini as the victim and the grandfather as the avenger. Yet the editing remains ambiguous, for it releases a strange dispersal of terror. The grandfather's gunshots are fired against an enemy who is not shown. As a result, they pull into their orbit Bertini's body much more than the enemy's image. It looks as if the actress is being victimized a second time, after the rape. Still, the children's presence and the intertitle "Revenge" help decrease the ambiguity, but the omission of the enemy is too problematic to be forgotten.

The diva's dream ends with a clear message about Bertini's newly found commitment to her country: "Such a terrible dream kindled the patriotic flame in the heart of Francesca Bertini." The implication is that the rape and the vendetta have exorcised the *capricci*, or tantrums, of the diva. Critics writing in Bertini's day as well as later historians applied infantilizing metaphors in their descriptions of the diva. In those days, an unmarried woman was always considered a child. In fact, Bertini's father chaperoned his daughter from contract to contract, from the lawyer's office to the producer's set.

The intertitle about the dream and patriotism is followed by the diva's second arrival on the set, this time in simple dark clothes and without too much fanfare. According to

Pina Menichelli in Amleto Palermi's *L'Età Critica* (1921). Courtesy Cineteca Nazionale, Rome.

film historian Roberto Paolella, this was not the original ending of the film.[32] After recalling his experience of *Mariute* as a spectator, Paolella reminds us that a coda was added to the narrative. In this segment—which is now lost and does not appear in the two surviving prints, one available through the Cineteca Nazionale of Rome, the other from the Library of Congress in Washington, D.C.—Bertini looks directly into the camera, thus breaking the narrative illusion. In the intertitles, she asks her public to invest in government bonds to support the war effort. She is the spokesperson for the Istituto Nazionale delle Assicurazioni (National Insurance Institute), which funded the film.

In comparison with other diva films, *Mariute* is an especially divided text. The strong-willed prima donna's personality, grafted onto the modern woman, is pitched against the values of the previous generation through the figure of the grandfather. He is the embodiment of a dying patriarchy, the representative of a world that precedes all forms of modernity: mechanized warfare, the cinema, and women's emancipation.

The real diva, not the fictional Mariute, has the responsibility of sending the political message. Such an assignment of patriotic agency makes the serious new woman emerge out of the clichés attached to the frivolous diva. Shortly before Bertini's arrival on the set, Camillo De Riso, one of her two male leads, addresses a little crowd. An iris shot isolates two old men, and an intertitle explains: "and with hardly any following, Camillo De Riso engages in a mysterious propaganda." It is apparent that Bertini is a better representative than De Riso for the national cause. This comparison between diva and actor suggests that the grandfather's violence not only stems from revenge, but also has to compensate for the weakness of a younger male generation.

If Bertini is to represent the Italian cause, which of her many real life and fictional roles will she play? How will her audience perceive her? Some might argue that if Bertini allows the nation's voice to speak through her silent body on film, she is nothing more than a ventriloquist dummy. Others might contend that Bertini has been hypnotized, since the dreamlike section of the film can be read as an implantation of nationalistic rhetoric into the actress's unconscious. Two iris shots, one at the very beginning and one at the very end, signal that the camera is moving in and out of the dreamer's mental boundaries. It is significant that the style of the sequence is realistic rather than surreal so the condensations and displacements of the dreamwork cannot express themselves visually. And this realistic style has nothing to do with technological limitations, for Giovanni Pastrone's *Cabiria* (1914) boasts an impressive dream sequence whose artificial style feeds a surreal effect. The open question here is whether Bertini as Mariute is just a puppet, or whether Bertini as a career woman, celebrity, and patriot is a presence strong enough to incorporate the victimized peasant woman. The latter fits the well-known stereotype of woman as land violated by the enemy.

Political involvement was one of the activities associated with the new woman of modernity. Without a doubt, Bertini's stance in *Mariute* was more honorable and admirable than Pina Menichelli's bad girl in *L'Età Critica* (1921), directed by Amleto Palermi. Here Menichelli plays no mater dolorosa. Instead she becomes a reckless teenager who drives a young officer of the Italian navy to suicide. In Donna Paola's 1919 book, *La Donna della Nuova Italia: Documenti del Contributo Femminile alla Guerra, Maggio 1915–Maggio 1917* (The Woman of the New Italy: Feminine Contributions to the War Effort, May 1915–May 1917), entire sections are explicitly devoted to feminism, nursing, female heroism, and propaganda, and it includes at the end a list of notable persons, organized according to Italian region and foreign cities (which enables her to include citizens living abroad or in the colonies). In supporting the war effort from the screen, Bertini was joining an illustrious crowd of female intellectuals and writers, including Gina Lombroso Ferrero, Teresa Labriola, Margherita Sarfatti, Ada Negri, and Annie Vivanti.[33]

Donna Paola's view of socially engaged femininity does not emerge from the pages of Ottorino Modugno's *Le Donne Mute* (The Silent Women), a study of actresses published in 1918. I shall here simply cite the stifling imperatives of the coda-like memorandum addressed to female readers who are also aspiring divas:

> 1. Remember that the cinema is an art form.
> 2. If you do not know that it is an art, do not call yourself actress, but silent woman.
> 3. Be modest, more modest, and even more modest.
> 4. Do not imagine yourself as someone you are not. . . .

5. You can see all your faults on screen: improve!
6. Do not think of yourself as a diva, because this vocabulary is overly theatrical.
7. Be a woman like all other women.
8. As an actress, remember that you have no words and you have to compensate with your expression.
9. Be dignified, but not arrogant.
10. Do not prostitute yourself in order to become a silent film actress.
11. Persuade yourself that no man's passion can give you the artistic talent you do not have.
12. Amen![34]

If Ottorino Modugno had gone to the premiere screening of *Mariute,* he would probably have had mixed feelings watching Bertini take a political stand in the coda. Modugno includes photos of Bertini and writes about her in his book. Since she presents herself as a *figlia d'arte,* he cannot associate her with the type he disapprovingly calls "a woman who is tired of typing." Still he manages to despise her origins and undermine her talent: "This woman made it all the way to the cinema when she was acting in a low-level theatrical company from Naples and when she was the humblest of actresses." Modugno is regrettably obliged to admit: "Francesca Bertini's one and only merit is to have brought a spark of originality to silent film. And like all original people, she had a lot of luck."[35] Shrewdly, after this concession, the writer switches to the Danish Asta Nielsen, and the implication is that the foreign actress is much worthier of artistic respect and approval as a career woman.

In 1918 the climate of opinion about women and war, on the one hand, and about women and cinema, on the other, was probably a composite of Paola's and Modugno's perspectives. Hence we can conclude that though Bertini's political voice in the coda might have been ventriloquized, at least she was no longer *muta* in the metaphorical sense of Modugno's derogative title. Despite the obvious soundlessness of silent film's intertitles, her support of suffering people during the war was, so to speak, loud and clear. Regardless of ideological disputes across Italian society between prowar futurist groups and antiwar socialist demonstrations, Bertini in *Mariute* chose to be a famous diva speaking with authority to her following, and this was a rare demonstration of a woman's political agency in public.

In *Mariute,* Bertini also manages to make the men around her look ineffectual, without coming across as the only source of their weakness. The force of the diva's on-screen image and her verbal appeal in the coda set up a certain competition between the grandfather—the man with the gun—and Bertini's shifting roles. Such a feeling of rivalry lingers on after the film has ended. In addition, the former soldier has compromised his masculine authority by working as an actor. It is worth mentioning here that in the genre of the diva film, men involved in the arts were most likely to become the victims of femmes fatales. In Giovanni Pastrone's *Il Fuoco* (1915), Pina Menichelli destroys a painter's mental health. The assumption behind this combination of ruthless diva and sensitive artist was that making art, just like making love, weakened the male. On the other hand, Modugno's diatribe against actresses springs from the conviction that the female brain is too small to fully master the meaning of "Art" with a capital *A.*

The elision of Mariute's husband in the

dream and the absence of a well-defined strong man for Bertini on the set suggest a certain distrust of youthful masculinity, namely, the generation of men most vulnerable to the femme fatale's spell. The distrust of male artists also explains why Camillo De Riso is less effective than the diva in discussing the political situation with the crowd of curious bystanders hanging around the set. I would speculate, therefore, that casting the grandfather as the heroic avenger in *Mariute* was symptomatic of an uneasiness not only with the unsettling power of the diva, but also with the unreliability of young males in a newborn nation with unstable boundaries.

By the early thirties, within a film culture completely transformed by the advent of sound, the demise of the silent divo offered the comedian Ettore Petrolini (1886–1936) an opportunity to parody the lounge lizards of the previous epoch through the character of "Gastone": "film actor, vaudeville artist, danseur, diseur, a regular of the bal-tabarins, playboy, a man of charm."[36] Most important is that, during his cabaret act as Gastone, Petrolini was making fun of the divo Alberto Collo, who worked frequently with Bertini. To return now to *Mariute* and to World War I, it is telling that, despite being late on the set, the diva enjoys more credibility and popularity than the returning veteran as the voice of national propaganda.

Mariute ends with Bertini as a sort of statuesque "Donna Italia," yet the issue of a woman's desire remains unresolved: the rape is too brutal a response to women's newfound power as producers and as consumers in Italian society. The political funding of the film by the state-owned National Insurance Company was not enough to channel all the energy of the actress into an Italian counterpart to the French Marianne, the 1789 revolutionary heroine. With an amazing feat of narrative elasticity, comparable to the dualistic organization of *Mariute*, Bertini personified the abstract ideal of the unified, national body politic, as well as a very real image of femininity in turmoil, divided between amusement and career, intellectualism and leisure, a transgressive profession and earning money. More specifically, Bertini's prowar stance was more in line with that of the wealthy *haute bourgeoisie*, given that opposition to the war was more frequent among working-class women.[37]

In a sense, the diva's cross-generic mobility within *Mariute*—half parody, half drama—corresponded to her powerful populist appeal, one aimed at men and women across all social classes. If this definition of Bertini's popularity still worked in 1918, it was becoming obsolete by 1922, at least in the pages of *Le Elegantissime*. Vanna Piccini there compares Donna Anna's highbrow tastes with her maid's humble outings: "Yesterday evening Madame la Marquise went to *Parsifal* . . . 'Yes, and I am exhausted. Five hours of Wagner makes you tired—it can kill you. What divine music!' Instead of Wagner's divine music that kills, Lisa thinks, she prefers *The Queen of the Cinematograph*, a lovely operetta."[38]

In Piccini's world of 1922, in the aftermath of Mussolini's rise to power, Bertini and her colleagues have lost their erotic charge, and have been corralled into a title that is safe even for boarding-school girls. "The Queen of the Cinematograph" is the inane correlative of Wagner's much more sublime and virile music—the music that overwhelms Donna Anna.

And yet only a few years before with *Mariute*, Bertini's dual citizenship in the past and the future, her status as an icon of patriotism and emancipation, was comparable to a tightrope-walking act across high and low classes to appeal to the broadest audience possible. A few quick examples from women's magazines should suffice to sketch the climate of opinion during the first phase of the diva's career. *La Donna,* for example, was a biweekly magazine founded in Rome by 1906 and published in Turin until 1916. In its illustrated pages, the following headings stand out: Articles by Matilde Serao; Literary Female Profiles; Advice on Beauty and Elegance; Etiquette; Kitchen and House; Health and Hygiene; Strauss's *Salomè;* Reports from Foreign Countries; Women and Industrialization; Fashion and Sports; Literary and Theatrical Reviews. A couple of covers show women driving cars and riding horses. Another example was *Regina* (1905–1908), a magazine that declared: "This magazine will be published in Naples and Paris, and the contributors will be the greatest French and Italian best-selling writers." In comparison with *La Donna, Regina*'s pages offer deeper glimpses into different social classes: one article is about the lunch break of factory women in Italy, but the same issue also carries reports of hunting parties and, literally, the "lifestyles of the rich and famous."

Both the diva film and the modern-woman film were in touch with foreign models; whether the female protagonist was a diva in a long film or a minor star in a short film, she was bound to be popular and controversial at the same time. Such a mixture of scandal and celebrity mirrored the cinema's position as a new medium at the center of an intricate web of favorable but also negative reactions. In the end, neither a female actress nor the cinema was as heavily criticized as the awkward male moviegoer impersonated by Vaser in his comedic shorts. This suggests that although change was primarily associated with the cinema and the women's movement, the real crisis was with the average young middle-class male who felt threatened by the gentle sex and professionally displaced in a difficult national economy.

CHAPTER 7

Tropes

OBSESSIONS AND TRAUMAS OF A GENRE

Even though only a small percentage of diva films have survived, most of the recovered or restored prints resemble one another in their settings, plots, themes, and construction of character. This is not to say that all diva films are exactly alike, but rather that a single sequence or a beautiful image is often easier to remember than the complicated and redundant narratives of the genre. With the diva film, storytelling tends to use the same situations and dilemmas over and over again. The term *trope* here means a confluence of strong elements—themes, motifs, imagery, symbols, plot situations, character types. The tension between narrative and spectacle in the melodramatic genre is a well-known topic of film criticism, but in the case of the diva film, this model alone cannot sufficiently explain why its storytelling can be incoherent, elliptical, erratic, and repetitive.[1] Possible explanations are missing footage or poorly developed plotlines, but I also think that the diva film deals with such traumatic material that narrative structure itself veers toward the delirious.

An evaluation of whether the diva film's narratives are well told—clear, developed, deep—often ends with a negative conclusion. Of all the films I have examined, only Leopoldo Carlucci's *Caino* uses a script that would qualify as a well-made play. This concept stems from Victorien Sardou's reputation in French theater for producing plots with a carefully thought-out architecture of incidents and coincidences, doublings and triangles. In *Caino,* the plot depends on two brothers and two sisters, and everything proceeds and precipitates toward the end with mathematical precision. In contrast to *Caino,* the typical diva film resembles a futurist crazy dress with one sleeve longer than the other, too many buttons on one side, and a slanted border at the bottom.

For all these reasons, it is far more satisfying to look at diva films through a comparative thematic framework. Taking this more iconographic and less narrative approach makes it apparent that the diva film was a weak but intense genre, a vulnerable, short-lived form that powerfully kindled the public's imagination.[2] This out-of-balance genre drew its life from strong iconic units—the visual equivalent of tropes—though it occasionally twisted them much more forcefully than the literature or the paintings of the period ever did. The diva film cries out about social issues while it also dazzles its viewers into an imaginary world that no literary description or theatrical performance could ever match.

The diva film knew that it could function like a quasi-surreal document, or documentary of the imagination, with a force of denunciation that anticipated 1940s postwar neorealism. That sober, documentary-like visual style is traditionally considered the extreme opposite of the escapist melodramas of the silent period. At the end of *Il Quadro di Osvaldo Mars*, a film with a violent plot built around a portrait of Salome, the police inspector declares, "I never dealt with so many ordinary people." This is a crucial reminder that the diva film dealt with ordinary cases and not with exceptional extremes. To be sure, two of the most common problems of private life in Italy at the beginning of the twentieth century were the conflict between men and women around divorce and adultery, and the rescue of children born out of wedlock and abandoned to an uncertain fate. Ultimately, the diva film analyzed the breakdown of the family, paying special attention to women's issues. Some diva films' handling of tropes was either so pessimistic about the present and the future, or so critical of ineffective rules of behavior, that despite their exotic and escapist settings, these melodramas exhibited the sociopolitical consciousness of docudramas.

The diva film showed that tropes flourish in a culture in which the handling of generic formulas is not based on the updating of conventions, but on a palimpsest-like layering of comparable situations. Comparisons across many diva films show that their historical context was not one informed by a sense of history as linear progression, but rather by a view of culture as a sort of thickly woven tapestry in which the threads of ancient episodes tend to confuse themselves with the weave of recent ones. Although grounded in this cultural tapestry of anxieties and desires, the tropes themselves did not always lead to renewal or to a process in which recurrence guaranteed an opening out to energizing possibilities. In the diva film, tropes comment on the blockage of any hope for improvement or on the illusory experience of relief; the narratives tend to end with social evils rooting themselves even more deeply in the fabric of daily life.

Illness and Music

In her book *Decadent Genealogies: The Rhetoric of Sickness from Baudelaire to D'Annunzio* (1989), Barbara Spackman explains that Gabriele D'Annunzio repeatedly included in his novels a female character who falls ill. This illness is not fatal—as tuberculosis is, for example, in Puccini's *La Bohème* (1896)—but productive. In fact, the heroine's subsequent convalescence amounts to a phase of erotic upheaval, which D'Annunzio celebrates as an opportunity for the male lover to fuse himself with a woman experiencing a radical transformation of her inner being. In D'Annunzio's *Il Piacere* (1889; *The Child of Pleasure*), for instance, Andrea Sperelli draws new energy from his encounter with Elena Muti when she is still suffering from fever, though the illness is receding.

In regard to D'Annunzio's suffering yet aroused heroines, Spackman comments:

> *The several rhetorics employed to characterize convalescence—that of conversion, that of a return to childhood, and that of feminization—intertwine in a complex and puzzling way. . . . The convalescent's conversion marks not a deeper division between mind and body, but the emergence of a new consciousness that can only be described in relation to this "other body." . . . "The new body" . . . is . . . characterized as feminine. Thus we might say that the "old woman" is expelled in order that the "new woman" might be put on.*[3]

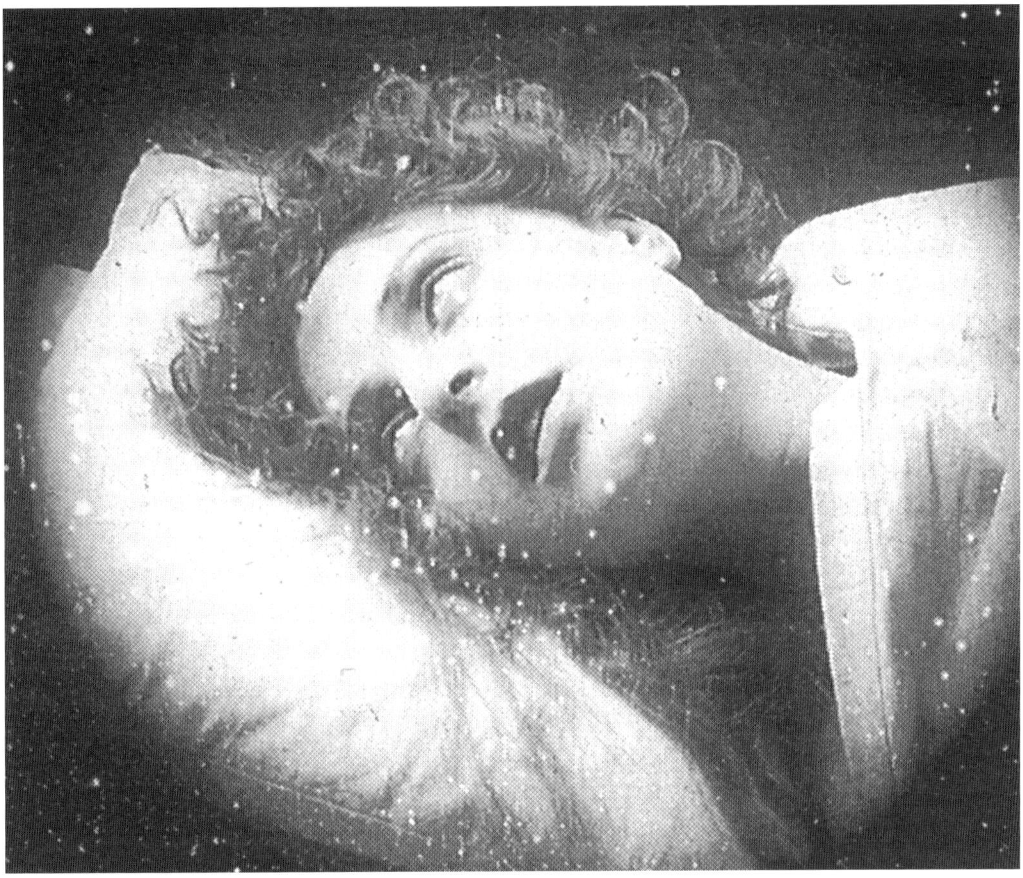

Pina Menichelli in Eugenio Perego's *La Storia di Una Donna* (1920). Courtesy Cineteca di Bologna.

Spackman underlines an important aspect of D'Annunzio's work: the problem of a division between mind and body—a masculine intellectual principle and a feminine intuitive counterpart—is resolved by using illness as a way to shed an old female body. D'Annunzio's solution to the double problem of reinventing gender roles in the social sphere and of acquiring a new relationship with oneself in the private sphere amounts to a process of borrowing. During the period of convalescence, the female patient resembles an androgynous creature—half female, half boyish—and she functions as an inspiration for D'Annunzio and his fictional alter egos, who seek new sexual and artistic identities through a woman's new level of energy.

In the diva film, especially in Lyda Borelli's performances, it is possible to find slim, androgynous female characters, while famous D'Annunzian novels such as *Il Fuoco* (1900; *The Fire*) and *The Child of Pleasure* are narratives centered on the problem of artistic inspiration; they show little or no concern for the world outside a circle of privileged individuals. In D'Annunzian erotic novels, the family unit is not at the heart of the narrative. By contrast, in diva films, family and marriage are crucial. Hence, illness and death strike not only women but also their innocent and helpless children. The stakes in the diva film are not always about art making, but they often switch to child-custody battles, separation proceedings, and the manipulative behavior of relatives.

By underlining the chronic ineffectiveness of the police and legal institutions, the diva film uses illness and death to denounce the husbands, companions, and fathers who manage to avoid any punishment despite their spying, blackmailing, pimping, gambling, and kidnapping. At the very beginning of Eugenio Perego's *La Storia di Una Donna* (1920), Pina Menichelli lies dying in a hospital bed. She is a woman without a future. The hopeful possibilities of convalescence—a renewal of energy and an erotic awakening—are not available to her. According to Spackman, children and convalescents have nothing to remember because they are people who, like amnesiacs, have lost their past, or else do not yet have one. The loss of memory produces a sort of clean slate, and an untapped flow of youthful energy often takes over the mental space previously occupied by haunting memories.[4]

In contrast to D'Annunzio's emphasis on leaving the past behind, *La Storia di Una Donna* revolves around the undying power of memory: problems from a woman's past, such as rape, homelessness, and the tension between romance and revenge, continue to haunt the narration in flashback, elicited from Menichelli's anonymous diary. The reason for these lingering memories is clear. Unameliorated by the period's laws, violence and poverty channel their urgency and injustice through the excessive features of melodrama. Hence, the long flashback spells out which past wrongs still impinge on present choices. Through the eyes of a young doctor reading the diary, we learn that the woman has chosen to be nameless. This choice, however, means something very different from Pina Menichelli's namelessness in *Il Fuoco*. For Pastrone's owl-woman, not having a name in *Il Fuoco* means to exist outside language, to be an unspeakable, perhaps mythical, kind of monster. But choosing not to have a name in *La Storia di Una Donna* calls attention to all the shame of women who have no legal rights, who must always depend on the words of men speaking either for them or against them. In this sense, *La Storia di Una Donna*—"The Story of One Woman"—means the story of innumerable women who were aware of and eager to denounce the abuses of ordinary life.

As the plot of *La Storia di Una Donna* unfolds, we learn from her diary that the dying woman has accidentally run into her first love, who had abandoned her with his child. Eager to settle old scores of jealousy and rejection, she decides to compromise him in the eyes of his current young mistress. Most importantly, even though she is still vulnerable to the man's charm, Menichelli is eager to seek some kind of revenge for the sake of her little boy.

Toward the end of the film, Menichelli fires a shot at her former lover, but he twists her arm and the bullet enters her own body. It is this self-inflicted wound that brings the protagonist to her deathbed. In this particular case, the diva film deviates heavily from D'Annunzio's theme of rejuvenation through convalescence, for the ending is based on a perverse scenario of female masochism triggered by male sadism.

The trope of illness, linked to childhood, adultery, or prostitution, is so frequent in the diva film that the three forms together compose a sort of supertrope inhabiting innumerable screen melodramas. In *La Piovra*

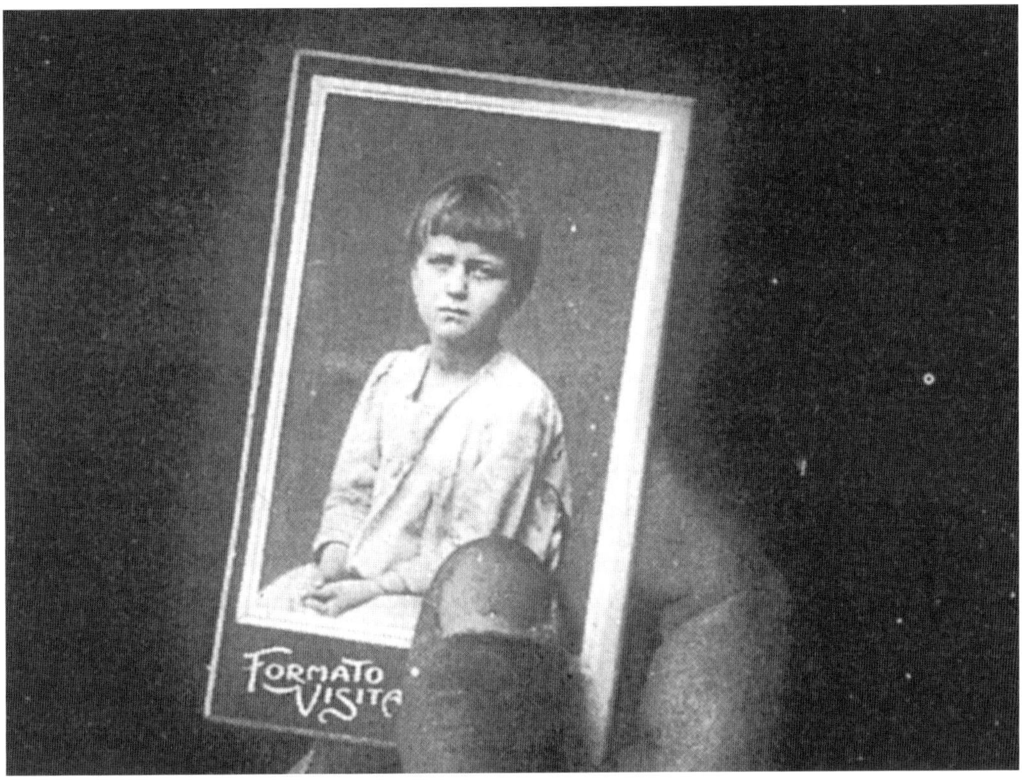

Pina Menichelli's son in Euginio Perego's *La Storia di Una Donna* (1920).

(1919; The Octopus), we reencounter precisely this triangulated and unavoidable trope: illness degenerates into death; accusations of adultery are based on gossip; and female independence nearly leads to death. In this film by Edoardo Bencivenga, Francesca Bertini is married to an extremely jealous husband who erroneously accuses her of having love affairs. He becomes so irate and insulted that he seeks a divorce. During the legal proceedings, Bertini becomes sick, but the thought of her son helps her recover.

Obliged to live with his father, the child misses his toys and a normal family life. Bertini is shown stricken with pain as she walks into her son's room. Kept away from his mother during the divorce proceedings, the child becomes seriously ill. In the meantime, his father and one of the father's best friends—a man called the "Octopus," Bertini's most evil but unsuccessful suitor—watch without empathy or concern as the child's situation deteriorates. Instead of improving, the little boy eventually dies. In short, the idea of childhood as a threshold leading to renewal does not fit in this diva film. *La Piovra* shows a father's indifference and neglect being responsible for the death of his own child.

Leopoldo Carlucci's *Caino* (1918), a film named after the biblical story of the first murderer, also involves illness and shock without recovery. To prove once again that D'Annunzian illness with a regenerative convalescence is impossible on the screen, I will have to summarize the film's convoluted plot. This is a worthwhile undertaking because the diva Elena Makowska plays the femme fatale in Carlucci's film. This coincidence of diva and femme fatale is an exception that can be verified with Pina Menichelli in *Il Fuoco* and *Tigre Reale*.

As the title itself suggests, Carlucci's *Caino* is a tale about two brothers in conflict. Raoul and Bruno, respectively a medical doctor and a farm manager, love the same woman, Elda, a tranquil country girl. At first Elda is involved with Bruno, and they kiss lovingly near the stables. On the other hand, Elda has a beautiful sister, Cecile, a singer who lives in Paris. The frivolous and insensitive Cecile is Elda's polar opposite.

Raoul takes Elda away from Bruno. Later he becomes involved with Cecile. Raoul courts Cecile inside a church while Bruno and Elda, who now share the same experience of loneliness and betrayal, watch the couple's passionate kissing. In the end, the heated affair between Raoul and Cecile runs its course, and Raoul decides to marry the quiet Elda. Urban images and postcard views of resorts appear only once during the narrative: when Raoul and Elda go on their honeymoon. In the couple's photographs from Milan, Lake Garda, and the Riviera, Cecile either stands next to Raoul, displacing Elda, or she dangerously hovers over the newlyweds.

Although he is married to Elda, Raoul follows Cecile into a life of grand hotels, musical intoxication, and gambling. Little by little, he falls deep into debt. Financial ruin is inevitable unless Raoul forges Bruno's signature on a check to the evil Lord Gaston, an implacable suitor of Cecile and a sort of cruel father of all fathers. As the manager of the family properties, Bruno is the stabilizing father figure for all the relatives in the countryside. Of course, he continues to live in the country, far from the corruptions of the city. Despite her marriage to Raoul, Elda is always lonely in the country; Bruno, who works all the time, is lonely too.

Because of the schemes of Lord Gaston—whose image is even intercut with that of a poisonous spider—and Raoul's forging of Bruno's signature, Bruno loses the farm and the family home. Even though Raoul is guilty of adultery, gambling, and ruining his family, it is Bruno who pays the most painful price, since he loses the woman he loved, the land he worked on, and the honor of his name. One more development complicates this already complicated plot: Raoul and Elda have a child together, baby Elina. To everybody's surprise, the infant looks just like Cecile. Society seems to be coming apart: good fathers lose their authority, and children's faces raise doubts about who their mothers are.

Crisis is in the air: Elda, in shock, rejects her own baby until she recovers her maternal instinct. However, the birth of Elina was so difficult that eventually Elda dies, and her corpse ends up inside an anatomical theater on an examination table under her husband Raoul's scientific scrutiny. Just before his medical lecture on the female body, Raoul hallucinates, transforming Elda into Cecile. Here, the superimposition of the two women's faces exposes the final unraveling of all identities and family relations.

The superimposition is significant because *Caino*, by its handling of filmic devices, blames the crisis of the family unit on representational technologies like the cinema and photography. Likewise, the femme fatale instigates all sorts of doublings and traumas because of unexpected or genealogically impossible similarities involving a biological reproduction.

Leopoldo Carlucci's *Caino* (1918). Courtesy Nederlands Filmmuseum, Amsterdam.

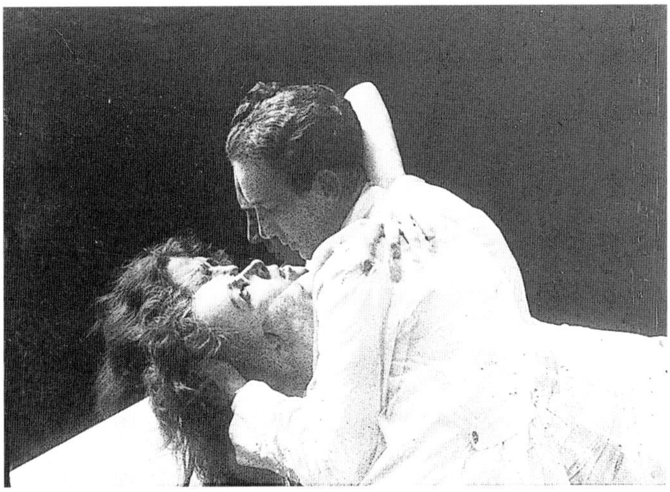

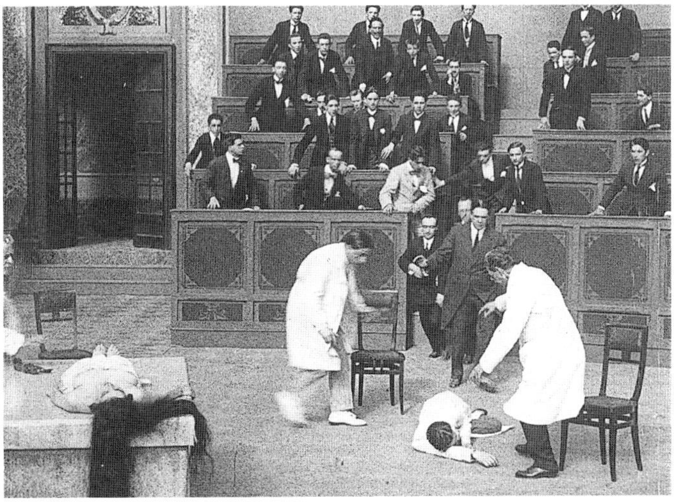

How does *Caino* end? The wretched Raoul returns to the farm after having spent years working in Libya, a colonial outpost. As a result of this experience, he has become a new and much more responsible man. Unaware of Raoul's positive transformation and full of anger over the past, Bruno, the good brother, behaves like Cain and kills his formerly bad brother. The horror is that he does so in front of the innocent Elina, who is now a young girl. After witnessing this act of violence by Bruno, whom she considers her father, and after beginning to understand that her true father might have been Raoul, who was trying to take her away from Bruno's house, young Elina goes completely mad, the innocent victim of a genealogy of family betrayals, abuses, and envy. The final twist is that before his fatal confrontation with Bruno, Raoul, who had done well in Africa, left a note containing enough money for Bruno to reacquire the land he had lost to Lord Gaston.

Caino's violent ending exemplifies a definitive denial of D'Annunzian convalescence; little Elina sees too much, a clear reminder of the role of visual perception in Freud's primal scene.[5] In *La Piovra,* the child dies. In *Caino,* the representative of the future, Elina, is forever damaged by the evil of those who should have set an example. In *Il Quadro di Osvaldo Mars,* a young girl sees the painter Osvaldo Mars kill himself in front of the portrait of a lascivious Salome. In this case, the child is an eyewitness to the tragic end of an adulterous affair between the painter and her own mother. In *Il Quadro di Osvaldo Mars,* muteness and shock are temporary, comparable to an illness. Eventually, it is only thanks to the girl's delirious narrative that the police are able to replace a hypothesis of murder with evidence of a suicide.

Not only does the diva film show children dying of mysterious illnesses or experiencing traumas, but it does not hesitate to stage the crisis of young males who are either too weak to resist women's allure or too reckless to be faithful to their wives. In *La Piovra,* for example, the evil Baron Petrovic is shaken by convulsions during an epileptic attack. Nineteenth-century medical science associated epilepsy mostly with men, in contrast to hysteria, which was considered a woman's disease. Men's unfaithfulness also affects the women who love them. In diva films, women faint—fainting, like hysteria, is a woman's problem—when they see with their own eyes that their companions are betraying them. This is exactly what happens to Lyda Borelli in *La Donna Nuda.*

In the role of Lolette, an affectionate young painter's model, the actress suffers a hysterical attack. Through a dark sliding-glass door, Lolette sees her lover, Pierre, flirting with a wealthy older woman. Because of her hysteric convulsions, Borelli's neatly tied hair comes loose and dances around her figure in a frenzy of pain and desperation. Falling ill, fainting, and the loosening of hair—all these situations signal either a weakening of the self or a discarding of conventions in the face of unbearably painful circumstances. Besides illness, fainting, unbound hair, trauma, death, and hysterical attacks, there are other reactions in the diva film that function as negative commentary on the theme of positive metamorphosis so dear to D'Annunzio.

To begin with, in the diva film and in D'Annunzio's writings, the playing of music leads either to a lowering of one's guard or to falling in love. In *Ma l'Amor Mio non Muore,* for instance, Elsa Holbein plays the piano while receiving flattering compliments from

Luisa Baccara (1892–1985) at the piano during one of her visits to Gabriele D'Annunzio's Vittoriale. Author's collection.

the spy, Moise Sthar. He steals her father's military documents, and the theft is responsible for Elsa's expulsion from home. Music, in this case, generates an endless chain of troubles instead of romance. During the second half of *Ma l'Amor Mio non Muore,* Elsa Holbein becomes Diana Cadouleur, a singer and dancer in the theater. It is in this new identity of "performer," or fallen woman, that Borelli meets the love of her life, Prince Maximilian, the heir to the duchy of Wallenstein. He is living incognito on the Riviera while convalescing after an illness. The key scene of his erotic reawakening happens when Diana plays the organ. Thus, her soon-to-be soul mate falls in love with her and the beauty of her music.

Sailing and Fire

The diva film's scenario of D'Annunzian convalescence is worth testing in relation to not only illness and music, but also the tropes of sailing and fire. One could argue that lakes and boats hold a special promise of fluidity. In *La Memoria dell'Altro,* in *Ma l'Amor Mio non Muore,* and in *Tigre Reale,* a happy romance is always marked by a couple taking a trip on the water or sailing off together into the sky of perfect love. It is worth noting, however, that in *Malombra,* Lyda Borelli, as Marina, repeatedly sails on a lake while dreaming of love and courtship. In her waking life, however, she is obliged by her uncle to live like a hermit. Marina seems oblivious of the rest of the world (even to the presence of a handsome boatman); she lies at the bottom of her vessel like a Pre-Raphaelite Ophelia. Through this horizontal and passive position, reminiscent of Ophelia's in John Everett Millais's (1829–1896) famous painting of the same name, she prefigures in reverse her demise at the end of the film.

Beautifully restored by the Cineteca di Bologna, *Malombra*'s ending is incomplete, but we can anticipate Marina's death if we embrace the outcome of Antonio Fogazzaro's novel on which the film is based. The last frame in the surviving print shows Marina leaving her uncle's estate by boat, rowing by herself, and standing up on the water for the first time. Significantly, Marina's shift from a horizontal to a vertical stance occurs only after she has provoked her uncle's death and killed her former lover, Corrado Silla. In line with the title of the novel and the film, Marina is an evil shadow, or *mal ombra*, in the sense that her appearance in the middle of the night seems to be gifted with evil and paranormal powers. Fogazzaro's tale of a female image endowed with the power to kill is not surprising since the writer was famously interested in all sorts of occult phenomena.

Marina's uncle, the family patriarch who persecuted Cecilia, Marina's female predecessor in the castle, looks toward the past. The dashing Corrado Silla, instead, stands out as a character linked to the future, to modernity and industrialization; he arrives by train, and his writing gives voice to Marina's repressed erotic longings. In a sense his little book, titled *A Dream*, replaces the D'Annunzian convalescence Marina is denied or is incapable of having. In other words, the transitional connotations of recovering from an illness give way to a complete loss of consciousness; instead of a twilight zone, dreaming opens up an alternative universe of fantasy. Yet there is no happy ending to Marina's dream of everlasting love with Silla.

By the end of *Malombra*, the fashionable writer has lost interest in Marina; he seems attracted to Edith, the daughter of Steinegge, the family's longtime accountant. Meanwhile Marina rejects every other suitor approved by her family, including a gentleman with whom she goes hiking in the mountains during a beautiful sequence probably shot on location in the deep rocky canyons around Lake Como. Marina's own awareness that her youth is wasting away is painfully evident when she lets innumerable roses fall on the carpets. All these flowers doomed to wither underline the inevitable passage of time and the frail illusions of love that is either not reciprocated or not meant to last. In sum, the film adaptation of Fogazzaro's narrative is either elusive or filled with lacunae, so that Marina's anger, Silla's volatile interest in her, and Edith's behavior toward both Marina and Silla are all difficult to evaluate.

Assunta Spina's deployment of the sailing trope is quite different from *Malombra*'s, but still in line with the alternation of renewal and crisis. The conflict begins as a result of an outing by water. Assunta sails to Posillipo with her girlfriends and Michele, her fiancé, to celebrate her name day. All the women ride in the same boat together; a detail that sets up a tension between Assunta's community of female friends and the prospect of structuring her life around only one man. During the feasting in Posillipo, Assunta's former lover, Raffaele, approaches her, which ignites Michele's jealousy. Later on, Assunta accepts Michele's offer to move to Naples and run a laundry next door to his butcher shop. For

Lyda Borelli overidentifies with a maternal role model in Carmine Gallone's *Malombra* (1917). Courtesy Cineteca di Bologna.

some time, Assunta and Michele get along quite well. We see them sailing in a boat at sunset, enveloped by an aura of romance. The trope of boating also concludes *Il Quadro di Osvaldo Mars*. The aristocratic wife accused of adultery is finally found to be innocent. Happily reunited, she and her husband leave for a long sea cruise in order to forget their previous troubles and rekindle their mutual affection.

Why did boating acquire this romantic connotation in the diva film? My guess is that the water's waves and ripples make such beautiful reflections when filmed in natural light that the trope might have grown out of a love affair between cinema and the light on the water. This also explains why there are so many fireplaces generating Caravaggesque effects in diva films. For example, in *Maman Poupée* and *Il Quadro di Osvaldo Mars*, the fireplace adds intimacy, warmth, and mystery to the otherwise trite formula of adultery and suspicion. The most flame-filled diva film is, of course, Giovanni Pastrone's *Il Fuoco*, with Pina Menichelli. It is also true that water and fire are most of all about movement, and this is significant in a film genre that comments on how difficult historical change can be.

In *La Storia di Una Donna*, Menichelli is a true diva because she is not just a femme fa-

Amleto Novelli in Giovanni Pastrone's *Il Fuoco* (1915; *The Fire*). Author's collection.

tale but also a mother, a young workingwoman, a rape victim, a prostitute, and a potential murderer. In *Il Fuoco*, Menichelli's role is much narrower, but unforgettable. Menichelli asks a painter (Febo Mari) to choose among three possible kinds of love affairs: the spark of an initial or limited meeting; the flame of passion and creativity for a while; and the ashes left after a final conflagration of everything and everybody. It is easy to see how, in this case, the fire is not only about the flame of love burning, but also about the problem of nourishing artistic productivity during and beyond the passage of time. *Il Fuoco* is a film about the antithesis between love and time, whose corrosive power is defied only by film, which preserves the movement of life in the moment of its happening. Bergson's favorite themes, such as subjectivity and temporality, are not difficult to recognize.

Carnival and Theater

The carnival is another diva film trope that warrants close examination because of its well-known ability to turn power relations upside down. Yet the carnival's promise of at least temporarily reversing situations of inequality does not always pan out in this genre, which is so conflicted about change. In particular, three films—*Carnevalesca, Rapsodia Satanica, Maman Poupée*—rely on the carnival or on costume parties to dramatize the lack of change or the impossibility of reversal. In *Maman Poupée*, for example, the carnival belongs exclusively to the children, so that the adult parents are stuck in their roles of betrayed wife and betraying husband. Despite Soava Gallone's efforts to forget adulthood and inhabit her children's world of make-believe, she belongs to a generation that is unable to change the frequency of adultery in married life. In addition, the children's costume parties do not pretend to be anything other than what they are: simple, innocent games with no reference to any reversal of power based on either class or gender. Sadly, during the children's carnival, the only example of reversal and revelation is Maman Poupée herself. She temporarily turns into the mindless and obedient mechanical doll that her marriage to an unfaithful and uncaring husband has forced her to become.[6]

The generational gap that awards the joys of the carnival only to the children in *Maman Poupée* does not apply to Amleto Palermi's *Carnevalesca*. In this second example, the carnival involves children and adults alike, but it does so in ways that are unsettling for all of them. The children fail to question the authority of older people over them, and instead mimic and amplify their parents' and mentors' thirst for power and control. By deranging the carnival—a feast of subversion—into a feast of consolidation, the children become even more abusive and disrespectful toward the adults than the adults are toward them. In this universe of arrogant youngsters, the adults cannot achieve any level of self-respect or authority to discipline others. Furthermore, in *Carnevalesca* the carnival does not occupy a limited section of the narrative; it takes over the entire story. It occurs three times, in the form of costume parties in different colors: white, red, and black. These chromatic changes mark a crescendo from peace to blood to death.

Soava Gallone. Author's collection.

Finally, *Carnevalesca*'s carnivals affect all members of society: the teachers are mocked and impotent; the judges are caricatures of themselves; the dishonest elements of society receive praise; and the honest folk are punished for crimes they have never committed. In short, by transforming the carnival from a circumscribed, temporary ritual into a limitless, endless way of life, Palermi's film depicts a society in which all representations are false; they amount to simulacra of what they are not. Thus, the carnival becomes a political allegory of a corrupt system on the edge of a precipice. The feasting allegorizes a society in an irreversible state of disarray and vulnerable to all kinds of illusions. One such illusion occurs when the royal entourage falls under the spell of a cloud of fireflies illuminating the darkest corner of the garden. This episode gives *Carnevalesca* a self-reflexive edge, since the fireflies produce the flickering light typical of cinematic projection. At the same time, this magic moment discloses how the kingdom of Malazia is immersed in a deceiving dream world, so only the dream-like images of the cinema can yield a reliable glimpse of what is really going on.

In contrast to *Carnevalesca*'s reduction of the whole narrative to a carnival, Nino Oxilia's *Rapsodia Satanica* devotes only one sequence to this trope: the indoor staging of a costume parade in which Alba (Lyda Borelli) appears as Salome. Alba enters her salon surrounded by guests in eighteenth-century garb. The eighteenth century is famous for its frivolous habits; its elaborate arabesque-like forms reappear also in *Maman Poupée* and *Carnevalesca*. In these films, the masked balls take place, respectively, in a walled garden and in a palatial hall, two spaces of containment far away from the public street.

Intertwined with the carnival trope, the theater is a space of spectacle and mirror-like relations between audience and performers. This mirror-like structure offers an opportunity to ponder the social framework of the diva film. In *Sangue Bleu,* for instance, Bertini can hardly tolerate the humiliation of the stage because it is the location of her downfall from aristocratic wife to prostitute. The intercutting between the space of the audience and the diva's tango of death is so emphatic, symmetrical, and mirror-like that the public itself ends up playing a role as a sort of collective voyeur. Thus, the on-screen audience instructs the offscreen film viewers in how to use the female body as a way of secretly looking at something either forbidden or painful, something literally on the threshold of life and death, of time past and time passing. In *Sangue Bleu*'s climactic sequence—the tango of death—Bertini stabs herself, but she does not die. Though this masochistic sequence is set in a theater, the intercutting between the diva and the audience makes the space so cinematic and self-reflexive that what is being staged can be viewed as a sort of pseudo–snuff film.

Originally from Argentina, the tango was supposed to be the dance of gauchos and of the ladies of the night. In the diva film, it is associated with bohemians, artists, anarchists, loafers, criminals, and prostitutes. Bertini's tango underlines the class divisions between the world of urban crime and the world of elegant spectators in the theater. Their tuxedos and jewels turn the viewers of the theater into one more spectacle, but one that is only for us—and we, of course, are an invisible set of viewers watching the theater sequence in the film. While the stage stands for society outside the upper classes, the best seats in the theater belong to the wealthy patrons who live in aristocratic villas with ominous wrought-iron gates protecting private property. One could say that the gate is also a visual trope in the diva film, but because this image applies to so many binary oppositions in the personal and social sphere, it is best to leave it there, in our memories, powerful and autonomous, the way that it must have felt to the viewers of the time, overwhelmed and yet seduced by the wealth of the aristocracy and the upper middle class.

At the end of *Il Fuoco,* Pina Menichelli walks into the lobby of a magnificent opera house and pretends not to recognize the painter she has seduced and abandoned. He looks like a derelict begging for a glance. Once again, the theater entertains those who have power and offers them a spectacle about those who struggle in the margins.

This situation of being alone in a crowd, which typifies the cinema, is related to the tropes of the carnival and the gambling casino. They all are concerned with appearance, spectacle, and risk, and also comment on the blurring of public and private spaces in modern life. During a carnival, the individual under the mask is alone in a crowd. In the gambling casino, winning or losing is always a lonely experience; there is no team play. Just as appearance no longer corresponds to reality during the carnival, class distinctions—including one's own identity—can be quickly destroyed by one spin of the roulette wheel. Shaped like a clock, the twirling roulette wheel becomes an icon of temporality out of control, for its suspenseful rotation relies on sheer chance, and no predictable sequence is possible.

The trope of the theater has aesthetic as well as social implications, since an older art form is repeatedly invoked as a framework for representation. There are additional sites of display that are analogous to the theater and punctuate the diva film as a genre. These places and situations include grand hotels, marble stairways, and banquets. They are scenic proofs that freewheeling imagination and making art rank much higher than linear logic and technology in the diva film. In this respect, miming, most memorable in *Sangue Bleu,* shows how the diva film defines making art. Miming is distinct from imitation because a mime creates a special emotional aura during the performance. By contrast, an imitating agent or a copying mechanism produces nothing new. Imitation is an invisible repetition; miming is more like a miraculous reproduction. One could say that, in contrast to mechanical reproduction's perfect copying, the diva film's mime-like redefinition of repetition through physical plasticity is another indication that a certain antimodern stance exists inside the modern paradigm of this genre film. But this antimodern stance is also based on the valuing of imaginative and nontechnological resources as ways of using the body and of performing, or even inventing, new forms of femininity as freely as possible.

Painting, Tattooing, Photography

The diva film used the trope of painting as well as that of theater to disclose ambivalent responses to technological modernity in Italy. In *Madame Tallien,* in *La Donna Nuda,* in *Il Quadro di Osvaldo Mars,* and in *Il Fuoco,* painting is primarily about the relation between artist and model. This approach invokes the story of Pygmalion, the sculptor who fell in love with his own beautiful statue. In *Madame Tallien* (1916), the canvas belongs to Élisabeth-Louise Vigée Le Brun, the female artist at the court of Marie Antoinette. This historical character is shown painting the Marquise Teresia de Fontenay, played by Lyda Borelli. From Vigée Le Brun's memoirs, we learn that her sitter eventually became known as Madame Tallien and that her beauty rivaled that of Madame Récamier.

Not only is it unusual in the genre of the diva film to see a female artist, but in this historical drama by Enrico Guazzoni (1876–1949), based on a play by Sardou, Borelli's character switches from model to painter when Teresia is shown at home painting a landscape. The revolution roams the streets and the countryside; it is safer for Teresia to work from memory instead of painting en plein air. In this film, painting is aligned with the royalists and used as a kind of mask on the wall. An oval portrait with a gilded frame covers the entrance to a secret tunnel leading to an unknown area of the house; there Borelli hides her secret lover, Jean Guérin. He is "the unattainable royalist" whom the implacable Robespierre chases all over Paris.

While Robespierre's troops search Teresia's home, a soldier stabs the painting, thus calling attention to the antithesis between the paintbrush of the elite and the knife of the masses. In this sense the popular medium of cinema is closer to the guillotine than to the canvas. Yet Guazzoni takes a much more conservative position, since he uses Madame Tallien's historical reputation as "Our Lady of Good Help" to argue that forgiveness is better than execution. In fact, Borelli's heroine became famous for her ability to save many royalists from death by pleading with her husband, Monsieur Tallien, a leader of the revolution. The French Revolution was characterized by extreme violence. By contrast, Italian history was unable to match, or else intentionally avoided, anything like the cruel upheaval of 1789 for the sake of a much slower, but also more uneven, adoption of modernity.

To be sure, *Madame Tallien* is about softening or humanizing the coldhearted politics and the unforgiving rationalism of the Enlightenment during the Reign of Terror. Whereas Antonio Gramsci repeatedly calls attention to the lack of a true revolution in Italian history, Guazzoni seems to feel that this lacuna was a piece of good fortune instead of a failure.[7] While Gramsci views the Enlightenment as the beginning of the modern era, Guazzoni makes sure that the compassionate Madame Tallien is chosen to march in public as the Goddess of Reason. Borelli's character, therefore, becomes the icon of an alternative, moderate modernity, one with no excess or trauma, safely rooted in the power of the ancien régime but also engaged in a dialogue with the new class in control of the masses. It is easy to see how Guazzoni used French history to show his support for Giovanni Giolitti's liberal-oligarchic government during the season of divismo.

This slippery, more fluid redefinition of modernity, in antithesis to the linear, surgical, and mathematical model of the Enlightenment, is ironically dramatized by a small episode enacting issues of social class, control, and excess. Before selecting Borelli as Goddess of Reason, Monsieur Tallien asks a laundress to play this role in the public procession. Flattered, the humble woman celebrates in a tavern, drinking so much that she becomes the opposite of anything or anyone rational. Clearly, she cannot perform as the Goddess of Reason for the whole city of Paris.

A more moderate view of who earns celebrity and who deserves execution belongs not only to Borelli but also to Monsieur Tallien. A humble printer before becoming a leader of the revolutionary movement, he criticizes Vigée Le Brun's portrait of Borelli, saying that it is accurate but fails to capture the model's hidden and passionate nature. Such a cautious yet insightful remark suggests how the diva film as a genre straddles the static beauty of pictorial reconstructions and the energy—erotic as well as kinetic—of intense dynamic sensations. The diva film oscillates between the highbrow citations of the historical genre and the fantastic chases of an adventurous or criminal plot. In the case of *Madame Tallien,* the attempt to incorporate the prestige of painting becomes most explicit when one of Guazzoni's intertitles refers to Watteau's garden scenes of games and courtship.

The ending of *Madame Tallien* suggests that a diva film with a historical topic ranks a bit lower than such monumental epics as *Quo Vadis?* (which Guazzoni brought to the screen in 1912). On the other hand, the diva film involves a higher frequency of art-historical allusions and orientalisms than the comedic genre or the contemporary drama. After saving once more the life of her royalist lover, Borelli marries the revolutionary Monsieur Tallien, who is less radical in his politics than his colleague Robespierre. Although his former profession as a printer aligns him with mechanical reproduction, he does not completely condemn Vigée Le Brun's artistry. Actually, he criticizes Vigée Le Brun for being too formulaic and superficial, which is why she has failed to depict Teresia's inner essence.

Finally, the image of Borelli painting alone at home is also significant in relation to women's rights and the way these issues are depicted in the shift from the ancien régime to the new order. Before the outbreak of the revolution and her involvement with Jean Guérin, the Marquise de Fontenay wanders in the park with her friends. There she surprises her husband kissing one of the maids. Humiliated in public, she declares that marriage over. In 1916, when Guazzoni shot *Madame Tallien,* the topic of divorce was highly controversial and widely debated in Italy. This feminist episode about a French woman's right to free herself from an unfaithful husband allows for a nice balance with the royalist allegiances of Borelli's character, and it is also consonant with Monsieur Tallien's desire for a less violent revolution than the one sought by Robespierre.

In the diva film, however, the erotic charge of high art, especially when it involves an orientalist topic, can become a serious cause of violence. In *Il Quadro di Osvaldo Mars,* Salome's upright full-length figure, her hand pointing toward the viewer, is an aggressive image. So impetuous is the portrait's aura that it functions like an index or an indictment, so much so that it ruins the reputation of an aristocratic woman. The poor Countess of San Giusto (Mercedes Brignone) looks just like the painter's model, who was also his former lover. Yet unlike her restless female double, who has forsaken her little daughter and her husband for the young painter, the countess is faithful to her spouse and leads a quiet, respectable life.

Either stylistically or thematically, high art—in the form of painting or sculpture—belongs to the diva film as much as orientalism does. To be sure, painting in *Il Quadro di Osvaldo Mars* has an impact on characters from three social classes and geographical locations: on the bohemian painter who lives in the city; on the peasant woman in the countryside, who meets the artist when he is working by the beach; and on an aristocratic urban couple. The central problem tying together all these strands is that a woman of wealth looks exactly like a woman of no means when they are dressed in Salome's clothing. In *Il Quadro di Osvaldo Mars,* a diva film structured like a criminal investigation, the crime is one of physical resemblance, manual reproduction, and visual likeness.

Interestingly, the painting is simultaneously an icon that is too powerful and an index that is weak. In fact, there is no murder, only a suicide in front of an image that is so precisely painted that it looks like a photograph. By occupying this fine line between excessive iconicity and weak indexicality, the photograph-like painting tells us more about photography's negative reputation in the diva film than about painting. Even when the enigma has been solved, one still wonders whether Salome's revealing orientalist dress or the painter's manual skill is more responsible for the physical resemblance between model and image.

Diva films such as *Madame Tallien* and *Il Quadro di Osvaldo Mars* can be said to reinforce traditional aesthetic values rather than those of mechanical reproduction. The Italian diva herself exemplifies the contradictory secularization of some lost divine aura. In this respect, it is also significant that many diva films exhibit a fascination with indelible, permanent marks, such as tattoos and scars. The leap here from paintings to scars may seem odd, but the point is that both these signs are made of marks that cannot be erased or removed. If they fade, such an occurrence goes against the grain of their everlasting or individualizing reputation. Someone's tattoo is either a mark of distinction or of marginality. In tribal cultures, the tattoo declares that the human body is a site for art. Likewise, painting has no value without a signature that at-

Francesca Bertini in *Assunta Spina* (1915). Courtesy Cineteca Nazionale, Rome.

taches the image to an individual with a unique touch.[8]

In *Assunta Spina,* Francesca Bertini's face is scarred; in *Il Fior di Male,* Lyda, a redeemed prostitute played by Borelli, is stabbed to death by a burglar with a tattooed hand. Thanks to this indelible mark, she realizes that her murderer is her own son. He came to execute her, as if his birth out of wedlock was Borelli's unforgivable original sin, which has haunted her all the way to death. In *Sangue Bleu,* Bertini's scar remains painful to think about, even after her reunification with her adulterous husband. These indelible signs, in turn, can also be seen as an adaptation of the mystical stigmata, a proof of fusion with the divine, a special kind of clue or mark left on the body by an invisible, transcendental force. This stress on branding the body may be a form of protest against the ephemeral and transitional nature of film.

In his work on early Russian cinema, Yuri Tsivian mentions the fashion of body painting celebrated in the futurist circles around Mikhail Larionov and Natalia Goncharova.[9] Antithetical to the irreversible tattoo of Italian diva films, the painted body of Russian futurism was a temporary and decorative reminder that had to be altered all the time. To be sure, the diva film's rejection of modernity was not based only on the alignment of painting and scarring. In line with Bergson's hostility to the snapshot's freezing of time, the diva film imbued photography with negative connotations. In *Il Quadro di Osvaldo Mars,* there are no photographs, but the negative reputation of this medium emerges, so to speak, from the implicit gap between painting and film. In fact, Mars's portrait looks like a photograph because the level of resemblance between sitter and painted image is extreme. At the end of the convoluted plot, the last intertitle, spoken by a police official, blames photographic accuracy on the art of portraiture: "Fatal resemblance!" The use of the word *fatal* indicates that no combination could be more explosive than a femme fatale plus photography plus the aura of painting layered over mechanical reproduction. The result is the most accusatory of indices. On the other hand, diva films also deny photography's indexical status or its reputation as objective and scientific evidence.

In *Sangue Bleu,* for example, a photograph misleads an adulterous husband into thinking that his estranged but faithful wife is also committing adultery. Countess Mira loses her reputation when she visits Jacques Wilson's bedridden mother. Two private detectives take her picture when she leaves with the evil mime Jacques, hoping that the photograph will be seen as evidence of an affair. In addition, the metonymic chain—mother, photography, and the alleged coupling of Mira with Jacques—brings to mind the envious mother described by Freud in one of his case studies: a young woman makes love to a man who is something of a father figure, when she thinks she hears a click of the camera. In her mind, this sound has to do with her mother spying on her from behind a curtain and taking her picture during this transgression.[10] Here the rejection of photography is interlaced with the theme of competition between mothers and daughters, another important trope in the diva film.

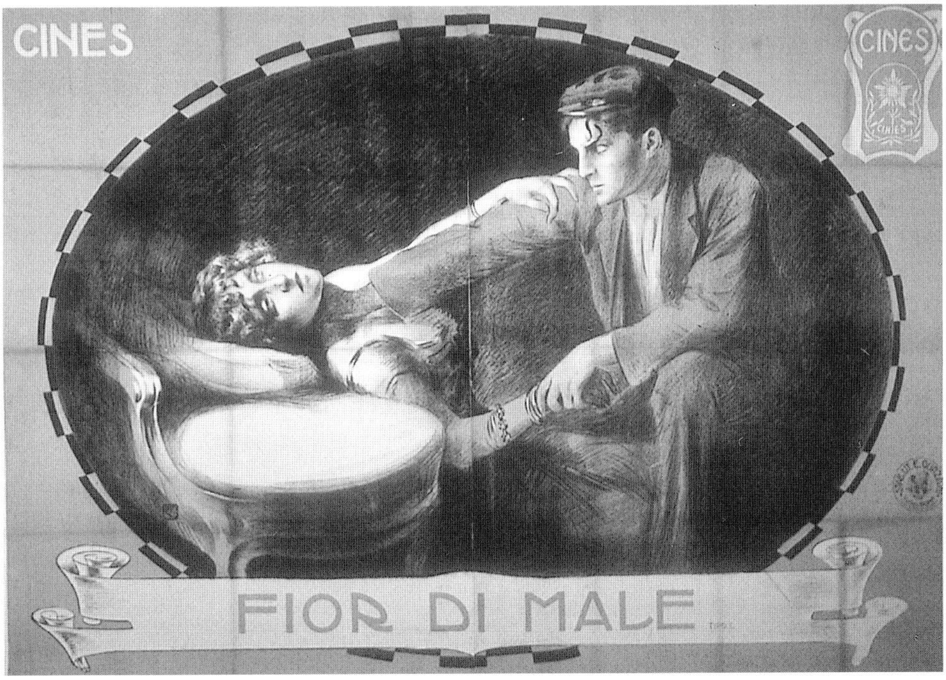

Lyda Borelli in *Il Fior di Male* (1915). Courtesy Nederlands Filmmuseum, Amsterdam, and Ripley's Film, Italy.

The Absent Father: Mothers and Daughters

Characters played by divas often lack supportive relatives as well as a man who can serve as a positive paternal figure. Of course, there are a few exceptions. In *La Donna Nuda,* for example, Lyda Borelli's Lolette finds a future life with her former protector, a painter much older than his colleague Pierre, who betrayed her. In *Il Quadro di Osvaldo Mars,* the traumatized girl lives with her father, who has been abandoned by his wife. Afraid to move toward the future, but also uncomfortable with upper-class privileges, the diva film would like to side with a new kind of stable and energetic middle class, which, though it cannot be found, is nonetheless constantly invoked by the films themselves. This sense of a social void where responsible fathers should be but are not is featured most dramatically in Bencivenga's *Mariute.* In this film, Bertini is a mother with only a grandfather in the home. Likewise, in *Il Processo Clémenceau* the sculptor Pierre is the son of a widowed mother; he hopes to find a male mentor in his wealthier friend, Constantino Ruiz. Through this powerful contact, Pierre eventually enters a higher social milieu, but it is in this world of young rakes open to selfishness and corruption that Pierre's schooling in vice begins.

The absence of the good father is a theme that appears also in Carmine Gallone's *Malombra,* since Marina, played by Borelli, has to accept the control of a much older uncle who treats her harshly. Even in *Caino,* the death of the old father is one of the reasons why his sons' rivalry for Cecile's attention escalates to the point of fratricide. Beyond the theme of the absent father, however, one more trope stands out with a special degree of force: the difficult, at times hostile, relations between mothers and daughters in many diva films.[11]

Michele's mother in *Assunta Spina* blames Bertini for having ruined her son. Present in the street when her son slashes Assunta's face, the old woman runs after her son, who is fleeing the police, to protect him from arrest. In *Il Processo Clémenceau,* Pierre Clemenceau's mother considers Bertini's Iza Dobronowska to be the source of all her son's financial problems. In *L'Età Critica,* Pina Menichelli is a rebellious young girl who does not listen to the older women who advise her to behave properly. In *Malombra,* Marina's circle of gossipy old aunts introduces Marina to a proper marriage candidate in an attempt to end her infatuation with the intellectual but volatile dandy Corrado Silla.

Indeed, *Il Fior di Male* and *La Donna Nuda,* both with Borelli, explore this same problem; it is also interesting to note that both of these films were directed by Carmine Gallone. In Pastrone's *Il Fuoco,* Febo Mari, in the role of an unknown painter, lives with his mother before he moves into The Nest of the Owls, Pina Menichelli's ominous castle.

On the other hand, Menichelli's decision to end the affair with the painter coincides with the return of her husband to the castle. This absent but influential male figure is introduced in the narrative through a telegram sent by a female friend to the diva; there is no direct communication between husband and wife. This model of power and silence parallels the dynamics between a cold foster father and a child afraid to be caught in the middle of some mischief. Most significantly, the female friend acts like a punitive yet cooperative mother who warns her misbehaving girl by using her husband's authority to restrain her.

All the preceding examples share a few common features: mothers are often minor characters with a tremendous impact on the lives of their sons and daughters-in-law; unwed mothers are unable to be mothers because they become prostitutes or murderers; daughters whose mothers were not prostitutes are often orphans and obliged to get along with either harsh father figures or insensitive aunts. Most importantly, there are two extreme cases that stand out: Marina's obsessive involvement with Cecilia, a maternal figure, in *Malombra*, and the painful scenario of mother and daughter loving the same man in *Il Fior di Male*, again with Borelli. Overall, the relations between these two generations of women amount to either an extremely brief episode that is, therefore, difficult to evaluate, or to an inference about family relations that is up to the viewer to figure out. It is as if the genre wanted to say that the bond between mother and daughter is important, but the diva films I have seen never show a mature and warm relation between two women.

Mercedes Brignon in *Il Quadro di Osvaldo Mars* (1921). Author's collection.

It is for this reason that one particular episode of female interaction in *La Donna Nuda* stands out for its intensity, but also for its peripheral placement in comparison with the main body of the narrative. In this film by Carmine Gallone, Borelli's Lolette visits the studio of a female painter, an older aristocrat who is having an affair with Pierre, the diva's companion. Neglected by her lover, Lolette poses for her rival. At first sight, the sequence seems to be organized horizontally: Lyda Borelli sits in the center of the frame with a huge neoclassical vase on her left. The painter sits in front of her canvas on the right. Anguished and suffering, Borelli repeatedly slumps, while the artist admonishes her to sit up straight. Here Borelli's acting style dramatizes the loss of the so-called pictorial pose, the beautiful and static offer of oneself as an elegant and formal object. In a larger sense, this sliding downward suggests a journey toward the domain of grottoes, the grotesque, the region where the self dissolves into monstrous reincarnations.

Borelli's increasing sense of weakness is emphasized by the eerie presence of the vase, a strong object, an amplified decorative detail whose function is to show the triumph of the ornamental, abstract register over the corporeal, figurative one. Most importantly, this unraveling of the self into ornament is a reminder that the baroque plasticity of the diva is as elegant and as sterile as the rococo designs embedded in the art nouveau style. I will mention here only that Adolf Loos's studies on ornament, tattooing, crime, and primitivism were published and well-received

Lyda Borelli in *Il Fior di Male* (1915). Courtesy Nederlands Filmmuseum, Amsterdam, and Ripley's Film, Italy.

in Italy in 1908, one year before Cesare Lombroso's death.[12] By then, the Italian criminal anthropologist had already studied the artwork of children, male criminals, and Russian female prostitutes, clumping all these categories under the label of primitive, arabesque-like, abstract, and degenerate art.

Why then is Borelli sliding toward the ground and sitting next to a huge object? These two details demonstrate that as soon as a woman is about to represent another woman, the model becomes unavailable for the artist; the possibility of female collaboration in reinventing the image of femininity is also denied. This denial is due to the pull of the earth and gravity, to the weight of history—that is, to the negative memory of previous images of women as beastly creatures. All these forces drive a wedge between the representer and the represented, the subject and the object of representation. In a sense, in the diva's days, Lombroso's pseudoscientific discourse, popularized by thousands of images and thousands of statistics unsupported by empirical evidence, stands between the huge vase and the empty canvas, between the model and the artist.

Yet there is another obstacle, invisible and powerful, that separates the two women. The relation between model and artist is only a variation on the theme of how a daughter can be torn between rejecting a mother's negative example and obeying the duty to imitate this female precedent, since she is a woman just like herself. Thus, the situation in *La Donna Nuda* in which two women who are not related by blood are competing for the same man becomes a pretext to meditate on the much closer relationship of artist and model, and on how this kind of creative rather than reproductive bond points to the difficult terrain between daughterly and motherly figures in the diva film.

This ambivalent link between mother and daughter, Cecilia and Marina, is the crucial topic of Gallone's *Malombra.* Marina overidentifies with this maternal figure and thereby suffers such a loss of self that she surrenders her subjectivity to the pull of the past. In *Malombra,* the relation between mother and daughter prefigures a collapse of origin and copy, referent and sign, into the narrative symbiosis of two women as the equivalent of a postmodern simulacrum. The latter is a particular kind of sign that does not represent something else by way of imitation, but pretends to be the thing in and of itself.

Cinematic representation means to make the world present again on the screen without ever eliminating difference. This is because the internal temporality of a certain moment in the world is bound to be always different from the external temporality of the filmic image, whenever it happens to be projected. The time of the original is always different from the time of the copy. By contrast, simulation marks the impossibility of distinguishing between similarity and sameness, and it does so to such an extreme that it reduces history to stifling repetition. The daughter must carry out revenge for the maternal figure, and Cecilia invades Marina's mind.

Mothers and daughters are similar, but they are never exactly the same; daughters struggle to develop individually, either by seeking a positive male model through the father or by trying to avoid being victimized as their female ancestors were. Marina goes further, punishing Cecilia's persecutor—her uncle—and her current male interest, Corrado Silla. It is fair to say that the diva film repeatedly asks this question through the mother-daughter trope: how can a victimized mother teach her daughter not to become a victim? This question is hardly ever answered, but there is, at least, one marginal character in one diva film who begins to set an example.

In *Il Processo Clémenceau,* Iza Dobronowska's aunt plays a crucial role in keeping track of her niece's financial interests and in showing her that she can choose between two men instead of considering herself forever bound to her first love, Pierre Clemenceau. In *Ma l'Amor Mio non Muore,* Elsa and her father live by themselves; she functions like a wife in taking care of her apparently widowed father.

Instead of a ménage à trois, the mother-daughter Oedipus complex deployed by the diva film concerns either the negative void between two generations or the negative repetition of one generation inside the next. It is an all-or-nothing situation in which negativity is multiplied by negativity. This model of identification between the spectator and the diva echoes the theme of self-effacement as a form of self-empowerment, typically associated with mystical practice. There is no mother in the story of Saint Theresa transfixed by the angel's spear and swelling with desire as she is about to fuse with the divine, the Absent One. In Saint Theresa's case, the mother's absence is not due to lack or separation but to plenitude and loss of self, for the mystical union between Saint Theresa and God is a fantasy that returns the daughter to the mother's womb, the locus of divine enthusiasm. Within mystical practice, God is both the mother and the father.

One wonders whether all these tropes have something in common, and I would say that they are at least brought together by a longing for the past, as shown by the rejection of photography and the emphasis on theatrical representation. Images of water and fire, of course, appeal to a fascination with physical movement and mental mobility, so that it is possible to say that their common orientation is not toward the earth, but in the direction of the sky. In a way, the mystical, utopian slant through which diva films compensate for their lacunae or resolve contradictions is not simply an appeal to spirituality, but also a form of procrastination and a diffusion of the issues into the void or some abstract level.

In keeping with Bergson's sense of life as an ongoing flow of energy, water and fire clash against static and oppressive architectural structures—palaces and gates, for example. This means that the enthusiasm about the cinema was genuine, yet the fear of historical and personal change was also strong. Such a divided stance was due to a crisis of political leadership and of positive family role models. It was as if the prospect of action, adulthood, and independent decisions was stifled or discouraged by a system of authority that would swing from overprotective behavior to paternalistic abuse. This is why neither mother figures nor fatherly characters are benevolent about letting go of outdated value judgments. Even carnivals fail: they set up models of destructive arrogance while reinforcing divisions and lack of respect for personal boundaries.

The tendency to mark bodies and paintings with scars and signatures suggests a frail sense of individuality and an obsession with leaving strong traces behind. Such a search for an everlasting memory echoes the ideal of an everlasting love, even though the diva film does not hesitate to stage loss, frailty, and the limits of appearances. In a sense, the wasteful spectacles, banquets, and gambling casinos of this genre are an appropriate updating and secularization of the religious memento mori, since consumption and randomness prevail over balance and rationality. Despite its painful depiction of women's lives and its punitive ideology, the diva film demonstrated the analytical power of early cinema in Italy. There a young medium was capable of producing beautiful yet highly critical and deep commentaries about all aspects of human experience in a changing society.

Nino Oxilia

BLUE BLOOD AND SATANIC RHAPSODY

Two surviving diva films, *Sangue Bleu* (1914) and *Rapsodia Satanica* (1915–1917), stand out because of the way they use orientalism and occultism to define the cinema as a medium involved with transformational or traumatic forces.[1] In addition, both films reflect on the nature of the medium itself by staging the problem of time's relation to space. Finally, both films were directed by Nino Oxilia (1889–1917), a creative personality involved in poetry, songwriting, and theater. Clearly, Oxilia's life and work warrant further archival research beyond the scope of this book.[2] Oxilia was born in Turin. As a young man he was a bohemian—that is, a member of the Turinese *Scapigliatura*—along with Guido Gozzano, another Turinese writer also involved in the cinema but less open to the new medium than Oxilia was. Gozzano's inclinations were more melancholic and conservative than Oxilia's. It might be going too far to call Oxilia a feminist, but he was a friend of the poet Guido Gozzano and the writer Amalia Guglielminetti, and this couple was engaged in debates about social reform and the emancipation of women. Turin was teeming with socialists, suffragettes, and ladies active in philanthropy and salons. Quick to appropriate all sorts of fashions and fads coming from Paris, Turin was also a strong center of filmmaking.

Vittorio Calcina, the first representative of the Lumière Brothers in Italy, was based there. Between the 1880s and 1890s, Turin became a city of patriotic piety, socialism, and the Italian Risorgimento, influenced by Edmondo De Amicis's heartbreaking feuilletons about immigration, poverty, and education. Antonio Gramsci, another native of Turin, split from the socialists in 1919 to found the Italian Communist Party that same year. Turin was the city of criminal anthropology and large urban projects, such as Cottolengo Hospital for the care of the handicapped. It was in Turin that Cesare Lombroso finally managed to get his chair at the university.[3]

The key component of the emerging industrial triangle with Milan and Genoa, Turin was different from other Italian cities because of its close ties to the scientific, secular tradition fostered by the Enlightenment across the Alps. The city was an enclave of industrialists and thrifty administrators such as Camillo Benso, Count of Cavour, or Giovanni Giolitti. All sorts of mystical and religious cults, as well as esoteric and exotic fashions, flourished there in reaction against mathematical certitudes that had been placed at the service of the Turinese liberal-conservative oligarchy.

Oxilia grew up in this Turinese climate of artistic experimentation, in which the beliefs

Maria Jacobini. Author's collection.

in satanic rituals developed next to the scientific testing of Angelo Mosso. More specifically, Oxilia started his artistic career in the theater as a writer, but he was quickly recruited by Arturo Ambrosio's production house. By 1912, Oxilia had become very close to Pier Antonio Gariazzo (1879–1963), a painter and filmmaker. A traveler and producer, Gariazzo was also the founder of Savoia Film, a company that specialized in contemporary dramas about family life, a crucial genre for the shift from the short to the long film.

Always eager to be informed about the latest trends, Gariazzo dabbled in philosophy, loved adventure, and sailed all the way to Indonesia, as some of his paintings of local landscapes and native women prove.[4] Turin was also the home of Adriano Tilgher, a minor philosopher who survived by working as a librarian. After a Crocean beginning, Tilgher became a disciple of Henri Bergson and managed to put together his own obscure book, *Arte, Conoscenza e Realtà* (1911; Art, Knowledge and Reality). Also familiar with the work of Pirandello on the comic vein, Tilgher published *Studi sul Teatro Contemporaneo* in 1922 and made a name for himself in Pirandellian criticism.

In this eclectic environment, the young Oxilia met his future fiancée, Maria Jacobini, a young woman who looked like Mary Pickford and was also the niece of a Vatican-based cardinal. Jacobini left her parents' house in Rome, amid great scandal, to become an actress and devote herself entirely to the cinema.[5] Oxilia fell in love with Maria and became her Pygmalion. In 1913, after many projects in the Turinese film environment, Oxilia signed a contract with Cines, a prestigious production house based in Rome, which asked him to work with Francesca Bertini on *Sangue Bleu* through its subsidiary company, Celio. In 1915, Oxilia wrote *Il Fior di Male*, a film beautifully interpreted by Lyda Borelli for the director Carmine Gallone.

In 1916, as the brief season of the divas was unfolding, images of blood, war, and death flooded the Italian screens. Oxilia shot a couple of newsreels set in the Balkans. His images were so gruesome that the censorship board intervened. In 1917, Oxilia died on the front line, blown to pieces by a bomb during the battle of Monte Tomba. He was one of many artists and intellectuals of that confused yet remarkable generation that died in World War I; the painter Umberto Boccioni and the architect Antonio Sant'Elia met the same fate. The diva film, thus, found itself lacking intellectual mentors to improve the genre and help it shed its clichés.

Overall, Oxilia's style as a director was quite fluid, and it is therefore difficult to determine exactly what he did or thought. In addition, his role as leader was submerged in a sort of cooperative authorship that prevailed within the energetic but chaotic film industry of that period. So open to experimentation was Oxilia that during the shooting of *Ananke* (1915; Fate), with Leda Gys, Maria Jacobini, and Maria's sister, Diomira Jacobini, he let the three divas handle most of the creative decisions and limited himself to the role of set designer. While his actresses directed themselves, the director put a lot of time into choosing fabrics for the sets. To be sure, Oxilia was well aware that textiles, along with other materials used in the construction of the décor, not only affect the light but also have a huge yet hardly noticeable impact on the atmosphere of the whole film.

What is sure, however, is that besides Bertini in *Sangue Bleu*, Borelli in *Rapsodia Satanica*, he also directed Pina Menichelli in *Il Papà* (1915; Daddy) and in *Il Sottomarino n. 27* (1915; Submarine 27), two films that unfortunately have been lost. Because Oxilia worked with the most important divas of his period, his reputation inside the industry was probably competitive with that of Mario Caserini, Carmine Gallone, and Giovanni Pastrone. Between 1912 and 1917, the year of his death, Oxilia was involved in the production of at least twenty-four films—all made one after another and at breakneck speed. It is hardly surprising that the modern dramas among these films explored controversial topics (family issues, gender roles, generational struggles, marriage crises), or that the diva films featured plots rife with love and death. There was no time to think, but at the same time there were a lot of ideas to play with.

Most of the diva films in Nino Oxilia's filmography have perished or cannot be found. On the other hand, his ideas about the cinema in *Sangue Bleu* and femininity in *Rapsodia Satanica* suggest that he was innovative, excited about his participation in a completely new creative environment, and sympathetic to women and the question of their future. After all, he had evolved from theater and song to film and set design, inspired by two major experimentalists in art nouveau: the Venetian-based Mariano Fortuny (1871–1949), an expert in textile and lighting design, and the American expatriate Loie Fuller (1862–1928), a choreographer and dancer. Beloved by the futurists, Fuller became incredibly famous by performing various kinds of watery serpentine movements through rippling fabric and glittering electric lights. Fortuny's fashion appealed to women sensitive to D'Annunzio's languid and exotic universe. He opened his couture house in 1906 and continued until 1946. Besides fashion, Fortuny worked in painting, photography—mostly clouds in various formations and trains speeding away—sculpture, architecture, etching, and stage lighting of a kind suited for Wagnerian total theater. He became famous for the Delphos gown, which was based on an ancient Greek style and sported innumerable thin pleats producing a sort of accordion effect.[6]

Sangue Bleu

As the narrative of *Sangue Bleu* demonstrates, orientalism presupposes an inevitable link between unattached women and sinful behavior. The title, which means "blue blood," reflects the film's concern about the purity

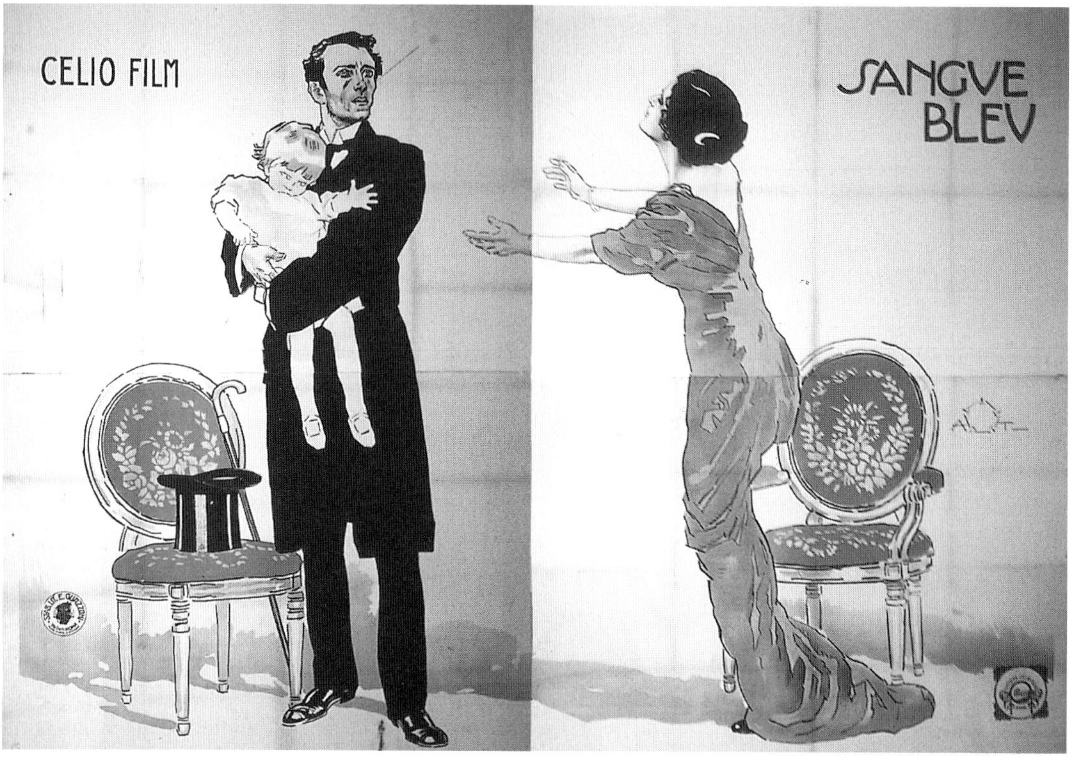

Nino Oxilia's *Sangue Bleu* with Francesca Bertini (1914; Blue Blood). Courtesy Nederlands Filmmuseum, Amsterdam.

of aristocratic bloodlines and is therefore a reminder of class superiority. Abandoned by her husband, Egon, for another woman, Countess Mira (Francesca Bertini) becomes involved with an evil mime, Jacques Wilson, a character with a name foreign in two different languages. The closer their entanglement, the worse her legal situation becomes. Eventually Mira loses custody of her little daughter, Liana. Alone and humiliated, she becomes a courtesan and, later, a disreputable woman of the stage. Mira's orientalist identity is a euphemism, a form of textual censorship to avoid stating outright that she is a prostitute. *Sangue Bleu* is not simply about a husband leaving his wife for another woman; it is a film about low self-esteem, depression, and loneliness. It deals with a forsaken wife who gives herself to an evil man, thus losing all self-respect.

This total loss of self on the part of the female protagonist coincides with one of the most metacinematic moments of *Sangue Bleu.* During a charity event at the house of the Marquis de Beaurivage, orientalism combines with an operatic element. Mira becomes a geisha during a bizarre spectacle that is halfway between badly filmed theater and a sophisticated meditation on the challenges of early cinema. While a pianist is playing underneath an improvised stage, Mira appears in the role of Cio-Cio-San, from Giacomo Puccini's *Madama Butterfly* (1904), wearing a kimono. At first she stands center stage; then she arranges some flowers; later she performs a tea ceremony. All of a sudden, Lieutenant

Pinkerton stumbles into her orderly and quiet space.

This first tableau vivant is about the encounter of East and West, and it is followed by a second composition that features great confusion and the piling up of bodies belonging to both races. After being wounded in some kind of colonial battle, Pinkerton is surrounded by his own soldiers, who try to steer him away from the Japanese woman. Likewise, the geisha is about to be taken away by her relatives, who are concerned that she loves the alien enemy. The third and final tableau shows the newlyweds embracing and displaying themselves to an audience that is enthusiastically clapping, pleased about this peaceful union between East and West. Yet there is a lot more to this happy ending, which was custom-made for a public proud of the conquest of the East and wealthier because of it. In contrast to the happy ending that concludes Mira's performance, the original opera's wedding scene is a sham, since Pinkerton plans to marry a "real" wife once he returns to the home. Near the beginning of Act I, Pinkerton and Sharpless, the consul in Nagasaki, toast Pinkerton's upcoming nuptials, and Pinkerton ends by drinking to the day when he will return to America and truly marry. The opera ends tragically: the geisha commits suicide after she discovers the truth, and after Pinkerton and his new American wife have taken away the son Cio-Cio-San had with Pinkerton.

Precisely because, in Puccini's opera, Cio-Cio-San takes the wedding ceremony more seriously than the sailor does, it makes sense to conclude that Oxilia's rewriting of the plot of *Madama Butterfly* in *Sangue Bleu* was meant not just to be edifying, but, much more significantly, to address openly issues of perception and illusionism. To begin with, two contiguous kinds of curtains draped on both sides of the stage—one thick and black, the other sheer and veil-like—separate the space of the performers onstage from that of the actors simply passing through the wings. This double framing, produced through the clever use of fabrics, underlines that something quite different is happening behind and around the stage during the main spectacle. Second, the filmic reenactment of *Madama Butterfly* happens just after an episode involving perception and photography, which I will now examine.

At the very beginning of their relationship, Mira naïvely thinks that Wilson is a good friend. In good faith she accompanies him to the countryside for a visit to his old, sick mother. This brief indoor scene is shot from a static camera placed well above the characters' eye level. Thus the eye of the camera intercepts the reflection of a chair in a mirror hanging next to the sick mother's bed. Although this visual detail is emphasized by the camera's unusual height and is easily accessible to the film viewers, the characters in the fictional space are completely unaware that the mirror within the frame of the filmic image offers information about offscreen space. Furthermore, the mirrored chair is shown in reverse, for it is only the reflection of an object on the other side of an invisible fourth wall.

This particular detail of the chair shown in reverse is meant to focus the film viewer's attention on the twists of direction that the screen—a sort of three-sided window open onto a believable world—requires in the interface; the diegetic, or narrative-based, mirror implies the invisible fourth side occupied by the camera. The scene immediately following this indoor sequence is staged outdoors. The camera is somewhat below waist level, and it voyeuristically adopts the point of view of two private detectives taking a photograph of Mira and Wilson leaving the mother's isolated house together in the Mira's motorcar.

Seen by itself, without a context, this photograph becomes an incriminating clue about an alleged affair between Mira and Wilson. Just as Puccini's Cio-Cio-San misinterprets the seriousness of the wedding, Egon thinks that this photograph proves Mira's adultery. The previous use of an actual mirror in the mother's house is also a reminder that the viewer outside the fiction sees more than do the characters in the fiction. By contrast, when a character looks at an image, he or she is not always in a position of power. Both Puccini's romantic geisha during the wedding and *Sangue Bleu*'s suspicious husband during the investigation are fooled by what they perceive and what they are told.

Such a split between seeing and knowing is explored again during the staging of *Madama Butterfly* before an audience familiar with the famous opera's plot but hostile to the thorny issue of miscegenation. To be sure, Puccini is diplomatic enough to soften miscegenation with adoption. This whole second half of the opera, involving the rearing and assimilation of a child of mixed race, disappears in the rehearsal organized by Wilson for the marquis's friends.

In Oxilia's *Sangue Bleu,* the three tableaux vivants already discussed are comparable to three flash cards or to the windows of a fast train, for they follow one another at an amazing speed. By 1914, in the development of the cinema as a technology, this effect of quick succession had been replaced by a slower, hence more intelligible, flow of images. It seems, therefore, that Oxilia decided to move his fiction back in time so that he might have the opportunity to comment on the earliest days of film. He was probably aware that the first flickering images of the new medium were linked with the term *psychocinematography,* describing the incredibly fast mental film of a whole life that a dying person experiences. Psychocinematography, in turn, was mostly associated with violent deaths, or with the dizzy feeling allegedly experienced during drowning or falling from a great height.

In *Sangue Bleu,* Oxilia exploits the tableaux vivants of an orientalist opera to document an important moment in the history of perception. He tells his contemporary viewers in 1914 something that he as a filmmaker already knows: at the very beginning of the century, the cinema was so new that it put unprecedented perceptual demands on the audience. That was why the perception of moving images amounted to a visually extraordinary experience—one, to be sure, comparable to trauma.

But there is more to the history of the term *psychocinematography,* for these two intensely visual media—film for technology, memory for the mind—were also associated with the power of invisible forces. The setting for Wilson's *Madama Butterfly* remains the same, namely, a mise-en-abyme of internal frames: the borders of the stage echo a door in the background, which, in turn, leads into a darker and more confused space—possibly the unrepresentable regions of the afterlife, far beyond the vanishing point of Albertian perspective. In "Lumen," an essay on spiritism from *Stories of Infinity* (1872), the astronomer and science-fiction writer Camille Flammarion (1842–1925) writes:

> *The regression of memory in relation to the most insignificant and remote events of human life is frequent in a variety of circumstances: when someone*

sleeps under the influence of drugs; during old age; when someone is delirious; or when death approaches. A comparable phenomenon to this one is the so-called psychocinematography *which takes place during violent deaths . . . and involves the visualizations of past events in the mind of the dying person. This flashing of images is as fast and confusing as the moving pictures of the cinematograph.*[7]

"Lumen" is not only a philosophical dialogue, but also the name of a cosmic spirit who reveals the scientific wonders of the celestial universe to Quaerens, a young seeker of knowledge. Within the pages of the essay, the author mixes empirical observations about the nature and speed of light with vivid speculations about such diverse subjects as reincarnation, time travel, the reversibility of history, and the ecology of other planets. "Lumen" is one of the first science fiction works to include detailed descriptions of alien lifeforms and the first to imagine, thirty years before Einstein's 1905 theory of relativity, the differences in perception that might result from traveling at velocities close to and beyond the speed of light. What is interesting in Flammarion's use of *psychocinematography* is that this word became so popular in the 1870s that it was able to persist in common parlance at least until 1912, when *L'Illustrazione Cinematografica* devoted a short article, entitled "Psicocinematografia," to the subject:

It is well-known that drowning is one of the most painful ways of dying; during the last minutes of life, the memories of the past come back in the mind. . . . Several explanations have been given about this phenomenon, and the most persuasive theory is the following: human thought puts its imprint or leaves its mark on the shapes and the feelings that move the individual, on the atmospheres that surround him. Hence it is possible that at a certain point, given a particular condition of the psyche, whatever is stored inside the memory sets on fire . . . these previously stored images. These very same images unfold one after another with the rush typical of the cinematograph when it moves its figures and makes them look as if they were existing in the present tense, even though its pictures are based on the past.[8]

It is amazing how close the paraphrase by the anonymous writer for *L'Illustrazione Cinematografica* is to Flammarion's original.

Oxilia's rendition of the most archaic form of cinema during the charade-like, mime-based staging of an opera is a clear meditation on the medium that he is using for his long feature film, *Sangue Bleu*. In fact, such a traumatic lack of narrative transitions from one tableau to the next would have been unthinkable in the theater. Introducing new performers and props onto a stage takes time, even if only a few moments. Each scene also transpires within a certain amount of time. But film, Oxilia seems to say, involves a completely different handling of temporality, one that resembles the mental processes of thinking and remembering much more than looking at and listening to something happening on a stage. The internal time of thought and memory does not match the external time of eye and ear.

Oxilia seems to conclude that the vanishing forms of theatrical melodrama and opera are comparable to people traumatized past the point of recovery by the speed and inner probing of the cinema. Likewise, a society in the midst of rapid colonial expansion is either incapable of coping with interbreeding or unable to regulate its frequency. And once these two situations have taken place within the media and the population, perceptual confusion takes over.

But there is more to Oxilia's distinction between theater and cinema. Besides Flammarion's writings, the Turinese filmmaker was probably aware of Giovanni Papini's 1907 journalistic scoop "La Filosofia del Cinematografo" ("Philosophy of the Cinematograph"), published in *La Stampa*.[9] In 1907, Oxilia was only seventeen, but the fact that a famous Italian intellectual like Papini would bother to write on film and philosophy in the popular press would have been no small event in Oxilia's bohemian circles.

Presaging Oxilia's comparison of film and theater in *Sangue Bleu,* Papini explains that the reason why the two eyes of cinema can be confused is that "these [spaces] or scenes of [impossible] transformations" change within a believable temporal framework that the theater can neither match nor suggest.[10]

The ability to alter time as well as space is the advantage that cinema has over theater and painting, since these two older media can work only by shaping space. Because of what it can do with time, Papini's cinema is the medium in which the impossible looks possible. And because of Papini's emphasis on time over space, his position is still aligned with Bergson's rejection of quantitative approaches in favor of qualitative and subjective ones.

The point here is that between 1907 and 1914, from Papini to Oxilia, the cinema matured; there was enough positive energy around the young filmmaker to sustain him during the production of *Rapsodia Satanica,* in 1915. This climate of openness to new ideas and cosmopolitan trends explains why Oxilia celebrated women's search for independence. Such a feminist use of a famous diva was no small statement, and it was also a compromising stance. It is interesting, therefore, to note that in comparison with his gambits for *Sangue Bleu* and Bertini, Oxilia took more risks the following year with *Rapsodia Satanica* and Borelli.

In *Sangue Bleu,* orientalism is associated with a geisha, a woman so immersed in the codes of the past that she believes too readily in the authenticity of a wedding ritual that appears correct. *Sangue Bleu* is nothing if not self-reflexive: it uses its own fast pace to point ironically at the failure of Mira's husband to understand even motionless images. Egon, who has been represented as powerful and arrogant—as one who believes himself entitled to commit adultery—suddenly comes across as naïve and old-fashioned. He is unable to read a single static image (the photograph of Mira) viewed in isolation. The combination of early cinema and orientalism is, for the jaded and cosmopolitan audience watching Mira's performance, a sort of mocking at the expense of Puccini's opera, whose ending is revealed and foreshadowed by Mira's static, portrait-like pose, which cites one more obsolete pictorial genre.

Wilson is in control of the rehearsal, but we may still wonder whose point of view this rush of three tableaux is meant to convey. As previously stated, in Flammarion's definition of *psychocinematography* these images grow out of the mind of someone experiencing a violent death. In *Madama Butterfly* and in *Sangue Bleu,* the only two characters who die violently are Cio-Cio-San and Countess Mira. The former commits suicide; the latter stabs her own bosom in an act of self-punishment after dancing the "tango of death" onstage. In other words, in both the opera and the film, women get the privilege of being in charge of the narrative's last word or life's final breath. But their cinema-like encounter with death is a statement of self-annihilation. On the one hand, Oxilia's film denies women any level of agency; on the other, *Sangue Bleu* is a remark-

Nijinsky in the *Blue God,* costumes designed by Leon Bakst. Bibliothèque Nationale de l'Opéra, Paris, France. Photo: Snark/Art Resource, N.Y.

Paul Poiret, *Sorbet,* evening ensemble (1912). Silk chiffon and satin, embroidered with glass beads and trimmed with fur. From Mme. Poiret's collection. Victoria and Albert Museum, London. © 2006 Artists Rights Society (ARS), New York/ADAGP, Paris. Photo: Victoria and Albert Museum, London/Art Resource, N.Y.

able achievement for its time, since—with Cio-Cio-San and Countess Mira—these women's last looks at their wasted lives anticipate Jean Cocteau's famous formulation of cinema as "death at work."[11]

In other words, the cinema is defined as a woman-bound form of spectacle that looks at the punishment or death of other women while simultaneously making women look at themselves and the world as if they were also about to die. Such a definition of the cinema is an interesting commentary on the diva film. Although it operated within a masochistic framework, the genre appealed to women by allowing them to see themselves and their own struggles. Whether this mirroring effect constituted a sadistic gesture from a director or a masochistic opportunity for the viewers, we shall never know.

My guess is that *Sangue Bleu* gave the audience a very believable story about the downfall of an innocent woman and about the mediocrity of a society based on compromises and double standards. Oxilia's film offered a measure of pain all women could share, thus developing a sense of solidarity. At the same time, Mira, as played by Bertini, is caught between empowerment and punishment. Her role is as contradictory as psychocinematography itself: a rush of movement, a mixture of images, a maximum of energy and life right before blindness, stillness, and death.

Sangue Bleu's ending is aristocratic and conservative. Egon and Mira reunite for the sake of their child. Their reunion seems hollow, for like the false wedding ceremony between Pinkerton and Cio-Cio-San, it is based on the need to protect a public reputation. Its purpose is to mislead whoever is looking at it from the outside. Such a statement in favor of the nuclear family was not surprising, even coming from a talented director like Oxilia, who, after all, had to counterbalance the cinema's reputation as a medium fostering social unrest and criminal behavior.

Rapsodia Satanica

Cinema's bad reputation as a conduit for evil flowing from the East to the West did nothing to slow down the orientalist vogue in early Italian film culture. To begin with, one of Borelli's dresses in Nino Oxilia's *Rapsodia Satanica* is based on the creations of the French couturier Paul Poiret and the lampshade look developed by Leon Bakst for Nijinsky in the role of *Le Dieu Bleu* (1912; The Blue God). Borelli's "lampshade" includes a shorter and wider gown with beautiful flowery embroidery and a narrow rim made of fur. The replacement of the belt with a lampshade layer flaring out, over, and below the waistline involves a tall flat bodice wrapped around the diva's bust in the Japanese style and a longer, simpler skirt underneath doubling the lampshade effect.

Borelli's flat-chested look strikes a note of contrast with an elaborate bow, also in the Japanese style, placed on her back. In line with the fashion of the day, which called for alternating simple features with complicated ones, Borelli's final look is neither archaic nor modern, neither feminine nor masculine. By mixing the organic with the inorganic, the furry with the flowery, the short with the long, the straight with the diagonal, the allusion to the cold climate of Russia with the oversized ornamentation of the Japanese kimono, Borelli's outfit exemplifies the ultimate orientalist montage of clichés about cultural perceptions and roles.

The lampshade garment is only one of the many costumes worn by Borelli in *Rapsodia Satanica*, whose plot seems driven by the dresses used and objects shown rather than by any significant action. Opening with Borelli dressed as a beautiful Salome, Oxilia's *Rapsodia* explores the transformation of the cruel femme fatale into the new woman of modernity, yet it also interrogates the cinema about its affinities with the outdoors, or the natural world, in contrast to the alliance between the theater and architecture, the indoors, and furniture. Oxilia's *Rapsodia* was shot and finished without music in 1914, but not distributed until 1917 because of unspecified difficulties. It seems that there was some rivalry with Mario Caserini, who was based in Rome and linked to Cines just like Oxilia. Perhaps Caserini was instrumental in holding up the film. One of the producers of the film at Cines was the Baron Alberto Fassini, also known as Alfa, who had strong ties with the Bank of Rome and financed the project.

Fassini brought in the composer Pietro Mascagni and asked him to write the music. After watching the film over and over again without intertitles, Mascagni felt strongly that the music should rule over the image. He declared that he envisioned a score at least fifty-five minutes long. As a result, Oxilia agreed to redo the ending so that the running time of the film would match the length of Mascagni's score. Some argue that *Rapsodia Satanica* stood on the shelf until 1917 because of Mascagni's endless revising. He was unwilling to declare he had completed the final version of the score until 1917, even though most of the music had been written by 1915.[12]

Sangue Bleu contains a mimed opera that refers to archaic cinema, which, in turn, is linked to theater. Two triangles battle with each other and overlap in *Sangue Bleu:* the first includes Mira, her husband, and his mistress; the second comprises Mira, Jacques Wilson, and Mira's husband. In contrast to *Sangue Bleu,* the plot of *Rapsodia Satanica* is thin, repetitive, and quickly summarized.

An old woman, Alba D'Oltrevita (Lyda Borelli), tired of wasting away and fearing death, makes a Faustian deal with the devil: she will be young and beautiful forever if she gives up romance—that is, smashes a small statue of Cupid. Yet Alba's statuette does not break. Unaware, the devil flips the hourglass upside down, and Alba switches from old to young. The owner of the Castle of Illusion, an obvious architectural allegory of the movie theater, Alba embodies not only the life-preserving power of the filmic image, but also the dream of reversing the death-bound flow of time.

In keeping with a self-reflexive reading of Oxilia's film, Alba's character can be linked to two separate images of time—two complementary views of the cinema involving two other famous female stars in silent film culture. The first image involves Ida Rubinstein, the famous Russian dancer from the Ballets Russes. Her first appearance on a Parisian stage in 1909 mesmerized the audience, especially when her body seemed to slowly emerge out of an unraveling, cocoon-like strip of cloth.[13] She looked like a butterfly leaving her chrysalis behind, or like a soul leaving a dead body. An ancient symbol of the immortal soul, the butterfly is a major icon of art nouveau.

The second image is a 1918 photograph of Theda Bara staring at an Egyptian mummy stored in a glass case. The first example is about the time of projection, whereas the second is about the cinema holding forever still a moment as unique and precious as the human body preserved through mummification.[14]

When they are combined, these two images spell out how each moment in film is suspended between a metaphysical ideal and an unavoidable physical decay: each frame wants to endure forever, yet each is flickering away at the same time. *Rapsodia Satanica* is an allegorical meditation on the inner and outer temporalities of the filmic image—that is, the filmic image is as transient as Alba's youth but, thanks to its photographic ontology, the image in film is also as long lasting as an Egyptian mummy.

Rapsodia's plot unfolds through episodes of jealousy and self-destruction involving Alba and two brothers who are both in love with her. Yet Borelli falls in love with palpitating nature, with life itself outside the walls of her castle. Alba's home is surrounded by a series of gardens, ranging from highly designed and cultivated plots to the forgotten corners where plants grow wild. While she is walking

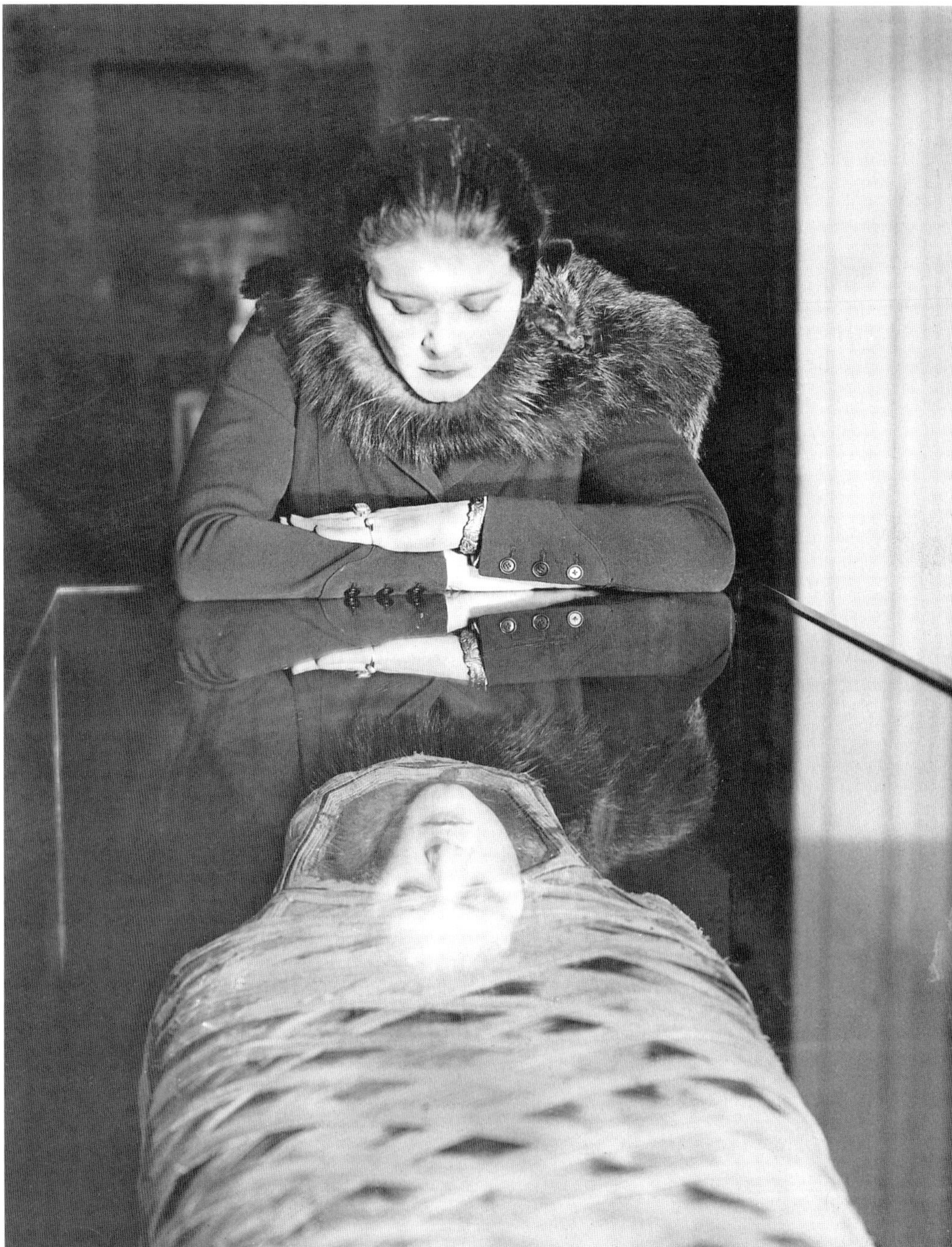

Theda Bara in *The Forbidden Path* (1918). MPTV.NET, Image Vault.

alone in a secluded corner of her huge park, she surprises a yellow butterfly resting on a flower. The distance between her and the object of her gaze is hardly established, so the cut from a close-up of her face to a close-up of the butterfly cannot complement each other within the system of the point-of-view shots. In the passage from one shot to the next, today's spectator can sense that the spatial proportions are off: the size of objects in the first shot looks awkward in relation to the size of those in the second.

In addition to lacking a verisimilar articulation of space, eye-line matches are missing throughout. Alba's gaze upon a group of musicians below her window is incomplete. The reaction shot necessary to legitimize the inference of a point-of-view shot is not there. These cannot be considered mistakes, since there were no rules in place at this point. That is why these particular examples are also responsible for the flavor and texture of the film, its rough edges and moments of surprise.

Despite the limitations (or virtues) typical of early cinema, the steady alternation between indoor and outdoor space suggests that Oxilia might have been wondering about film's special kinship with nature, which arises from its birth out of the camera obscura, the time of exposure, and the sun. The director's energy seems to be torn between cramped art-historical allusions in the sets, on the one hand, and the spontaneous flow of water and the coruscation of light in the garden, on the other. Of course, most shots of the landscape include carefully arranged micronarratives of youthful groups horseback riding or dancing in the remotest background layers of the shot. Even nature is combed and choreographed.

Yet the use of natural lighting in the outdoor sequences, the feeling of fresh air, and the thin fabrics used for the costumes indicate that the cinema functions at its very best with intangible, quasi-invisible materials. On the other hand, inside the Castle of Illusion, mirrors and chiaroscuro lighting produce a thick, alluring sense of mystery around Alba. Oxilia's filmmaking in *Rapsodia Satanica* mixes an older, indoor, "primitive" theatrical mode with attempts toward a more advanced, outdoor, and modern method. Likewise, Alba experiences senility first, then youth.

Dressed as Salome during the opening costume party, Borelli slowly advances from the background to the foreground of the shot. The outline of her figure is almost lost in the crowded composition: rococo furniture and statuettes, arabesque-like stuccoes, walls covered with pictures of all sizes, oriental rugs, curtains, tapestries, animal skins, gilded frames, and bibelots surround the famous diva. Despite its redundant quality—the guests bowing over and over again like puppets on a timer—this kitschy scene is worth analyzing, for it exemplifies a certain kind of mentality that stretches from private property through the sphere of female domesticity to public sites for women's consumption in the city. The point here is that the cinema is a sort of geographical link and storage space between the home and the department store.

In discussing how modernity in Italy was less modern, so to speak, than that in other countries, the historian Adrian Lyttelton remarks: "Foreign observers were struck by the traditionalism of the middle class, most of whose wealth was still kept in land, furniture and houses rather than in bank deposits or shares."[15] While Lyttelton's interpretation stresses the conservative behavior of the Italian upper middle class, the literary critic Mario Praz offers a more historical and less geographical perspective about rooms crowded with objets d'art arranged as if in a museum. In his *La Filosofia dell'Arredamento* (1945; Philosophy of Furniture), Praz stresses not only the triumph of bad taste, but also its international outreach. Just as the diva's orientalist costume is made up of eclectic cultural sources, domestic interiors masquerade as colonialist or museological atlases of the non-Western world:

We have seen Egyptian furniture designed on the basis of drawings by Hope . . . and reserved for the Egyptian room planned in an illustration of Household Furniture. *Leaving the craftsmen's virtuosity aside, these furnishings looked just right for the theatre. And this is the problem with most Regency household furniture. The rooms either cite this style or that one: Greek, Egyptian, Gothic, Indian, Chinese, they amount to a masquerade. To put it in Miss [Mary Russell] Mitford's words, after she visited Rosedale Cottage: "Every room is a masquerade: the Chinese living room with vases . . . pagodas, the Egyptian library all covered with hieroglyphs, and crowded with crocodiles and sphinx-like furniture. Think about a sofa in the shape of a crocodile and think of an ottoman in the guise of a sphinx! They sleep under Turkish tents and they have lunch in a Gothic chapel."*[16]

Keeping in mind Praz's observation that furniture abounds both in the antiquarian Italian household and in the British home adorned with colonial trophies, it is difficult to tell whether Italian interiors were truly more packed than the average living rooms in other European countries. One thing is certain: in Italy, France, or England, the glamorous images of the diva film and the sparkling displays of the department stores were an all-consuming cosmopolitan phenomenon closely related to the rise of female consumerism and stardom across Europe and America.

As early as 1889, even before the official invention of the cinema, the journalist Emilia Nevers was quick to remark that the modern city was the seed of all this dazzle and glitter as well as of this creation, i.e., the department store, that pulls into its public orbit even the most secluded domestic space:

The department store, the art world, the seduction of women through window-shopping is nothing new. All of a sudden, from a dark basement or a ground floor, where the merchandise is hidden or ignored, we see a new kind of look capturing our attention. It has to do with the rise of bigger department stores, more beautiful ones, enhanced by an army of perfectly groomed and polite shopping assistants, with windows in which all the novelties are arranged fantastically or artistically. Along the streets, where the gaslit lampposts have replaced the old ones lit by oil, or under Edison's whitish, moon-like electric lightbulb, one discovers, little by little, something like a magic display. . . . At first silent and closed, the houses in the city acquire life, variety, and they open their eyes to incredible possibilities; they open their thoughts to the surrounding world that they were about to forget, submerged as they were in urban monotony. From the shop to the department store—from the ground floor to the first floor—the department store expands, the merchandise needs more and more room, it acquires a new look, it takes on a new elegance, a whole new environment is built around the commodities, a sort of stage—a few rooms are not enough, it is necessary to have a whole house, and the house becomes a place, and the place a palace that turns into a gigantic mansion by acquiring incredible proportions, until it becomes a small city, a whole world by itself.[17]

By describing the shift from window-shopping to being overwhelmed by the department store, Nevers suggests that as "urban monotony" increases, the display of goods will become increasingly necessary. This implies that modernity is gray, uniform, and anonymous; hence, colors, lights, the miniaturization of huge things, and the enlargement of small items are required to bring this new landscape back to life and to entertain the eye. By the end of Nevers's description, the transformation of the department store into an aristocratic palace raises the issue of a certain nostalgia for an antidemocratic or a prebourgeois past, when hierarchical distinctions were oppressive yet protected aesthetic values.

Whether or not Lyttelton's and Praz's remarks apply to the filmic image as such, it would be too easy, and also quite wrong, to dismiss *Rapsodia Satanica* on the basis of comments about its orientalist kitsch. Furniture, ornament, and drapery are much more than gratuitous decorative details: they offer Oxilia an opportunity to emphasize plasticity, molding, and relief—namely, depth of field—within the diva film, which was still trying to mediate between the impression of reality and a certain degree of *horror vacui,* or fear of empty spaces.

An art-historical term, *horror vacui* refers to the anxiety of filling in an empty background that otherwise would be too reminiscent of the shadowy flatness of archaic projection. It is quite telling that the devil literally walks into the narrative of *Rapsodia* by leaving the dark void of an overly gilded pictorial frame, which seems both to contain and to compensate for a ghastly area of unrepresentable emptiness. Furthermore, in a film in which the surfaces of mirrors reflect multiple images, such a dance of interacting projections makes up for a static camera.

Halfway through the film, during the sequence about her newly found independence from the devil, the mediation of the mirror between Alba and her reflection in the glass is most effective. When she turns to face the camera, the image of her back suggests the mental, and therefore insubstantial, nature of the barrier of an invisible fourth wall. By using the mirror to turn the body into a reflection, Oxilia underlines its illusionistic and constructed nature, hence its potential for collapse. Here the mirror is no instrument of narcissistic self-deception, but rather a means of visualizing a space that leads to a kind of magical realm beyond which it might be possible to be yourself and nothing but yourself.

A film heavily backed by bankers, *Rapsodia* was shot in extremely lavish locations and was released with an original musical score written by a major composer. It is not surprising, then, that *Rapsodia Satanica* deployed a highly selective use of color that was designed not so much to increase its documentary realism as to underline its fantastic poetic moments. In this case, color truly fulfilled Papini's protosurrealist definition of the filmic image. As we learn from Pier Antonio Gariazzo, the cold gray of photography appeared to be a major aesthetic limitation, so much so that it is not surprising Bergson thought of mechanical reproduction as an ally of science and an enemy of fantasy.

The point here is that this narrow definition of photography was a major challenge for the diva film to overcome, since its cinema was meant to be seductive and emotionally charged. Gariazzo wrote: "Quite brutally, the merciless, cold, destructive medium photography proposed to us, from time to time, a series of ugly and barren sights, and it removed us from a vague dream filled with colors and beautiful forms to take us into a monotony of grey mountains, waters, and cities, all of them resembling one another, inhabited by people just like us, small and petty little towns."[18]

Perhaps to compensate for a widespread negative view of photography, Oxilia learned from fashion designer Mariano Fortuny—one of Borelli's favorite artists—how to develop chromatic effects for *Rapsodia*. In his laboratory, on the Venetian island of Giudecca, Fortuny used the *pochoir* (stenciling) technique to add silver and golden threads in the form of printed or woven arabesques to the surface of precious fabrics such as velvet, silk, linen, and organza.

In Oxilia's film, the pochoir technique imbues the lifeless, rigid clichés of the story with an unprecedented emotional force. The stenciling, or pochoir, in color makes the film's images look softer. As a result, the diva's wardrobe includes clothes of yellow, blue, pink, or green; a window absorbs the light and becomes as yellow as the large butterfly that epiphanically promises Alba a future beyond the devil. During Alba's reacquisition of youth and the coming of all sorts of spring festivals, the trees are green; Borelli's veils are pink in opposition to the devil's red cape.

In the end, color, just like life in motion, seems to belong to the outdoors and to costume, thus hinting at film's special power to tune in to subtle changes in the body, behavior, and in the natural world. In his book about the making of *Diva Dolorosa*, Peter Delpeut aptly comments on the difference between the diva films in black-and-white and the humanization that color brings to *Tigre Reale* with Pina Menichelli:

> *The copy from Turin had soft pink and clear blue tones. I only knew the black-and-white version. But with the color version of* Tigre Reale, *I understood once and for all that monochrome coloring is essential for the appreciation of silent film. The black-and-white copies we knew were usually copies of original colored nitrate films. In the copying process, it is impossible to produce a pristine black-and-white picture. The film material is insensitive to particular colors; it cannot read them and translate them into gray scales or tones. The color areas are incompatible with a clear black-and-white scheme. Films like* Tigre Reale *for years were screened with grey tones. . . . Everything seemed to drown into a dull blur. Copying the original color brings life back to the story and makes the film as a whole more visually accessible.*[19]

Finally, it is significant that clothes, along with Oxilia's choice of locations and sets, help the diva direct her performance. In fact, Lyda Borelli wore several of Fortuny's most famous dresses for the shooting of *Rapsodia*, as if she wanted to trademark the film beyond the screen into the worlds of fashion and stage art. During the planning of *La Memoria dell'Altro*, Borelli wrote a letter to producer Alberto Fassini in which she stressed over and over again the importance of clothes in her work and her admiration for Fortuny.[20] The diva's body, the celluloid of film, the application of color—these three levels seemed to converge in the project of transforming photographic coldness into film's magic.

Borelli, Boccioni, and Oxilia

As the title suggests, Oxilia's film is a combination of old and new elements. The plot of *Rapsodia*—the word comes from the Greek verbs *rhaptein* and *aidein,* which mean "to sew" and "to sing," respectively—is stitched together, transformative, and transgressive. Through the well-known characters of Salome and Faust, Oxilia rehashes the themes that feminine beauty is lethal and ephemeral and that eternal youth is a reward worthy of any sacrifice. Much more refreshing than these worn-out ideas are the meaningful transformations of setting and mood that Alba experiences when she leaves the Castle of Illusion for fresh air; when she contemplates the beautiful yellow butterfly in the garden; and finally when, after scattering dying flowers on the floor and playing the piano, she acknowledges the painful return of wrinkles on her face. She knows she has broken her pact with the devil and that there is no turning back. It is precisely during this memorable scene of veils and mirrors bathed in Caravaggesque chiaroscuro lighting that the viewer senses the possibility of unexpected prodigies refreshening the stale story line Oxilia has followed up to this point.

The film ends not with the same old grotesque Alba of the first sequence, but with a new, stronger, ethereal creature who emerges from the glowing twilight hour, the see-through fabric, and the reflecting surfaces of the mise-en-scène. This alchemy of sunset, cloth, and glass is not only a combination of flexible materials whose mutability is reminiscent of film's sensitivity to time's fleeting moments; it is also a protective envelope for the diva's definitive inner change, which arrives at the moment of her greatest despair: the devil has just withdrawn his promise of eternal youth. The play of veils, the glow of candles, and the dance-like motions caught by the looking glass function as a nurturing chrysalis: they enable the butterfly-woman of the future to be born. And she comes to life against all odds. Thus, an artificial icon of the art nouveau period—the real butterfly that Alba saw in the garden—becomes her alter ego as well as the symbol of her search for a new identity outside the rules of the castle.

With a surprising twist of the traditional story line, Oxilia does not make Alba return to her stuffy chambers; instead, he edits a close-up of a cold, indifferent mirror, a reference to aging, with a low-angle shot of an ominous black door slowly opening to a terrace overlooking a forest. Moving from indoors to outdoors, the filmmaker concludes this transitional sequence by juxtaposing a frontal view of Borelli, in all her toylike smallness, with a monumental Egyptianate threshold. The diva's hieroglyphic and rigid figure grows in size as she faces and walks toward the camera, but this view is suddenly replaced by one of her receding back becoming smaller. Without a doubt, Oxilia's radical switch from a frontal to a rear view of Borelli underlines the crossing of a rigid boundary inside herself and in the society she lives in. It also makes apparent the link between the relativity of perception and the subjectivity of motion, a conceptual pairing that the invention of cinema brought to the forefront of daily experience; further, it reinforces Bergson's denial of a stable and objective view of the world.

In the end, the veils fluttering dancingly behind her, around her, and toward her announce the death of Salome. The old-fashioned femme fatale is gone once and for all, replaced by Alba's transformation into the new woman of modernity. By modeling her movements on Loie Fuller's famous choreography of soft fabrics, Alba becomes a sort of marvelous abstract being, faceless and bodiless but radiating immense freedom, lightness of spirit, and energy.

Fuller mobilized the arabesque line of art nouveau into utopian apparitions of mystery and power. The famous American dancer represented leaping flames, becoming a butterfly in flight, while the outlines of endless abstract designs induced sensations of fear, surprise, and enchantment in the audience.

Borelli's movements on the terrace are so reminiscent of Fuller's approach that the director and the diva could be said to have coauthored the whole sequence. One example of Borelli's lucid awareness about the deep ties between fashion and film comes from her preface to Mario Carli's worthless novel *Retroscena* (1915; Backstage). This is how the actress writes about her own insights on questions of movement and gender:

> *Reading your novel has produced a strange impression in me: I have found in you a sensitivity—or better, a gamut of sensations—that I would call feminine. . . . I say this not because I find your imaginative path to be either weak or frail, but simply to underline one of its most fundamental traits: the suppleness of your imagination. After all, we need to get rid of the superstition that women are weak and shallow. There are a lot of men who are weaker and shallower than any woman, hence it is an absolute commonplace to call us the weak sex. . . . I am very interested in your fascination with clothes, with the question of a woman's elegance, with that fantastic and, without a doubt, complicated world which is a woman's wardrobe. I, just like you, believe that a wardrobe is a sort of poetic medium or instrument.*[21]

So aware was Borelli of the power of clothes to generate autonomous forms of movement with a storytelling power of their own, that she invoked *la poesia delle vesti.* Borelli was describing the way that pleats and folds, like analogies and metaphors in poetry, can yield a glimpse of hidden physical energies and half-formulated thoughts. The latter are, by definition, difficult to externalize, represent, or even express, not only to others but even to oneself. Hence, Borelli seems to suggest that clothes send messages to oneself that nobody else would even know, and that clothes narrate to other people the histories of many different worlds.

Female narcissism is a constant theme in the visual arts of the nineteenth century, and this convention reappears in the first half of *Rapsodia* when Alba looks at her image reflected on the surface of a pond in her garden. By contrast, in the sequence set on the terrace, Borelli hides her body in a swirl of fabrics. This turn toward disembodiment—and, therefore, abstraction—suggests that Oxilia's melodrama aligns itself with modernist experimentation. In this respect, echoes of Boccioni's "plastic" or "transcendental" dynamism can be found in Borelli's use of veils. Through Fuller's choreography, Oxilia and Borelli elevate the standard diva film into a futurist-oriented form of experimental visual poetry.

On March 30, 1907, the painter Umberto Boccioni noted in his diary that he accidentally saw an elegant young actress: "Yesterday I saw a young actress who was so elegant that I thought that if I could study using that woman as a model, perhaps I could find what I am really looking for. This one or another one, as long as she carries in herself a whole musical range of movements that I find very typical of elegant twentieth-century women."[22] In 1907, Boccioni was not yet a futurist painter. That would happen after he met Marinetti in 1909, the year of the first *Futurist Manifesto.* In fact, he was still working in a divisionist mode and, even though he did not mention Borelli's name, the link between an actress, clothes, and motion spells out

Umberto Boccioni, *Il Romanzo di Una Cucitrice* (1908; *The Story of a Seamstress*). Oil on canvas. Private collection. Photo: Alinari/Art Resource, N.Y.

Borelli, since this was both the way she described herself and the way contemporary reviewers characterized her over and over again.

When Boccioni described his neighbor Ines in his diary, he again observed that clothes in motion could become a spiritual epiphany about a woman's soul.[23] Boccioni's remarks about Ines contain words very similar to the ones used for Borelli, since he was writing about the way he saw modern life more than about Ines. In keeping with his search for a personal and contemporary abstract style, the clothed surface of Ines's figure in *Il Romanzo di Una Cucitrice* (1908; *The Story of a Seamstress*) is not only flat and two-dimensional, but it dissolves into streaks and filaments of colored lights that are on the way to becoming futurist abstraction.

By 1911, when Marinetti announced *The Futurist Manifesto of Painting,* Boccioni was well along in his transition from divisionism to futurism. In fact, inspired by Lyda Borelli, he had concluded in his diary: "I can feel that I want to paint whatever is the new, the fruit of our industrial age."[24]

Influenced by the writings of Max Nordau and Otto Weininger on evolutionary theory and sexuality, Boccioni, like the rest of the futurists, saw women as inferior creatures. Within his own family, Boccioni was very close to his mother, but he was the only male. Thus he enjoyed always being the center of attention. By invoking a new era, therefore, the artist was not necessarily thinking about women's emancipation, but was using the female image as a springboard for finding his own creative direction. For Boccioni,"new" did not mean the new woman with a new set of rights and opportunities. It meant, instead, a novel conception of space and time in relation to the mind and the body. It was not until 1913, with the sculpture *Forme Uniche della Continuità nello Spazio* (*Unique Forms of Continuity in Space*), that Boccioni elaborated his Bergsonian theory of"plastic dynamism," another way of phrasing the reversibility of image and object, external matter and mental projection. For the painter, the viewing subject and the art object should interpenetrate or intersect simultaneously and reshape each other.

Upon closer examination, Boccioni's sculpture is unique, because it seems to take off within a 360-degree space. It is also unique because for Boccioni—and Bergson alike—every moment in time is different, and therefore, unique. All of a sudden the metal frees itself from gravity. Its energy level is so rotational that it seems to aspire to become a propeller, another object reminiscent of Fuller's masterful control of veils. When one wave of fabric peaks, the dancer anticipates the next one. For Boccioni, continuity in space must synthesize three dimensions so as to suggest a fourth, mental one, immersed in time and invisible. The latter is a leap into the unknown: the fourth dimension is about the projection of new configurations and forces unfolding in another space and in another time, which the mind can only imagine and wonder about.

One might argue that Boccioni's famous sculpture is a mixture of old and new because its engagement with motion alludes to the Louvre's Nike of Samothrace (Winged Victory) as a model. The famous ancient sculpture seems to leap beyond its stasis, but it projects itself in only one direction. By contrast, Boccioni's *Unique Forms* achieves the paradox of a stubborn singularity within an unstable multiplicity, so his sculpture does not simply appear to be exploring several possible trajectories of motion at the same time; instead, it looks completely different according to the angle of vision chosen by the observer. The observer, in turn, is led to think that there are many sculptures contained in one, and that each is turning into another within an open-ended ever-changing simultaneity rather than within a series of facets based on some kind of deconstructive plan or original source in disarray. It may seem impossible to link Oxilia's statements about filmic specificity to Boccioni's "plastic dynamism," but the director did think of the cinema as a kind of antitheater operating between sculpture and dance.

During a survey taken by Alberto Cavallaro and published in *La Vita Cinematografica* in 1913, Oxilia declared:

The cinema, a corollary of the theatre? No, the cinema is an autonomous art form, with a specificity of its own. It is absolutely different from theatre. For it does possess . . . its own deep and courageous grace. And as far as people saying that the cinema is a new art? Yes it is, in its form, but not in regard to issues of creativity. Perhaps it is a transformation of the art of posing which Euripides valued so much, after all, precisely because it is the simplest, the dance of human passions—trans-

Umberto Boccioni, *Forme Uniche della Continuità nello Spazio* (1913; *Unique Forms of Continuity in Space*). Bronze, $43^7/_8 \times 34^7/_8 \times 15^3/_4$ in. (111.4 × 88.6 × 40 cm.). Acquired through the Lillie P. Bliss Bequest (231.1948). Museum of Modern Art, New York. Photo: Digital Image © Museum of Modern Art. Licensed by Scala/Art Resource, N.Y.

formed for our modern mentality. . . . I would call the cinema the art of silence in the sense that it is an art of sculptures, one following the other.[25] *(emphasis added)*

It is remarkable that Oxilia separates cinema from high art and associates it with dance, the body, and emotions without feeling insecure. Form, he says, can be sculptural—that is, artistic—but not its source of creativity. Of course, because of photography's bad reputation, he does not use the word *mechanical*, but the appeal to corporeality invokes a physiology of the moving image, "the dance of human passions," whose changing shapes are external and introspective at the same time.

Oxilia, Bergson, and Fuller

Time and motion, according to Boccioni, were the most effective indications of a higher, transcendental, dynamic reality. Little did he know that these two elements amounted to what the cinema—a medium the painter had no respect for—is all about. But what is of interest here is another issue. To assume, as Bergson did, that the temporal side is experientially more significant than the spatial and measurable aspect can also be a way of distinguishing between the futurist and cubist agendas. In fact, the futurist way of setting the object in motion was different from the cubist approach.

According to the cubists, motion was an effect of showing the same thing from several sides at once. Hence, the cubist strategy was fundamentally spatial and metonymic. An example is warranted here. Marcel Duchamp's cubist painting *Nude Descending a Staircase No. 2* (1912) is about motion: the elements of a single figure are rearranged in line with a metonymic scattering of parts to proclaim the disintegration of the body—namely, the cohesive figure of classical painting—which has shattered into multiple fragments of broken but still homogenous pieces. Instead of producing a radical transformation of the one into a heterogeneous multiplicity of parts, cubist movement radically remapped an old hierarchy so that single parts could come into contact with previously inaccessible areas of the canvas without losing their shared texture. Homogeneity in cubism meant that space prevailed over time. Regardless of the cubist breakdown of the corporeal features of the original body, the single figure under deconstruction retained its identity and did not become someone or something else. In a word, cubist analytical fragmentation differed from futurist willful metamorphosis.[26]

For the futurists, by contrast, motion was not the result of dismantling a figure into its elements, but rather the inner origin of a transformation that would allow multiple beings—flames, birds, flowers, smoke, women, ghosts, snakes, wings, feathers, clouds, waves—to coexist simultaneously within the same leap of a metaphorical kind of imagination. There is something totemic and animistic about the futurist approach, while cubism is a scientific and analytical procedure. Simultaneity, of course, has to do with time, although the futurist approach is more visionary than experimental.

It is indeed this multiplicity of forms—one replacing another, which, in turn, becomes something else altogether—that explains the parallels between Lyda Borelli's performance at the end of *Rapsodia Satanica*, Loie Fuller's dancing, Boccioni's *Unique Forms of Continuity in Space*, the title of a sculpture that can be used as a shrewd paraphrasing of Oxilia's definition of the cinema: an original

Marcel Duchamp, *Nude Descending a Staircase No. 2* (1912). Oil on canvas, $57\frac{7}{8} \times 35\frac{1}{8}$ in. (147×89.2 cm.). The Louise and Walter Arensberg Collection, 1950. Philadelphia Museum of Art. © 2006 Artists Rights Society (ARS), New York/ADAGP, Paris/Succession Marcel Duchamp. Photo: Philadelphia Museum of Art/Art Resource, N.Y.

art form with its own specificity, but also halfway between sculpture and dance, movement and stasis. To be sure, Alba's spiritual changes in *Rapsodia* manifest themselves through the yellow butterfly, the glowingly lit bridal veil in front of the mirror, and the unstable fabrics attached to her hieratic silhouette. Each of these visualizations, whether it stresses wings or cloth or both, is characterized by a metaphorical attempt to define femininity according to transformational tropes of art nouveau: from the woman-butterfly to the woman-cloud, from nature to heaven, within the usual Catholic dilemma of elevation or sublimation.

Precisely because Fuller's method was closer to the futurists—and later, to the surrealists—than to the cubist sensibility, it is fair to say that her dances appealed more to a wild imagination. In true Bergsonian fashion, Fuller's spectacles demonstrated that creativity could stem from an emphasis on imagination over logic, intuition over intellect. And this is also why she did not conceive of her choreography along the step-by-step approach of cubism. The latter required a rearrangement of parts leading to a dispersion of the centrality of the self into several disjointed and spatially competing points of view. Much more in line with a surrealist mentality based on allusions, mysteries, replacements, and automatism, Fuller developed the overall geography of her veils from one metaphor to the next. Thanks to a relentless routine of technological research and test, only Fuller had a sense of the complete construction that she would set in motion with an uncanny sense of rhythm, between instinct and control, intuition and intelligence, feeling and information.[27]

From Fuller to Boccioni, to Borelli and Oxilia, this associational and analogical approach resonated with the creative energy of Henri Bergson's élan vital, while also appealing to the Romantic ancestry of the diva film as a genre of love and death, growth and decay. To be sure, Bergson's highly attended lectures were one of the highlights of the period, which was characterized by little-known yet crucial links between feminism and occult practices, Bergsonism and the esoteric tastes of the Ballets Russes. In his essay "Bergson," from a collection about the history of philosophy, *Ventiquattro Cervelli* (1922; *Four and Twenty Minds*), Papini underlines that educated women were Bergson's most fervent admirers:

> *Since 1910 Henri Bergson . . . has been the most famous philosopher on the surface of the earth, admired by the women* cerebrali *who fill up the Collège de France. Some old-fashioned commentator has decided that Bergson's philosophy is worth nothing at all, and that it will pass after a brief celebrity, just like the chairs from the Viennese Secession and the dancers of the Ballets Russes. Such a rushed conclusion stems from having seen the usual "blue-stocking ladies" agitate themselves in front of the author of* Matter and Memory, *along with the usual dandies who want to be in touch with the latest fads but who are really the last individuals to know anything at all.*[28]

Again Papini loves and hates Bergson, just as before he imitated him but also betrayed his text of 1907. In this passage, the Florentine thinker will not be so stupid as to say that Bergson is a fad, but the fact that he is so popular perhaps triggers the Italian's envy, so he does not hesitate to conclude that Bergson's audience amounts to feminists and dandies rather than other colleagues in philosophy. On the one hand, evidence exists that Boccioni read Bergson's *Matter and Memory* in the public library of Milan.[29] On the other, Borelli's ongoing attachment to the theater, regardless of her tremendous success on the screen, perhaps explains why in both Caserini's *Ma l'Amor Mio non Muore* and in Oxilia's *Rapsodia,* Borelli had to play Salome at all costs. Thus the link between Borelli and Boccioni is complex, since it excludes movement on the screen, while movement in real life is how the actress seduces the painter into new ideas about his art.

In contrast to this intricate web of negative and positive attitudes about old and new—between Boccioni and Borelli, cinema and theater, and cinema and painting—the ties between the American dancer Loie Fuller and Henri Bergson are much more straightforward. The relation of her movements to his philosophical sense of life as a form of constant change open to both the past and future—namely, duration—has been eloquently discussed by Tom Gunning:

> *One would be hard put to conceive of a better image of Bergson's contrasting, new, dynamic understanding of duration than the dances of Loie Fuller. "In reality," Bergson claimed, "the body is changing form at every moment; or rather there is no form, since form is immobile and the reality is movement. What is real is the* change of form: *form is only a snapshot view of a transition." If form is a snapshot of a transition, Fuller's dance, as the art of motion, seemed to offer forms dissolved by the cinema.*[30] *(emphasis in the original)*

Gunning's research on Fuller and Bergson expands our understanding of how Bergson's thought can be applied to the pre–World War I cinema in ways that go beyond the philosopher's views on Marey's motion studies at the end of the nineteenth century. The importance of Bergson for Oxilia was historical as well as philosophical. If Bergson was on Oxilia's intellectual horizon in Turin, his key ideas reached the filmmaker mixed with many other fads, patterns, and obsessions from that period. This was why Bergson in Italy became "Bergsonism."

For instance, the contamination of Bergson's ideas with Wagnerian and Nietzschean echoes became most explicit a few years after Oxilia's death, in Ricciotto Canudo's *Helen, Faust and Us,* written in 1920 but published only in 1927. Canudo's title alone is a simple summary of Oxilia's plot for *Rapsodia:* Helen of Troy stands for beauty, Faust stands for aging, and, the pronoun *us* brings in the dimension of temporality, since the audience of cinema changes each time. But besides the Paris-based and therefore geographically distant Canudo, Oxilia's longtime friend Pier Antonio Gariazzo was one of the many popularizers of Bergson, through his book *Teatro Muto* (1919). With a rhetoric much more futuristic than Canudo's—who was always very careful to write in a style between D'Annunzio's and Marinetti's—Gariazzo originally composed this paragraph in 1918 while serving as a soldier on the front line:

> *We want to dream for our future a theatre made of shiverings instead of analysis; we do not want a theatre made of narratives, with long byzantine convolutions, but we want life itself transformed by art through a prismatic refraction: disassembled into its most beautiful colors: one beam after another. We shall remove from the Book of Time grey, monotone pages in such a way to lengthen and intensify Time itself. We shall fill each single instant of our universe by opening up to every possible vibration. Let the prism [cinema] turn around and yield its luminous reverberations so that our ever-shifting life can move from a black to a purple dress, while every single emotion in our soul palpitates. This is my wish!!*[31]

It is worth noting that the image of the prism was frequent yet mysterious in those days. Of course, I am tempted here to compare Gariazzo's prism to film critic Antonio Chiattone's use of the "living arabesque" in relation to Borelli in 1948. More specifically, the prism stood for the dream of an avant-garde cinema in contrast to mainstream productions and diva films. Despite the multifaceted construction of this cultural type, the diva was no prism open to the future, according to most intellectuals before World War I, who perceived her in negative terms.

Interestingly, the diva Borelli had the honor to enter and exit the world of futurism at will and to move in and out of Bergson's lecture room along with other women *cerebrali* just like her. There seemed to be a confused yearning for a new aesthetic that never came about, but that Gariazzo was trying to articulate by invoking the need for marvelous abstractions. In short, Gariazzo's formula was made up of Boccioni's longing for an artistic and willful kind of transcendence through plastic dynamism, and Bergson's spiritualism heightened with a futurist cult of vibrations and chromatism. Notwithstanding what the diva's period thought of itself, its cinema, and its icons, it would be worthwhile to revisit Italian futurism in the light of French surrealism, at least as far as the category of the marvelous is concerned. Furthermore, in antithesis to cubism, Italian futurism and French surrealism were two art movements with a strong analogical and metaphorical orientation. For example, before Pierre kills his wife in *Il Processo Clémenceau*, there is a strange insert of a moon being obscured by clouds. Although the iconography includes no eye and no razor blade, the image of the moon presiding over a fatal sexual encounter anticipates the sadistic connotations of Luis Buñuel and Salvador Dali's *Un Chien Andalou* (1928).

To conclude, although Oxilia's *Rapsodia Satanica* associated Borelli with Fuller and the new woman of the future, the ending of his film, in which the devil prevails over Alba, produces a precarious compromise between the past and the present, between the interiors of the castle and the open, outdoor spaces of tomorrow. In fact, Alba's dance of veils on the terrace is not enough to protect her from Satan's punishment. The last few images of *Rapsodia* show Borelli lost in a thick forest until she ends up under the devil's cape in an attitude of resigned subordination. Another protosurrealist moment occurs in *La Piovra* when the stalker's arms stretching toward Francesca Bertini belong not only to her anxious imagination, but also to the moving shadow of Murnau's famous vampire in *Nosferatu* (1922), a German expressionist film beloved by the French surrealists.

Rapsodia's punitive ending is typical for a diva film, but Oxilia, being young and ambitious, may have hidden another level of interpretation in his standardized conclusion. One may speculate that the devil not only embodies Catholic ideas about women and sin, but also stands for occult forces comparable to the cinema itself, a medium suspended between magic and technology. Only Lucifer has the power to reverse time's forward-moving trajectory. This is why Oxilia's *Rapsodia* can only be *Satanica*, because, even though he aligns women's emancipation with cinema's creativity, in the end he seems to side more with his medium (cinema) and the occult (Satan) rather than with the diva's impossible search for romantic love and eternal beauty.

Such a conclusion is not surprising. Whereas the orientalism of *Sangue Bleu* was filtered through Puccini's *Madama Butterfly*, here Oxilia is the Turinese bohemian who chooses the devil, the first mentor of anticonformist choices. Such a stance entails not only a rejection of scientific positivism in favor of Bergsonism, but also a sliding toward the future, without necessarily becoming futurist. Hence, in Oxilia's film, the cinema is defined as a kind of youthful and carefree defiance of history. We see here the rise of a model hostile to the aestheticizing imperative of the Italian cultural tradition, which was steeped in archeology and the past. Space, aging, and history were the diva's enemies—the components of a stale, theatrical kind of cinema she wished to leave behind. By contrast, temporality and cloth, rather than architecture and the female body, paved the way for the mysterious fourth dimension: so difficult to represent outside the conventions of calendars and clocks, and so precious and profoundly subjective an experience that science and magic, positivism and spiritualism fought over its redefinition and appropriation.

Conclusion

Beyond the Femme Fatale

I hold Menippo's whip, I flog lust, weaknesses, the manners and the vices of my time. And for the wholesome spirits of the world, I sing about first love.

FEBO MARI, *Il Fauno* (The Faun), 1917

Diva is a book about an age and a sensibility that may be gone, but whose intense debates showed an admirable seriousness of intent and ambition toward results. In a society shaped by the values of classical beauty and Renaissance humanism, Italian modernity negotiated technology with aesthetics, mass regimentation with individual defiance. Sadly, these efforts did not include a meaningful transformation of gender roles. Regardless of its failure to lead the way toward a cinematic avant-garde, the diva film was much more than just escapist melodrama. Rather, this genre turned into an alarming survey of major social problems, such as prostitution, adultery, and out-of-wedlock births. This is why I have stressed the documentary streak buried in the diva film's overcrowded wardrobes or in its arabesque-like plots highlighted by stunning outdoor sequences featuring gardens, seascapes, mountainous terrain, and shimmering lake surfaces.

Caught between Filippo T. Marinetti's futurist avant-garde and Gabriele D'Annunzio's symbolist-decadent style, the diva and early Italian film culture did not evolve to the experimental level that some intellectuals and filmmakers had hoped for. Notwithstanding the way that Mussolini's Fascism blocked women's march toward emancipation, the diva film as a genre demonstrates the crucial importance of three themes: first, the influence of Henri Bergson's philosophy of time and motion on early Italian film culture; second, the explanatory power of the oxymoron of belatedness and utopia to characterize the cultural specificity of Italian modernity; and third, the eccentric self-consciousness of a filmmaking tradition that collapsed the premodern with the postmodern by feeling out of synch with northern Europe.

Without a doubt, Italian cinema produced images hinting at the presence of powerful and invisible forces. Often these images were associated not only with occultism and orientalism, but also with the contradictions of femininity itself. Although most producers and performers, writers and artists, were aware of Bergson, Nietzsche, and Wagner, this whole generation was overshadowed by two competing discourses on gender roles: one from the Catholic Church and the other from Cesare Lombroso's criminal anthropology.

Someone may ask what the legacy of the

Italian film diva can teach us about the way we write film history today. To begin with, the Frankfurt School's discourse on modernity does not capture the flavor of the anomalous experience of early Italian cinema. This eccentric modernity is more comparable to a postcolonial development after World War II than to a process of industrialization in a leading northern European society before World War I. Furthermore, while the Italian middle-class film audiences were enthusiastic about the moving image, the major thinkers in the culture were diffident of the cinema and, for the most part, either insensitive or blind to women's contributions on the screen. A perusal of film journals of the period suggests that there was a concerted effort either to desexualize the diva or to turn her into a devastating and inexplicable force of nature. Except for Febo Mari's statement in *Il Fauno* about flogging lust, I found no evidence in the trade magazines of a concern for social justice in regard to women and children. The focus of the commentary was usually on acting style and narrative; references to prostitution, rape, or orphanages were usually absent.

Whereas Walter Benjamin underlined the disjunctions of cinematic perception, and Siegfried Kracauer pointed out the quasi-abstract, ornamental qualities of the filmic image as a sort of mass hieroglyph, Benedetto Croce and Antonio Gramsci alike underestimated over and over again the power of popular culture and continued to believe in a cohesive class-based subject. Furthermore, while Benjamin and Kracauer were interested in the cinema as a mixed form of perception shuttling between the irreconcilable poles of memory and amnesia, Croce and Gramsci held on to a sort of stable Hegelian compromise between the frantic urban life required by modernity and a humanist belief in equilibrium, harmony, and gradual change. While Gramsci advocated for the working class, Croce remained tied to an elitist view.

In contrast to Croce and Gramsci, only Giovanni Papini and Luigi Pirandello emerged as adventurous Italian thinkers in regard to the cinema. While Papini intertwined a cosmic gaze with the events of daily life, Pirandello in *Shoot!* spelled out all the stages of an irreversible male crisis. Serafino Gubbio, Pirandello's protagonist, has many negative anxieties. By contrast Varia Nestoroff, Pirandello's diva, has positive epiphanies about herself, life, and the world of the future.

A figure of temporality based on metaphor, metamorphosis, and flights of the imagination, the diva was more than just an embodiment of women's struggle to reinvent themselves. In fact, she stood for a whole nation torn between old and new. It is precisely this eccentric kind of modernity, that makes the study of the Italian silent diva extremely valuable for future research about film stardom in non-Western cultures or in developing countries today. In those contexts, layers and webs of regional, peripheral, and tribal formations often collide with a superficial and forced implantation of industrial methods imported from the outside but hardly assimilated in the indigenous microstructures of feeling and behavior.

The key words of this study have been arabesque and grotesque, verticality and the close-up, élan vital and memento mori, metaphor and metamorphosis, circus and aviation, Laocoön and Icarus—namely, serpentine shapes and aerial impulses. This book's central thesis is that the Italian silent diva was a combination of the femme fatale and the modern woman, but unlike any other European or American star of her period, she also exhibited a strong mater dolorosa aspect that tapped into Catholic-mystical artistic and religious traditions.

My overview of the relationship between the diva and Italian modernity has been that mechanical reproduction in the form of photography was perceived negatively by theorists such as Ricciotto Canudo and Pier Antonio Gariazzo. By contrast, cinema's free-flowing energy could still aspire toward the achievement of pictorial effects, especially through color, lighting, and fabrics. Thus, the diva film's intense pictorialism enabled the genre to achieve a much more positive reputation than cold black-and-white photography. In short, in the diva film the unprecedented technological possibility to make temporality visible through motion intertwined itself with the theme of fading beauty and life passing by.

Through *Diva,* I have also demonstrated that the landscape of Italian stardom was much more complex than the standard accounts of the period have acknowledged. While minor stars prevailed in short action-oriented narratives, the diva was born out of the marriage of orientalism and the long film. Orientalism, in turn, was a key element of cinema's involvement with occultism, science, and perceptions of cultural differences. The filmic image of the period was so imbued with exotic and esoteric connotations that this particular definition of the cinema has become obsolete today. Thus, while it may be possible to establish parallels and contrasts between silent divas and female stars from other periods of Italian film history, the bottom line is that the study of early cinema releases a way of looking at movement, and a feeling for space and time, that cannot match our current and habitual expectations as viewers.

In the wake of Italian culture's ambivalent reception of modernity, one could say that the diva was a modern phenomenon that "mimed" a premodern form. At the same time, the Diva icon pushed for the birth of some hybrid postmodern being, one halfway between the ethereal and the grotesque, between metaphysical suspension and surrealist hallucination. The reference to "miming," here, is intentional. Somehow, in early Italian film, a medium by definition split between motion and stillness, élan vital and memento mori, the power of performance based on intuition and timing counted more than acting styles based on rigid formulas and group coordination. Within a curvilinear style, Francesca Bertini emphasized elegance and desperation; Borelli underlined complexity and melancholia; and Menichelli embraced luminosity and defiance. While a fairly conformist and predictable behavior was the only way to fit into mass society, the diva's persona oscillated between extremes of criminal deviancy and aristocratic solitude. On the other hand, the diva's asymmetrical relation to her mass audience, explains her enormous power to affect mores, develop a following, and trigger all sorts of anticonformist fashions.

By exhibiting a strong attachment to antimodern values such as uniqueness and creativity, the diva's mime-like, performative, and intuitive acting could range from Bertini's sobriety to Borelli's baroque to Menichelli's playful cruelty. As a cultural type linked to qualitative variations of behavior, the diva was meant to function as an antidote to the measurable and quantifiable features of mechanical reproduction. Even the most hysteric scenes in the diva film, despite their convulsive and therefore repetitive and automatic outbursts, exhibit a choreographic gracefulness mixed with uncanny deformation. A shape in constant motion trying to leap out of her old self, the diva demonstrated her support of an aesthetic based on flow and continuity, in clear defiance of the fragmented and monotonous actions practiced in the modern factory. As a result of its stress on corporeal plasticity, the diva's acting style is between neorealist improvisation and nineteenth-century theatrical codes. At the same time, the Italian diva ignored the step-by-step plan of coherent psychological construction typical of Hollywood stardom. This is the case because the Italian diva was about a sadomasochistic spectacle at odds with agency and self-esteem.

Generally speaking, cinematic stardom itself is a visual solution to the problem of overcoming the finite nature of human life and providing some empowering alternative that makes people feel worthwhile about being on the earth. As a star, the Italian diva was close to being a religious icon. My attention to the history of ideas and to religious systems of belief in this study is meant to show that the cinema is a sort of secular mass cult. It was this appreciation of the aura of live performance that became competitive with the newly born eye of the camera. In Italy, this social technology leaned toward the miraculous, the magical, the occult, and the marvelous, but in the particular case of the diva film, it did so without the dismemberments of Georges Méliès or the shocks of French surrealism. The entire moving line of the diva's body produced a sort of fluid emotional writing meant to anticipate the development of camera movement and make visible the invisible: namely, an inner self struggling against its socially constructed stereotype. This struggle, however, had no happy ending. The conclusion of *Carnevalesca*, to take a specific example, is a statement of lonely defeat. After surviving family intrigues and murderous plots, Lyda Borelli becomes the queen of Malazia. But the narrative ends with her murdering her own faithful and loving husband, who, ironically, is innocent of all scheming and plotting for the throne. The diva's loss of trust in anyone, even the person closest to her heart, provides a measure of the damage that a society filled with corruption, double standards, secrets, and innuendoes inflicts not only on the public life of its citizens, but, most dangerously, on their private ways of feeling and being in the context of family life. In the end, the diva film is a tremendous document about unjust suffering in women's lives and painful anguish in children's minds.

But there is more to this genre. First, because it combines dazzling exoticism with sociopolitical issues, the diva film speaks to the surrealist principle of photographic ontology being a mixture of fact and hallucination. It is well known that surrealism flourished in France and not in Fascist Italy. But the usefulness of the diva film's hidden documentary vocation is that it should invite a reconsideration of futurism as an avant-garde movement in search of marvelous moments. This is why futurism was open to daily life combined with impossible visions, and eager for on-location nocturnal scenes transfigured by artificial lighting.

Second, because it exasperates gesture and feeling, the diva film echoes Anton Giulio Bragaglia's photodynamic agenda of making visible the invisible. This curiosity about the visualization of interiority addresses, on the one hand, Bergson's interest in the subjectivity of time, and, on the other, Bazin's sense that the cinema is the only twentieth-century medium capable of returning to us today the flavor of a particular experience in time from the point of view of a whole generation. And the memory of the past can only help our present to better understand itself.

The end of the diva's story is that the cinema alone was not sufficient to bring about new legislation in favor of women in the period following World War I. However, this new medium did change models of perception, to the point of contributing to the quest for equality between the sexes. In Giovanni Pastrone's *Tigre Reale,* Pina Menicelli sits alone in the back of an elegant car. Wrapped in a luxurious fur coat, she eats rose petals and rides into the mysteries of the night. Her moving reflection on the car window intersects with the streaming lights of the modern city. She is the city that does not sleep, and she is the night of a new era about to begin. Like a spectatrix in the movie theater, she can consume glamorous narratives while dreaming about everlasting youth, beauty, and love. The fresh rose petals are images of a magic time preserved on screen, feeding the diva's desire for the happiness she would like to find.

This cross-over of embodied motion and visual flow turns the diva Menicelli into a modern female viewer, while it separates her forever from a long artistic history of static women confined inside the home and standing alone by an open window. By using a car to stage a motion-filled perception, Pastrone reasserts in positive terms the alliance between femininity and the cinema. In other words, the divas and the women who admired them on screen were "futurists" at heart, in the best sense of the term.

Even if the diva's struggle fell short of its aesthetic and political ambitions, its trajectory remains most instructive for us today. In fact, the diva films continue to speak about the future and about those who are oppressed. Most important, this obscure and uneven genre that lasted the span of a star shooting across the night, calls attention to the fact that modernity did not happen in a singular mode. Rather, major historical transitions of international resonance manifested themselves through different models of temporalities, competing spatial configurations, and, most of all, heterogeneous cultural sensibilities.

Portraits

BIOGRAPHICAL PROFILES OF ACTRESSES*

These profiles were freely translated and edited by Angela Dalle Vacche from Vittorio Martinelli, *Le Dive del Silenzio*, Cineteca del Comune di Bologna (Bologna: Le Mani, 2001).

Francesca Bertini (Elena [Taddei] Vitiello), 1892 (Florence)–1985 (Rome). Reared by a middle-class family, Bertini started out on the Neapolitan stage: when she was eighteen she played an extra in *Assunta Spina*, the famous melodrama that Salvatore di Giacomo had originally written for the actress Adelina Magnetti. Here Bertini was noticed by the managers of Film d'Art, an Italian branch of French Pathé, so in 1910, after playing the role of a female slave in *Salomè*, she became the protagonist in innumerable films featuring female heroines from opera, literature, and theater: Juliet, Cordelia, Francesca Da Rimini, Isotta, and Bianca Cappello, among others. When production houses decided to switch from the short to the long film, Bertini immediately understood that this format change opened up opportunities for her career as well. While Film d'Art stubbornly clung to the short form, Bertini moved on to Celio (Rome), where she excelled in contemporary dramas and long films. In 1914, Bertini played a role *en travesti*, a rare practice in Italian acting, when she took on the male character of Pierrot for *L'Histoire d'un Pierrot*. Bertini's involvement with Celio ended in 1914 with the provocative and successful *Sangue Bleu* (Blue Blood), directed by Nino Oxilia. A few months later, Bertini signed a contract with Caesar Film and appeared in *Nelly La Gigolette* (1914), a drama set in an urban working-class milieu. This role paved the way for her popular success with the filmic adaptation of *Assunta Spina* (1915), a performance that sanctioned the diva's mobility across operatic and realist registers within melodrama. Despite her inclination for unconventional choices, Bertini had to resign herself to many predictable bourgeois roles based on literary and theatrical sources: *The Lady of the Camellias* (1915), *Odette* (1918), *Tosca* (1918), *Frou Frou* (1918), and *La Contessa Sara* (1919). By 1921 the actress had decided to retire, and so she turned down a lucrative contract with the American production house Fox and married a wealthy count, Paul Cartier. Critics from her period and historians today agree that Bertini managed to construct her own image on-screen and offscreen with a special degree of self-consciousness and success. After sharing a small Roman apartment with her seamstress, she died in poverty.

*Thaïs Galitzky is not included because I have not been able to find enough information.

Lyda Borelli, 1884 (Rivarolo Ligure, La Spezia)–1959 (Rome). Borelli started her theatrical acting career in Rome at age fifteen, playing in *La Veine,* by Alfred Capus. Shortly afterward she was involved in *La Figlia di Jorio* (Jorio's Daughter), by Gabriele D'Annunzio, along with such famous theater performers as Ruggero Ruggeri, Virginio Talli, Irma Grammatica, and Oreste Calabresi. By 1905, Borelli had become the "first young actress," next to Eleonora Duse, and she appeared as prima donna with Ruggero Ruggeri in 1909. Borelli's range onstage was remarkable: she was the title character in *Salomè* (1910), by Oscar Wilde; she also worked in *Il Ferro,* by Gabriele D'Annunzio; *La Sfumatura,* by Francis de Croisset; and even in a vaudeville atmosphere in *La Presidentessa,* by Hennequin and Veber. By the time Gloria Film (Turin) hired Borelli in 1913 for *Ma l'Amor Mio non Muore (Everlasting Love)*, she was already a famous and highly developed actress. Immediately after this success with Mario Caserini, who launched the format of the diva film, Borelli played a female pilot in *La Memoria dell'Altro* (1913), with Mario Bonnard in the male lead. While moving from Turin to Rome with Cines, Borelli brought to the screen *La Donna Nuda* (1914; The Nude Woman), *La Marcia Nuziale* (1915; The Wedding March), and *La Falena* (1916; The Moth)—three texts by Henry Bataille. Audiences raved about Borelli, and young women imitated all her gestures. Borelli also starred in *Madame Tallien* (1916), *Malombra* (1917), *La Storia dei Tredici* (1917; The Story of Thirteen), *Carnevalesca* (1918), and *Una Notte a Calcutta* (1918; A Night in Calcutta). One of Borelli's most interesting films was *Rapsodia Satanica* (1917), by Nino Oxilia, a revisitation of Faust's pact with the devil. Borelli's career in the cinema was intense but brief, since she left the screen in 1918 to marry Count Vittorio Cini and settle in his palazzo in Venice. Borelli's early retirement was interrupted only by two patriotic exceptions. In 1918 she appeared in *L'Altro Esercito o La Leggenda di Santa Barbara*—a war-propaganda documentary in which she played Santa Barbara, the protector of fighting soldiers. After Italy's painful defeat at the Battle of Caporetto, in 1917, the actress also agreed to appear in a short film titled *Per la Vittoria e per la Pace* (1918; For Victory and for Peace).

Soava Gallone (Stanislava Winawer), 1880 (Warsaw)–1957 (Rome). While vacationing in Sorrento with her mother and brother to recover from a failed marriage, Stanislava (called Soava) met Carmine Gallone, a writer a bit younger than she. The couple married and moved to Rome in 1911. Their debut in the world of theater did not go well; his play, *Coriolanus,* failed, and she had a strong foreign accent that did not help onstage. They both decided to turn to silent cinema; there her foreign origin would not be a handicap. Thanks to mediation by director Nino Oxilia, in 1914 Cines hired Soava and Carmine, who soon became the director of a series of films set on the Amalfi coast and starring his beautiful wife. While these landscape films were praised abroad for their beauty, it was only with *Avatar* (1916) and *La Chiamavano Cosetta* (1917; She Was Called Cosetta) that Soava achieved celebrity. Carmine, however, limited her appearances on-screen to two films a year because he did not want to overuse her delicate and refined appeal. Once her fortunes declined, Soava followed her husband abroad during different professional engagements from 1927 to 1936. Soava's best titles include *La Storia di un Peccato* (1918; The History of a Sin); *Il Bacio di Cirano* (1919;

Cyrano's Kiss); *Maman Poupée* (1919), based on a subject by Washington Borg; *Amleto e il Suo Çlown* (1920; Hamlet and His Clown); *Nemesis* (1920); *La Cavalcata Ardente* (1925; The Fiery Squadron); and *Celle Qui Domine* (1927), based on the novel *She Who Squandered Men,* by May Edginton.

Leda Gys (Giselda Lombardi), 1892 (Rome)–1957 (Rome). Thanks to the Roman poet Trilussa (Carlo Alberto Salustri, 1871–1950), Lombardi signed a contract with Cines and acquired her screen name, Leda Gys. By 1913 she had already starred in short adventure films directed by Baldassarre Negroni, who was one of the most important directors of the early 1910s. Between 1913 and 1914, Gys divided her time between Cines and Celio, working in short and medium-length films in a variety of genres: contemporary bourgeois dramas, comedies, and costume films. Besides Negroni, Gys worked with Enrico Guazzoni, Ivo Illuminati, and Giulio Antamoro. Notwithstanding these different directorial personalities, Gys specialized in positive female roles, playing naïve or innocent young women caught in evil webs and manipulated by family members and suitors. Gys's canonization as a diva took place when she portrayed Mary in *Christus* (1916), a film shot on location in Egypt and Palestine. After becoming quite successful in Spain, Gys also worked for the Neapolitan Elvira Notari and interpreted texts written by Victorien Sardou. In 1917 she shifted her energies from Rome to Naples, where she starred in socially conscious serials and literary adaptations of texts by Giovanni Verga, Dario Nicodemi, and Gabriele D'Annunzio, under the direction of Gustavo Lombardo. Gys eventually married Lombardo and settled at Lombardo Films. The titles worth remembering from the twenties are *I Figli di Nessuno* (1921; Nobody's Children), *Trappola* (1922; The Trap), and *Santarellina* (1923; Little Saint). During the same decade, Gys participated in film productions that Eugenio Perego made in the Neapolitan dialect: *Vide Napuli e po' mori!* (1924), *Napule e . . . niente cchiù!* (1928), and *Napule è 'na canzona* (1927). Gys retired in 1929 to raise her son, Goffredo (1920–2005), who sat on the board of Titanus, a production company founded by his father, Gustavo, in 1908.

Maria Jacobini, 1892 (Rome)–1944 (Rome). Jacobini stood out as the diva who specialized in girl-next-door roles. In contrast to the emphatic acting style of some divas, her approach was understated. Her first films were produced by Savoia Film (Turin) around 1910; some of the titles reveal Jacobini's tendency to play femmes fatales: *Pantera* (1912; The Panther), *La Zingara* (1913; The Gypsy Woman), *L'Onta Nascosta* (1913; The Hidden Shame), *Giovanna d'Arco* (1913; Joan of Arc), *Ananke* (1915; Fate), *Come le Foglie* (1917; Like the Leaves)—a play by Giuseppe Giacosa, with direction by Gennaro Righelli—and *Addio Giovinezza!* (1918; Good-bye, Youth!), by Augusto Genina. The latter film was dedicated to her fiancé, Nino Oxilia, killed the year before in the war. During the twenties, Jacobini and Righelli became a couple, and they made *Il Viaggio* (1921; The Journey), based on a novella by Luigi Pirandello; *Amore Rosso* (1921; Red Love), based on a novel by Théophile Gautier; and the ethnographic *Cainà* (1922), shot in Sardinia. In 1923, Righelli and Jacobini begin to work in Germany, thanks to producer Jakob Karol. After the release of *Bohème* (1923), the pair worked all over Europe and even shot on location in Africa, with occasional visits to Italy and

France for Jacobini. In fact, she starred in *La Bocca Chiusa* (1925; The Closed Mouth), by Guglielmo Zorzi; *Beatrice Cenci* (1926); *Il Carnevale di Venezia* (1927; Venetian Carnival); and *Maman Colibrì* (1929), by Julien Duvivier. The advent of sound damaged Jacobini's career, and by 1937 she had begun to teach acting at the prestigious Centro Sperimentale di Cinematografia in Rome. There she mentored many important actresses, including Adriana Benetti, Clara Calamai, Elli Parvo, and Alida Valli. Jacobini's sister, Diomira, was also an actress during the silent period, but she never attained Maria's fame.

Diana Karenne (Leocadia Konstantin), 1888 (Danzig)–1940 (Aachen [Aix-la-Chapelle]). Karenne arrived in Turin around 1915 and became involved with Eugenio Maria Pasquali, who directed her in *Passione Tsigana* (1916; Gipsy Passion). After making a few more films in collaboration with Pasquali, Karenne began to write her own scripts, direct herself, and even produce the posters for her films. After declaring that her major source of inspiration was Asta Nielsen, Karenne was a constant presence on Italian screens between 1916 and 1920. Most of her films have been lost, however, which makes it difficult to assess her acting style and screen persona as a diva. Eccentric in her clothes and makeup offscreen, and notorious for her assertive personality, she played Mary Magdalene in *Redenzione* (1919; Redemption) for Carmine Gallone. After the Italian film industry collapsed, Karenne moved to Berlin and Paris, where she acted in *Marie Antoinette, das Leben einer Königin* (1922; Marie Antoinette, the Love of a King), by Rudolf Meinert; *Casanova* (1927), by Alexander Volkoff, with Ivan Mosjouskine; and *Rasputins Liebesabenteuer* (1928; *Rasputin, the Holy Sinner*). The advent of sound marked the end of Karenne's career; she retired to Aachen (Aix-la-Chapelle) with her husband. She came out of retirement only briefly, for an appearance in *Manon Lescaut* (1940) by Carmine Gallone. That same year, Karenne died of injuries sustained during a bombing raid.

Elena Makowska (Helena Woyniewicz), 1893 (Krivoi Rog, Ukraine)–1964 (Rome). Daughter of a Polish engineer, Makowska was born in the Ukraine during one of her father's assignments while he was working for a Russian-Belgian company. At sixteen, Elena was briefly married to a Warsaw lawyer, Julien Makowsky, whom she left to go to Milan and take singing lessons. After a debut in the world of opera, as Amelia in *Un Ballo in Maschera* (A Masked Ball) and Elena in *Mefistofele*, Makowska turned to cinema with *Romanticismo* (1915), produced by Ambrosio Film in Turin. After this successful debut, she made at least forty films between 1915 and 1920. Critics agreed that Makowska was beautiful, but critical evaluations improved once she started working for a series of different production houses. She was Ophelia in *Hamlet* (1917), for Rodolfi; for Itala, she became the evil Elena in *Addio Giovinezza!* (1918; Good-bye, Youth!); and for Gladiator Films, she appeared as the title character in *La Dame en Gris* (1919; The Lady in Gray). Once the Italian film industry entered its crisis period, Makowska moved to Germany, where she continued to work in film in Warsaw and Berlin, and married the actor Karl Falkenberg. The thirties were marked by a third marriage, this time to an Englishman, and a return to her native Poland to perform in a few operas. She was Micaela in *Carmen*, and she also appeared in a few operettas—for instance, *Eine Frau Die Weiss Was Sie Will* (1932;

A Woman Knows What She Wants), by Oscar Straus. After the German invasion of Poland, Makowska was arrested as a British citizen and deported to Berlin. From there, she was transferred to a concentration camp for four years. Eventually released, thanks to an exchange of prisoners, Makowska immediately joined the theater ensemble of the Polish army, for which she performed until the end of the war. Makowska spent her last years in Italy and managed to appear in *La Valigia dei Sogni* (1953; The Suitcase of Dreams), an interesting film by Gianni Comencini, director of Cineteca Italiana of Milan. This work shows Makowska as an old woman playing herself and looking at her own beautiful image in a silent film. The audience bursts into laughter out of contempt for the period's exaggerated style of acting. Comencini's film underlines how arrogant audiences can be; it also stresses the need for film preservation and underscores the educational value of film history for recovering the flavor of an era.

Pina Menichelli (Giuseppina Menichelli), 1890 (Castroreale, Messina)–1984 (Milan). Daughter of Sicilian actors trained to perform in dialect, the young Menichelli, after a rather superficial start in the theater, decided to work in cinema. Between 1913 and 1914, she appeared in approximately forty films for Cines, either as the protagonist or in some significant role. Director Nino Oxilia paired Menichelli with Ruggero Ruggeri for an epic film titled *Il Sottomarino n. 27* (1915; Submarine no. 27), and in *Papà* (1915), based on a comedy by Robert de Flers and Gaston Armand de Caillavet. Augusto Genina directed Menichelli, again with Ruggeri in the male lead, in *Lulu* (1914), based on a play by Carlo Bertolazzi; and in *Il Grido dell'Innocenza* (1914; Innocent Cry), *Giovinezza Che Trionfa!* (1914; Youth That Wins!), and *I Misteri del Castello di Monroe* (1914; The Mysteries of Monroe Castle). In *Zuma* (1913), Baldassarre Negroni transformed Menichelli into a husband stealer. Nino Martoglio cast her in his *Romanzo* (1913; Romance), while Enrico Guazzoni, after working with Menichelli in *Alma Mater* (1915), asked her to play Cleopatra in *Cajus Julius Caesar* (1914). During the editing of this film, however, Menichelli's character was completely eliminated from the narrative. Notwithstanding this episode, Menichelli was the protagonist in other films by Guazzoni—for instance, *Scuola d'Eroi* (1914; School for Heroes). It was in this historical film, set during the Napoleonic era, that Giovanni Pastrone is said to have noticed Menichelli for the first time. Although the actress had already been on the covers of film journals, it was her shift to Itala and Pastrone that turned her into a major diva. Inspired by the title of Gabriele D'Annunzio's eponymous novel, Pastrone's *Il Fuoco* (The Fire), with Menichelli, was released in 1915. In addition, a novella by Giovanni Verga, *Tigre Reale* (1916; Royal Tiger), was the source of another film success. After these two major hits with Pastrone, Menichelli abandoned her femme fatale roles for a more modern and socially charged character: a single mother obliged to live like a high-class prostitute in Amleto Palermi's *La Storia di Una Donna* (1920; The Story of One Woman). But the titles in Menichelli's filmography go on and on: *Padrone delle Ferriere* (1919; The Railway Owner); *Seconda Moglie* (1922; Second Wife); *Romanzo di un Giovane Povero* (1919; The Story of a Poor Young Man); and *La Donna e l'Uomo* (1923; Man and Woman), which was shot mostly in England. By this point Menichelli had become tired of playing tormented, melodramatic roles, so she turned to playwright Georges Feydeau, who offered her the opportunity to display her talents in more agile and comic parts in *La Dame de chez Maxim's* (1923) and *Occupati d'Amelia* (1925; Take Care of Amelia). She retired to Milan in 1923, and the next year married Baron Carlo Amato, who had been the producer for much of her work at Rinascimento Films.

Archival Locations and Filmography

Locations of Films Viewed by Author

Although in my researches I dealt with a variety of short and early films, this filmography lists only the Italian diva films or films with major diva roles (modern woman, femme fatale, or mater dolorosa) discussed in this book. The institution at which a viewing occurred was not always responsible for the restoration of the film seen. Rather, the archive may have acquired the copy from another source, which may or may not have been indicated in the credits or in the logo of the print I was able to examine. All of my information about casts, dates, and lengths is based on comparing data found in Aldo Bernardini's *Archivio del Cinema Italiano*, vol. 1: *Il Cinema Muto, 1905–1931*, and consulting plot summaries in the annual issues of *Il Cinema Muto Italiano* that were edited by Aldo Bernardini and Vittorio Martinelli and published by Biblioteca di Bianco e Nero. Finally, I have also used informal filmographic information obtained by the archives where I saw the films.

Filmography

Note: *VC*: visto di censura *(censorship visa, the governmental certification required for a film to be produced and shown in Italy).*

Length: length (in meters) of the celluloid film which has survived from a particular print.

L'Amazzone Mascherata (1913). Director: Baldassarre Negroni. VC #2591, issued 21 February 1914. Length: 1,606 m. Studio: Celio Film. Title in Spain: *La Amazona disfrazada* (6 May 1914); title in the Netherlands: *De Geheimzinnige Amazone;* alternate title in the Netherlands: *De Geheimzinnige paardrijdster;* title in France: *L'Amazone masquée.* Screened at Nederlands Filmmuseum, Amsterdam.

Assunta Spina (1915). Directors: Gustavo Serena and Francesca Bertini. VC #9173, issued 29 May 1915. Length: 1,690 m.; length of restored print: 1,324 m. Duration: 55 min. Studio: Caesar Film. Source: drama by Salvatore Di Giacomo (1909). Screenplay: Gustavo Serena and Francesca Bertini. Cinematography: Alberto Carta. Story: Alfredo Manzi. Cast: Francesca Bertini, Gustavo Serena, Carlo Benetti, Alberto Albertini, Antonio Cruicchi, Amelia Cipriani, Alberto Collo. Screened at Cineteca di Bologna, Bologna.

The restoration of this print was carried out by Cineteca di Bologna, Bologna, and Cineteca Italiana, Milan, and was based on two copies: one from Milan, without intertitles, and one from Cinemateca Brasileira, São Paulo, with intertitles in Portuguese.

Caino (1918). Director: Leopoldo Carlucci. VC #13120, issued 1 January 1918. Length: 1,781 m. Studio: Corona Films, Turin. Source: an Arabic novella. Cinematography: Arnoldo Ricotti. Cast: Elena Makowska, Luigi Cimara, Achille Majeroni, Luigi Duse, Elda Bruni-De Negri, Ettore Mazzanti, Mary-Cleo Tarlarini, Contessa Henry, Bruno Leveson, Raoul Leveson. Screened at Nederlands Filmmuseum, Amsterdam.

Carnevalesca (1918). Director: Amleto Palermi. VC #13199, issued 1 January 1918. Length: 1,755 m.; length of restored copy: 1,500 m. Duration: 55 min. Studio: Cines, Rome (1906). Story: Lucio D'Ambra. Cinematography: Giovanni Grimaldi. Cast: Lyda Borelli (Lyda), Livio Pavanelli (Luciano), Renato Visca (Luciano as a child), Mimi (Lyda as a child). Screened at Cineteca di Bologna, Bologna.

The color of the Bologna print of *Carnevalesca* was restored using the Noël Desmet method from the Cinémathèque Royale de Belgique, Brussels.

Cenere (1917). Directors: Febo Mari and Arturo Ambrosio, Jr. VC #12166, issued 11 January 1916. Length: 914 m. Studio: Società Anonima Ambrosio, Turin. Source: novel by Grazia Deledda. Title in France: *Les Cendres du passé.* Screened at Cineteca di Bologna, Bologna.

La Donna Nuda (1914). Director: Carmine Gallone. VC #3084, issued 15 April 1914. Length: 1,600 m. Studio: Cines (1906). Title in Spain: *La Mujer desnuda* (March 1914; length: 1,950 m.). Screened at Cineteca di Bologna, Bologna.

L'Età Critica (1921). Director: Amleto Palermi. VC #16011, issued 5 January 1921. Length: 2,135 m. Studio: Rinascimento Film. Title in Sweden: *Den Farliga åldern* (Stockholm; 4 May 1925; length: 1,993 m.). Screened at Cineteca Nazionale, Rome.

Il Fauno (1917). Director: Febo Mari. VC #12769, issued 6 June 1917. Length: 1,325 [1,385] m. Studio: Società Anonima Ambrosio, Turin. Story and screenplay: Febo Mari. Cinematography: Giuseppe Vitrotti. Cast: Febo Mari (myth/Faun), Nietta Mordeglia (Faith), Elena Makowska (Female), Vasco Creti (Art), Oreste Bilancia (Shrewdness), Ernesto Vaser (the cart-man), Fernando Ribacchi, Giuseppe Pierozzi (gamblers). Screened thanks to Mondadori Video (PAL format).

Il Fior di Male (1915). Director: Carmine Gallone. VC #8317, issued 29 March 1915. Length: 1,500 m. Studio: Cines (1906). Title in the Netherlands: *Kinderen der zonde.* Screened at Nederlands Filmmuseum, Amsterdam; print with Dutch intertitles.

Il Fuoco (1915). Director: Piero Fosco [Giovanni Pastrone]. VC #10838, issued 8 December 1915. Length: 1,100 m. Studio: Itala Film, Turin. Title in Spain: *El Fuego* (Madrid; 7 April 1916; length: 1,069 m). Screened at Museo del Cinema, Turin.

L'Histoire d'un Pierrot (1914). Director: Baldassarre Negroni. VC #2546, issued 14 February 1914. Length: 1,200 m. Studio: Italica Ars/Celio Film. Title in U.S.: *Pierrot the Prodigal* (8 June 1914); title in France: *L'Histoire d'un Pierrot;* title in Spain: *Historia de un Pierrot* (February 1914). Screened at Library of Congress, Washington, D.C.

Ma l'Amor Mio non Muore (1913). Director: Mario Caserini. VC #1462, issued 1 December 1913. Length: 2,600 m. Studio: Film Artistica "Gloria", Turin. Story: Emiliano Bonetti, G. Monleone. Cinematography: Angelo Scalenghe. Cast: Lyda Borelli (Elsa Holbein), Mario Bonnard (Prince Maximilian), Vittorio Rossi Pianelli (Colonel Julius Holbein), Emilio Petacci (Colonel Theubner), Camillo de Riso (theater manager Schaudard), Gian Paolo Rosmino (Moise Stahr), Dante Cappelli (Grand Duke of Wallenstein), Maria Caserini Gasparini (Grand Duchess of Wallenstein), Gentile Miotti, Letizia Quaranta, Felice Metellio, Antonio Monti (a general). Title in Spain: *Pero mi amor no muere* (October 1913); title in France: *Mais mon amour ne meurt pas!* (October 1913); title in U.S.: *Everlasting Love* (17 January 1914; 6 reels). Screened at the Museum of Modern Art, New York.

Madame Tallien (1916). Director: Enrico Guazzoni. VC #12193, issued 8 November 1916. Length: 1,855 m. Screening time: 80 min. Studio: Palatino Film, Rome. Source: from the eponymous drama by Victorien Sardou. Screenplay: Enrico Guazzoni. Cinematography: Gabriele Gabrielian. Cast: Lyda Borelli (Teresia Cabarrus, Madame Tallien), Amleto Novelli (Tallien), Renzo Fabiani (Robespierre), Ruggero Barni (Guérin), Ettore Baccani (Fontenay), Roberto Spiombi (a young abbott), Orlando Ricci. Screened thanks to Mondadori Video (PAL format).

The restoration of this print was carried out by Cineteca di Bologna and Cinémathèque Française, Paris. Two copies were used: one from Cineteca Italiana, Milan, and one from Cinémathèque Française.

Malombra (1917). Director: Carmine Gallone. VC #12374, issued 17 January 1917. Length: 1,705 m. Studio: Cines (1906). Subject: from the eponymous novel (1881) by Antonio Fogazzaro. Screenplay: Carmine Gallone. Cinematography: Giovanni Grimaldi. Cast: Lyda Borelli (Marina Di Malombra), Amleto Novelli (Corrado Silla), Giulia Cassini-Rizzoto (Contessa Salvador), Berta Nelson, Francesco Cacace-Galeota, Augusto Mastripietri (Conte Cesare), Amedeo Ciaffi, Noemi De Ferrari, Consuelo Spada (Edith), Giorgio Fini. Screened at Cineteca di Bologna, Bologna.

The restoration of this print was based on two copies: one with Italian intertitles and one from SODRE (Servicio Oficial de Difusión, Radiotelevisión y Espectáculos), Montevideo, with Spanish intertitles.

Maman Poupée (1919). Director: Carmine Gallone. VC #14035, issued 1 March 1919. Length: 1,840 m. Screening time: 95 min. Studio: Olympus Film, Rome. Story: Washington Borg. Cinematography: Giulio Rufini, Emilio Guattari. Screenplay: Piero Guidotti. Cast: Soava Gallone (Susetta di Montalto, aka Maman Poupée), Bruno Emanuel Palmi (the husband), Mina D'Orvella (the rival), Mario Cusmich. Screened at Cineteca di Bologna, Bologna.

Mariute (1918). Director: Edoardo Bencivenga. VC #13506, issued 1 May 1918. Length: 743 m. Studio: Caesar Film/Bertini Film, Rome. Story: Robert de Flers. Cinematography: Giuseppe Filippa. Screenplay: Alfredo Manzi. Cast: Francesca Bertini (herself and Mariute), Gustavo Serena, Livio Pavanelli, Camillo De Riso (themselves), Alberto Albertini (the veteran). Screened at Library of Congress, Washington, D.C., and at Cineteca Nazionale, Rome.

La Memoria dell'Altro (1913). Director: Alberto Degli Abbati. VC #2084, issued 24 December 1913. Length: 1,650/2,000 m. (six parts). Studio: Film Artistica "Gloria", Turin. Story: Baronessa De Rege. Cinematography: Angelo Scalenghe. Cast: Lyda Borelli (the aviatrix Lyda), Mario Bonnard (Mario Alberti), Vittorio Rossi Pianelli (the prince of Sèvre), Letizia Quaranta (Cesarina), Felice Metellio (the journalist), Emilio Petacci. Title in France: *La Mémoire de l'autre* (April 1914; length: 1,623 m.); alternate title in France: *Jusqu'à la mort.* Screened at Cineteca Nazionale, Rome.

Il Nodo (1921). Director: Gaston Ravel. VC #16260, issued 1 July 1921. Length: 1,598 m. Studio: Caesar Film/Bertini Film. Screened at Cineteca Nazionale, Rome.

La Piovra (1919). Director: Edoardo Bencivenga. VC #14108, issued 1 May 1919. Length: 1,687 m. Screening time: 85 min. Studio: Caesar Film/Bertini Film, Rome. Story: V. Brusiloff. Screenplay: Vittorio Bianchi. Cinematography: Giuseppe Filippa. Screenplay: Alfredo Manzi. Cast: Francesca Bertini (Daria Oblosky), Amleto Novelli (Petrovich, the "octopus"), Livio Pavanelli (Maurizio Grafenthal), Giovanni Schettini (Marchese Di Francavilla). Screened at Cineteca di Bologna, Bologna.

Il Processo Clémenceau (1917). Two episodes: *Iza bimba,* VC #12822, issued 1 July 1917; length: 1,079 m.; *Iza donna,* VC #12823, issued 1 July 1917; length: 1,354 m. Director: Alfredo De Antoni. Studio: Caesar Film. Screened at Cineteca di Bologna, Bologna.

The restoration of this print was based on two copies, one found in the Valencia Film Archive and one in the Saragoza Film Archive. The Castilian intertitles in both copies have been translated into Italian, and the original graphic style has been maintained as much as possible.

Il Quadro di Osvaldo Mars (1921). Director: Guido Brignone. VC #16171, issued 1 June 1921. Length: 1,446 [1,266] m. Studio: Rodolfi Film, Turin. Cinematography: Anchise Brizzi. Cast: Mercedes Brignone (Anna Maria Di San Giusto), Domenico Serra (Osvaldo Mars), Giovanni Cimara (the husband), François-Paul Donadio, Armand Pouget. Screened at Cineteca di Bologna, Bologna.

Rapsodia Satanica (1917). Director: Nino Oxilia. VC #12873, issued 1 July 1917. Length: 905 m. Studio: Cines (1906). Story: Alfa (Alberto Fassini), Fausto Maria Martini. Screenplay: Alfa. Intertitles: Fausto Maria Martini. Music: Pietro Mascagni. Cinematography: Giorgio Ricci. Cast: Lyda Borelli (Countess D'Oltrevita), Andrea Habay (Tristano), Ugo Bazzini (Mephisto), Giovanni Cini (Sergio), Alberto Nepoti. Title in France: *La Rhapsodie satanique.* Screened at Cineteca di Bologna, Bologna.

The restoration of this print, based on one copy, was conducted by Cinémathèque Suisse, Lausanne; Cineteca di Bologna; and Cineteca Italiana, Milan.

Sangue Bleu (1914). Director: Nino Oxilia. VC #3772, issued 1 August 1914. Length: 1,308 m. (5 acts). Studio: Celio Film, Rome. Story: Alberto Fassini. Screenplay: Guglielmo Zorzi. Cinematography: Giorgio Ricci. Cast: Francesca Bertini (Princess Elena Di Montvollon), André Habay, Angelo Gallino, Fulvio Perini (Countess Simone de la Croix), Anna Cipriani (Diana), Elvira Radaelli, Amedeo Ciaffi. Title in Spain: *Sangre Azul* (July 1914); title in the Netherlands: *Het Lijden van een vrouw;* alternate title in the Netherlands: *Vorstin van Montecabello.* Screened at Nederlands Filmmuseum, Amsterdam; print with Dutch intertitles.

La Serpe (1920). Director: Roberto Roberti. VC #14749, issued 1 January 1920. Length: 1,580 m. Studio: Caesar Film/Bertini Film. Screened at Cineteca Nazionale, Rome.

La Storia di Una Donna (1920). Director: Eugenio Perego. VC #14745, issued 1 January 1920. Length: 2,000 m. [restored version: 1,290 m.] Screening time: 70 min. Studio: Rinascimento Film, Rome. Story and screenplay: Amleto Palermi. Cinematography: Antonino Cufaro. Cast: Pina Menichelli, Luigi Serventi (Paolo), Livio Pavanelli (Fabiano). Screened at Cineteca di Bologna, Bologna.

La Terra Promessa (1913). Director: Baldassarre Negroni. VC #76 1 December 1913. Length: 939 m. Studio: Celio Film. Title in UK: *The Land of Promise* (9 June 1913; length: 3,100 feet); title in France: *La Terre promise* (6 June 1913; length: 939 m.); title in the Netherlands: *Het Land van belofte.* Screened at Nederlands Filmmuseum, Amsterdam.

Thaïs (1917). Directors: Anton Giulio Bragaglia and Riccardo Cassano. VC #12429, issued 30 January 1917. Length: 1,446 m. Studio: Novissima Film, Rome. Story: A. G. Bragaglia. Screenplay: A. G. Bragaglia and R. Cassano. Cinematography: Luigi Dell'Otti. Set design: Enrico Prampolini. Cast: Thaïs Galitzky (Vera Preobrajenska/Thaïs), Ileana Leonidoff (Bianca Stagno-Bellincioni), Mario Parpagnoli (Count San Remo), Augusto Bandini (Oscar), Dante Paletti, Alberto Casanova (two suitors). Title in France: *Les Possédées.*

Tigre Reale (1916). Director: Piero Fosco [Giovanni Pastrone]. VC #11662, issued 20 June 1916. Length: 1,742 m. Studio: Itala Film, Turin. Source: novel by Giovanni Verga (1873). Cinematography: Giovanni Tomatis, Segundo de Chómon. Cast: Pina Menichelli (Countess Natka), Alberto Nepoti (Giorgio La Ferlita, ambassador), Febo Mari (Dolski, woodskeeper), Valentina Frascaroli (Erminia), Gabriel Moreau (Count de Rancy), Ernesto Vaser (drugstore owner), Enrico Gemelli, Bonaventura Ibañez. Title in France: *La Tigresse royale;* title in Spain: *Tigre real* (Madrid; 28 October 1916). Screened at Museo del Cinema, Turin.

Una Tragedia al Cinematografo (1913). Director: Enrico Guazzoni. VC #196, issued 1 December 1913. Length: 166 m. Studio: Cines (1906). Cast: Pina Menichelli (Clara, the wife); Ignazio Lupi (Antonio, the husband); Bruto Castellani (owner of the cinematograph theater). Title in France: *Une Tragédie au cinéma en carnaval* (13 June 1913; length: 166 m.); title in Great Britain: *Cinema Tragedy at Carnival Time* (26 June 1913; length: 566 ft.); title in the Netherlands: *Een Treurspel in de bioscoop.* Screened at Nederlands Filmmuseum, Amsterdam.

Notes

Introduction

(See Bibliography for full publication details.)

1. Edgar Morin, *Les Stars*, 21.

2. For my biographical profiles I have mostly relied on Vittorio Martinelli, *Le Dive del Silenzio*.

3. On art nouveau, see Giovanna Massobrio and Paolo Portoghesi, *La Donna Liberty*; and Debora Silverman, *Art Nouveau in Fin-de-Siècle France*. For the study of visual form, illustrious models are Henri Focillon, *The Life of Forms in Art*; and Yves Alain Bois and Rosalind Krauss, *Formless: A User's Guide*.

4. Gian Piero Brunetta, "Il Divismo."

5. Aldo Bernardini, *Cinema Muto Italiano*, vol. 3, *Arte, Divismo, Mercato, 1910–1914*, 203.

6. Carol Ockman and Kenneth Silver, eds., *Sarah Bernhardt: The Art of High Drama*. My observations on Bernhardt in this study are based on what I learned from the splendid exhibition at the Jewish Museum in New York and from this book, the catalogue edited by the cocurators.

7. William Weaver, *Duse: A Biography*, 220.

8. Professor Mark Seymour from the Department of History at the University of Otago, Dunedin, New Zealand, told me that Waldo Commandini in 1920 also proposed the introduction of civil divorce, in the wake of the proposed Sacchi Law (1919). See Mark Seymour, *Debating Divorce in Italy: Marriage and the Making of Modern Italians*.

9. Bram Dijkstra, *Evil Sisters: The Threat of Female Sexuality and the Cult of Manhood*. The Italian diva is such a quagmire of artistic references that all the illustrations in Bram Dijkstra's *Idols of Perversity: Fantasies of Feminine Evil in Fin-de-Siècle Culture* can be useful to future researchers in women's studies and early Italian cinema.

10. The expert on hysteria and female deviancy in Italy was not Sigmund Freud, but the criminal anthropologist Cesare Lombroso (1835–1909). On this topic, see Giorgio Colombo, *La Scienza Infelice: Il Museo di Antropologia Criminale*, and Mary Gibson, *Prostitution and the State in Italy, 1860–1915*.

11. Mira Liehm, *Passion and Defiance*, 19–21.

12. On the diva, the femme fatale, and opera, see Catherine Clement, *Opera, or the Undoing of Women*; Wayne Koestenbaum, *The Queen's Throat: Opera, Homosexuality, and the Mystery of Desire*; and Susan Leonardi and Rebecca Pope, *The Diva's Mouth: Body, Voice, Prima Donna Politics*.

13. On the arabesque and the grotesque, see Antonio Chiattone, "La Diva Muette," 68; Mary Russo, *The Female Grotesque: Risk, Excess and Modernity*, 17–51; and Wolfgang Kayser, *The Grotesque in Art and Literature*. The reader may want to consult Gino Gori, *Il Grottesco nell'Arte e nella Letteratura*, an especially interesting source. In his preface to the book, Italian cultural theorist Massimo Bontempelli links the cinematic grotesque to Bergson's philosophy, which I discuss in Chapter 1 in relation to the diva and temporality. Also on Bergson, the cinema, and Italy in the twenties, see Santino Caramella, *Bergson*; Francesco Ogliati, *La Filosofia Bergsoniana e il Realismo*; and Ogliati, *La Filosofia di Enrico Bergson*.

14. Gilles Deleuze, *Cinema 2: The Time-Image*.

15. For this study, the most important philosophical text is Henri Bergson, *Creative Evolution*. See also Windon Carr, "Time and History in Contemporary Philosophy; with Special Reference to Bergson and Croce."

16. Aldo Bernardini, *Cinema Muto Italiano*, vol. 1, *Ambienti, Spettacoli, Spettatori, 1896–1904*.

17. Noel Burch, *Life to Those Shadows*, 138.
18. Aldo Bernardini and Vittorio Martinelli, *Roberto Roberti: Direttore Artistico*, 8.
19. Angela Dalle Vacche, *The Body in the Mirror: Shapes of History in Italian Cinema*, 3–17. In 1901 the illiteracy rate was 48 percent.
20. Grazia Deledda, *Ashes* (*Cenere*).
21. Giovanni Marchesi, "Cinema e Letteratura: Cinema Muto Italiano e Le Letterature Straniere, 1914–1931."
22. Peter Wollen, "Salome," *Paris/Manhattan: Writings on Art*, 110-111.
23. Janet Staiger, *Bad Women: Regulating Sexuality in Early American Cinema*.
24. Massimo Cardillo, *Tra Le Quinte del Cinematografo: Cinema, Cultura e Società in Italia, 1900–1937*. It is interesting to note that around 1916, during the planning of *Cenere* (1917), Eleonora Duse switched from *la film* to *il film* in her letters to Giovanni Papini. On this point, see Olga Signorelli, "L'Epistolario di *Cenere*," 20, 25; compare, for example, *la film* (20) with *mio film* (25).
25. Edmondo De Amicis, *Cinematografo Cerebrale* (1907).

Chapter 1

1. "Matter or mind, reality has appeared to us as a perpetual becoming. It makes itself or it unmakes itself, but *it is never something made*. Such is the intuition that we have of mind when we draw aside the veil which is interposed between our consciousness and ourselves." Henri Bergson, *Creative Evolution*, 272 (emphasis in the original).
2. "Of becoming we perceive only states, of duration only instants." Bergson, *Creative Evolution*, 273.
3. Ibid., 298–299.
4. Cesare Lombroso and Guglielmo Ferrero, *The Female Offender* (1893); see also Luigi Bulferetti, *Cesare Lombroso*. This is the best study I have ever read on Lombroso: besides establishing the Darwinian training of this scientist, Bulferetti goes into the legacy of Giambattista Vico's cyclical view of time for mid-nineteenth-century Italy and explains how his philosophy of history became a stifling system of repetition within circularity in Lombroso's work. Finally, Bulferetti explores Lombroso's Jewish origins, his mother's influence on his university career, and his lifelong career struggle against the Catholic Church.
5. Bergson, "The Cinematographical Mechanism of Thought and the Mechanistic Illusion," in *Creative Evolution*, 306.
6. Bergson, "The Vital Impetus," in *Creative Evolution*, 89–97; for the difference between élan vital and natural instinct, see 167–175. On the concept of élan vital, see Lorenzo Giusso, *Bergson*: "Now it is something like a projection of the unconscious, totally parallel to the natural instinct; now it becomes a mystical leap upward and a magic collapse downward, into the absolute at the very same time" (98).
7. On the crucial differences between Bergson's philosophy and Catholicism, see Kenneth Silver, *Esprit de Corps: The Art of the Parisian Avant-garde and the First World War, 1914–1925*, 216n55.
8. On the visual culture and scientific debates surrounding Bergson and Marey, and on the difference between cubism and futurism, see Marta Braun, *Picturing Time: The Work of Étienne-Jules Marey, 1830–1904*.
9. On Debussy's popularity in Italy, see Valerio Castronovo, Renzo De Felice, and Pietro Scoppola, "L'Età Liberale," 67.
10. Benedetto Croce, *Estetica come Scienza dell'Espressione e Linguistica Generale*, 102.
11. "Perception is never a mere contact of the mind with the object present; it is impregnated with memory-images which complete it as they interpret it." Bergson, *Matter and Memory*, 33.
12. On Nietzsche's eternal return, see Allan Megill, *Prophets of Extremity*, 83–84 and 96–97. On Vico's philosophy of temporality and its implications for Italian cinema, see Dalle Vacche, *Body in the Mirror*, 3–17. On Nietzsche in Italy, see Gaia Michelini, *Nietzsche nell'Italia di D'Annunzio*.
13. Martin Jay, "Sartre, Merleau-Ponty, and the Search for a New Ontology of Sight."
14. On Lombroso's atavism, see George Hersey, *The Evolution of Allure: Sexual Selection from the Medici Venus to the Incredible Hulk*, 121–123.
15. On the contact between Bergson and Croce, see Simona Cigliana, *Futurismo Esoterico*, 243–266. This book was very helpful to me.
16. On Bergson and Italy, see Franco Zambelloni, "Bergson e la Filosofia Italiana, 1900–1915."

The most important article for understanding Papini's role in mediating between Bergson and Italian culture is Luca Mazzei, "Quando il Cinema Incontrò la Filosofia: Il Caso di Giovanni Papini." Of course, see also Giovanni Papini, "La Filosofia del Cinematografo."

17. Luca Mazzei, "Quando il Cinema Incontrò la Filosofia: Il Caso di Giovanni Papini," 69.

18. In "Quando il Cinema Incontrò la Filosofia," Mazzei cites this appropriation of Nietzsche (85n31) without, however, mentioning the name of the German philosopher.

19. Walter Benjamin, "The Work of Art in the Age of Mechanical Reproduction," *Illuminations* 241–242.

20. Mazzei, "Quando il Cinema Incontrò la Filosofia," 85n12.

21. Ibid., 69.

22. Ibid., 81n67.

23. On Athanasius Kircher, see Laurent Mannoni, *The Great Art of Light and Shadow: Archeology of the Cinema*, 20–27.

24. Deleuze, *Cinema 2*.

25. André Bazin, "The Ontology of the Photographic Image," 15.

26. Ibid., 16.

27. On this point about Federico Fellini's *La Strada* (1954), see Gian Piero Brunetta, *Storia del Cinema Italiano dal 1945 agli Anni Ottanta*: "In Fellini's work . . . it is possible to recognize echoes from Bergson's philosophy or from the writings of Emmanuel Mounier and Alberguin, with some surrealist influences" (445). On the other hand, it is also useful to compare the following dialogue from *La Strada*, between the Angel and Gelsomina, with Mazzei's reference to Papini's citing of William Blake on "how to see a whole world inside a grain of sand" ("Quando il Cinema Incontrò la Filosofia," 74n33). In Brunetta, the dialogue between Fellini's two characters goes as follows: "You will not believe it, but everything which exists in this world, has some kind of purpose. . . . For example, take that little stone over there . . . even this little stone is useful for something . . . I am not sure for what, but I know that it is there for a reason. This is so because if the little stone was useless, then everything means nothing . . . even the stars" (*Storia del Cinema Italiano*, 451). In short, Brunetta seems to suggest a connection between Fellini and French Personalism via Bergson on the theme of the interrelatedness of all things, human and nonhuman. And according to Mazzei, this theme is not far from Papini's sense that the cinema is the world spiritualized.

28. Giovanni Papini, ed., *La Filosofia dell'Intuizione*.

29. Giovanni Papini, *Ventiquattro Cervelli*.

30. Mazzei, "Quando il Cinema Incontrò la Filosofia, 83."

31. Sebastiano Arturo Luciani, "L'Idealità del Cinematografo."

32. Bergson, "Plato and Aristotle," in *Creative Evolution*, 315–327.

33. Luciani, "L'Idealità del Cinematografo," 206.

34. In "The Ontology of the Photographic Image," Bazin begins to formulate his theory of *montage interdit*: "It is not for me to separate off, in the complex fabric of the objective world, here a reflection on a damp sidewalk, there the gesture of a child" (15).

35. Bazin states that all plastic arts, including photography and cinema, are characterized by a "mummy complex": "If the plastic arts were put under psychoanalysis, the practice of embalming the dead might turn out to be a fundamental factor in their creation" ("The Ontology of the Photographic Image," 9).

36. Georges Sorel, *Reflections on Violence*.

37. Luigi Pirandello, *Shoot! The Notebooks of Serafino Gubbio, Cinematograph Operator*.

Chapter 2

1. D'Annunzio's essay can be found in *Giovanni Pastrone: Gli Anni d'Oro del Cinema Italiano*, edited by Paolo Cherchi Usai, 113–122; for Gozzano's essay, see *Poesie e Prose*, edited by Alberto De Marchi, 1167–1175. On the cover of *Rivista Sapic* (1 April 1914), a monthly film trade journal with offices in Via del Tritone, Rome, I found another logo with a woman caught in a filmstrip's serpentine coils. In this case, however, the coils are carefully arranged to spell *SAPIC*. The woman's shoulders are bare, but she wears a skirt that covers one side of a rotating globe featuring either the outline of some island (Java, Indonesia?) or perhaps the black silhouettes of two Javanese puppets.

2. On Amalia Guglielminetti and her period in general, with special attention to magazine illustrators, see Rossana Bossaglia, A. Braggion, and M. Guglielminetti, *Dalla Donna Fatale alla Donna Emancipata: Iconografia Femminile nell'Età del Deco.*

3. Gozzano's three stories, "Pamela-Film," "Il Riflesso delle Cesoie," and "I Sandali della Diva," may be found in *Poesie e Prose,* edited by Alberto De Marchi.

4. Gozzano, "I Sandali della Diva," 549.

5. Freud's essay can be found in volume 18 of *The Standard Edition of the Complete Psychological Works of Sigmund Freud,* translated and edited by James Strachey.

6. D'Annunzio, "Del Cinema tografo Considerato come Strumento di Liberazione," 122.

7. On D'Annunzio, the cosmopolitan cultural scene, and aviation, see Peter Demetz, *The Air Show at Brescia, 1909.* This book is a little jewel of historical and cultural analysis.

8. D'Annunzio, "Del Cinema Considerato come Strumento di Liberazione," 122.

9. On Guido Gozzano and his unrealized project for a film about the life of Saint Francis, see Sinibaldo Piro, "La Film di Gozzano," and Piro, "Le Meravigliose Frodi [Fronde?] nel San Francesco Di Gozzano." See also Mariarosa Masoero, ed., *Guido Gozzano: San Francesco D'Assisi.*

10. On Walter Benjamin's "Origin of German Tragic Drama" (1916), see Angela Dalle Vacche, ed., *The Visual Turn: Classical Film Theory and Art History,* 4. And see also Walter Benjamin, *The Origin of German Tragic Drama.*

11. Croce, *Estetica:* "But if the symbol is looked upon as separable—if the symbol can be expressed on the one side, and the thing symbolized on the other—we fall back again into the intellectualist terror: the pretend symbol is the exposition of an abstract concept, it is an *allegory,* it is science, or art that apes science" (57; emphasis in the original).

12. In *Estetica,* Croce devotes a section of chapter four to his critique of the symbol and allegory: "Thus those pictures and compositions, each of which is an individual inexpressible by logic, are resolved into universals and abstractions" (58).

13. These observations are based on my experiences in the state school system between 1968 and 1974.

14. Benedetto Croce, "The Advance of Culture and Spiritual Unrest, 1901–1914," 248.

15. Ibid.

16. Ibid., 246.

17. Ibid., 242.

18. Ibid., 255.

19. Benedetto Croce, "Letter to Luigi Chiarini." Also see Giorgio Ghezzi, "Benedetto Croce e il Cinema come Arte."

20. Antonio Gramsci, *Selections from the Cultural Writings,* 334–335 and 376–378.

21. On Enrico Ferri, see Papini, *Ventiquattro Cervelli,* 237–262. On Ferri and the detective novel, see also Gramsci, *Cultural Writings,* 369–370.

22. On Gramsci and Ibsen, see Gramsci, *Cultural Writings,* 70–73.

23. On Gramsci's views about working-class women leaving the family, see Gramsci, *Cultural Writings,* 70–73.

24. For Casati, see Dario Cecchi, *Corè: Vita e Dannazione della Marchesa Casati.* This is the best biography of the socialite.

25. For Gramsci on the theater and the cinema, see Gramsci, *Cultural Writings,* 54–56.

26. On Lyda Borelli, see Antonio Gramsci, *Letteratura e Vita Nazionale,* 334–336.

27. On the progressive views of Cesare Lombroso's daughters, Gina and Paola, see Delfina Dolza, *Essere Figlie di Lombroso: Due Donna Intellettuali tra '800 e '900.* Progressive or reformist though they were, Lombroso's daughters repeated his work in several ways.

28. Gramsci, "Some Aspects of the Sexual Question—Americanism and Fordism," in *Selections from the Prison Notebooks,* 294–298.

29. Renate Holub, *Antonio Gramsci: Beyond Marxism and Postmodernism,* 196.

30. Holub, *Antonio Gramsci,* 198. Gramsci's awareness of Taylorism also helps us understand his conflicted views about futurism, an avant-garde movement inspired by Bergson's anti-Tayloristic philosophy of time. "Taylorism" refers to the approach to management and to industrial and organizational psychology initiated by Frederick Winslow Taylor in his 1911 monograph *The Principles of Scientific Management.*

31. Franca Angelini, "Dal Teatro Muto all'An-

titeatro: Le Teorie del Cinema all'Epoca del *Si Gira*," 78.

32. Pirandello, *Shoot!* 139.

33. P. Adams Sitney, "The Autobiography of a Metonymy," 223–233.

34. Bernardini and Martinelli, *Roberto Roberti*, 8.

35. Pirandello, *Shoot!* 40–41.

36. Ibid., 120.

37. On mechanical reproduction involving a separation between soul and hands, Pirandello describes a violinist who has to accompany an automatic pianoforte: "The soul which moves and guides the hand of the man, which now passes into the touch of the bow, now trembles in the fingers that press the strings, is obliged to follow the register of this automatic instrument" (*Shoot!* 20).

38. On Pirandello's relationship with Anton Giulio Bragaglia in regard to a filmic adaptation of *Shoot!* see Nina Da Vinci Nichols and Jana O'Keefe Bazzoni, *Pirandello and Film*, 10–11. See also Mario Verdone, "Anton Giulio Bragaglia," 11.

39. Pirandello, *Shoot!* 83.

40. Bazin, "The Ontology of the Photographic Image," 13.

41. Pirandello, *Shoot!* 84.

42. Tom Gunning, "Introduction: The Diva, the Tiger, and the Three-Legged Spider," in Pirandello, *Shoot!* xiii.

43. Regarding humor, the irrational, and the Freudian unconscious, the reader may want to keep in mind that Freud wrote *The Joke and Its Relation to the Unconscious* in 1905, five years after Bergson tackled the same topic and three years before Pirandello did. For biographical and photographic details about Pirandello's extremely difficult family life, see Luciani, *Luigi Pirandello: Una Biografia per Immagini*, especially 66–67. *L'Esclusa* (The Female Outsider) may be found in Pirandello, *Tutti i Romanzi*, 1–158.

44. See Luciani, *Luigi Pirandello*, 82.

45. *Suo Marito* (Her Husband) may be found in Pirandello, *Tutti i Romanzi*, 837–1043. On Grazia Deledda and women's issues, see Deledda, *After the Divorce* (1902).

46. Giovanni Lista, *Futurism and Photography*, 13–47.

47. Anton Giulio Bragaglia, "Le Questioni," in *Fotodinamismo Futurista*, 2–3. Although 1913 is the official founding year of photodynamism, Bragaglia started working on these issues as early as 1910.

48. Mary Ann Doane, *The Emergence of Cinematic Time*, 86–88.

49. Anton Giulio Bragaglia, *L'Evoluzione del Mimo*, 240–241. It would be interesting to compare this passage to Siegfried Kracauer's insights from 1927 on the cinema as a mass ornament.

50. On *scenoplastica*, see Anton Giulio Bragaglia, *L'Evoluzione del Mimo*, 288. Enrico Prampolini's definition of *scenoplastica* in the context of his collaborations with Bragaglia is cited in Castronovo, De Felice, and Scoppola, "L'Età Liberale," 68. Note that *Thaïs* (1917) can easily be confused with *Perfido Incanto* (1918), another film by Bragaglia. The credits of *Perfido Incanto* include Thaïs Galitzky again, but not Ileana Leonidoff. According to Aldo Bernardini and Vittorio Martinelli in their *Bianco e Nero* volume on 1918, the owner of Novissima Film during the shooting of *Perfido Incanto* was Gustavo Lombardo. Yet the precise economic history of Bragaglia's Novissima Film production house remains obscure to this day.

51. In 1917, Diana Karenne took over Novissima Film. See Mario Verdone, *Cinema e Letteratura del Futurismo*, 59.

52. Millicent Marcus, "Anton Giulio Bragaglia's *Thaïs*, or, the Death of the Diva, the Rise of Scenoplastica, and the Birth of Futurist Cinema," 76.

53. For *La Cinematografia Futurista* (1916; *Futurist Cinematography*), see Michael Kirby and Victoria Kirby, *Futurist Performance*, 120–142. On photodynamism and the cinema, see also Caroline Tisdall and Angelo Bozzolla, "Photodynamism and Futurist Cinema," in *Futurism*, 137–152.

54. On futurism and women, see Tisdall and Bozzolla, "Futurism and Women," in *Futurism*, 153–164.

55. On the 1913 manifesto "Immaginazione senza Fili e la Parole in Libertà" ("Imagination without Strings and Words in Freedom"), see Tisdall and Bozzolla, "Literature and Theatre," in *Futurism*, 89–110.

56. On the consequences of the controversial and delayed arrival of Freud's work in Italy, see Michael David, *La Psicanalisi nella Cultura Italiana*.

57. Ghislaine Wood, *Art Nouveau and the Erotic*, 24.

Chapter 3

1. See her "Rhetorical Veils: Textuality and the Femme Fatale." The reader should keep in mind that Loie Fuller created a dance about Salome.

2. Edward Said, *Orientalism.*

3. In *Creative Evolution,* Bergson defines the élan vital thus: "*Life does not proceed by the association and addition of elements, but by dissociation and division*" (89; emphasis in the original), adding later: "Life is, more than anything else, a tendency to act on inert matter" (96).

4. The argument that the Italian diva channeled petit-bourgeois feelings of anger toward the aristocracy after the mediocre results of the 1911–1912 campaign in Libya is the central thesis of Brunetta, "Il Divismo," 173–196.

5. In 1999, Ethiopian filmmaker Haile Gerima, who teaches at Howard University, made an excellent documentary about Adwa. The video version of *Adwa* is distributed by Mypheduh Films, Inc., Washington, D.C.

6. Adrian Lyttelton, "Italian Culture and Society in the Age of *Stile Floreale,*" 10–31.

7. Alberto Boschi, "La Donna Nuda," 233–242.

8. Ibid., 241.

9. Lyttelton, "Italian Culture and Society," 11.

10. A good source on the Ballets Russes is Lynn Garafola and Nancy Van Norman Baer, eds., *The Ballets Russes and Its World, 1909–1929.*

11. The futurists were also interested in the fourth dimension. See Linda Henderson, "Italian Futurism and the Fourth Dimension."

12. See Cecchi, *Corè.*

13. Tito Alacci, *Le Nostre Attrici Cinematografiche,* 155.

14. On the cinema and the Maria Tarnowska scandal, see Roberto Paolella, "La Decadenza del Divismo in Italia."

15. On the transformation of Maria Tarnowska into a sort of suffering, mystical creature, see Annie Vivanti, *Circe: Il Romanzo di Maria Tarnowska* (1912).

16. Lombroso and Ferrero, *La Donna Delinquente* (1893).

17. Sander Gilman, *Difference and Pathology: Stereotypes of Sexuality, Race, and Madness,* 95–99.

18. Piero Pesce-Maineri, *I Pericoli Sociali del Cinematografo,* 15.

19. Arnaldo Monti, "Il Fascino della Bellezza Muliebre nella Cinematografia," 39–40.

20. Gaetano Strazzulla, "Storia della Censura Cinematografica in Italia," 8–21.

21. Ibid, 8–9. See also *La Vita Cinematografica* (Turin), "Una Circolare dell'Onorevole Giolitti ai Prefetti per un'Attiva Sorveglianza sulle Rappresentazioni Cinematografiche," 28 February 1913; and Bortolo Belotti, *Politica del Costume.*

22. Enrico Ferri, *Studi sulla Criminalità ed Altri Saggi,* 9.

23. Valentine de Saint-Point, *La Femme dans la Littérature Italienne,* 21.

24. For anyone studying the import-export history of early Italian cinema, the best place for film trade journals is the National Public Library of Florence.

25. This fact was confirmed to me by Aldo Bernardini in conversation during the Udine International Film Conference, March 2004.

26. See Ricciotto Canudo, "Il Trionfo del Cinematografo"; this 1908 essay also reappears in the guise of an abstract in *La Rivista Fono-Cinematografica* (Turin) 3–4 (26 January 1909); the essay was also recycled in a new version called "La Naissance d'un Sixième Art—Essai sur le Cinématographe," in the magazine *Les Entretiens Idéalistes* (Paris), 25 October 1911. Canudo's most important and best-known book is *L'Usine aux Images* (1927; The Image Factory). On Canudo, see Giovanni Dotoli, ed., *Ricciotto Canudo, 1877–1977.*

27. Giovanni Dotoli, "Il Cinema, Arte Totale Nasce con Canudo," 295.

28. Ibid.

29. Ibid.

30. Germana Orlandi Cerenza, "L'Éros, la Déraison, il Doppio nei *Libérés* di Canudo," 335n32.

31. Dotoli, "Il Cinema," 294. One of Canudo's best friends in Paris was the Italian painter Ardengo Soffici, who used Bergson's "élan vital" as the title of his autobiography, which depicts him as a reckless young man. See Ardengo Soffici, *Il Salto Vitale: Autoritratto d'Artista Italiano nel Quadro del Suo Tempo* (1954).

32. For Cézanne's views on photography, see Edoardo Bruno, "L'Officina Immaginifica," 303–307.

33. Anna Paola Mossetto, "Ricciotto Canudo: La

Nascita di una Sesta Arte: Saggio sul Cinematografo," 369.

34. Ibid., 368. Canudo as quoted by Mossetto; emphasis added.

35. Bazin, "The Ontology of the Photographic Image," 12.

36. See the January–February 1914 issue (numbers 1–2) of the bimonthly *Montjoie*.

37. In my view, Valentine de Saint-Point is a minor figure, but her life alone is worth writing a novel about. She dabbled in many arts and in many circles, but her ideas were confused and derivative. For whoever may be so inclined, here are some helpful sources: M. Barry Katz, "The Women of Futurism"; Henri Le Bret, *Essai sur Valentine de Saint-Point;* Jacques Reboul, *Notes sur la Morale d'une Annonciatrice: Valentine de Saint-Point;* Abel Verdier, "Une Étrange Arrière-Petite-Nièce de Lamartine: Valentine de Saint-Point (1875–1953)"; and Valentine de Saint-Point, *Manifeste de la Femme Futuriste,* edited and annotated by Jean-Paul Morel.

38. For example, Canudo published two previous texts, *Les Artistes* (1904) and *La Plume* (1905), which then appeared together as *Les Métamorphoses* (1908).

39. See Tisdall and Bozzolla, "Futurism and Women," in *Futurism,* 153–164.

40. According to Jean-Paul Morel, the term *cérébriste* was developed, with positive connotations, during the 1880s in the writings of Paul Bourget, Rémy de Gourmont, and Octave Mirbeau; see Morel's edition of Saint-Point, *Manifeste de la Femme Futuriste,* 45. The term was also included in the *Dictionnaire Historique d'Argot* (1881) by Lorédan Larchey.

41. The masculine features of woman and the feminine features of man are discussed by Otto Weininger in *Sex and Character* (1903).

42. For *nevrosico,* see Paolo Mantegazza, *Il Secolo Nevrosico.*

43. Fausto Maria Martini, "L'Esule Delusa: Diana Karenne."

44. Diana Karenne uses the term *cerebrale* in Martini, "L'Esule Delusa," 63.

45. Canudo and Saint-Point were both familiar with René Guénon, *L'Ésotérisme de Dante* (1912).

46. On Saint-Point in Egypt, see Faouzia Zouari, "Valentine de Saint-Point: Un Itinéraire de l'Occident à l'Orient, 1875–1953."

Chapter 4

1. On the cinema, the airplane, and subjectivity, see Paul Virilio, *War and Cinema: The Logistics of Perception.* On the cinema and the train, see Lynne Kirby, *Parallel Tracks: The Railroad and Silent Cinema.* An excellent source on aviation and European culture is Robert Wohl, *A Passion for Wings: Aviation and the Western Imagination, 1908–1918.*

2. The Versailles Treaty (1919) prohibited Germany from developing an air force of its own. By contrast, Italy produced the first theoretician of the air, General Giulio Douhet. Born in Caserta in 1869, Douhet began to write about aviation issues in 1909. In his major book *Il Dominio dell'Aria* (1921), which was translated into several languages, he argued that the air force was so new a weapon that it was best to develop it independently of the army or the navy. This insight proved to be wrong during World War II, when coordination became the name of the game. In addition, Douhet maintained that the development of military aircraft marked the beginning of total war, in which combat would be taken beyond the battlefield and trenches and into the cities and factories. He was especially interested in the use of bombing campaigns to break down the morale of the civilian population. Unfortunately, Douhet's second theory was well received by Hermann Goering (1893–1946), who organized Nazi Germany's Luftwaffe, and by the American Curtis E. LeMay (1906–1990), who oversaw the bombing of Hiroshima. Douhet's name also remains attached to the tragedies of Guernica and Dresden, and, most of all, to Hitler's Battle of Britain.

3. Pirandello, *Shoot!* 71.

4. Ibid.

5. Filippo Tommaso Marinetti, *Mafarka le Futuriste: Romain Africain* (1909). This is not the only work in which Marinetti turns to the airplane; in fact, the explosion of the fad happened in the 1930s with futurist aerial painting and aerial poetry. Other relevant works by Marinetti are *The Monoplane of the Pope* (1911); *The Bombing of Adrianapolis* (1912), written during the Libyan campaign; and *L'Aereopoema del Golfo di La Spezia* (1937). *Canto Uo-*

mini e Macchine della Guerra Mussoliniana (1940), written before Marinetti left for the Russian front, is dedicated to two famous aviators, Italo Balbo and Bruno Mussolini. Finally, shortly before he died, Marinetti wrote one more piece: *L'Aereopoema di Cozzarini, Primo Eroe dell'Esercito Repubblicano.* On the place of the airplane in futurist iconography, see Enrico Crispolti, *Il Mito della Macchina ed Altri Temi del Futurismo* (1969); and Enrico Falqui, *Bibliografia ed Iconografia del Futurismo* (1988).

6. D'Annunzio published *Forse Che Sí, Forse Che No* in 1910; the whole novel is about aviation and an erotic quadrangle. Valuable information about D'Annunzio, the cinema, and the airplane can be found in Wohl, *Passion for Wings,* 114–122; Tommaso Antongini, *D'Annunzio,* 129–145, 471–473; and Cardillo, *Tra Le Quinte del Cinematografo,* 122–123.

7. Cecchi, *Corè,* 84–86.

8. On Marinetti, metaphors, and women, see Cinzia Sartini Blum, *The Other Modernism: F. T. Marinetti's Futurist Fiction of Power.*

9. Edith Hamilton, *Mythology: Timeless Tales of Gods and Heroes,* 139–140.

10. Nino G. Caime, "Personalità Femminili della Scena Italiana: Lyda Borelli," 19.

11. Michela De Giorgio, *Le Italiane dall'Unità ad Oggi: Modelli Culturali e Comportamenti Sociali,* 253–259.

12. Ibid., 209–253.

13. Fausto Montesanti, "La Parabola della Diva," 7–8.

14. De Giorgio, *Le Italiane,* 220–222. On fashion and flying, see Karla Jay, "No Bumps, No Excrescences: Amelia Earhart's Failed Flight into Fashions," in *On Fashion,* ed. Shari Benstock and Suzanne Ferris, 76–94.

15. De Giorgio, *Le Italiane,* 221.

16. Claudia Salaris, *Aero . . . : Futurismo e Mito del Volo,* 90.

17. This contact between Karenne and D'Annunzio is documented in the archives of Il Vittoriale. On D'Annunzio's androgynous women and ventriloquist dandies, the best source is Barbara Spackman, *Decadent Genealogies: The Rhetoric of Sickness from Baudelaire to D'Annunzio.*

18. [Diana Karenne], "Lega Aerea Nazionale," Archivio Generale LXV, 4, Il Vittoriale degli Italiani, Gardone Riviera, Italy.

19. Frances A. Yates, *Astraea: The Imperial Theme in the Sixteenth Century.*

20. On Baracca, see Marcello Berti, *Francesco Baracca: Una Vita per il Volo.* Readers with a special interest in Astrea and all her colleagues, should see Alberto Farassino and Tatti Sanguineti, "Amazzoni dell'Aria e Danzatrici della Prateria," in *Gli Uomini Forti;* on *Justitia* (1919), Astrea's most important film, see the *Bioscope* (London), 4 January 1920; on "La Farfalletta," see Paolo Cherchi Usai and Livo Jacob, eds., *I Comici del Muto Italiano,* 42–43.

21. On the popularization of a strong female type, see the very humorous novelette by Edmondo De Amicis, *Amore e Ginnastica* (1892). In contrast to the stereotype of the femme fragile, Astrea and her sisters are comparable to Maciste, the heroic athlete who stars in Pastrone's *Cabiria* (1914).

22. For the term *gynandry,* see Cynthia Secors, "Androgyny: An Early Reappraisal." On androgyny and flying, see Naomi Ritter, "Art and Androgyny: The Aerialist." On the grotesque, see Russo, *Female Grotesque,* 17–51; and Kayser, *Grotesque in Art and Literature.*

23. Kayser, *Grotesque in Art and Literature,* 33, 39.

24. Russo, in *Female Grotesque,* is right in associating the grotesque with risk and stunt rather than utopia and performance, or metamorphosis and freedom. The equivalent of this connection between risk and modernity, but through the "stunt" of gambling reduced to a throw of the dice, is discussed by Mary Ann Doane, "The Erotic Barter: Pandora's Box," in *Femmes Fatales: Feminism, Film Theory, Psychoanalysis,* 142–162.

25. On New York City and Fortunato Depero, see Serena Aldi, "Depero e Il Cinema."

26. The connection between procreation and eugenic theory is especially strong in the work of Paolo Mantegazza (1831–1910); see his *The Sexual Relations of Mankind.*

27. De Giorgio, *Le Italiane,* 259. In an endnote (343n15), De Giorgio cites Ester Danesi-Traversari, "A Volo, su Roma," *La Donna* 17 (5 February 1921). On a miniature world seen from an aerial point of view, see also Susan Stewart, *On Longing: Narratives of the Miniature, the Gigantic, the Souvenir, the Collection.*

28. On dreams and flying, with case studies involving male as well as female patients, see Sigmund Freud, *The Basic Writings of Sigmund Freud*, ed. A. A. Brill, 356–357.

29. Sibilla Aleramo, "Il Mio Primo Viaggio Aereo" (1925), 45–53.

30. On mysticism, see Annarita Buttafuoco, "Vite Esemplari: Donne del Primo Novecento": "The mystical coefficient of some models proposed by women at the beginning of the century is well-known: it is not a coincidence that figures such as Ersilia Maino or Alessandra Ravizza, whether they liked it or not, were commonly defined as 'lay saints.' It was not just a formula for paying homage to their extraordinary commitment to ill and poor people, but it also made apparent the perception of a sort of religious halo stemming from their personalities. In writing to Ersilia Maino and comparing her to the Madonna of Seven Pains, Maria Montessori adds: 'It is certainly true that your figure is shrouded in religiosity and inspires a religious feeling as well.' On the other hand, Alessandra Ravizza was called Madonna of the Poor" (153).

31. On women mystics, see Caroline Walker Bynum, *Holy Feast, Holy Fast: The Religious Significance of Food to Medieval Women;* Cristina Maria Mazzoni, "Virgin Births and Hysterical Pregnancies: Neurosis and Mysticism in French and Italian Literature at the Turn of the Century;" Angela Dalle Vacche, "Still Life and Feminine Space," in *Cinema and Painting: How Art is Used in Film*, 221–245; and Nick Mansfield, *Masochism: The Art of Power.*

32. For an excellent discussion of gender and modernity based on well-circumscribed case studies and on cultural theory, mostly relevant to England and France, see Rita Felski, *The Gender of Modernity*.

33. Horst Bredekamp, "The Question of Movement: Sculpture and Machine," 1–9.

34. Giovanni Lista, *Loie Fuller, Danseuse de la Belle Époque*. In Claude Chabrol's film *Rien ne va plus* (*The Swindle*) (1997), a dance performance with sticks and veils is extremely reminiscent of Loie Fuller's method: the body of the dancer completely disappears into waves of movement.

Chapter 5

1. Lombroso and Ferrero, *Criminal Woman*, trans. Rafter and Gibson, 7.

2. According to the Migrant Information Programme, "Trafficking in Women for Sexual Exploitation to Italy," IOM (International Organization for Migration), June 1996: "The Merlin Law of 1958 decriminalized prostitution [in Italy] if it is practiced privately, forbids prostitution in brothels, and criminalizes those who exploit prostitutes or lead women into prostitution, including foreign women. Such crimes are punishable even if committed in a foreign country" (cited at http://www.uri.edu/artsci/wms/hughes/italy.htm).

3. On acting schools and their ambiguous reputation, see "Scuola per Film," *Cine-Gazzetta* 1, no. 18 (3 May 1917), n.p.

4. Gibson, *Prostitution in Italy*, 147.

5. Ibid., 126.

6. The film's plot could easily have been drawn from one of the examples in Gibson, *Prostitution in Italy*, 162–164.

7. Carl Ipsen, "The Annunziata Scandal of 1897 and Foundling Care in Turn-of-the-Century Italy." Cristina Jandelli demonstrated that Francesca Bertini was born out of wedlock and that her real name was Elena Taddei (*Le Dive Italiane del Cinema Muto*, 31–33). According to Jandelli, this problem of origins haunted Bertini throughout her life.

8. Reinhold Heller, *The Earthly Chimera and the Femme Fatale: Fear of Woman in Nineteenth-Century Art*, 19.

9. Salvatore Ottolenghi, *The Sensitivity of Women*, cited in Gibson, *Prostitution in Italy*, 138.

10. Gloria Chianese, *Storia Sociale della Donna in Italia, 1800–1900*, p. 113.

11. Marcus Verhagen, "The Poster in Fin-de-Siècle Paris: 'That Mobile and Degenerate Art'," 115.

12. Ockman and Silver, *Sarah Bernhardt*, 29n9.

13. Bragaglia, *L'Evoluzione del Mimo*, 240. In an article on Anton Giulio Bragaglia, Mario Verdone cites William James's awareness that movement is comparable to vertigo: "At the beginning, movement gives us a sensation of confusion whose primitive form can best be understood in the light of vertigo as a phenomenon" ("Anton Giulio Bragaglia," 124).

14. Cesare Molinari, *L'Attrice Divina: Eleonora Duse nel Teatro Italiano fra i Due Secoli,* 237–261.

15. Ibid., 165–205.

16. William Weaver, "Duse and the Art of Silence," 44–51.

17. Duse to Papini, as cited in Olga Signorelli, "L'Epistolario di *Cenere.*" Papini was impressed with *Cenere* (27). Signorelli also recounts Duse's first visit to the cinema: she saw Francesca Bertini in *Odette* by Sardou (19).

18. Iole Ribolzi, *Storia Aneddotica del Cinema Italiano,* 7. On Duse's hostility to the close-up, see also Mario Gromo, *Cinema Italiano:* "The close-up frightens me. I would rather retreat into solitude. [If there is no other way around it], I prefer the shadow or a quick profile" (40).

19. On the invasive use of the close-up, see Annie Vivanti, "La Cinematografia Applicata alla Scienza Chirurgica," 9–10.

20. Kristen Ina Grimes, "Visual Structure and Class Delineation in Duse's *Cenere,*" 63–72.

21. Ibid., 67.

22. Jose Pantieri, ed. *Lyda Borelli,* 33.

23. Jolanda Hawkins, "Eleonora Duse, Our Contemporary," 47.

24. Alfredo Panzini, cited in Antonio Baldini, "Vent'Anni Dopo *Ma l'Amor Mio non Muore,*" 7–8.

25. Robert de la Sizeranne (1866–1932), cited in Montesanti, "La Parabola della Diva," 61n4.

26. D'Annunzio, *Forse Che Sí,* cited in Montesanti, "La Parabola della Diva," 64n3.

27. Salvador Dali, cited in Montesanti, "La Parabola della Diva," 65–66n3.

28. Virgilio Tosi's reference to the screen as a "vertical white sheet" comes from the press of the period (*La Vita Cinematografica* [Turin], 18 February 1908, n.p.) in response to Doctor Camillo Negro's *Neuropatologia* (1908), on which Roberto Omegna also worked. On Nielsen's vertical acting in contrast to the Italian diva's pictorial style, see Ben Brewster and Lea Jacobs, *Theatre to Cinema: Stage Pictorialism and the Early Feature Film,* 116–119.

29. Fortunato Depero's letter to F. T. Marinetti on May 27, 1930, from 116 West 49th Street reads: "Dear Marinetti, Words in Freedom. I have the profound sensation of having finally broken through the crust of the earth, which was closing on me and setting up an obstacle against my great destiny. Horses made of Light/Joy rumble inside my heart. Guaranteed Futurist Triumph. The psychological vertigo is daily rhythm. Yours Depero. Ultra-ultra-ultra winning dynamo" (manuscript 1919, Fondo Depero, MART, Rovereto, Italy).

30. Papini, "La Filosofia del Cinematografo," cited in Maria Adriana Prolo, *Storia del Cinema Muto Italiano,* 27–29.

31. On Nielsen, see also Janet Bergstrom, "Asta Nielsen's Early German Films;" Corinna Muller, "Genèse de la Structure du Star System en Allemagne;" Robert C. Allen, "Asta Nielsen: The Silent Muse." On *The Abyss* as an example of so-called "primitive cinema," see Burch, *Life to Those Shadows,* 186.

32. Engberg, *Asta Nielsen: Europe's First Film Star,* 4.

33. See Caspar Tyberg, *An Art of Silence and Light: The Development of Danish Film Drama to 1920.*

34. In a famous section in *Der Sichtbare Mensch* (1924; The Visible Man), Béla Balázs writes about Asta Nielsen's acting to explain his notion of polyphonic mimicry. In English, see Béla Balázs, "Asta at the Mirror." See also Balázs, "Asta Nielsen's Eroticism"; this wonderful piece originally appeared in *Der Tag* (26 April 1923).

35. It might be interesting to pursue more research on possible comparisons between Balázs's notion of the natural language of gestures and the concept of inner speech put forward by Russian formalist Boris M. Eixenbaum. This concept was first addressed in Eixenbaum's 1927 essay "Problemy kino-stilistiki," translated into English as "Problems of Cinema Stylistics."

36. On autosuggestion and acting as trance, see Engberg, *Asta Nielsen,* 12; and Tyberg, *Art of Silence and Light,* 126.

37. Heide Schlüpmann, "Asta Nielsen: A Girl with No Fatherland," 197.

38. *Chicago Record,* 12 February 1925.

39. On the exceptional use in *The Abyss* of shots comparable to actual close-ups, see Tyberg, *Art of Silence and Light,* 100–101.

40. Mary Ann Doane, "Film and Masquerade: Theorizing the Female Spectator," 74–75.

41. *New York Telegraph,* 7 October 1917.

42. On different theories of the close-up, see Angela Dalle Vacche, "Alain Cavalier's *Thérèse:* Still Life and the Close-Up as Feminine Space," in *Cinema and Painting,* 221–245. One revealing comment

about Duse's rejection of the close-up and her passive view of the maternal role is cited in Signorelli, "L'Epistolario di *Cenere*": "I would remain in the shadow, the way a mother should next to her son" (24).

43. Ribolzi, *Storia Aneddotica*, 7.

44. On Francesca Bertini and her admiration for Nielsen, see Angela Dalle Vacche, "Francesca Bertini: La Donna è Mobile," 186. Vanina's story is from Stendhal's *Chroniques Italiennes;* Roberto Rossellini also used it as a source for his film *Vanina Vanini* (1961).

45. Ribolzi, *Storia Aneddotica*, 7.

46. See, for example, a review in *Film* (21 June 1914). On Benjamin Christensen's *The Mysterious X*, see Brewster and Jacobs, *Theatre to Cinema*, 197–200.

47. Quoted in Aldo Bernardini and Vittorio Martinelli, "*La Terra Promessa*," in *Il Cinema Muto Italiano: I Film degli Anni d'Oro*, 285.

48. Vittorio Martinelli, "Nino Oxilia," in Redi, *Cinema Italiano Muto, 1905–1916*, 71–86.

49. Colette (Sidonie-Gabrielle Colette), "Lettres à Marguerite Moreno" (August 1928), cited in Laura Mariani, *Sarah Bernhardt, Colette e L'Arte del Travestimento*, 212n130.

50. Pantieri, *Lyda Borelli*, 46.

51. Lyda Borelli, "Preface," in Mario Carli, *Retroscena: Romanzo*, 7–8.

52. Salvatore Di Giacomo's activities as a journalist explain why he coauthored *Mala Vita: Scene Popolari Napoletane* with Goffredo Cognetti.

53. Andrea Bisicchia, ed., *Assunta Spina/Salvatore Di Giacomo* (Milan: Mursia, 1986), 21. Benedetto Croce, Giuseppe Ceci, Mariano D'Ayala, and Salvatore Di Giacomo, *La Rivoluzione Napoletana del 1799;* see also Di Giacomo, *La Prostituzione in Napoli nei Secoli 15,16, e 17*.

54. Frank M. Snowden, *Naples in the Time of Cholera, 1884–1911*.

55. Matilde Serao, *Il Ventre di Napoli* (1906), 99–101.

56. On the laundry trade and the spread of cholera in Naples in 1884, see Snowden, *Naples in the Time of Cholera*, 97; on the failure of rebuilding and the *questione meridionale* (southern question), see 360–367.

57. Franco Schlitzer, *Salvatore Di Giacomo: Ricerche e Note Bibliographiche*, 603.

58. Aria: "A term normally signifying any closed lyrical piece for solo voice (exceptionally for more than one voice) with or without instrumental accompaniment, either independent or forming part of an opera, oratorio, cantata or other large work" (*New Grove Dictionary of Music and Musicians*, 2nd ed., [New York: Oxford Univ. Press, 2001], s.v. "aria," 1:887).

Chapter 6

1. Lucia Re, "Futurism and Feminism," 257.

2. Antonio Gramsci, *Cultural Writings*, 216.

3. Giuseppe Lelio Arrighi, *La Storia del Femminismo*.

4. Maria Rosa Cutrufelli et al., *Il Novecento delle Italiane: Una Storia da Raccontare*.

5. Angela Bianchini, *Voce Donna: Momenti Strutturali dell'Emancipazione Feminile*, 276.

6. Whereas Italian women voted for the first time in 1947, in England and in Germany women began to vote in 1918, and in the United States in 1919.

7. Matilde Serao, "The Cigarette: Can Women Smoke?" in *Saper Vivere: Norme di Buona Creanza*, 221–223.

8. All these issues come up one by one in Sibilla Aleramo, *Una Donna*.

9. Luigi Dal Pane, as cited in Gibson, *Prostitution in Italy*, 63.

10. Gibson, *Prostitution in Italy*, 99.

11. Gloria Chianese, "Il Movimento Suffragista tra Interventismo e Neutralismo," in *Storia Sociale della Donna in Italia, 1800–1900*, 47–68.

12. Gibson, *Prostitution in Italy*, 112.

13. Chianese, "Il Movimento Suffragista," 51.

14. Gibson, *Prostitution in Italy*, 110.

15. Chianese, "Il Movimento Suffragista," 51.

16. On the difference between the short film (which flourished from 1907 to 1910) and long film (1910–1913), see Aldo Bernardini, "Francesca Bertini," in *Le Dive*, 3–38.

17. Pierre Sorlin, "The Coming War," in *European Cinemas, European Societies, 1939–1990*, 23–51.

18. Monica Dall'Asta, "Pearl White e le Altre Eroine del Serial: L'Avvento della Donna d'Azione nel Cinema Muto," in *Cantami O Diva: I Percorsi del Femminile nell'Immaginario di Fine Secolo*, ed. Silvana Sinisi, 207–219. See also Dall'Asta, "Donne Avventurose del Cinema Torinese," in *Cabiria e il Suo*

Tempo, ed. Paolo Bertetto and Giovanni Rondolino, 354–364.

19. I have checked all the relevant bound volumes of *La Vita Cinematografica* at the Cineteca Italiana (Milan).

20. My conclusions about the reception of American stars in Italy, reached after consulting *La Vita Cinematografica* at the Cineteca Italiana (Milan), match those of Riccardo Redi. See Riccardo Redi, *Cinema Muto Italiano, 1896–1930*, 74–83.

21. Ricciotto Canudo, *L'Officina delle Immagini*, 151.

22. De Amicis, *Amore e Ginnastica* (1892) was inspired by the De Santis Law, concerning physical education in the school system.

23. This piece of information comes from Rosita Levi Pisetzky, *Il Costume e la Moda nella Società Italiana*, 347.

24. Ibid., 353–360.

25. Angelo Mosso, cited in De Giorgio, *Le Italiane*, 242–243.

26. Bernardini, "Francesca Bertini," 7–10.

27. Prolo, *Cinema Muto Italiano*, 57.

28. Lista, *Futurism and Photography*, 14.

29. Ibid.

30. Alfredo Maria Cavagna, *Il Cinema: Ieri, Oggi, Domani*, 85.

31. Vanna Piccini, *Le Elegantissime*, 221–222.

32. Roberto Paolella, cited in Vittorio Martinelli, *Il Cinema Muto Italiano, 1918*, 141.

33. Donna Paola (Baronchelli-Grosson), ed., *La Donna della Nuova Italia: Documenti del Contributo Femminile alla Guerra (Maggio 1915–Maggio 1917)*.

34. Ottorino Modugno, *Le Donne Mute*, 107.

35. Ibid., 66–68.

36. Giulio Cesare Castello, *Il Divismo: Mitologia del Cinema*, 35.

37. Paola Lombroso, *Caratteri della Femminilità*, viii.

38. Piccini, *Le Elegantissime*, 222.

Chapter 7

1. On spectacle and narrative flow in melodrama, see Christine Gledhill, *Home Is Where the Heart Is: Studies in Melodrama and the Woman's Film*.

2. On weak genres in Italian film history, see Dalle Vacche, *Body in the Mirror*, 3–17.

3. Spackman, *Decadent Genealogies*, 69–71.

4. In *Decadent Genealogies*, Spackman writes: "Memory plays a major role in both the scene of convalescence and in hysteria. For Freud and Breuer diagnosed hysteria as an illness deriving from memory . . . The cure, then, consists in forcing—through hypnosis . . . —the patient to remember. But while the patient's task is to remember and tell all, the doctor's task is to induce forgetfulness, to induce the traits of convalescence" (118).

5. The Freudian primal scene—a scenario in which a child is traumatized by seeing the parents making love—was originally diagnosed through a case study of a patient known as the Wolf-Man (*der Wolfsmann*), who was actually Sergei Konstantinovitch Pankejeff (1886–1979), a Russian aristocrat from Odessa. Freud's title for this case study, written in 1914 and published in 1918, was "From the History of an Infantile Neurosis." On women and the primal scene, see Elisabeth Young-Bruehl, ed., *Freud on Women: A Reader*, 160–162, 307–308.

6. The reference here is to Jacques Offenbach's opera *Les Contes d'Hoffmann* (1881; *The Tales of Hoffmann*) and to Olympia, the mechanical doll with whom Hoffmann falls in love. Offenbach's libretto was based on three short stories by E. T. A. Hoffmann, a German writer and composer of the Romantic era. Coppelius, Olympia's inventor, sells Hoffmann magic glasses that make Olympia appear as a real woman. On automatons, see Lois Rostow Kuznets, *When Toys Come Alive: Narratives of Animation, Metamorphosis, and Development*.

7. On Gramsci's theory that Italy in 1860 failed to have a revolution comparable to the 1789 French Revolution, see Dalle Vacche, *Body in the Mirror*, 131n8. See also Gramsci, *Cultural Writings*, 216.

8. On tattooing, see Angela Dalle Vacche, "Kenji Mizoguchi's Five Women and Utamaro: Film between Woodblock Printing and Tattooing," in *Cinema and Painting*, 197–220.

9. Yuri Tsivian, "Russia, 1913: Cinema in the Cultural Landscape."

10. The title of Freud's case study is "A Case of Paranoia Running Counter to the Psychoanalytic Theory of the Disease" (1915); see Mary Ann Doane, *The Desire to Desire: The Woman's Film of the 1940s*, 131–133.

11. On the mother-daughter bond, see Young-Bruehl, *Freud on Women*, 160–162, 307–308.

12. On Adolf Loos, his Anglophile orientation, and European impact, see Janet Stewart, *Fashioning Vienna: Adolf Loos' Cultural Criticism*. In *Ornament and Crime* (1908), Loos attacked the decorative values of Viennese art nouveau and advocated a severe and linear modernist style that adhered to the principle of form following function. Loos's dislike of ornament was based on his belief that backward societies used decorations (tattoos, feathers, beads), whereas advanced cultures did not waste their time on these superfluous and colorful elements.

Chapter 8

1. Rossana Bossaglia, *Gli Orientalisti Italiani: Cent'Anni di Esotismo, 1830–1940*.

2. All my information on Nino Oxilia comes from Vittorio Martinelli, "Nino Oxilia," 71–86. For an overview of women and intellectual life in Turin, see Donatella Alesi, "La Donna, 1904–1915: Un Progetto Giornalistico Femminile di Primo Novecento."

3. Luigi Bulferetti, *Le Ideologie Socialistiche in Italia nell'Età del Positivismo Evoluzionistico, 1870–1892*.

4. Paolo Zappa, *La Legione Straniera: Tavole e Disegni di Pier Antonio Gariazzo*.

5. Vittorio Martinelli, *Il Dolce Sorriso di Maria Jacobini*.

6. No early-cinema specialist, as far as I know, has dealt with Mariano Fortuny's lighting machines. I have visited the Museo Fortuny in Venice several times, and it appears that there is a warehouse full of stage contraptions worth investigating. Those interested may contact Dr. Silvio Fuso, Centro di Documentazione Palazzo Fortuny, at Silvio.Fuso@comune.Venezia.it. For an overview of Fortuny's work, see Anne-Marie Deschodt and Doretta Davanzo Poli, *Fortuny*.

7. Camille Flammarion, *Lumen*, xlviii. Flammarion was a friend of Henri Bergson and Loie Fuller.

8. "Psicocinematografia," *L'Illustrazione Cinematografica* 1, no. 1 (15 January 1912): 51.

9. Giovanni Papini, "La Filosofia del Cinematografo," reprinted in Prolo, *Cinema Muto Italiano*, 27–29.

10. Ibid., 28–29.

11. On the history of this idea, see Naomi Greene, *Pier Paolo Pasolini: Cinema as Heresy*: "The important role Pasolini conferred upon montage in individual films led him, in fact, to what may have been his most personal and striking analogy. Evoking Sartre's belief that only at the moment of death can we judge the significance of a life, as well as Cocteau's epithet that cinema captures 'death at work,' he drew a kind of metaphysical contrast between, on the one hand, the infinite long take (or plenitude of the real) inherent in cinema and, on the other, the limitations (culminating in death) imposed by montage on individual films" (100).

12. Ermanno Comuzio, "*Rapsodia Satanica* (1915) e la Musica di Mascagni." See also Stefano Vaccarino, "Un Metodo d'Analisi del Rapporto Musica-Immagine per *Rapsodia Satanica* di Mascagni-Oxilia," in *A Nuova Luce*, ed. Michele Canosa, 267–86.

13. On this interpretation of Rubinstein's image on stage, see Joe Lucchesi, "An Apparition in a Black Flowing Cloak: Romaine Brooks's Portraits of Ida Rubinstein," in Whitney Chadwick, *Amazons in the Drawing Room: The Art of Romaine Brooks*, 73 and 86n5.

14. On the association of Andre Bazin's mummy complex with Theda Bara, see Mary Ann Doane, "Aesthetics and Politics," 1229–1235.

15. Adrian Lyttelton, "Italian Culture and Society," 21.

16. Mario Praz, *La Filosofia dell'Arredamento*, 182. The title of this book comes from Edgar Allan Poe's essay "The Philosophy of Furniture" (1840).

17. Emilia Nevers, *Vita Moderna: Studi Sociali*, 35–36.

18. Pier-Antonio Gariazzo, *Il Teatro Muto*, 100.

19. Peter Delpeut, *Diva Dolorosa: reis naar het einde van een eeuw*, 24.

20. José Pantieri, ed., *Lyda Borelli*, 60.

21. Carli, *Retroscena*, 7–8. *Retroscena: Romanzo* was reprinted as *Marvana: Mistero d'Amore*.

22. Umberto Boccioni, "Diari: Primo Taccuino, January 6–September 12 (1907)," in *Gli Scritti Editi ed Inediti*, 239.

23. The most exhaustive account of Boccioni's complicated relationship with his model Ines can be found in Gino Agnese, "Solo con Ines," *Vita di Boccioni*, 47–54.

24. Although there is no direct reference to

Borelli in Boccioni's text, the editor has placed the name *Borelli* as note 1 under the date of the diary entry.

25. Nino Oxilia, as quoted in Redi, *Cinema Italiano Muto,* 83.

26. For my juxtaposition of futurism with cubism, I was influenced by Braun, *Picturing Time.*

27. Giovanni Lista, *Loie Fuller: Danseuse de la Belle Époque,* 154.

28. Giovanni Papini, "Bergson," in *Ventiquattro Cervelli,* 317. In this same collection, Papini dedicates essays to the Lombrosian Enrico Ferri and to the philosopher Giambattista Vico.

29. Flavio Fergonzi, "On the Title of the Painting *Materia,*" in *Boccioni/Materia: A Futurist Masterpiece and the Avant-Garde in Milan and Paris,* ed. Laura Mattioli Rossi, 51.

30. Tom Gunning, "Loie Fuller and the Art of Movement: Body, Light, Electricity and the Origins of Cinema," in *Camera Obscura, Camera Lucida: Essays in Honor of Annette Michelson,* ed. by Richard Allen and Malcolm Turvey, 86–87.

31. Gariazzo, *Il Teatro Muto,* 331.

Bibliography

Agnese, Gino. *Vita di Boccioni.* Florence: Camunia, 1996.

Alacci (Alacevich), Tito. *Le Nostre Attrici Cinematografiche.* Florence: Bemporad, 1919.

Aldi, Serena. "Depero e Il Cinema." Thesis, University of Udine, 2000.

Aleramo, Sibilla. *La Donna e Il Femminismo: Scritti, 1897–1910.* Rome: Editori Riuniti, 1978.

———. *Una Donna.* Turin and Rome: STEN, 1906.

———. "Il Mio Primo Viaggio Aereo." In *Gioie d'Occasione* (1930), 45–53. Milan: Mondadori, 1954.

Alesi, Donatella. "La Donna, 1904–1915: Un Progetto Giornalistico Femminile di Primo Novecento." *Italia Contemporanea* 222 (March 2001): 43–63.

Allen, Richard, and Malcolm Turvey, eds. *Camera Obscura, Camera Lucida: Essays in Honor of Annette Michelson.* Amsterdam: Amsterdam Univ. Press, 2003.

Allen, Robert C. "Asta Nielsen: The Silent Muse." *Sight and Sound* 42, no. 4 (Fall 1973): 205–209.

Angelini, Franca. "Dal Teatro Muto all'Antiteatro: Le Teorie del Cinema all'Epoca del *Si Gira.*" In Lauretta, *Pirandello e il Cinema,* 65–84.

Antliff, Mark. *Inventing Bergson: Cultural Politics and the Parisian Avant-Garde.* Princeton, N.J.: Princeton Univ. Press, 1993.

Antognini, Tommaso. *D'Annunzio* (1938). Freeport, N.Y.: Books for Libraries Press, 1971.

Aristarco, Guido. "Il Leopardo, l'Orso e la Tigre." In Genovese and Gesù, *La Musa Inquietante di Pirandello,* 105–107.

Arrighi, Giuseppe Lelio. *La Storia del Femminismo.* Florence: Razzolini, 1911.

Bade, Patrick. *Femme Fatale: Images of Evil and Fascinating Women.* New York: Mayflower Books, 1979.

Baer, Nancy Van Norman, comp. *The Art of Enchantment: Diaghilev's Ballets Russes, 1909–1929.* San Francisco: Fine Arts Museum of San Francisco; New York: Universe Books. Distributed by St. Martin's, 1988.

Balázs, Béla. "Asta at the Mirror." In *Film Theory and Criticism: Introductory Readings,* 4th ed., edited by Gerald Mast et al., 265–267. New York: Oxford Univ. Press, 1992.

———. "Asta Nielsen's Eroticism." In *Hungarofilm Bulletin* 1, no. 14–15 (1984). Originally published in *Der Tag,* 26 April 1923.

Baldini, Antonio. "Vent'anni Dopo: *Ma l'Amor Mio non Muore.*" *Scenario* 2, no. 1 (January 1933): 7–8.

Baronchelli-Grosson, Paola, ed. *La Donna della Nuova Italia: Documenti del Contributo Femminile alla Guerra (Maggio 1915–Maggio 1917).* Milan: R. Quintieri, 1917.

Baudot, Francois. *Poiret: Memorie della Moda.* Florence: Franco Cantini, 1998.

Bazin, André. "The Ontology of the Photographic Image." In *What Is Cinema?* 1:9–16. Essays selected and translated by Hugh Gray. Berkeley and Los Angeles: Univ. of California Press, 1967.

Belotti, Bortolo. *Politica del Costume.* Milan: Unitas, 1924.

Benjamin, Walter. *Illuminations* (1936). Translated by Harry Zohn. Edited and with an introduction by Hannah Arendt. New York: Schocken, 1986.

———. *The Origin of German Tragic Drama* (1928). Translated by John Osborne. London and New York: Verso, 2003.

Benstock, Shari, and Suzanne Ferris, eds. *On Fashion*. New Brunswick, N.J.: Rutgers Univ. Press, 1994.

Bentivoglio, Mirella, and Franca Zoccoli. *Women Artists of Italian Futurism*. New York: Midmarch Arts Press, 1997.

Bergson, Henri. *Creative Evolution*. Translated by Arthur Mitchell. Mineola, N.Y.: Dover, 1998. Originally published as *L'Évolution créatrice* (Paris: Alcan, 1907).

———. *Laughter: An Essay on the Meaning of the Comic*. Translated by Cloudesley Shovell, Henry Brereton, and Fred Rothwell. New York: Macmillan, 1911. Originally published as *Le Rire: Essai sur la signification du comique* (Paris: Alcan, 1900).

———. *Matter and Memory*. Translated by Nancy Margaret Paul and W. Scott Palmer. London: George Allen and Unwin, 1911. Originally published as *Matière et mémoire* (Paris: Alcan, 1896).

———. *Time and Free Will*. Translated by F. L. Pogson. New York: Macmillan, 1910. Originally published as *Essai sur les données immédiates de la conscience* (Paris: Alcan, 1889).

Bergstrom, Janet. 1990. "Asta Nielsen's Early German Films." In *Prima di Caligari: Cinema Tedesco, 1895–1920*, edited by Paolo Cherchi Usai and Lorenzo Codelli, 162–185. Pordenone, Italy: Biblioteca dell'Immagine, 1990.

Bernardini, Aldo. *Cinema Muto Italiano*. Vol. I: *Ambiente, Spettacoli e Spettatori, 1896–1904*. Vol. II: *Industria e Organizzazione dello Spettacolo, 1905–1909*. Vol. III: *Arte, Divismo e Mercato, 1910–1914*. Rome and Bari: Laterza, 1980–1982.

———. "Francesca Bertini." In *Le Dive*, 3–38. Bari: Laterza, 1985.

Bernardini, Aldo, and Vittorio Martinelli. *Il Cinema Muto Italiano: I Film degli Anni d'Oro; 1913, Prima Parte*. Turin: Nuova ERI, 1994.

———. *Roberto Roberti: Direttore Artistico*. Pordenone: Le Giornate del Cinema Muto, 1985.

Bertellini, Giorgio. "Mute Visuality: Notes around D'Annunzio and the Expressive Bodies of Italian 'Hysterical Cinema.'" Paper presented at the annual conference of the Society of Cinema Studies, Ottawa, Canada, 1997.

Bertetto, Paolo, and Gianni Rondolino, eds. *Cabiria e il Suo Tempo*. Turin: Museo Nazionale del Cinema; Milan: Il Castoro, 1998.

Berti, Marcello. *Francesco Baracca: Una Vita per il Volo*. Lugo di Romagna: Walberti, 1991.

Bianchini, Angela. *Voce Donna: Momenti Strutturali dell'Emancipazione Femminile*. Milan: Bompiani, 1979.

Biondi, M. *Tavoli e Medium: Storia dello Spiritismo in Italia*. Rome: Gremese, 1988.

Bisicchia, Andrea, ed. *Assunta Spina/Salvatore Di Giacomo*. Milan: Marisa, 1986.

Blom, Ivo. "*Il Fuoco* or the Fatal Portrait: The XIX Century in the Silent Cinema." *Iris* 14–15 (Autumn 1992): 55–66.

———. "Das Gestische Repertoire: Zur Korpersprache von Lyda Borelli." *Kintop* 7 (1998): 69–83.

———. *Jean Desmet and the Early Dutch Film Trade*. Translated by James Lynn. Amsterdam: Amsterdam Univ. Press, 2003.

Blom, Ivo, and Nelly Voorhuis, eds. *Il Primo Cinema Italiano, 1905–1945*. Amsterdam: Mechano, 1988.

Blum, Cinzia Sartini. *The Other Modernism: F. T. Marinetti's Futurist Fiction of Power*. Berkeley and Los Angeles: Univ. of California Press, 1996.

Boccioni, Umberto. *Gli Scritti Editi e Inediti*. Milan: Feltrinelli, 1971.

Bois, Yves Alain, and Rosalind Krauss. *Formless: A User's Guide*. New York: Zone Books, 1997.

Boschi, Alberto. "La Donna Nuda." In Canosa, *A Nuova Luce*, 233–242.

Bossaglia, Rossana. *Gli Orientalisti Italiani: Cent'Anni di Esotismo, 1830–1940*. Venice: Marsilio, 1998.

Bossaglia, Rossana, Anna Braggion, and Marziano Guglielminetti. *Dalla Donna Fatale alla Donna Emancipata: Iconografia Femminile nell'Età del Deco*. Nuoro: Ilisso, 1993.

Bozzolla, Angelo, and Carolyn Tisdall. *Futurism*. London: Thames and Hudson, 1977.

Bragaglia, Anton Giulio. "L'Arcoscenico del Mio Cinematografo." *Penombra* 2, no. 1 (January 1919): 21–24.
———. "Un Duello con Ida Rubinstein." In *La Maschera Mobile*, 272–280. Foligno: Franco Campitelli, 1916.
———. *L'Evoluzione del Mimo*. Milan: Ceschina, 1930.
———. *Fotodinamica Futurista* (1912). Turin: Einaudi, 1980.
Braun, Martha. *Picturing Time: The Work of Étienne-Jules Marey, 1830–1904*. Chicago: Univ. of Chicago Press, 1992.
Bredekamp, Horst. "The Question of Movement: Sculpture and Machine." In *The Lure of Antiquity and the Cult of the Machine: The Kunstkammer and the Evolution of Nature, Art, and Technology*, 1–9. Translated by Allison Brown. Princeton, N.J.: Markus Wiener, 1995.
Brewster, Ben, and Lea Jacobs. *Theatre to Cinema: Stage Pictorialism and the Early Feature Film*. Oxford: Oxford Univ. Press, 1997.
Brunetta, Gian Piero. "Il Divismo." In *Storia del Cinema Italiano, 1895–1945*, 173–196. Rome: Riuniti, 1979.
———. *Storia del Cinema Italiano dal 1945 agli Anni Ottanta*. Rome: Riuniti, 1982.
Bruno, Edoardo. "L'Officina Immaginifica." *Filmcritica* 22, no. 5 (November 1977): 303–307.
Bruno, Giuliana. *Streetwalking on a Ruined Map: Cultural Theory and the City Films of Elvira Notari*. Princeton, N.J.: Princeton Univ. Press, 1993.
Bulferetti, Luigi. *Cesare Lombroso*. Turin: Unione Tipografico–Editrice Torinese, 1975.
———. *Le Ideologie Socialistiche in Italia nell'Età del Positivismo Evoluzionistico, 1870–1892*. Florence: Le Monnier, 1951.
Burch, Noel. *Life to Those Shadows*. Translated and edited by Ben Brewster. Berkeley and Los Angeles: Univ. of California Press, 1990.
Buttafuoco, Annarita. "Vite Esemplari: Donne del primo Novecento." In *Svelamento: Sibilla Aleramo, Una Biografia Intellettuale*, edited by Annarita Buttafuoco and Marian Zancan. Milan: Feltrinelli, 1988.
Bynum, Caroline Walker. *Holy Feast, Holy Fast: The Religious Significance of Food to Medieval Women*. Berkeley and Los Angeles: Univ. of California Press, 1987.

Caime, Nino G. "Personalità Femminili della Scena Italiana: Lyda Borelli." *La Donna* (Turin), 5 February 1911.
Callari, Francesco. *Pirandello e il Cinema*. Venice: Marsilio, 1991.
Camerini, Claudio. "Histoire d'un Pierrot." *Immagine* 7 (1984): 23–26.
———. "Recitazione Muta: Italia Almirante Manzini e il Codice della Diva." *Immagine* 1 (1981): 13–14.
Camerini, Claudio, and Riccardo Redi. *Tra Una Film e l'Altra: Materiali sul Cinema Muto Italiano, 1907–1920*. Venice: Marsilio, 1980.
Canosa, Michele, ed. *A Nuova Luce: Cinema Muto Italiano*. Bologna: CLUEB, 2000.
———. "Il Crepuscolo dei Divi (Muti ed Italiani)." *Cinegrafie* 4 (1991): 119–126.
Canudo, Ricciotto, ed. *Montjoie*, nos. 1–2 (January–February 1914). Special issue on dance, Ida Rubenstein, and Valentine de Saint-Point.
———. *L'Officina delle Immagini*. Edited by Mario Verdone. Rome: Edizioni di Bianco e Nero, 1966. Originally published as *L'Usine aux Images* (Geneva: Office central d'édition, 1927).
———. "Il Trionfo del Cinematografo." *Nuovo Giornale* (Florence), 25 November 1908. Reprinted in *Filmcritica*, no. 278 (1977): 295–302.
Caramella, Santino. *Bergson*. Milan: Athena, 1925.
Cardillo, Massimo. *Tra le Quinte del Cinematografo: Cinema, Cultura, e Società in Italia, 1900–1937*. Bari: Edizioni Dedalo, 1987.
Carli, Mario. *Marvana: Mistero d'Amore*. Milan: Alpes, 1927.
———. *Retroscena: Romanzo*. Preface by Lyda Borelli. Milan: Lombardo, 1915.
Carr, Windon. "Time and History in Contemporary Philosophy; with Special Reference to Bergson and Croce." *Proceedings of the British Academy* 8 (1918): 1–19.

Castello, Giulio Cesare. *Il Divismo: Mitologia del Cinema.* Roma: Eri, 1957.

Castronovo, Valerio, Renzo De Felice, and Pietro Scoppola. "L'Età Liberale." In *L'Italia del Novecento,* 1–76. Turin: UTET Libreria, 2004.

Catella, Elsa. "L'Attività Artistica di Lyda Borelli nella Storia del Teatro dal 1894 al 1917 e nell'Immediato Dopoguerra." Thesis, University of Padua, 1970–1971.

Cavagna, Alfredo Maria. *Il Cinema: Ieri, Oggi, Domani.* Turin: Marietti, 1945.

Cecchi, Dario. *Corè: Vita e Dannazione della Marchesa Casati.* Bologna: L'Inchiostroblu, 1986.

Cerenza, Germana Orlandi. "L'Éros, La Déraison, Il Doppio nei *Libérés* di Canudo." In Dotoli, *Ricciotto Canudo,* 325–338.

Chadwick, Whitney. *Amazons in the Drawing Room: The Art of Romaine Brooks.* Chesterfield, Mass.: Chameleon Books, and Berkeley and Los Angeles: Univ. of California Press, in association with the National Museum of Women in the Arts, 2000.

Cherchi Usai, Paolo, ed. *Giovanni Pastrone: Gli Anni d'Oro Del Cinema Italiano.* Turin: UTET, 1986.

Cherchi Usai, Paolo, and Livio Jacob, eds. *I Comici del Muto Italiano.* Pordenone: Cineteca del Friuli, 1985.

Chianese, Gloria. *Storia Sociale della Donna in Italia, 1800–1900.* Naples: Guida, 1980.

Chiattone, Antonio. "La Diva Muette." *La Revue du Cinéma* 13 (18 May 1948): 67–71.

Chiavarelli, Lucio, ed. *La Belle Epoque.* Rome: Gherardo Casini, 1966.

Cigliana, Simona. *Futurismo Esoterico: Contributi per una Storia dell'Irrazionalismo Italiano fra Ottocento e Novecento.* Rome: Edizioni La Fenice, 1996.

Cine-Gazzetta. "Scuola per Film." 3 May 1917.

Clement, Catherine. *Opera, or the Undoing of Women.* Translated by Betsy Wing. Minneapolis: Univ. of Minnesota Press, 1988.

Colette, (Sidonie-Gabrielle). *Lettres à Marguerite Moreno.* Edited and annotated by Claude Pichois. Paris: Flammarion, 1959.

Colombo, Giorgio. *La Scienza Infelice: Il Museo di Antropologia Criminale.* Turin: Boringhieri, 1975.

Comencini, Luigi. *La Valigia dei Sogni: Restauro di un Ricordo.* Edited by Matteo Pavesi. Milan: Il Castoro, 1997.

Comuzio, Ermanno. "*Rapsodia Satanica* (1915) e la Musica di Mascagni." *Cineforum* 27, no. 261 (January–February 1987): 7–12.

Connelly, Frances. *Modern Art and the Grotesque.* Cambridge: Cambridge Univ. Press, 2003.

Costa, Mario. *Histoire d'Un Pierrot: Riproduzione Cinematografica della Pantomima Musicale Eseguita dalla Celio Film di Roma; Riduzione Letteraria di Tommaso Sillani; Disegni di Aleardo Terzi sul Libretto di F. Beissier.* Roma: Pacca, 1914.

Costantini, Costanzo. *La Diva Imperiale: Ritratto di Francesca Bertini.* Milan: Bompiani, 1982.

Crispolti, Enrico. *Il Mito della Macchina ed Altri Temi del Futurismo.* Trapani: Celebes, 1969.

Croce, Benedetto. "The Advance of Culture and Spiritual Unrest, 1901–1914." In *History of Italy, 1871–1915,* 237–255. Translated by Cecilia M. Ady. Oxford: Clarendon Press, 1929.

———. "Il Concetto di Barocco." In *Conversazioni Critiche,* 150–153. Bari: Laterza, 1932.

———. *Estetica: Come Scienza dell'Espressione e Linguistica Generale; Teoria e storia* (1902). Edited by Giuseppe Galasso. Milan: Adelphi, 1990.

———. "Letter to Luigi Chiarini." *Bianco e Nero* (December 1948): 3–4.

———. *Storia dell'Età Barocca in Italia.* Bari: Laterza, 1953.

———. *Studi Storici sulla Rivoluzione Napoletana del 1799.* 2nd. edition. Rome: Loescher, 1897.

Croce, Benedetto, Giuseppe Ceci, Mariano D'Ayala, and Salvatore Di Giacomo. *La Rivoluzione Napoletana del 1799.* Naples: Morano, 1899.

Cutrufelli, Maria Rosa, et al. *Il Novecento delle Italiane: Una Storia ancora da Raccontare.* Rome: Riuniti, 2001.

Dagrada, Elena. *International Bibliography on Early Cinema.* Quebec: Domitor, 1995.

Dall'Asta, Monica. "Donne Avventurose del Cinema Torinese." In *Cabiria e il Suo Tempo,* edited by Paolo Bertetto and Giovanni Rondolino, 354–364. Turin: Museo Nazionale del Cinema; Milan: Il Castoro, 1998.

———. "Pearl White e l'Altre Eroine del Serial: L'Avvento della Donna d'Azione nel Cinema Muto." In *Cantami O Diva: I Percorsi del Femminile nell'Immaginario di Fine Secolo,* edited by Silvana Sinisi, 207–219. Cava de'Tirreni: Avagliano, 1999.

Dalle Vacche, Angela. "Asta Nielsen: Motion, Emotion, and the Close-Up." *Framework* 43, no. 1 (Spring 2002): 76–94.

———. *The Body in the Mirror: Shapes of History in Italian Cinema.* Princeton, N.J.: Princeton Univ. Press, 1992.

———. *Cinema and Painting: How Art Is Used in Film.* Austin, Tex.: Univ. of Texas Press, 1996.

———. "Femininity in Flight: Androgyny and Gynandry in Early Silent Cinema." In *A Feminist Reader in Early Cinema,* edited by Jennifer Bean and Diane Negra, 444–475. Durham, N.C.: Duke Univ. Press, 2002.

———. "Francesca Bertini: La Donna è Mobile." *Cinegrafie* 12 (1999): 52–65.

———. "Love Everlasting: The Legacy of the Italian Diva." In Farinelli and Passek, *Stars au Féminin,* 89–106.

———. "Nino Oxilia's *Satanic Rhapsody* (1915–1917) with Lyda Borelli." *CINémas: Revue des Études Cinématographiques* 16, no. 1 (August 2005): 93–117.

———, ed. *The Visual Turn: Classical Film Theory and Art History.* New Brunswick, N.J.: Rutgers Univ. Press, 2003.

Dalle Vacche, Angela, and Gian Luca Farinelli, eds. *Silent Divas of Italian Cinema: Passion and Defiance.* Milan: Edizioni Olivares, 2000.

Dalrymple Henderson, Linda. "Italian Futurism and the 'Fourth Dimension.'" *Art Journal* 41, no. 4 (Winter 1981): 317–323.

Damerini, Gino. *D'Annunzio e Venezia* (1943). Venice: Albrizzi-Marsilio, 1992.

D'Annunzio, Gabriele. *Forse Che Sí, Forse Che No* (1910). Milan: Mondadori, 1982.

———. "Del Cinematografo Considerato come Strumento di Liberazione e come Arte di Trasfigurazione" (1914). In *Giovanni Pastrone: Gli Anni d'Oro del Cinema Italiano,* edited by Paolo Cherchi Usai, 113–122. Turin: UTET, 1986.

David, Michael. *La Psicanalisi nella Cultura Italiana.* Turin: Boringhieri, 1970.

De Amicis, Edmondo. *Amore e Ginnastica* (1892). Turin: Einaudi, 1971.

———. *Cinematografo Cerebrale* (1907). Edited by Biagio Prezioso. Rome: Salerno Editrice, 1995. Originally published in *L'Illustrazione Italiana* 34, no. 1 (December 1907): 532–533.

De Giorgio, Michela. *Le Italiane dall'Unità ad Oggi: Modelli Culturali e Comportamenti Sociali.* Bari: Laterza, 1992.

Deledda, Grazia. *After the Divorce.* Translated from the Italian by Susan Ashe. Evanston, Ill.: Northwestern Univ. Press, 1995. Originally published as *Dopo il divorzio* (Turin: Roux e Viarengo, 1902).

———. *Ashes.* Translated by Jan Kozma. Madison, N.J.: Fairleigh Dickinson Univ. Press, 2004. Originally published as *Cenere* (Milan: Fratelli Treves, 1910).

Deleuze, Gilles. *Cinema 2: The Time-Image.* Translated by Hugh Tomlinson and Robert Galeta. Minneapolis: Univ. of Minnesota Press, 1989.

Delpeut, Peter. *Diva Dolorosa: Reis naar het einde van een eeuw.* Amsterdam: Muelenhoff, 1999.

———, dir. *Lyrical Nitrate (Lyrisch Nitraat).* 35mm, 50 min. Netherlands, 1991. New York: Zeitgeist Films.

Demetz, Peter. *The Air Show at Brescia, 1909.* New York: Farrar, Straus, and Giroux, 2002.

Depero, Fortunato. Letter to Marinetti, dated May 1930, from 116 West 49th St., New York, New York. Fondo Depero, Manuscript 1919. Rovereto: MART.

Deschodt, Anne-Marie, and Doretta Davanzo Poli. *Fortuny.* New York: Abrams, 2001.

Di Giacomo, Salvatore. *La Prostituzione in Napoli nei Secoli 15, 16, e 17.* (1899). Naples: Edizioni del Delfino, 1968.

Di Giacomo, Salvatore, and Goffredo Cognetti. *Mala Vita: Scene Popolari Napoletane.* Naples: Bideri, 1889.

Dijkstra, Bram. *Evil Sisters: The Threat of Female Sexuality and the Cult of Manhood.* New York: Knopf, 1996.

———. *Idols of Perversity: Fantasies of Feminine Evil in Fin-de-Siècle Culture.* New York: Oxford Univ. Press, 1986.

D'Incerti, Vico. "*Assunta Spina* (1914): Vecchio Cinema Italiano." *Ferrania* 6 (June 1952): 1–16.

———. "Le Dive: Vecchio Cinema Italiano." *Ferrania* 5, no. 10 (October 1951): 17–34.

Doane, Mary Ann. "Aesthetics and Politics." *Signs* 30, no. 1 (Autumn 2004): 1229–1235.

———. *The Desire to Desire: The Woman's Film of the 1940s.* Bloomington: Indiana Univ. Press, 1987.

———. *The Emergence of Cinematic Time: Modernity, Contingency, the Archive.* Cambridge, Mass.: Harvard Univ. Press, 2002.

———. *Femmes Fatales: Feminism, Film Theory, and Psychoanalysis.* New York: Routledge, 1991.

———. "Film and Masquerade: Theorizing the Female Spectator." *Screen* 23, no. 3–4 (September–October 1982).

Dolza, Delfina. *Essere Figlie di Lombroso: Due Donne Intellettuali tra '800 e '900.* Milan: Angeli, 1990.

Dotoli, Giovanni. "Cerebrismo Canudiano ed Estetica Totale." In Dotoli, *Ricciotto Canudo,* 97–112.

———. "Il Cinema, Arte Totale Nasce con Canudo." *Filmcritica* 22, no. 5 (November 1977): 295–302.

———. *Nascita della Modernità: Baudelaire, Apollinaire, Canudo, il Viaggio dell'Arte.* Fasano: Schena, 1995.

———. ed. *Ricciotto Canudo, 1877–1977.* Proceedings of the Congresso Internazionale nel Centenario della Nascita, Bari–Gioia del Colle, 24–27 November 1977. Fasano: Grafischena, 1978.

Douhet, Giulio. *Il Dominio dell'Aria: Saggio sull'Arte Guerra Aerea.* Rome: Stabilimento poligrafico per l'amministrazione della guerra, 1921. Published in English as *The Command of the Air,* translated by Dino Ferrari (New York: Coward-McCann, 1942).

Dyer, Richard. *Heavenly Bodies: Film Stars and Society.* London and New York: BFI-Macmillan, 1986.

Eixenbaum, Boris M. "Problems of Cinema Stylistics" (1927). In *Russian Formalist Film Theory,* edited by Herbert Eagle, 55–80. Slavic Materials 19. Ann Arbor: Univ. of Michigan Press, 1981.

Engberg, Marguerite. *Asta Nielsen: Europe's First Film Star.* Berkeley: University Art Museum and Pacific Film Archive, 1996.

Falqui, Enrico. *Bibliografia ed Iconografia del Futurismo* (1959). Florence: Le Lettere, 1988.

Farassino, Alberto, and Tatti Sanguineti. *Gli Uomini Forti.* Milan: Mazzotta, 1983.

Farinelli, Gian Luca, and Jean-Loup Passek. *Stars au Féminin: Naissance, Apogée, et Décadence du Star System.* Paris: Centre Pompidou; Bologna: Cineteca del Comune di Bologna, 2000.

Felski, Rita. *The Gender of Modernity.* Cambridge, Mass.: Harvard Univ. Press, 1995.

Fergonzi, Flavio. "On the Title of the Painting *Materia.*" In *Boccioni/Materia: A Futurist Masterpiece and the Avant-Garde in Milan and Paris,* edited by Laura Mattioli Rossi, 47–52. New York: Solomon R. Guggenheim Foundation, 2004.

Ferri, Enrico. *Studi sulla Criminalità ed Altri Saggi.* Turin: Bocca, 1901.

Flammarion, Camille. *Lumen.* Rome: Voghera, 1907.

Focillon, Henri. *The Life of Forms in Art.* Translated by Charles Beecher Hogan and George Kubler. New Haven, Conn.: Yale Univ. Press; London: H. Milford, Oxford Univ. Press, 1942.

Fogazzaro, Antonio. *Malombra* (1881). Florence: Vallechhi, 1971.

Freud, Sigmund. *The Basic Writings of Sigmund Freud* (1938). Translated and edited by A. A. Brill. New York: Modern Library, 1995.

———. "Dreams and Delusions in Jensen's *Gradiva.*" (1907). In *The Standard Edition of the Complete Psycho-*

logical Works of Sigmund Freud, vol. 18. Translated and edited by James Strachey. London: Hogarth Press, 1959.

Garafola, Lynn, and Nancy Van Norman Baer, eds. *The Ballets Russes and Its World.* New Haven, Conn.: Yale Univ. Press, 1999.

Gariazzo, Pier Antonio. *Il Teatro Muto.* Turin: Lattes, 1919.

Genovese, Nino, and Sebastiano Gesù, eds. *La Musa Inquietante di Pirandello: Il Cinema.* Palermo: Bonanno, 1990.

Gerima, Haile, dir./prod. *Adwa: An African Victory.* Video, 97 min. Washington, D.C.: Mypheduh Films, 1999.

Ghezzi, Giorgio. "Benedetto Croce e il Cinema come Arte." *Il Mulino: Rivista Mensile di Attualità e Cultura* 21–22 (July–August 1953): 371–377.

Gibson, Mary. *Prostitution and the State in Italy, 1860–1915.* 2nd ed. Columbus: Ohio State Univ. Press, 1999.

Gili, Jean. "Thaïs." *Immagine* 2 (1986): 1–7.

Gilman, Sander. *Difference and Pathology: Stereotypes of Sexuality, Race, and Madness.* Ithaca, N.Y.: Cornell Univ. Press, 1985.

Giusso, Lorenzo. *Bergson.* Milan: Bocca, 1948.

———. *Il Ritorno di Faust: Henri Bergson.* Naples: Tirrenia, 1929.

Gledhill, Christine. *Home is Where the Heart Is: Studies in Melodrama and the Woman's Film.* London: British Film Institute, 1987.

Gori, Gino. *Il Grottesco nell'Arte e nella Letteratura: Comico, Tragico, Lirico.* Rome: Stock, 1926.

Gozzano, Guido. "Il Nastro di Celluloide e i Serpi di Laocoonte." *La Donna* (5 May 1916). Reprinted in *Poesie e Prose,* edited by Alberto De Marchi, 1167–1175. Milan: Garzanti, 1966.

———. "Pamela-Film." In *Poesie e Prose,* edited by Alberto De Marchi, 736–743. Milan: Garzanti, 1966.

———. "Il Riflesso delle Cesoie." In *Poesie e Prose,* edited by Alberto De Marchi, 690–697. Milan: Garzanti, 1966.

———. "I Sandali della Diva." In *Poesie e Prose,* edited by Alberto De Marchi, 546–558. Milan: Garzanti, 1966.

Gramsci, Antonio. *Letteratura e Vita Nazionale.* Roma: Riuniti, 1971.

———. *Selections from the Cultural Writings.* Edited by David Forgacs and Geoffrey Nowell-Smith. Translated by David Boelhower. Cambridge, Mass.: Harvard Univ. Press, 1985.

———. *Selections from the Prison Notebooks* (1926–1934). Edited and translated by Quintin Hoare and Geoffrey Nowell-Smith. New York: International Publishers, 1972.

Greene, Naomi. *Pier Paolo Pasolini: Cinema as Heresy.* Princeton, N.J.: Princeton Univ. Press, 1990.

Grimes, Kristen Ina. "Visual Structure and Class Delineation in Duse's *Cenere.*" *La Fusta* 11 (Fall 1997–Spring 1998): 63–73.

Gromo, Mario. *Cinema Italiano, 1903–1953.* Milan: Mondadori, 1954.

Guénon, René. *L'Ésotérisme de Dante* (1912). Paris: Gallimard, 1974.

Guglielmi, Guido. *La Prosa Italiana del Novecento: Umorismo, Metafisica, Grottesco.* Turin: Einaudi, 1986.

Guglielminetti, Marziano. "Dal Futurismo al Grottesco." In *La Contestazione del Reale,* edited by Enrico Cavacchioli. Naples: Liguori, 1974.

Gunning, Tom. "The Diva, the Tiger, and the Three-legged Spider." In Pirandello, *Shoot!* vii-xiv.

———. "Loie Fuller and the Art of Movement: Body, Light, Electricity and the Origins of Cinema." In Allen and Turvey, *Camera Obscura, Camera Lucida.*

Hamilton, Edith. *Mythology: Timeless Tales of Gods and Heroes* (1942). New York: Penguin, 1989.

Hawkins, Jolanda. "Eleonora Duse, Our Contemporary." Master's thesis, Hunter College, City University of New York, 2000.

Heller, Reinhold, ed. *The Earthly Chimera and the Femme Fatale: Fear of Woman in Nineteenth-Century Art.* Published in conjunction with an exhibition organized for the David and Alfred Smart Gallery, University of Chicago. Chicago: David and Alfred Smart Gallery, 1981.

Hersey, George L. *The Evolution of Allure: Sexual Selection from the Medici Venus to the Incredible Hulk.* Cambridge, Mass.: MIT Press, 1996.

Holub, Renate. *Antonio Gramsci: Beyond Marxism and Postmodernism.* London and New York: Routledge, 1992.

L'Illustrazione Cinematografica. "Psicocinematografia." 15 January 1912, 51.

Ipsen, Carl. "The Annunziata Scandal of 1897 and Foundling Care in Turn-of-the-Century Italy." *Journal of Modern Italian Studies* 4, no. 1 (1999): 1–29.

Jandelli, Cristina. *Le Dive Italiane del Cinema Muto.* Palermo: L'Epos, 2006.

Jay, Karla. "No Bumps, No Excrescences: Amelia Earhart's Failed Flight into Fashions." In Benstock and Ferris, *On Fashion,* 76–94.

Jay, Martin. "Sartre, Merleau-Ponty, and the Search for a New Ontology of Sight." In *Downcast Eyes: The Denigration of Vision in Twentieth-Century French Thought,* 263–328. Berkeley and Los Angeles: Univ. of California Press, 1993.

Jewell, Keala. *Monsters in the Italian Literary Imagination.* Detroit: Wayne State Univ. Press, 2001.

Katz, M. Barry. "The Women of Futurism." *Women's Art Journal* 7, no. 2 (Fall 1986–Winter 1987): 3–13.

Kayser, Wolfgang. *The Grotesque in Art and Literature* (1963). Translated by Ulrich Weisstein. New York: Columbia Univ. Press, 1981.

Kirby, Lynne. *Parallel Tracks: The Railroad and Silent Cinema.* Durham, N.C.: Duke Univ. Press, 1997.

Kirby, Michael, and Victoria Kirby. *Futurist Performance.* New York: Paj Publications, 1986.

Koestenbaum, Wayne. *The Queen's Throat: Opera, Homosexuality and the Mystery of Desire.* New York: Vintage, 1993.

Kuryluk, Ewa. *Salome and Judas in the Cave of Sex: The Grotesque; Origins, Iconography, Techniques in Art and Literature.* Evanston, Ill.: Northwestern Univ. Press, 1987.

Kuznets, Lois Rostow. *When Toys Come Alive: Narratives of Animation, Metamorphosis, and Development.* New Haven, Conn.: Yale Univ. Press, 1994.

Lant, Antonia, with Ingrid Periz, eds. *Red Velvet Seat: Women's Writing on the First Fifty Years of the Cinema.* London: Verso, 2006.

Larchey, Lorédan. *Dictionnaire Historique d'Argot.* 9th ed. Paris: Editions Dentu, 1881.

Lauretta, Enzo, ed. *Pirandello e il Cinema.* Agrigento: Centro Nazionale Studi Pirandelliani, 1978.

Le Bret, Henri. *Essai sur Valentine de Saint-Point.* Nice: Aux Éditions de "l'Aloès," 1923.

Leonardi, Susan J., and Rebecca A. Pope. *The Diva's Mouth: Body, Voice, Prima Donna Politics.* New Brunswick, N.J.: Rutgers Univ. Press, 1996.

Lessing, Gotthold Ephraim. *Laocoön: An Essay upon the Limits of Painting and Poetry* (1766). Translated by Ellen Frothingham. Mineola, N.Y.: Dover, 2005.

Liehm, Mira. *Passion and Defiance: Film in Italy from 1942 to the Present.* Berkeley and Los Angeles: Univ. of California Press, 1984.

Lista, Giovanni. *Loie Fuller: Danseuse de la Belle Époque.* Paris: Stock/Éditions d'Art Somogy, 1994.

———. *Futurism and Photography.* London: Merrell, 2001.

Lombroso, Cesare. *L'Uomo di Genio in Rapporto alla Psichiatria, alla Storia ed all'Estetica.* 6th edition. Turin: Fratelli Bocca, 1894; Rome: Napoleone, 1971 (17th edition).

Lombroso, Cesare, and Guglielmo Ferrero. *Criminal Woman, the Prostitute, and the Normal Woman.* Translated and with a new introduction by Nicole Hahn Rafter and Mary Gibson. Durham: Duke Univ. Press, 2004. Originally published as *La Donna Delinquente, La Prostituta, e La Donna Normale* (Turin and Rome: Roux, 1893). Originally published in English as *The Female Offender* (London: Unwin, 1893).

Lombroso, Paola. *Caratteri della Femminilità*. Turin: Bocca, 1909.

Loos, Adolf. *Ornament and Crime* (1908). Selected and with an introduction by Adolf Opel. Translated by Michael Mitchell. Riverside, Calif.: Ariadne Press, 1998.

Lucchesi, Joe. "An Apparition in a Black Flowing Cloak: Romaine Brooks's Portraits of Ida Rubinstein." In Chadwick, *Amazons in the Drawing Room*, 73–87.

Luciani, Luigi. *Luigi Pirandello: Una Biografia per Immagini*. Cavallermaggiore: Gribaudo, 2001.

Luciani, Sebastiano Arturo. *Il Cinema e le Arti*. Taranto: Barbieri, 2001.

———. "L'Idealità del Cinematografo." *Penombra* 2, no. 1 (January 1919). Reprinted in Camerini and Redi, *Tra una Film e l'Altra*, 206–209.

Lyttelton, Adrian. "Italian Culture and Society in the Age of *Stile Floreale*." *Journal of Decorative and Propaganda Arts* 13 (Summer 1989): 10–31.

Mannoni, Laurent. *The Great Art of Light and Shadow: Archaeology of the Cinema*. Translated and edited by Richard Crangle. Exeter, UK: Univ. of Exeter Press, 2000.

Mansfield, Nick. *Masochism: The Art of Power*. Westport, Conn.: Praeger, 1997.

Mantegazza, Paolo. *Il Secolo Nevrosico*. Florence: Berbera, 1887.

———. *The Sexual Relations of Mankind*. New York: Eugenics Publishing Co., 1925.

Marchesi, Giovanni. "Cinema e Letteratura: Cinema Muto Italiano e le Letterature Straniere, 1914–1931." *Immagine* 29 (1994–1995): 4–27.

Marcus, Millicent. "Anton Giulio Bragaglia's *Thaïs*, or, the Death of the Diva, the Rise of Scenoplastica, and the Birth of Futurist Cinema." *South Central Review* 13, no. 2–3 (Summer–Fall 1996): 63–81.

Mariani, Laura. *Sarah Bernhardt, Colette e L'Arte del Travestimento*. Bologna: Il Mulino, 1996.

Marinetti, Filippo Tommaso. *Lussuria Velocità*. Milan: Modernissima, 1921.

———. *Mafarka the Futurist: An African Novel* (1910). Translated by Carol Diethe and Steve Cox. London: Middlesex Univ. Press, 1998. Originally published as *Mafarka le Futuriste: Romain Africain* (Paris: Sansot, 1910).

———. "Uccidiamo il Chiaro di Luna" (April 1909). In *Teoria ed Invenzione Futurista*, 13–24. Milan: Mondadori, 1968.

Martinelli, Vittorio. "Asta!" In *1911: La Nascita del Lungometraggio*, edited by Riccardo Redi, 19–20. Roma: CNC Edizioni, 1992.

———. *Il Cinema Muto Italiano 1918*. Rome: Nuova Eri, 1991.

———. "Diana Karenne." *Immagine* 18 (1991): 13–21.

———. *Le Dive del Silenzio*. Cineteca del Comune di Bologna. Bologna: Le Mani, 2001.

———. *Il Dolce Sorriso di Maria Jacobini*. Rome: Associazione Italiana per le Ricerche del Cinema, 1994.

———. "L'Incanto Perfido di Thaïs." *Immagine* 17 (1991): 1–9.

———. "Nascita del Divismo." In *Storia del Cinema Mondiale: L'Europa*, edited by Gian Piero Brunetta, 1:221–250. Turin: Einaudi, 1999–2001.

———. "Nino Oxilia." In Redi, *Cinema Italiano Muto: 1905–1916*, 71–86.

———. *Pina Menichelli: Le Sfumature del Fascino*. Rome: Bulzoni, 2002.

Martinelli, Vittorio, and Riccardo Redi. "Due Registi e Un Produttore [*Thaïs*]." *Immagine* 17 (1991): 8–10.

Martini, Fausto Maria. "L'Esule Delusa: Diana Karenne." In *Penombra* 1, no. 2 (July 1918): 61–64.

Masoero, Mariarosa, ed. *Guido Gozzano: San Francesco d'Assisi*. Alessandria: Edizioni dell'Orso, 1997.

Massobrio, Giovanna, and Paolo Portoghesi. *La Donna Liberty*. Rome and Bari: Laterza, 1983.

Mazzei, Luca. "Quando il Cinema Incontrò la Filosofia: Il Caso di Giovanni Papini." *Bianco e Nero* 63, no. 3–4 (May–August 2002): 68–87.

Mazzoni, Cristina Maria. "Virgin Births and Hysterical Pregnancies: Neurosis and Mysticism in French and Italian Literature at the Turn of the Century." PhD diss., Yale University, 1991.

Megill, Allan. *Prophets of Extremity: Nietzsche, Heidegger, Foucault, Derrida.* Berkeley and Los Angeles: Univ. of California Press, 1985.

Michelini, Gaia. *Nietzsche nell'Italia di D'Annunzio.* Palermo: Flaccovio, 1978.

Mingozzi, Gianfranco, ed. *Francesca Bertini.* With a filmography by Vittorio Martinelli. Recco: Le Mani, 2003.

———, dir. *The Last Diva (L'Ultima Diva: Francesca Bertini).* Video, 85 min. Italy, 1982. New York: Kino Video.

Modugno, Ottorino. *Le Donne Mute.* Florence: Cecconi, 1918.

Moe, Nelson J. "Production and Its Others: Gramsci's 'Sexual Question.'" *Rethinking Marxism* 3, no. 3–4 (Fall–Winter 1990): 218–237.

Molinari, Cesare. *L'Attrice Divina: Eleonora Duse nel Teatro Italiano fra i Due Secoli.* Rome: Bulzoni, 1985.

Montesanti, Fausto. "La Parabola della Diva." *Bianco e Nero* 13, no. 7–8 (July–August 1952): 55–72.

Monti, Arnaldo. "Il Fascino della Bellezza Muliebre nella Cinematografia." *La Vita Cinematografica* 5, no. 18 (15 May 1914): 39–40.

Morel, Jean-Paul, ed. *Valentine de Saint-Point.* Paris: Editions Mille et Une Nuit, 2005.

Morin, Edgar. *Les Stars.* Paris: Éditions du Seuil, 1957.

Mossetto, Anna Paola. "Forme e Strutture del Film nel Primo Ricciotto Canudo." *Cinema Nuovo* 22, no. 225 (October 1973): 358–360.

———. "Ricciotto Canudo: La Nascita di una Sesta Arte; Saggio sul Cinematografo." *Cinema Nuovo* 22, no. 225 (October 1973): 361–371.

Muller, Corinna. "Genèse de la Structure du Star System en Allemagne." In Farinelli and Passek, *Stars au Féminin,* 131–141.

Nevers, Emilia. *Vita Moderna: Studi Sociali.* Turin: L'Ufficio del Giornale delle Donne, 1889.

Nichols, Nina Da Vinci, and Jana O'Keefe Bazzoni. *Pirandello and Film.* Lincoln: Univ. of Nebraska Press, 1995.

Nielsen, Asta. *Den Tiende Muse.* Copenhagen: Gyldendal, 1945.

Ockman, Carol, and Kenneth E. Silver, eds. *Sarah Bernhardt: The Art of High Drama.* Published in conjunction with an exhibition at the Jewish Museum, 2 December 2005–2 April 2006. New Haven, Conn.: Yale Univ. Press, 2005.

Olgiati, Francesco. *La Filosofia Bergsoniana e il Realismo.* Milan: n.p., 1935.

———. *La Filosofia di Enrico Bergson.* Turin: Bocca, 1914.

Ovid. *Metamorphoses.* Translated and with notes by Charles Martin. Introduction by Bernard Knox. New York: Norton, 2004.

Palmieri, Eugenio Ferdinando. *Vecchio Cinema Italiano.* Venice: Zanetti, 1940.

Pantieri, José. *Album del Cinema Muto Italiano, n. 1.* Rome: Edizioni del MICS (Museo Internazionale del Cinema e dello Spettacolo), 1991.

———, ed. *Lyda Borelli.* Rome: Edizioni del MICS, 1993.

Paolella, Roberto. "La Decadenza del Divismo in Italia." *Sequenze* 12, no. 10–11 (June–July 1950): 6–8. "Il Divismo" issue, edited by Fausto Montesanti.

———. *Storia del Cinema Muto.* Naples: Giannini, 1956.

Papini, Giovanni. "Bergson." In *Four and Twenty Minds: Essays,* 317–326. Selected and translated by Ernest Hatch Wilkins. New York: Crowell Co., 1922.

———. *Il Crepuscolo dei Filosofi.* Milan: Società Editrice Lombarda, 1906.

———."La Filosofia del Cinematografo." *La Stampa* (Turin) 41 (18 May 1907): 2–4.
———, ed. *La Filosofia dell'Intuizione: Enrico Bergson; Introduzione alla Metafisica ed Estratti di Altre Opere.* Lanciano: Carabba, 1909.
———. *Ventiquattro Cervelli: Saggi non Critici.* Ancona: Puccini e Figli, 1913.
Pesce-Maineri, Piero. *I Pericoli Sociali del Cinematografo.* Turin and Genoa: Marsano, 1922.
Piccini, Vanna. *Le Elegantissime.* Milan: Ravagnati, 1922.
Piccioli, Angelo."Colei Che Attendiamo." *Apollon* 1, no. 2 (1916): 1–4.
Pirandello, Luigi."L'Esclusa" (1893–1901). In *Tutti I Romanzi,* 1–158. Milan: Mondadori, 1944.
———. *Shoot! The Notebooks of Serafino Gubbio, Cinematograph Operator* (1915). Authorized translation by C. K. Scott Moncrieff. Chicago: Univ. of Chicago Press, 2005.
———."Suo Marito [Giustino Roncella Nato Boggiolo]" (1911). In *Tutti I Romanzi,* 837–1043. Milan: Mondadori, 1944.
———. *L'Umorismo: Saggio* (1908). 2nd ed. Florence: Battistelli, 1920.
Piro, Sinibaldo."La Film di Gozzano." *Carte Segrete* 27 (January–March 1975).
———."Le Meravigliose Frodi [Fronde?] nel San Francesco di Gozzano." In *Cinema Nuovo* 24 (1976).
Pisetzky, Rosita Levi. *Il Costume e la Moda nella Società Italiana.* Turin: Einaudi, 1995.
Praz, Mario. *La Filosofia dell'Arredamento: I Mutamenti nel Gusto della Decorazione Interna attraverso i Secoli dall'Antica Roma ai Nostri Tempi* (1945). 20th ed. Milan: TEA, 1993.
———. *The Romantic Agony* (1930). New York: Oxford Univ. Press, 1966.
Prezzolini, Giuseppe."La Filosofia di Enrico Bergson." In *La Teoria Sindacalista.* Naples: Perrella, 1909.
Prolo, Maria Adriana. *Storia del Cinema Muto Italiano,* vol. 1. Milan: Poligono, 1951.

Re, Lucia."D'Annunzio, Duse, Wilde, Bernhardt: Il Rapporto Autore/Autrice tra Decadentismo e Modernità." *Modern Language Notes* 117, no. 1 (January 2002; Italian issue): 115–152.
———."Futurism and Feminism." *Annali d'Italianistica* 7 (1989): 252–271.
Reboul, Jacques. *Notes sur la Morale d'une Annonciatrice: Valentine de Saint-Point.* Paris: Eugène Figuiere, 1912.
Redi, Riccardo, ed. *Cinema Italiano Muto: 1905–1916.* Mostra Internazionale del Nuovo Cinema "Verso il Centenario." Rome: CNC Edizioni, 1991.
———. *Cinema Muto Italiano: 1896–1930.* Biblioteca di Bianco e Nero, Saggistica, n. 2. Venice: Marsilio, 1999.
———."Un Film di Lucio d'Ambra" [*L'Illustre Attrice Cicala Formica*]. *Immagine* 5 (1987): 1–6.
Renzi, Lisetta."Donne Angeliche e Demoniache: Tra la Cultura Europea e Cinema Muto Italiano." *Cinegrafie* 4, no. 7 (1994).
Renzi, Renzo, ed. *Sperduto nel Buio: Il Cinema Muto Italiano e il Suo Tempo, 1905–1930.* With the collaboration of Michele Canosa, Gian Luca Farinelli, and Nicola Mazzanti. Bologna: Cappelli, 1991.
Ribolzi, Iole. *Divi e Dive: Faccende e Vicende del Cinema 1913.* Milan: Stellissima, 1943.
———. *Storia Aneddotica del Cinema Italiano.* Varese: Maj e Malnati, 1945.
———. *Vecchio Cinema Italiano.* Milan: Nuova Aurora, 1940.
Ritter, Naomi."Art and Androgyny: The Aerialist." *Studies in Twentieth-Century Literature* 13, no. 2 (Summer 1989): 173–193.
Riva, Massimo."Per Speculum Melancholiae: The Awakening of Reason Engenders Monsters." In Jewell, *Monsters in the Italian Literary Imagination,* 279–296.
Rognoni, Luigi. *Cinema Muto dalle Origini al 1930.* Roma: Bianco e Nero, 1952.
Russo, Mary. *The Female Grotesque: Risk, Excess, Modernity.* New York: Routledge, 1995.

Sadoul, Georges."Le Cinéma Italien." In *Histoire du Cinéma Mondial des Origines à Nos Jours,* 89–94. Paris: Flammarion, 1949.
Said, Edward. *Orientalism.* New York: Pantheon, 1978.

Saint-Point, Valentine de. *La Femme dans la Littérature Italienne.* Paris: Eugene Figuiere, 1911.

———. *Manifeste de la Femme Futuriste.* Edited and annotated by Jean-Paul Morel. Paris: Éditions Mille et Une Nuits, 2005.

Saladin, Linda Ann. "Rhetorical Veils: Textuality and the Femme Fatale." PhD diss., University of California at Irvine, 1985.

Salaris, Claudia, ed. *Aero . . .: Futurismo e Mito del Volo.* Rome: Parole Gelate, 1985.

Savio, Francesco. *Visione Privata: Il Film "Occidentale" da Lumière a Godard.* Rome: Bulzoni, 1972.

Schlitzer, Franco. *Salvatore Di Giacomo: Ricerche e Note Bibliographiche.* Florence: Sansoni, 1960.

Schlüpmann, Heide. "Asta Nielsen: A Girl with No Fatherland." *Cinegrafie* 12: Divine Apparitions, 1999.

Secors, Cynthia. "Androgyny: An Early Reappraisal." *Women's Studies* 2 (1974): 161–169.

Serao, Matilde. *Saper Vivere: Norme di Buona Creanza.* 19th ed. Florence: Passigli, 1989. Originally published Naples: Tocco, 1900.

———. *Il Ventre di Napoli* (1906). Rome: Vito Bianco, 1973.

Seymour, Mark. *Debating Divorce in Italy: Marriage and the Making of Modern Italians.* New York: Palgrave Macmillan, 2006.

Sheehy, Helen. *Eleonora Duse: A Biography.* New York: Knopf, 2003.

Sighele, Scipio. *Eva Moderna.* Milano: Fratelli Treves, 1910.

Signorelli, Olga. "L'Epistolario di *Cenere.*" *Bianco e Nero* 19, no. 12 (1958): 18–28.

Silver, Kenneth E. *Esprit de Corps: The Art of the Parisian Avant-Garde and the First World War, 1914–1925.* Princeton, N.J.: Princeton Univ. Press, 1989.

Silverman, Debora. *Art Nouveau in Fin-de-Siècle France: Psychology, Politics, and Culture.* Berkeley and Los Angeles: Univ. of California Press, 1989.

Sitney, P. Adams. "The Autobiography of a Metonymy." In Pirandello, *Shoot!* 223–233.

Snowden, Frank M. *Naples in the Time of Cholera, 1884–1911.* Cambridge: Cambridge Univ. Press, 1995.

Soffici, Ardengo. *Il Salto Vitale: Autoritratto d'Artista Italiano nel Quadro del Suo Tempo.* Florence: Vallecchi, 1954.

Sorel, Georges. "I Cattolici contro Bergson." In *L'Europa sotto la Tormenta.* Milan: Corbaccio, 1932.

———. *Reflections on Violence* (1908). Edited by Jeremy Jennings. Cambridge: Cambridge Univ. Press, 1999. Originally published as *Réflexions sur la Violence* (Paris: Rivière, 1946).

Sorlin, Pierre. *European Cinemas, European Societies, 1939–1990.* New York: Routledge, 1991.

———. "First Generation: The World in a Dark Room." In *Italian National Cinema: 1896–1996,* 16–43. New York: Routledge, 1996.

Soro, Francesco. *Splendori e Miserie del Cinema: Cose Viste e Vissute da un Avvocato.* Milan: Consalvo, 1935.

Spackman, Barbara. *Decadent Genealogies: The Rhetoric of Sickness From Baudelaire to D'Annunzio.* Ithaca, N.Y.: Cornell Univ. Press, 1989.

Staiger, Janet. *Bad Women: Regulating Sexuality in Early American Cinema.* Minneapolis: Univ. of Minnesota Press, 1995.

Stamp, Shelley. *Movie-Struck Girls: Women and Motion Picture Culture after the Nickelodeon.* Princeton, N.J.: Princeton Univ. Press, 2000.

Steele, Valerie. *The Corset: A Cultural History.* New Haven, Conn.: Yale Univ. Press, 2001.

Stewart, Janet. *Fashioning Vienna: Adolf Loos' Cultural Criticism.* New York: Routledge, 2000.

Stewart, Susan. *On Longing: Narratives of the Miniature, the Gigantic, the Souvenir, the Collection.* Durham, N.C.: Duke Univ. Press, 1993.

Strazzulla, Gaetano. "Storia della Censura Cinematografica in Italia." *Inquadrature* 9–10 (October 1961–September 1962): 8–21.

Taylor, Frederick Winslow. *The Principles of Scientific Management.* New York: Harper and Brothers, 1911.

Tilgher, Adriano. *Arte, Conoscenza, e Realtà.* Turin: Bocca, 1911.

———. *Studi sul Teatro Contemporaneo, Preceduti da un Saggio su l'Arte come Originalità e i Problemi dell'Arte.* Rome: Libreria di scienze e lettere, 1928.

Tisdall, Caroline, and Angelo Bozzolla. *Futurism.* London: Thames and Hudson, 1997.

Tortora, Matilde, ed. *Lettere di Matilde Serao a Eleonora Duse.* Naples: Graus, 2004.

Tosi, Virgilio, dir. *Un Pioniere del Cinema Scientifico: Roberto Omegna, 1876–1948.* Video, 49 min. Rome: Istituto Luce, 1974.

Tsivian, Yuri. "Russia, 1913: Cinema in the Cultural Landscape." *Griffithiana* 50 (1994): 125–148.

Tyberg, Caspar. "An Art of Silence and Light: The Development of Danish Film Drama to 1920." PhD diss., University of Copenhagen, 1996.

Vaccarino, Stefano. "Un Metodo d'Analisi del Rapporto Musica-Immagine per *Rapsodia Satanica* di Mascagni-Oxilia." In Canosa, *A Nuova Luce,* 267–284.

Varaldo, Alessandro. *Profili d'Attrici e Attori.* Florence: Barbera, 1926.

Varnedoe, Kirk. *A Fine Disregard: What Makes Modern Art Modern.* New York: Abrams, 1989.

Verdier, Abel. "Une Étrange Arrière-Petite-Nièce de Lamartine: Valentine de Saint-Point (1875–1953)." *Annales de l'Académie de Macon* 3, no. 50 (1970–1971): 147–159.

Verdone, Mario. "Anton Giulio Bragaglia." *Bianco e Nero* 26, no. 5–6 (May–June 1965; special issue on futurism).

———. "Arte Totale, Critica Totale." *Filmcritica* 22, no. 5 (November 1977): 308–312.

———. "I Bragaglia e la Fotodinamica." *Immagine* 30: 17–21.

———. *Cinema e Letteratura del Futurismo* (1968). Calliano: Manfrini, 1990.

Verhagen, Marcus. "The Poster in Fin-de-Siècle Paris: 'That Mobile and Degenerate Art.'" In *Cinema and the Invention of Modern Life,* edited by Leo Charney and Vanessa R. Schwartz, 103–129. Berkeley and Los Angeles: Univ. of California Press, 1995.

Veroli, Patrizia. *Baccanti e Dive dell'Aria: Donne Danza e Società in Italia, 1900–1945.* Perugia: Edimond, 2001.

Villiers de L'Isle-Adam, Auguste. *Tomorrow's Eve.* Translated by Robert Martin Adams. Urbana: Univ. of Illinois Press, 2001.

Virilio, Paul. *War and Cinema: The Logistics of Perception.* Translated by Patrick Camiller. London: Verso, 1989.

Virmaux, Alain, and Alain Brunet. *Colette et le Cinéma.* Paris: Fayard, 2004.

Virmaux, Alain, and Odette Virmaux, eds. *Colette at the Movies: Criticism and Screenplays.* Translated by Sarah W. R. Smith. New York: Ungar, 1980.

La Vita Cinematografica (Turin). "Una Circolare dell'Onorevole Giolitti ai Prefetti per un'Attiva Sorveglianza sulle Rappresentazioni Cinematografiche." 28 February 1913, 11.

Vivanti, Annie. "La Cinematografia Applicata alla Scienza Chirurgica." *La Rivista Cinematografica* 2, no. 21 (10 November 1921): 9–10.

———. *Circe: Il Romanzo di Maria Tarnowska* (1912). Milan: Quintieri, 1921.

Weaver, William. *Duse: A Biography.* New York: Harcourt Brace Jovanovich, 1984.

———. "Duse and the Art of Silence." In Dalle Vacche and Farinelli, *Silent Divas of Italian Cinema,* 44–55.

Weininger, Otto. *Sex and Character.* Vienna: Braumüller, 1903; London: Heinemann, 1906; New York: Putnam's Sons, 1906; Turin: Fratelli Bocca, 1912.

Wohl, Robert. *A Passion for Wings: Aviation and the Western Imagination, 1908–1918.* New Haven, Conn.: Yale Univ. Press, 1994.

Wollen, Peter. "Salome." In *Paris/Manhattan: Writings on Art,* 101–112. London: Verso, 2004.

Wood, Ghislaine. *Art Nouveau and the Erotic.* New York: Abrams, 2000.

Yates, Frances A. *Astraea: The Imperial Theme in the Sixteenth Century.* London: Routledge and Kegan Paul, 1975.

Young-Bruehl, Elisabeth. *Freud on Women: A Reader.* New York: Norton, 1990.

Zagarrio, Vito. "*Mariute*: Un Metafilm del Muto." *Immagine* 6 (1983): 5–10.

Zambelloni, Franco. "Bergson e la Filosofia Italiana, 1900–1915." *Filosofia* 2, no. 3 (July 1970): 331–360.

Zappa, Paolo. *La Legione Straniera: Tavole e Disegni di Pier Antonio Gariazzo.* Turin: Edizioni della Cicogna, 1945.

Zouari, Faouzia. "Valentine de Saint-Point: Un Itinéraire de l'Occident à l'Orient (1875–1953)." PhD diss., Université de la Sorbonne Nouvelle, Paris III, 1983.

Index

Italic page numbers refer to illustrations.

About the author

A specialist in the intersection of aesthetic theory and film history, Angela Dalle Vacche was born in Venice, Italy, and came to the United States in 1978. She has graduate degrees in American Studies and in Film Studies from Mount Holyoke College and the University of Iowa. She has been the recipient of a Fulbright Travel Grant, a Mellon Fellowship, a Rockefeller Bellagio Grant, and a Leverhulme Distinguished Professorship at the University of London, Birkbeck College, History of Art. Her retrospective, Italian Silent Divas, for the 2000 New York Film Festival was voted as "Best Event of the Year" by Art Forum. Dalle Vacche has worked with the Cineteca di Bologna, The Nederlands Filmmuseum, Anthology Film Archive in New York, and DAMS/Gorizia in Italy. She lectures internationally, most recently in Portugal, Vienna, and Dublin.

While teaching at Vassar College, Yale University, and Georgia Institute of Technology, she has become a leading voice in Italian film studies, an internationally recognized specialist in European cinema, and she is highly regarded for having opened the field of film studies to the history of art.

Angela Dalle Vacche's books include *The Body in the Mirror: Shapes of History in Italian Cinema*, Princeton 1992; and *Cinema and Painting: How Art Is Used in Film*, University of Texas, 1996. She has edited two anthologies: *The Visual Turn: Classical Film Theory and Art History*, Rutgers 2002; and with Brian Price, *Color, The Film Reader*, Routledge, 2006.

Currently, besides organizing every year the African and the Japanese Film Series at Georgia Tech, Dalle Vacche is working on a new book, *André Bazin and the Visual Arts*.

PHOTOGRAPHER: *Angela Cumberbirch*